D1009407

Tony Harcup is Senior Lecturer at the Department of Journalism Studies, University of Sheffield. His publications include *Alternative Journalism, Alternative Voices* (2013), *Newspaper Journalism* (with Peter Cole, 2010), *The Ethical Journalist* (2007), and *Journalism: Principles and Practice* (2004).

SEE WEB LINKS

To find recommended web links for this and many other Oxford reference titles, visit http://global.oup.com/booksites/reference/ when you see this sign.

Oxford Paperback Reference

The most authoritative and up-to-date reference books for both students and the general reader.

Accounting
Animal Behaviour
Archaeology
Architecture and Landscape Architecture
Art and Artists
Art Terms
Arthurian Literature and Legend
Astronomy
Battles
Bible
Biology
Biomedicine
British History
British Place-Names
Business and Management
Card Games
Chemistry
Christian Church
Classical Literature
Classical World
Computing
Construction, Surveying, and Civil Engineering
Cosmology
Countries of the World
Critical Theory
Dance
Dentistry
Earth Sciences
Ecology
Economics
Education
English Etymology
English Grammar
English Literature
English Surnames
Environment and Conservation
Everyday Grammar
Film Studies
Finance and Banking
Foreign Words and Phrases
Forensic Science
Geography
Hinduism
Human Geography
Humorous Quotations
Idioms

Irish History
Islam
Kings and Queens of Britain
Law
Law Enforcement
Linguistics
Literary Terms
London Place-Names
Mathematics
Marketing
Mechanical Engineering
Media and Communication
Medical
Modern Slang
Music
Musical Terms
Nursing
Opera Characters
Philosophy
Physics
Plant Sciences
Plays
Pocket Fowler's Modern English Usage
Political Quotations
Politics
Popes
Proverbs
Psychology
Quotations
Quotations by Subject
Reference and Allusion
Rhymes
Rhyming Slang
Saints
Science
Scottish History
Shakespeare
Slang
Social Work and Social Care
Sociology
Statistics
Superstitions
Synonyms and Antonyms
Theatre & Performance
Weather
Weights, Measures, and Units
Word Origins
Zoology

Many of these titles are also available online at
www.oxfordreference.com

A Dictionary of

Journalism

TONY HARCUP

OXFORD
UNIVERSITY PRESS

OXFORD
UNIVERSITY PRESS

Great Clarendon Street, Oxford, OX2 6DP,
United Kingdom

Oxford University Press is a department of the University of Oxford.
It furthers the University's objective of excellence in research, scholarship,
and education by publishing worldwide. Oxford is a registered trade mark of
Oxford University Press in the UK and in certain other countries

First Edition published in 2014
Impression: 1

Published in the United States of America by Oxford University Press
198 Madison Avenue, New York, NY 10016, United States of America

British Library Cataloguing in Publication Data
Data available

Library of Congress Control Number: 2013956092

ISBN 978-0-19-964624-1

Printed in Great Britain by
Clays Ltd, St Ives plc

Preface

This first *Oxford Dictionary of Journalism* is what it says: a dictionary, not an encyclopedia. It defines more than 1,300 terms and has another 150 or so signpost entries. For each one, even the handful of longer entries that have slipped in, the gist of the definition is contained within the first sentence; indeed, some entries consist of just one sentence. Of course, many of the terms defined have lives and meanings away from journalism, but what they do in their own time is no concern of this dictionary. Therefore, entries deal only with uses in relation to journalism as it is practised and/or studied. Contested concepts or explanations are highlighted where deemed necessary and many entries point to web links and further reading suggestions that will help with deeper exploration; at the same time, detailed cross-referencing offers breadth.

This is not an account driven by the 'great men' and 'great women' of journalism so there are no biographical entries. However, individuals *do* matter, and the appendix includes a list of some of the people named in the dictionary and some of the entries in which they crop up. A chronology is also included, which provides a route through the historical events and developments considered in selected entries. A word of warning, though: real life is always messier and more overlapping for those living it than might appear in any timeline constructed with the benefit of hindsight.

Thanks are due to Judith Wilson, Joanna Harris, Karen Bunn, and everyone else at Oxford University Press who has helped make this project a reality; also to Terry for feedback and all-round support, and to Parkrun for managing to get me away from the computer and books at regular intervals even with a deadline looming.

Finally, if a dictionary is to be convenient as well as useful it cannot include every possible term or every potential explanatory nuance; however, I would be pleased to receive readers' comments or suggestions for any future edition, and these can be sent via the publishers.

TH

Contents

Contents

AAN *See* ASSOCIATION OF ALTERNATIVE NEWSWEEKLIES.

ABC *See* AMERICAN BROADCASTING COMPANY.

ABC *See* AUDIT BUREAU OF CIRCULATION.

ABC *See* AUSTRALIAN BROADCASTING CORPORATION.

ABCe A section of the *Audit Bureau of Circulation established in 1996 to measure the audience reach of *digital media in the UK but which has since been subsumed into the core functions of the ABC.

ABC News A major broadcast news network in the USA that is engaged in a *ratings battle with *NBC. ABC News is the news arm of the *American Broadcasting Company, which is itself part of the Walt Disney Company, and its flagship shows include *Good Morning America*, *Nightline*, and *This Week*.

above-the-fold An item that appears in the top half of the front page of a large-format *newspaper (*see* BROADSHEET; BERLINER). Traditionally this is seen as the most prominent location for a story because of its visibility even when the newspaper is folded in half, for example while on display in a newsagent's shop. An item might be placed above-the-fold because it is seen as the most important and/or the most appealing. Sometimes also used to refer to items that can be seen on a website without scrolling down. *See also* BELOW-THE-FOLD.

above-the-line Online material written by journalists as opposed to *user-generated content. The text of an online news story or feature is referred to as being above-the-line when, beneath it, there is a facility for readers to post comments on it. The author of an item that is above-the-line may sometimes respond to readers' comments below, and some sites encourage or even require their journalists to be involved in the *curation or management of such online discussion. *See also* YOUR COMMENTS.

absolute privilege The term used for the law whereby journalists in the UK cannot be sued for *defamation for reporting a court case, providing their report is fair, accurate, and published contemporaneously. The law of *privilege recognizes that there is a *public interest in the media being free to report on justice being done, and being seen to be done, including the reporting of allegations, denials, and evidence that ultimately may not be found to be true. Members of Parliament are also covered by absolute privilege for any allegations they make in parliamentary debates, committees, and questions, but media reports of such allegations are covered only by *qualified privilege.

academization of journalism The process whereby journalism in many countries has become largely a graduate occupation, with new recruits having increasingly been exposed to the academic study of journalism (*journalism studies) alongside *training in journalistic skills. Debate over the benefits or otherwise of such academization can be sharp and occasionally abusive, with many journalists dismissing study of the media as a 'Mickey Mouse subject' taught by phoneys who know nothing about life in a *newsroom, and many academics accusing journalists of anti-intellectualism and being afraid of critical scrutiny. *Compare* INDENTURES. *See also* JOURNALISM EDUCATION.

access The privileged admittance to news organizations and outlets that some sections of society are said to enjoy, while others tend to be marginalized or overlooked. Studies suggest that, although the *journalist–source relationship is complex, there is a tendency for more socially and economically powerful individuals and organizations routinely to have advantageous access to the media in general and to journalists in particular. *See also* PRIMARY DEFINERS; REPRESENTATION.

Accrediting Council on Education in Journalism and Mass Communications (ACEJMC) The body that accredits more than a hundred professional journalism courses in US universities and colleges. Formed in 1945 as the American Council on Education in Journalism, it adopted its current name in 1980.

((⊕)) SEE WEB LINKS
• ACEJMC accredited courses

accuracy Obtaining and transmitting information that is as correct and truthful as can be ascertained given the *constraints under which journalists operate. The discovery, recording, and reporting of accurate information is widely regarded as fundamental to journalism because, without accuracy (or at least the quest for it) 'information' becomes misinformation and therefore ceases to be journalism. Accuracy covers everything from the correct spelling of a name and the correct *attribution of a *quote through to coverage of more complex issues such as scientific breakthroughs and political arguments. Journalistic accuracy entails precision, exactitude, *verification, cross-checking, and the use of specific rather than vague information or language; it also implies that a journalist's own assumptions have been questioned (*see* REFLEXIVE PRACTICE). A commitment to accuracy is subsumed within the ideals of *objectivity, *impartiality, and *investigative journalism, but other forms of journalism also make claims for the accuracy of the information conveyed and the importance of accuracy is a common theme of journalists' *codes of conduct. However, this quest for accuracy can be problematic; a perfectly accurate account of a source's words (supported by a recording or a verbatim note) may actually be inaccurate if the source is mistaken (or is deliberately misleading the journalist). Such limitations on accuracy, combined with the fast pace and other constraints typically involved in the production of journalism, have led to the work of journalists being described as the striving for the most accurate version of the *truth obtainable within the time available. What appears to be accurate today may tomorrow be shown to be doubtful or inaccurate, in which case a commitment to accuracy will result in the publication of a *correction or clarification. *See also* FACTICITY; FACTS; TRUTHINESS.

Ace in the Hole The title of a film (dir. Billy Wilder, 1951) showing how an unscrupulous journalist tramples over the lives of ordinary people and manipulates reality to create a story that will sell better. There have been countless films made about journalism, but this is widely seen as one of the most savage critiques of journalistic *ethics ever produced. The film was also released under the title *The Big Carnival*.

ACEJMC *See* ACCREDITING COUNCIL ON EDUCATION IN JOURNALISM AND MASS COMMUNICATIONS.

active audience A conceptualization of a media *audience as actively involved in the ways in which any particular item or *text may be understood. Theories about the active audience counter the *hypodermic model in which journalists and other creators of media output are said to be able to inject messages into the minds of a passive audience. Advocates of the concept of the active audience argue that audience members bring their own knowledge, experiences, expectations, attitudes, predispositions, and prejudices to any media text and that such factors may have the effect of filtering out some messages or creating a prism through which material is viewed. Since the advent of *online journalism, *user-generated content, and *social media, the phrase 'active audience' is also sometimes used to refer to the way in which audience members can now interact more directly and immediately with journalists and other audience members. *See also* ENCODING, DECODING.

active voice *See* ACTIVE WRITING.

active writing A style of writing that uses the **active voice** rather than the passive, placing the emphasis on people saying and/or doing things rather than a *style in which things are said and done. One of George *Orwell's six rules of writing is 'never use the passive where you can use the active' (*Politics and the English Language*, 1946), and journalists' adherence to this is one of the key stylistic differences between journalistic writing and more academic forms of writing. Active writing is an important element of the *training of journalists, whether on the job or on courses of further or higher education. *See also* LANGUAGE OF NEWS.

activist journalism The use of journalistic skills within *activist media to report on, and inspire political engagement with, one or more issues. Activist journalists are typically activists first and journalists second, with the latter function serving the former. *See also* ALTERNATIVE JOURNALISM; NATIVE REPORTING; OPPOSITIONAL REPORTING.

activist media Newspapers, magazines, online, and other forms of media produced by and for individuals and groups engaged in social and political campaigning and organizing. Although the phrase is most commonly associated with left-wing causes it can also be applied to media produced by the far-right. *See also* ACTIVIST JOURNALISM; ALTERNATIVE MEDIA; FEMINIST MEDIA.

actuality The sound of an event captured as it happens and available to be used as *audio in *broadcast or *online journalism. *Compare* ATMOS; FACTUALITY.

ad *See* ADVERTISEMENT.

add-par An additional paragraph of *copy to be added to a story already in the editorial system.

Advance Publications *See* CONDÉ NAST; NEW ORLEANS TIMES-PICAYUNE.

adversarial journalism 1. A combative or oppositional style of journalism that rejects *impartiality in favour of taking sides, deliberately blurring *reporting and *opinion. Adherents of adversarial journalism emphasize that it retains a journalistic attachment to *verification and the *truth; it does not imply twisting the facts of a story to support a cause, merely to draw conclusions from those facts and to not be afraid of pointing the finger at whoever is judged to be to blame. Critics counter that selective use of information interwoven with comment can turn reporting into *propaganda, simultaneously damaging trust in journalism and lowering the quality of discussion within the *public sphere. *See also* ADVOCACY JOURNALISM; ALTERNATIVE JOURNALISM; CAMPAIGNING JOURNALISM; INVESTIGATIVE JOURNALISM; JOURNALISM OF ATTACHMENT.
2. A phrase sometimes used as criticism of a form of broadcast *interview that is almost ritualistically antagonistic and is often said to generate more heat than light.

advert *See* ADVERTISEMENT.

advertisement (advert, ad) A paid-for message appearing within an identifiable slot on commercial TV, radio, online, or in newspapers or magazines. *See also* ADVERTISERS; ADVERTISING; ADVERTISING FEATURE.

advertisers Organizations (or individuals) that pay for *advertisements to appear in commercial media. Advertisers have been known to attempt to use their economic power to influence editorial content, for example by withdrawing advertising (or threatening to) from newspapers that criticize or investigate them. Such direct intervention is rare and a more prevalent influence is probably the way

a

stories and subjects are selected to attract key advertisers' target audiences. *See also* ADVERTISING; EDITORIAL INDEPENDENCE.

advertising The placement of *advertisements within commercial media. Advertising is the main form of income for many employers of journalists, especially commercial broadcasters, magazines, the *'quality' press, and *free newspapers. Popular media demand a mass audience to attract mass advertising, whereas the heavier press depend on delivering smaller, targeted audiences for more niche advertising markets. Commercial media operate in a dual market, whereby the publication/programme is one product (with the audience as consumers) and the audience itself is another product (access to which is bought by the advertisers). Popular and *mid-market *tabloid newspapers typically rely rather less on advertising and more on income from sales of the publication itself. A decline in advertising can result in editorial cutbacks or closures, while an increase in advertising can fund expansion. Advertising can also impact on journalism by skewing editorial coverage to appeal more to certain advertiser-friendly audiences; that is, the audiences most sought after by advertisers. The *internet has proved hugely disruptive of traditional advertising markets and, in most instances, so-called *legacy media companies (especially in *print journalism) have (so far) only been able to compensate in digital advertising income a tiny fraction of what they have lost. *See also* ADVERTISERS; ADVERTISING FEATURES; CONSTRAINTS.

advertising feature (ad feature, advertorial) A paid-for article in a newspaper or magazine designed to accompany one or more *advertisements. Despite being made to look similar to editorial content, and often being written by the publication's regular editorial staff, the power to approve or reject *copy is often given to the advertiser. *Ethical concerns arise if advertising features are not clearly labelled as such, as this can be seen as misleading readers and potentially breaching *trust between journalists and audience. Any of the terms for advertising feature may occasionally be used to disparage a piece of journalism for being too uncritical, as in 'it reads just like an advertorial for the company'. *See also* ADVERTISERS; EDITORIAL INDEPENDENCE.

advocacy journalism A form of *reporting that is designed to speak up for a particular cause, policy, campaign, organization, nation, section of the population, neighbourhood, or even an individual. Advocacy journalism eschews a commitment to formal *objectivity, *impartiality, or giving both sides of a story an equal hearing, although it tends to be less aggressive in tone than *adversarial journalism. However, as with adversarial and *campaigning journalism, critics object to the blurring of comment and facts that is implicit (and sometimes explicit) within such reporting. *See also* ALTERNATIVE JOURNALISM; BIAS; PEACE JOURNALISM; PROPAGANDA; PUBLIC RELATIONS.

AFP *See* AGENCE FRANCE-PRESSE.

Agence France-Presse (AFP) A multimedia news and picture agency that began life in 1835 as the Havas agency in Paris, said to be the world's first *news agency. Now with 200 bureaus in 150 countries, its international income overtook that from France in 2011.

(⊕) SEE WEB LINKS
• English-language version of AFP homepage

agency The power of individual journalists to control their own practice and/or to influence the output of the media organizations for which they work. Some academic critiques of journalism appear to allow little room for journalistic agency or *autonomy, arguing that journalism itself remains largely unaltered even when the individuals producing it change. However, many anecdotal accounts of journalism by journalists themselves arguably over-privilege agency by downplaying the impact of structural forces on constraining the ability of individuals to actively intervene in their working environment. To argue that journalists have agency is not to deny that journalists operate within constraints, but to suggest that structural forces do not totally determine individuals' actions. *See also* CONSTRAINTS. *Compare* AGENCY, NEWS.

agency, news An organization that supplies *copy, still *pictures, *video footage and/or *audio to media organizations on a commercial basis. Such agencies may operate on a local or specialist basis employing just one or two journalists, on a national basis (such as the *Press Association in the UK), or on an international basis (such as *Reuters). *Compare* AGENCY. *See also* FREELANCE JOURNALISTS.

agency copy The *text of a story (or part of a story) supplied by a *news agency (*see also* AGENCY, NEWS).

agenda-setting The notion that the media play a significant role in amplifying certain issues, increasing their salience within the *public sphere and constructing parameters within which debate will be seen as legitimate. Associated with a study by Maxwell McCombs and Donald Shaw of the US presidential election campaign of 1968, the premise of agenda-setting is that although media coverage may not be able to tell people what to think on a given issue (*compare* HYPODERMIC MODEL), it may be influential in telling people what issues to think *about*. More recent academic research raises the possibility that the media agenda may be influenced by the public as much as the other way around. *See also* AMPLIFICATION; GATEKEEPING; MEDIA EFFECTS.

aggregation The process whereby an online news service, often without employing any journalists of its own, brings together material and/or gathers *hyperlinks to material from a variety of other sources. *See also* BUZZFEED; GOOGLE NEWS; NEWS AGGREGATION; NEWSVINE.

agony aunt A *columnist for a newspaper or magazine who invites readers to write in about personal problems, very often involving relationships or sex in one way or another, and who then dispenses advice in the column, creating a curious mix of prurience and public service. Agony aunts, and the occasional agony uncle, almost universally dislike the term as a description of someone who writes an advice column or problem page, but they seem to be stuck with it. *See also* LADIES' MERCURY.

air Where broadcasting is said to happen. To run a piece of *broadcast journalism is to put it on air, and *live interviews take place while the participants are on air. *See also* DEAD AIR.

airbrushing The alteration or 'improvement' of a *photograph, today also known as Photoshopping, *digital manipulation, or digital retouching. Alterations can range from the innocent tidying up of a picture, by removing a distracting shadow or cloud, for example, to modifications that might change a picture's meaning. There are occasional controversies over the practice, ranging from debates about the *ethics of making women in magazines seem unnaturally thin to allegations of political *bias about somebody being removed from, or added to, a picture that purports to depict a specific event of some historical or political import.

AJA *See* AUSTRALIAN JOURNALISTS' ASSOCIATION.

AJE *See* ASSOCIATION FOR JOURNALISM EDUCATION.

alert A message sent to *newsdesks by a *news agency, or a *public relations operation, warning of a major piece of *breaking news and indicating that more information will follow in due course. An alert may also be sent out to correct erroneous information previously distributed or to highlight the legal implications of a particular story.

algorithmic journalism The use of computer software to transform data and other material into a *story that resembles a piece of human journalism, by following a pre-programmed structure and formula. *Compare* COMPUTER-ASSISTED REPORTING. *See also* HARVESTING CONTENT.

(((⊕))) SEE WEB LINKS

• *Wired*: 'Can an algorithm write a better news story than a human reporter?'

Al Jazeera A television network established in 1996 in Doha, the capital of Qatar, with financial backing from that country's ruling emir. Since its launch as a niche satellite TV broadcaster with a mission to present an Arab perspective on international events, Al Jazeera has grown into a substantial network broadcasting to around 220 million households in more than 100 countries, with 3,000 staff working out of bases in Doha, London, and Washington DC, plus more than 60 bureaus in other countries. Its output includes separate *24-hour news channels in Arabic and English, *documentary and sports channels, and websites in both Arabic and English. Al Jazeera also claims to be the most watched news channel on *YouTube, with its videos being viewed approximately 2.5 million times each month. With many of its bureaus based in the global south, and journalists recruited from a wide range of countries with numerous languages between them, Al Jazeera offers something of an alternative perspective on global affairs (*compare* CULTURAL IMPERIALISM). Its access to people, organizations, and locations that Western journalists sometimes struggle to reach has given it a succession of *scoops especially from war and conflict zones; however, a number of Al Jazeera personnel have been attacked and even killed in the course of their work. Al Jazeera has its own code of *ethics, which declares, amongst other things, that it will 'adhere to the journalistic values of honesty, courage, fairness, balance, independence, credibility, and diversity, giving no priority to commercial or political over professional considerations'. The code also commits the broadcaster to 'recognize diversity in human societies with all their races, cultures, and beliefs, and their values and intrinsic individualities, so as to present unbiased and faithful reflection of them'.

Further reading: H. Miles, *Al Jazeera* (2006).

(((⬤))) SEE WEB LINKS

• Al Jazeera code of ethics

all human life is there The claim made for itself by the *News of the World*. Often used as a motto beneath the newspaper's *masthead as well as in its own promotional campaigns, it was used to signify the *News of the World*'s willingness to report on people's foibles in addition to covering the big social and political issues of the day. The slogan had ceased to be used by the time the newspaper closed in 2011 following the *hackgate revelations.

Alliance for Audited Media A membership organization that supplies independently verified information on *circulation and audience reach of commercial media to the US and Canadian *advertising industries. It was founded as the Audit Bureau of Circulations in 1914 and adopted its current name in 2012.

Alliance of Independent Press Councils of Europe (AIPCE) A fairly loose network of press councils and other organizations with a role of regulating or self-regulating journalism in around 30 European countries. Formed in 1999, the alliance brings together organizations around principles such as that regulation of editorial content should be independent of government and that it is neither possible nor desirable to impose on journalists an international or global code of ethics. AIPCE has no formal membership structure or central secretariat but runs an annual conference, normally held in a different country each year. *See also* ETHICS; SELF-REGULATION.

(((⬤))) SEE WEB LINKS

• Organizations participating in AIPCE

all-rounder A story or other item that is not *exclusive and is supplied to a number of media organizations by a *freelance journalist or *news agency. *See also* ON SPEC.

all the news that's fit to print The motto adopted by the *New York Times* at the end of the 19th century to distinguish itself from what it saw as the more disreputable *yellow press of the time. The slogan, sometimes described as the most famous seven words in US journalism, can still be seen today, next to the *masthead on the front page of the newspaper's print edition.

All the President's Men The title of a book (Bernstein and
Woodward, 1974) and film (dir. Alan Pakula, 1976) that tell the story
of how *Washington Post* journalists Bob Woodward and Carl Bernstein
uncovered the *Watergate scandal in the United States; widely seen as
an exemplar of *investigative journalism. *See also* DEEP THROAT.

Further reading: C. Bernstein and B. Woodward, *All the President's Men* (1974).

alternative journalism The more journalistic elements of
*alternative media; that is, alternative media practices that involve
*reporting and/or commenting on factual and/or topical events.
Alternative journalism typically takes place in relatively open and
participatory, non-professionalized and non-commercial media
organizations, often utilizing collective and non-hierarchical working
methods. Implicit in alternative journalism is a rejection and critique of
many of the established practices of mainstream journalism, with the
consequence that alternative journalists may see themselves as working
to different *news values, covering different *stories, giving access to a
different cast of news actors and *sources, operating to an alternative set
of *ethics, and in effect operating as a form of *watchdog on mainstream
journalistic organizations that like to portray themselves as watchdogs.
Precisely what might be labelled 'alternative journalism' will differ over
time and space; some journalistic writing styles and subject matter
that were the preserve of alternative media in the 1960s and 1970s are
now much more common within the mainstream media of both the
USA and the UK, for example. Alternative media and alternative
journalism have tended to be regarded as of marginal interest to the field
of *journalism studies, but this has been changing since the turn of the
century with scholars such as Chris Atton, John Downing, Susan Forde,
and Clemencia Rodriguez amongst those arguing that we should extend
our gaze beyond the mainstream. *See also* ACTIVIST JOURNALISM;
ALTERNATIVE PRESS; AMATEUR JOURNALISM; CITIZEN JOURNALISM;
HYBRIDITY; NATIVE REPORTING; OPPOSITIONAL REPORTING; PEACE
JOURNALISM; RADICAL JOURNALISM; UNDERGROUND PRESS.

Further reading: C. Atton and J. Hamilton, *Alternative Journalism* (2008).
S. Forde, *Challenging the News: The Journalism of Alternative and Community
Media* (2011).
T. Harcup, *Alternative Journalism, Alternative Voices* (2013).

alternative media Media projects, often run by untrained and
unpaid activists, that reject and/or challenge the conventions and

structures of mainstream commercial or state-funded media.
*Alternative and *radical journalism can be found within many
examples of alternative media, but countless other forms of
expression that have little or no connection to journalism have also
been labelled as alternative media, including graffiti, flyposting,
badge-making, pamphleteering, experimental film-making, creative
writing, music distribution, and *fanzine production. Alternative media
may be defined as *media output produced by its (potential) *audience
and can be seen as serving and as helping to form what might be
described as an *alternative public sphere in which groups and
individuals on the margins of mainstream culture and media can form
communities of interest within which they can communicate and
debate issues of mutual interest. *See also* ACTIVIST MEDIA;
EMPOWERMENT; REPRESENTATION.

alternative press Newspapers and magazines that adopt and adapt
many of the conventions of journalism to publish informative material
that questions or opposes that which is commonly found in
*mainstream journalism. The alternative press tends to be open to the
involvement of non-professionals, and many mainstream journalists
obtain initial experience of journalism by contributing to alternative
titles. Historically, alternative newspapers and magazines have tended
to be financially challenged and short-lived but that has not necessarily
diminished their influence. Since the turn of the century there has been
a shift towards publication online, either in addition to, or, increasingly,
instead of print. *See also* ALTERNATIVE JOURNALISM; FEMINIST MEDIA;
RADICAL PRESS; UNDERGROUND PRESS.

Alternative Press A monthly US music magazine that began as a
*fanzine in Cleveland, Ohio, in 1985 and which grew to become an
influential full colour print product plus multimedia digital *brand.

alternative public sphere A conceptual space for information-
sharing, discussion, and debate amongst those sections of the population
that reject mainstream discourse. Drawing on the Habermasian concept
of the bourgeois *public sphere, in which mainstream media are said to
be amongst the locations for such public discussion that does take place,
scholars writing about *alternative media and *alternative journalism
posit the existence of an alternative public sphere (or a *counter public
sphere) that is simultaneously served by and partially formed by such

alternative media. In recent years scholars have increasingly been writing about the existence of multiple and overlapping public spheres rather than one mainstream sphere and one alternative sphere; similarly, citizens may move between spheres or even participate in several simultaneously. *See also* PLEBEIAN PUBLIC SPHERE.

amateur journalism Journalism produced without the payment of either fee or wage. This can range from an individual hobbyist publishing a niche newsletter for circulation amongst a small number of fellow enthusiasts to an *alternative media collective producing revelatory *investigative journalism for a sizeable yet not commercially viable audience. Somewhere between these two extremes might be special-interest or *hyperlocal *bloggers whose output incorporates a range of journalistic techniques but who do not (yet) make any money from their efforts. *See also* ALTERNATIVE JOURNALISM; CITIZEN JOURNALISM; USER-GENERATED CONTENT; VILLAGE CORRESPONDENT.

ambient journalism Journalism that is produced, distributed, and received continuously via new communications technology such as *social networking, *microblogging, and *Twitter, becoming an almost invisible yet virtually ever-present factor in many people's lives. Such journalism may originate from paid journalists and mainstream media organizations, *user-generated content, or a mixture of the two. *Compare* SLOW JOURNALISM. *See also* DIGITAL MEDIA; DIGITAL NATIVES; ONLINE JOURNALISM.

American Broadcasting Company (ABC) A major US commercial television and entertainment network that forms part of the Disney empire. The network's *ABC News is a major employer of journalists.

American Journalism Review A discussion journal about journalism that stopped its print version and became digital-only in 2013. It began as the *Washington Journalism Review* in 1977, and since 2011 it has been owned by the Philip Merrill College of Journalism.

(((🌐))) SEE WEB LINKS
• The *AJR* archive

American Prospect A liberal but politically unaligned magazine based in Washington DC and published every two months. Launched in 1990, it is a non-profit publication that relies for its survival on donations from sympathizers.

American Society of News Editors (ASNE) An organization of editors and journalism trainers that, since its formation in 1922 as the American Society of Newspaper Editors, has lobbied in support of journalistic freedom and *First Amendment rights; it adopted its current name in 2009. ASNE holds annual *awards for journalists and, every March from 2005 onwards, it has organized a *Sunshine Week to draw public attention to the importance of open government and *freedom of information.

(((()))) SEE WEB LINKS

• ASNE website

American Spectator A monthly magazine surveying the US political scene from the right of centre, first published in 1924.

America Online *See* AOL.

amplification The way in which a particular phenomenon or point of view may acquire disproportionate importance or prevalence as a result of being selected for media coverage. Examples include the way in which public fear of crime may result from journalists' tendency to report the most unusual and extreme cases, thereby arguably creating an impression that society is more dangerous than it actually is. Similarly, the operation of *news values results in some more newsworthy diseases attracting much more media coverage than others that might in fact pose more of a risk to most citizens. Particular perspectives can also be amplified if journalists make disproportionately frequent invitations to certain organizations to state their case on an issue, either because of deliberate *bias or simply because such organizations have slick and well-resourced *public relations operations and readily available contributors. *See also* AGENDA-SETTING; MEDIA EFFECTS; MORAL PANIC; PRIMARY DEFINERS.

analogue A pre-digital form of broadcast media output that relies on the transmission of electromagnetic waves. The term is sometimes used metaphorically to refer to what are perceived to be old-fashioned or *legacy media. *Compare* DIGITAL MEDIA.

anchor A US term for the *presenter of a TV news programme. *See also* NEWSREADER.

anecdote Details of a particular incident that may be included in a story to help paint a wider picture and/or to add *entertainment value.

Anecdotes are found more often in *features or *colour pieces than in news and may be used to help explain how the participants in a story behaved, felt, or reacted; anecdotes may also be humorous or moving. Some academics are critical of journalism for placing too much emphasis on anecdotes and 'anecdotalism' rather than evidence obtained by academic-style study.

angle The particular way in which a story is approached and/or introduced as well as the elements of a story that are selected for added emphasis. A journalist taking an angle on a story is not to be confused with a journalist taking a politically biased stance on a story.
See also PEG.

anniversaries Occasions on which old stories can be made to seem fresh again thanks to an anniversary, especially when the number of years that has passed ends in a zero or a five.

anonymous source (anonymity, confidentiality, confidential source) 1. A person who *leaks information to a journalist or other organization (such as *WikiLeaks) without the recipient necessarily knowing the identity of the *source. Such sources might leak information for any number of reasons, ranging from malice and mischief to seeking to prevent crime, expose wrongdoing, or protect life. An example of an anonymous source is Sarah Tisdall (1960–), a clerk with the Foreign Office in the UK who in the 1980s secretly supplied the *Guardian newspaper with a photocopy of a confidential document concerning the arrival in the UK of US cruise missiles; the newspaper did not know who its source was but, after making some checks on the likely veracity of the leaked document, published a story based on its contents. The government pursued the newspaper through the courts in an effort to identify the source of the leak; having lost its legal fight to protect its source, the *Guardian* reluctantly handed over the photocopy, and markings on it led to the identification and arrest of Sarah Tisdall, who was eventually jailed under the *Official Secrets Act. The then *Guardian* editor Peter Preston subsequently reflected that the newspaper should have destroyed the document as soon as the story had been written but not yet published, before the commencement of legal action by the government. In 2007 the website *WikiLeaks* was established with the declared intention of allowing sources to leak information safely and anonymously.

2. Confidential source A person whose identity is known to the journalist but who supplies information on the understanding that they will not be identified as the source, or who agrees to give a broadcast interview only on condition that their face is obscured and/or voice disguised.

Journalists are trained that *on-the-record identifiable sources are best, but there is broad agreement that there are circumstances when using an anonymous source is the only way to break a story. A source may wish to place information in the public domain but may wish to remain anonymous because they fear embarrassment, losing their job, being prosecuted, physical reprisals, or even death. However, anonymous sources are not necessarily lone individuals speaking out about what they perceive as an injustice; they might just as easily be *spin doctors trying to plant stories to damage a rival or to 'fly a kite' that can subsequently be denied. Before agreeing to confidentiality, a journalist will have to weigh up arguments for and against, including whether the source can be believed, why the source does not wish to go public, what other evidence can be produced to support the source's story, how the identity of the source might be kept secret, and whether the *public interest inherent in the story outweighs the lack of transparency and *trust involved in publishing information without a named source. An example of a confidential source is Dr David Kelly, the scientist whose *off-the-record briefing of *BBC journalist Andrew Gilligan over the 2003 Iraq war was followed by a major confrontation between the UK government and the BBC, the death of Dr Kelly, and the instigation of an official inquiry chaired by Lord Hutton. Perhaps the most famous confidential source in journalistic history is *Deep Throat, who secretly provided *Washington Post journalists with tips, leads, and confirmation of information during their *Watergate investigation into the United States' White House under President Richard Nixon in the early 1970s. Reporters Woodward and Bernstein protected the identity of Deep Throat for more than 30 years, until 2005, when the source's own family revealed him to be Mark Felt, who had been second-in-command of the Federal Bureau of Investigation (FBI) while leaking information. *See also* HUTTON REPORT; SHIELD LAW; WHISTLEBLOWER.

anti-communism One of the five 'filters' of Edward Herman and Noam Chomsky's *propaganda model of the media; they argued that an atmosphere of anti-communism, particularly within the USA, resulted in a tendency for journalists to stick to safe subjects and *sources for fear of being labelled a communist or fellow traveller. Since the fall of the Berlin Wall and the end of the Cold War, the bogeyman role previously played by the Soviet Union and communists has arguably been transferred to Islamic fundamentalists. *See also* FLAK; MCCARTHYISM.

Anyone Here Been Raped and Speaks English? A question shouted repeatedly by a television reporter from the UK to women and children fleeing newly independent Zaire, according to a book of that title by foreign correspondent Edward Behr (1926–2007). The story is often told as an example of the insensitivity of journalists chasing a story. *See also* ETHICS.

Further reading: E. Behr, *Anyone Here Been Raped and Speaks English?* (1985).

AOL A US mass media online giant that employs some journalists directly to produce original content for its websites and in 2011 paid a reported $315 million (US dollars) to buy the *Huffington Post*.

AOP *See* ASSOCIATION OF ONLINE PUBLISHERS.

AP *See* ASSOCIATED PRESS.

apology An expression of a news organization's regret and remorse over the publication or broadcast of a story that was inaccurate, unjustifiably intrusive, or in some other way was deemed to contravene either the law, a code of ethical guidelines, or both. News organizations traditionally resist apologizing or offering *corrections on the grounds that such a public admission of fallibility might cause the audience to regard the product as a whole as unreliable and not to be trusted; those rare apologies that do appear tend to be the result of legal action for *defamation, with the wording typically drafted by lawyers. In recent years many news organizations have become quicker to offer some form of clarification or correction of erroneous information. Such corrections may be facilitated by a *readers' editor in the hope that *trust in a news outlet might actually be increased by the prompt correction of errors, although full and unreserved apologies remain relatively rare in journalism. *See also* RETRACTION.

apostrophe An important punctuation mark, the misuse of which is common among those training to be journalists and the correct use of which is a matter of pride for a good *sub-editor. *See also* GRAMMAR.

app An application or program for a computer, phone, or *tablet device that is designed, for example, to allow users to receive media output including digital editions of newspapers and magazines, or to attract users to a media organization's particular *brand.

April fool spoofs Hoax items that are run, in a spirit of playfulness, on the first day of April. The UK media, in particular, has a tradition of running elaborate hoaxes, two of the most famous of which are BBC *Panorama*'s 1957 'investigation' into the European spaghetti harvest and the *Guardian* newspaper's 1977 travel supplement to a little-known group of tropical islands, 'roughly in the shape of a semicolon', called San Serriffe (where everywhere and everyone was named after terms used in printing and typesetting). *See also* SPOOF.

(((•))) SEE WEB LINKS

• The BBC's spaghetti hoax
• The *Guardian*'s April Fool's hoaxes

Archant A Norwich-based publisher of regional newspapers, magazines, and websites in the UK, whose flagship titles include the *Eastern Daily Press* and the *East Anglian Daily Times*. Archant is consistently one of the top ten publishers of provincial newspapers in the UK, ranking seventh in 2013 with an average weekly *circulation of 1.6 million copies. It publishes more than 60 titles, around half of which are *freesheets.

archetypes People in the *news who are presented as if they somehow represent a group, a phenomenon, a trend, and/or as a mythic figure such as the hero, the villain, or the *victim. *See also* MYTH; REPRESENTATION; STEREOTYPING; TROPE.

archive 1. A news organization's internal collection of *cuttings, *pictures, *video, *audio, *letters, and other potentially useful documents. Whether material is stored in a collection of tatty brown envelopes or in a fully digitized electronic library, it needs to be indexed, cross-referenced, and be searchable by journalists working on stories. Very large news organizations might employ archivists or librarians to manage such material.

2. Back issues of a printed publication, or previously broadcast programmes, which in some cases will be available to the public.

Areopagitica A pamphlet written and published in 1644 by the English poet John Milton (1608–74) that articulated the case against *censorship and in favour of unlicensed printing and publishing. Arguing for the 'unbridled pen', Milton's pamphlet appeared during the political and social flux of the English Revolution (or Civil War), when all sides in the conflict used *pamphlets and other printed material to comment on events and put forward their arguments, and after which the republican government reimposed similar restrictions on free expression to restrictions that had existed under the monarchy. *Areopagitica* proved influential in subsequent arguments about a *free press and was cited in public debates that led to the lapsing of the *Licensing Act in 1695, which effectively ended prepublication censorship of *printing and paved the way for the emergence of the UK newspaper industry. *See also* DEMOCRACY; PUTNEY DEBATES.

(((●))) SEE WEB LINKS
• Text of *Areopagitica*

Arizona Republic A US daily newspaper (and website) published in Phoenix and covering the state of Arizona. It is now part of the *Gannett empire and is one of the top 25 US newspapers in terms of *circulation.

art The preferred generic term in many US newsrooms to cover *photographs as well as other forms of graphical illustration such as maps or *cartoons.

Article 19 A UK-based charity that campaigns for freedom of expression and in defence of journalism around the world. Formed in 1987 and named after the clause of the United Nations' *Universal Declaration of Human Rights that asserts the right to freedom of opinion and expression, its first campaign was on behalf of Zwelakhe Sisulu (1950–2012), an editor who was detained without trial by the apartheid government in South Africa. Sisulu was freed the following year. *See also* CENSORSHIP; HUMAN RIGHTS.

(((●))) SEE WEB LINKS
• Article 19's English-language website

artist's impression A painting or drawing of somebody in the news most commonly seen in media reports of court cases in the UK where filming and photography are normally prohibited (and where the sketch has to be done from memory after a brief visit to the courtroom by the artist).

Asian Media Information and Communication Centre (AMIC) A Singapore-based charity, formed in 1971, that promotes the development of media throughout the Asia-Pacific region. Its activities include researching media issues and organizing *awards.

(((∰))) **SEE WEB LINKS**
• AMIC homepage

Asian values in journalism A set of ideas articulated during the 1990s that rejected the primacy of the individual citizen's freedom of expression and/or right to know in favour of a form of journalism that emphasized societal harmony and collective interests. Seen by its supporters as a useful application of journalism in the service of national or regional development, critics have on occasions accused the Asian values 'movement' of being insufficiently critical of those in positions of power within society. *See also* DEVELOPMENT JOURNALISM.

ASNE *See* AMERICAN SOCIETY OF NEWS EDITORS.

Associated Newspapers A UK national media company whose flagships are the *Daily Mail* newspaper and the *Mail Online* website. Other titles include the *Mail on Sunday* and the free distribution newspaper *Metro*. Associated Newspapers forms part of A&N Media, which also includes a series of specialist property, travel, and employment websites and, until they were sold in 2009 and 2012 respectively, included the London *Evening Standard* and the *Northcliffe group of regional newspapers. A&N Media itself forms part of the DGMT plc (Daily Mail and General Trust), a London-based international conglomerate of media, digital, and events businesses that is listed on the London Stock Exchange. The company was founded by the Rothermere family and the family remains the biggest shareholder, with Lord Rothermere being the company chairman.

Associated Press (AP) A major *news agency owned by its subscribers within the US newspaper and broadcasting industries and operating on a not-for-profit basis to supply coverage of events across all media platforms. It was founded in 1846 when five newspapers in New York combined to pay for a pony express route through Alabama to allow readers in the north to hear news of the war with Mexico faster than the Post Office could deliver it. AP then made use of the *new technology known as the *telegraph. It is still based in New York and now employs more than 2,000 journalists, covering every US state as well as many countries overseas. AP likes to call itself 'the Marine corps of journalism—always first in and last out'.

Association for Education in Journalism and Mass Communication (AEJMC) An organization of *journalism studies academics, journalism trainers, and communication studies scholars working in the USA and Canada that was formed in 1912 as the American Association of Teachers of Journalism. Among other activities, the AEJMC publishes *Journalism & Mass Communication Quarterly*. *See also* JOURNALISM EDUCATION.

(((●))) SEE WEB LINKS
• The AEJMC centennial website

Association for Journalism Education (AJE) A network of lecturers and professors who teach journalism within universities in the UK and Ireland. Formed in 1997, the AJE aims to bring together those who train students in the vocational skills required to work as journalists, those whose focus is on the more academic elements of *journalism studies, and those who straddle what is often seen as the practice/theory divide. The AJE holds regular conferences and seminars, and in 2012 it launched a peer-reviewed open-access online journal, *Journalism Education. See also* ACADEMIZATION OF JOURNALISM; HACKADEMY; JOURNALISM EDUCATION; TRAINING.

(((●))) SEE WEB LINKS
• AJE website

Association of Alternative Newsweeklies (AAN) A network of more than 100 local alternative newspapers that are published in the USA and Canada. Since its formation in 1978, AAN has brought together publications that, in its own words, can demonstrate 'a strong focus on local news, culture and the arts; an informal and sometimes profane style; an emphasis on point-of-view reporting and narrative journalism; a tolerance for individual freedoms and social differences; and an eagerness to report on issues and communities that many mainstream media outlets ignore'. *See also* ALTERNATIVE PRESS; UNDERGROUND PRESS; VILLAGE VOICE.

(((()))) SEE WEB LINKS
• Directory of AAN members

Association of British Editors An organization set up in 1985 to provide a forum primarily for national newspaper editors in the UK that allowed them to meet independently of *proprietors. Membership extended to editors in other sections of the media before the association merged with the *Guild of Editors in 1999 to form the *Society of Editors.

Association of Magazine Media A New York-based organization that brings together publishers of more than 900 *magazines in the USA. Formed in 1919, and known as the Magazine Publishers Association (MPA) until 2010, it now covers online and multi-platform magazines in addition to print titles, and its research activity includes studies of magazine *brands on *social media and *tablet devices. It has retained the abbreviation MPA.

(((()))) SEE WEB LINKS
• MPA website

Association of Online Publishers (AOP) A trade body formed in 2002 to represent the digital publishing industry in the UK, the membership of which now includes major broadcast and print companies with online operations. The association publishes a regular *Digital Landscape Report*, which compiles details of the latest research of interest to digital publishers. *See also* ONLINE JOURNALISM.

(((()))) SEE WEB LINKS
• AOP news feed about digital media

astroturfing The creation of a false or exaggerated impression of grassroots support. The *comments facilities of news organizations' websites and *blogs can be bombarded with posts, often from one or two users with multiple online identities, to create an impression of widespread public concern about an issue where little or no genuine public concern may exist. The phenomenon of astroturfing (which gets its name from a term for artificial grass) is highlighted as one reason why journalists ought not to assume that online opinion is necessarily the same as *public opinion. *See also* HOAXES.

Atex A form of editorial *content management system (CMS) developed by the UK software company of the same name and used by

numerous media companies in different countries. The system has
proved attractive to managers because of the potential savings involved,
for example by cutting the jobs of *sub-editors. But the way it has
sometimes been utilized has been criticized by some journalists who see
it as downplaying the more human elements of subbing such as
creativity and *fact-checking. In 2010 the *National Union of Journalists
(NUJ) complained that the way the CMS system was being used on some
newspapers was undermining journalists' quest for *accuracy and the
ability of editors to edit; the complaint was prompted by a newspaper
company's instructions to editors that they no longer had to read every
story before publication. *See also* TEMPLATES.

Athenian Mercury *See* LADIES' MERCURY.

Atlanta Journal-Constitution A daily newspaper and online news
operation covering the US city of Atlanta, Georgia. The current title was
created in 2001 from a merger of two formerly rival newspapers: the
Atlanta Constitution, first published in 1868, and the *Atlanta Journal*,
which dates from 1883. Today the *Atlanta Journal-Constitution* is one of
the top 25 US newspapers in terms of *circulation.

Atlantic Monthly A US magazine and online platform that focuses on
politics and culture. Based in Washington DC, it is the flagship
publication of the Atlantic Media Company and was an early adopter of
digital publishing in the 1990s. Launched in 1857, the *Atlantic* was
among the first to publish the writing of Mark Twain.

atmos (atmosphere) The natural background sound, also known as
wildtrack, that is recorded on (or broadcast *live from) location and is
designed to add authenticity to a piece of *audio. *Compare* ACTUALITY.

attachment, journalism of *See* JOURNALISM OF ATTACHMENT.

Attitude A gay *lifestyle magazine published in the UK since 1994 that
specializes in making cover stars of celebrities (such as the West Ham
United footballer Matt Jarvis) who, although they may not themselves be
homosexual, are happy to pose for pictures and/or be interviewed. In
2012 *Attitude* presented *Times* columnist Caitlin Moran with its
Honorary Gay of the Year award, and in 2013 readers of the magazine
voted Olympic diver Tom Daley 'the sexiest man in the world'. *See also*
GAY MEDIA.

attribution Ascribing information and/or opinion to the *source or sources from which it originates so that members of the audience are not left asking, 'How do they know this?' or, 'Who says so?'. Attribution is therefore regarded as a key element of journalistic practice that tells the reader or viewer how a news organization knows what it is reporting, and confirms that journalists are not simply giving their own versions of events. Attribution can involve direct *quotes, *indirect quotes, *soundbites, citations of documents, references to other media, and *links to original material. It is normally as specific as possible, although there are occasions when the use of *anonymous or confidential sources mean the journalist may give few clues as to precisely where information has come from. Such stories still require some attribution so the audience knows that there *is* a source even if they do not know the identity. Some proponents of *investigative and *campaigning journalism regard journalism-by-attribution as a form of cop-out on the grounds that it absolves the reporter from deciding whose account is closer to the *truth of a matter, thereby reducing reporting to something closer to stenography.

audience The people who consume journalism, who may be *Twitter followers, website *users, TV *viewers, radio *listeners, or *readers of magazines and newspapers. Audiences may be divided into market segments based on demographics or areas of interest, and access to their eyes and/or ears will in turn be sold on to *advertisers (with the exception of the audience for non-commercial media such as the *BBC). News organizations are constantly searching for new audiences while trying to retain their existing ones. To this end, many publishers embark on extensive audience research, including the use of focus groups, and the findings are often used to adjust editorial priorities and decisions over what to cover and how (much to the dismay of those journalists who disdain any commercial influence on their craft). Although (some) members of the audience have long contributed to media via *letters to the press and later through radio and TV *phone-ins, the advent of the *internet and then *social media has seen an exponential growth in interaction between news organizations and their audiences. It may still be only a minority of audience members who communicate directly with journalists and other producers of media output, but it is a much bigger minority than in *analogue days and the speed of communication can be much faster, even instant.

See also ACTIVE AUDIENCE; AUDIT BUREAU OF CIRCULATION; IMAGINED AUDIENCE; NATIONAL READERSHIP SURVEY; RATINGS; TROLLING; USER-GENERATED CONTENT; YOUR COMMENTS.

audio The sound recorded (or broadcast *live) for use on radio, TV, online, or via mobile devices. *See also* ACTUALITY; ATMOS; AUDIOBOO; RADIO JOURNALISM.

AudioBoo A website and *app that allows users to upload and share *audio clips online or via smart phones. Whereas broadcast and online journalists can use AudioBoo to post extracts of a story, listeners can also use it to draw attention to any mistakes that make it on *air. One of the most shared clips since the app was launched in 2009 was of *Today presenter James Naughtie mispronouncing the name of senior politician Jeremy Hunt.

(((∰))) SEE WEB LINKS
• Top 10 AudioBoo moments

audio slideshow The combination of still *pictures with one or more forms of *audio as a way of telling a story online. An audio slideshow typically lasts four or five minutes and often incorporates music as well as clips from interviews. It is a web-specific form of reporting that can be used as part of the journalism mix for both serious and light stories, often following initial coverage and adopting something of a reflective tone. *See also* ONLINE JOURNALISM.

Audit Bureau of Circulation (ABC) A membership organization that, since 1931, has been supplying independently verified information on sales and the audience reach of commercial media to the UK *advertising industry. *See also* ABCE.

Australian A national daily *broadsheet newspaper in Australia that is part of the *Murdoch empire, having been launched by Rupert Murdoch himself in 1964. In the following decade the paper experienced what has been described as the first strike by journalists over an ethical issue at an Australian newspaper, when staff objected to what they saw as *biased and unfair coverage of the 1975 general election campaign. *See also* ETHICS.

Australian Broadcasting Corporation (ABC) The *public service broadcaster of Australia, created through the Australian Broadcasting Commission Act of 1932. Its early news on the radio was simply read aloud from the newspapers but by 1939 it was breaking stories on air, including the outbreak of the Second World War. ABC TV News launched in 1956, online output followed in 1995, and ten years later its *24-hour news operation began as the first free-to-air rolling news channel on Australian television.

(⊕) SEE WEB LINKS

• ABC News 24 website

Australian Independent Media Inquiry *See* FINKELSTEIN REPORT.

Australian Journalists' Association (AJA) The trade union for journalists in Australia from 1910 to 1992, when it became part of the *Media Entertainment and Arts Alliance.

autocue An electronic device with a screen, on which a *script can be displayed directly in front of a TV *presenter or *newsreader; the script will be scrolled through at the appropriate speed, allowing the presenter to appear to look directly into the camera while reading.

autocutie A term for TV news and sport *presenters who are thought to have been employed more for their appearance than for their ability. *See also* SEXISM.

autonomy The freedom to work without being directly controlled, censored, or micro-managed. Within journalism the concept of autonomy may refer to an absence of state *censorship or system for *licensing journalists, the extent to which editors may or may not be free of proprietorial and commercial interference, the way in which journalists may or may not be expected to adopt a preconceived editorial line on an issue, and the extent to which reporters in the field have the freedom or otherwise to decide from which locations to report, when, and how. Media theorists tend to refer to journalists enjoying only a limited, constrained, or licensed form of autonomy whereby individuals may take some decisions, have some influence, and push some boundaries, but only up to a point. *See also* AGENCY; CONSCIENCE CLAUSE; CONSTRAINTS; EDITORIAL INDEPENDENCE.

Avaaz An online movement of international activists and 'clicktivists' that, since its launch in 2007, has mobilized people both on the streets and on the internet in support of what it describes as 'people-powered politics'. Its campaigns have included a particularly

high-profile one against the power of the *Murdoch empire. *See also*
ACTIVIST MEDIA; NETIZEN.

(⊕) SEE WEB LINKS
• Avaaz English-language website

awards Prizes and/or marks of recognition that are awarded to
individual journalists, teams of journalists, or particular media outlets.
Awards are typically presented at ceremonies that can be seen as
celebrations of excellence in journalism or as orgies of self-
congratulation, depending on who has won and who has lost. In the
USA, winning the *Pulitzer Prize is widely regarded as the pinnacle of
journalistic achievement. *See also* LITTLE JIMMY.

B

backgrounder A piece that accompanies or follows a *news item and gives further historical or other contextualizing information or analysis.

bad news An event that has negative connotations for those involved and which is deemed by journalists to be *newsworthy. This is expressed in the adage that, for the media, the only good news is bad news. Bad news can vary from death, disaster, and other forms of *tragedy, to less serious examples of misfortune, such as a punter who has lost a winning lottery ticket. However, as with millions of other events that happen in the world every day, the process of *selection means that only a tiny fraction of potential bad news items ever become news; additional factors that come into play range from other *news values to logistical questions about the location of journalists and the availability of *pictures. *Compare* GOOD NEWS. *See also* NEGATIVITY.

BAJ *See* BRITISH ASSOCIATION OF JOURNALISTS.

balance Even-handedness and fairness in assessing and presenting different sides of an issue, argument, or conflict (*compare* BIAS). The notion of balance does not necessarily require a strict stopwatch-measured evenness between the time devoted to different sources, nor does it imply that all viewpoints be treated equally (a story about the murder of a child need not be balanced by interviewing a spokesperson for child killers, for example). Rather, balance within journalism requires that journalists approach stories with open minds and report matters fairly, having regard to the evidence, and acknowledging the existence of different explanations and interpretations. *See also* IMPARTIALITY; OBJECTIVE JOURNALISM.

Baltimore Sun A daily newspaper covering the state of Maryland in the USA from 1837 onwards. Since 2000 the paper and its online operations have been owned by the Tribune Company of Chicago.

A semi-fictionalized version of the newspaper featured in the acclaimed television crime drama *The Wire* (2002–08), created by former *Baltimore Sun* reporter David Simon (1960–).

(((●))) SEE WEB LINKS

• *Baltimore Sun* on *The Wire*

banner A style of *headline or *advertisement that is big, bold, often run across the full width of a page, and difficult to avoid. *See also* BANNER HEADLINE.

banner headline A *headline set in a large font, typically across the width of a page, and in some *tabloid newspapers taking up virtually the entire front page.

Bar of Shame *See* SIDEBAR OF SHAME.

Bauer Media A giant German-based international media company that, in the UK, owns *Angling Times*, *Closer*, *FHM*, *Grazia*, *Heat*, *Mojo*, *Q*, *Take a Break*, *Yours*, *Zoo*, many other magazine and online *brands, plus a string of radio stations.

BBC (British Broadcasting Corporation) The UK-based *public service broadcaster that is a major provider of *news, *current affairs, and much else on radio, television, and online, employing around 20,000 people including up to 7,000 journalists producing an estimated average of 120 hours of news broadcasting every day. It is the largest news broadcasting organization in the world.

Formed in 1922 by a group of radio manufacturers (including Marconi) as the British Broadcasting Company, from the start it was independent from *advertisers because it was funded by a Post Office *licence fee. On 1 January 1927 it became the British Broadcasting Corporation, established by royal charter. The first BBC Director-General was John Reith (1889–1971), an engineer who had been general manager of the original company and had campaigned for the royal charter; he was duly elevated to Sir John. It was Reith who established the BBC's ethos of informing, educating, and entertaining (*see* REITHIAN PRINCIPLES). The charter, which is renewed periodically, sets out the objectives, obligations, and powers of the BBC and the *BBC governors (now the *BBC Trust), creating a funding structure for the corporation that frees it from direct commercial considerations as it does not rely on *advertising. Nor is the BBC a directly state-run or state-funded broadcast organization (with the exception of the *BBC World Service prior to 2014), although its much-prized operational independence is tempered by the role of politicians in appointing governors and trustees and in setting the level of the licence fee.

News was extremely limited in the early days of the BBC, with brief summaries and *bulletins broadcast on radio only after 7 pm so as not to compete with newspapers, and, until such restrictions were relaxed in 1928, not covering any political, industrial, or religious topics that were deemed controversial. The bulk of its stories were supplied by news agencies such as *Reuters and, in contrast with the press, BBC news was from the start formally committed to *impartiality. On Good Friday 1930, BBC radio famously declared that there was no news to report that evening, but the role of news on the BBC and the numbers of its own journalists grew in the rest of that decade, not least with the launch of the Empire Service (forerunner of the World Service). The first half-hour radio news programme was broadcast in 1944 (at 9 pm on the evening of D-Day), and then a fledgling form of television news began in 1948, modelled in part on cinema *newsreels. The following decade saw a number of major developments, including: longer form current affairs journalism on television with *Panorama (launched in 1953); news programmes specifically designed for TV (from 1954); and a modernizing shake-up of BBC television news in response to the arrival of competition from the commercial *ITN (launched in 1955). The year 1957 saw two further developments which contributed to giving BBC journalism a more independent and less deferential tone: the launches of *Tonight* as the first television programme to tackle topical issues every weekday and of *Today*, which gradually grew to become *the* agenda-setting radio programme in the UK.

New services and new technologies have been incorporated into the BBC's news output over subsequent decades, including: the launch of local radio (with BBC Radio Leicester, in 1967); the first TV news broadcast in colour (*Newsroom*, in 1968); the creation of an on-screen text-based information service (*Ceefax*, in 1974); breakfast news on TV (1983); *rolling news on radio (1991); *BBC News 24* on television (1997); and online services (also launched in 1997 but which have developed hugely since, with a network of regional news websites and, from 2007, the iPlayer digital catch-up service).

The corporation's journalism across all platforms and outlets is required to abide by the *BBC editorial guidelines, which are issued and reviewed by the BBC Trust. Trustees set BBC strategy but day-to-day management is in the hands of the BBC Executive, headed by the Director-General (who is hired and fired by the Trust). The history of the BBC is punctuated by crises and outbreaks of tension with governments of the day, which have often been prompted by disputes over the independence of BBC journalism at times of conflict such as Suez (1956), the Falklands War (1982), Iraq (2003, *see* HUTTON REPORT), and Northern Ireland (repeatedly, *see* REAL LIVES).

In 2012 the BBC was plunged into a wholly self-inflicted crisis over its initial failure to take seriously allegations of child sex abuse by TV 'personality' Jimmy Savile (1926–2011), which emerged after he had died. Director-General George Entwistle became the shortest-lived holder of that office in BBC history when he lost his job after just 54 days in the wake of what was widely seen as a particularly poor interview on the *Today* programme, which followed a *Newsnight* story that had led to the false identification of a lord as a paedophile, which in turn followed *Newsnight* dropping an investigation into Savile while the BBC ran gushing tributes to him (*see* POLLARD REVIEW). Such own goals are seized on gleefully by much of the UK's commercial media, especially by the *Daily Mail* and newspapers in the *Murdoch empire, which often need little prompting to accuse the BBC variously of *bias, wasting public money, or stifling competition. Earlier, *News Corporation's James Murdoch told the 2009 Edinburgh Television Festival that 'state-sponsored journalism' such as that provided by the BBC threatened the plurality of news provision. BBC journalism tends to be accused by the right of pandering to a liberal or left-wing metropolitan elite, whereas critics from the left see it as overly deferential towards, and uncritical of, the ruling forces in society. However, not all criticisms emanate from commercial rivals or political activists: the BBC's own journalists have on many occasions expressed dismay at the corporation's tendency to employ ever more highly paid managers even when cutting the jobs of relatively low-paid journalists, producers, and researchers. There have also been accusations of bullying. The BBC is unusual in that internal criticisms and disputes are typically reported on the organization's own news programmes in the same way as other stories are covered, with critics being given airtime and senior bosses being interrogated by journalists who are, in effect, their employees. Following criticisms of BBC journalism in the Hutton Report of 2004, the BBC established its own College of Journalism in an effort to educate new and existing staff alike in the ways of the BBC's brand of reporting (*see* NEIL REPORT).

In 2010 the BBC licence fee was frozen until 2016–17 and government funding of the World Service was withdrawn from 2014; both decisions have led to cutbacks across the BBC, including in broadcast and online news and current affairs. *See also* BIMEDIA JOURNALISM; BROADCAST JOURNALISM; OFCOM; ONLINE JOURNALISM; RADIO JOURNALISM; TELEVISION JOURNALISM.

(⊕) SEE WEB LINKS
• BBC College of Journalism website

BBC editorial guidelines The rules, values, and standards established by the *BBC to guide its entire output, including *news and *current affairs. The guidelines cover everything from *impartiality, election coverage, and responses to hostage-taking, to the portrayal of nudity, secret filming for comedic effect, and the integrity of 'makeover' programmes. They apply to all of the corporation's editorial content, including that originated by *freelance journalists or independent production companies, across the BBC's websites, magazines, and social media output, in addition to its *broadcast journalism. The guidelines incorporate and add to the UK's more general broadcasting regulations laid down by *Ofcom. The guidelines, which can be searched online and are used as a daily reference point by BBC journalists, are reviewed and reissued by the *BBC Trust every five years.

(⊕) SEE WEB LINKS
• BBC editorial guidelines

BBC governors The governing body of the *BBC before the *BBC Trust took over that role in 2007 in the wake of the *Hutton Report. From their creation in 1927, the BBC governors were dominated by loyal members of the UK establishment who at times of conflict were often said to adopt a deferential posture described by critics as a 'pre-emptive cringe'. Appointed by the monarch on the advice of governments of the day, governors occasionally asserted their independence by defending the integrity of BBC journalism when it came under fire from politicians, while at other times they stood accused of craven subservience (*see* REAL LIVES).

(⊕) SEE WEB LINKS
• BBC governors' archive

BBC Trust The governing body of the *BBC since 2007 when it replaced the *BBC governors following criticism of the previous regime in the *Hutton Report. The Trust sets the BBC's strategy, issues the *BBC editorial guidelines, decides how to spend the *licence fee, conducts reviews of the corporation's output and policy, and hears appeals from people dissatisfied with the response of BBC management to complaints. Members of the Trust (trustees) are formally appointed by the monarch, acting on the recommendation of the prime minister of the UK. *See also* POLLARD REVIEW; OFCOM; STATUTORY REGULATION.

((())) SEE WEB LINKS
• Current BBC trustees

BBC World Service A news, current affairs, education, and entertainment service run by the UK-based *BBC and broadcast to the rest of the world. Launched in 1932 as the Empire Service, using shortwave radio and broadcasting only in English, by the outbreak of war in 1939 it was also broadcasting in seven additional languages, including French, German, and Italian. A year later the service was broadcasting 78 news bulletins every day in 34 languages, including Hindi, and by 1945 that had risen to 45 languages, including Arabic. The Empire Service had changed its name in 1943 to the General Overseas Service and only in 1965 did it become the World Service. Its history has seen periods of expansion into, and retreat from, different territories and languages, partly in response to world events and partly prompted by financial considerations. Traditionally the service has been funded not by the BBC's *licence fee but directly by the UK Government via the Foreign and Commonwealth Office. Despite such direct state funding, the *BBC editorial guidelines are applied to World Service output and the BBC has resisted pressures to run it as a *propaganda outfit, leading to occasional tensions with governments of the day. This funding arrangement will change, following a decision by David Cameron's Government in 2010 that, from 2014 onwards, the service would have to be paid for from the licence fee. The World Service still broadcasts via shortwave radio but is today a multimedia broadcaster, delivering content in 28 languages via AM and FM radio, digital satellite television, cable, online, and via wireless handheld devices, to a weekly audience estimated to be around 166 million people. For most of its history the service was synonymous with Bush House, its London headquarters, but in 2012 staff were relocated to Broadcasting House, also in London. *Compare* VOICE OF AMERICA.

(((•))) SEE WEB LINKS

• World Service leaves Bush House

beat Primarily a US term for the subject matter or geographical area that a *reporter might be assigned to cover, as in 'the crime beat' or 'the Washington beat'. Reporters might still be expected actually to beat (walk) streets and stalk corridors in person but today they are even more likely to be required to monitor *social media for potential stories and *sources as well as to develop a network of *contacts who may provide *tips or with whom rumours may be checked. Beat reporters are expected to become founts of all knowledge on their area or topic; as they are wont to say, they have to know when anyone so much as coughs, spits, or farts on their *patch. A beat reporter who is scooped by a rival is likely to be frowned upon by the *newsdesk. *See also* SPECIALIST.

Bebo A *social networking website that, as with *Facebook, will often be used by journalists looking for information on, pictures of, and contact details for people who suddenly find themselves in the news (for example by being a *victim or alleged perpetrator of a violent crime). *See also* DIGITAL DOORSTEPPING; INTRUSION.

Belfast Newsletter Believed to be the world's oldest surviving general daily newspaper, having been first published in 1737. Since 2005 it has been part of the *Johnston Press stable and, as a result, there has been some speculation that the *Newsletter* might become a weekly.

Belfast Telegraph A daily newspaper published in Northern Ireland since 1870 and owned since 2000 by *Independent News & Media.

below-the-fold An item that appears in the bottom half of the front page of a large format newspaper (*see* BROADSHEET; BERLINER), giving it less visibility or prominence, especially when the newspaper is folded in half, for example while on display in a newsagent's shop. This space is sometimes used for more quirky, humorous stories or *colour pieces that provide a contrast with the more serious news above it. The term may also refer to items that cannot be viewed on a website without scrolling down. *See also* ABOVE-THE-FOLD.

Berkshire Hathaway An investment company run by multi-billionaire Warren Buffett (1930–) (the fourth richest man on the planet, according to *Forbes*) that in 2012–13 began buying local newspapers in the USA, including the *Omaha World-Herald* and the *Tulsa World*, prompting a number of commentators to question whether newspapers were necessarily doomed to vanish after all.

Berliner A *newspaper format larger than a *tabloid but smaller than a traditional *broadsheet although, like the latter, it requires a horizontal fold for display in a shop; the standard Berliner page size is 470 mm by 315 mm. The Berliner size is used by some serious newspapers such as *La Stampa* (Italy), *La Vanguardia* (Spain), and *Le Monde* (France), although not currently by newspapers in the German city after which it derives its name. Use of the Berliner was pioneered in the UK by the *Guardian*, which spent a reported £50 million on a new printing operation in 2005 to switch to a format that editor Alan Rusbridger saw as allowing for the retention of the newspaper's broadsheet approach in a more reader-friendly size. Although it has been seen primarily as a European format, the Berliner crossed the Atlantic in 2006 when the *Lafayette Journal & Courier* became the first of several US newspapers to adopt it.

Berrow's Worcester Journal A weekly published in the UK city of Worcester that claims to be the oldest surviving commercial newspaper in the world, having been published (albeit as an irregular news-sheet in the early years) since 1690. Some scholars doubt the connection between that earlier publication and the paper proper, which was launched as the *Worcester Post-man* in 1709, later becoming the *Worcester Journal*; the name of one of the newspaper's 18th-century owners was subsequently inserted into the title to distinguish it from a rival publication, and it stuck. Today it is owned by *Newsquest. *See also* LOCAL JOURNALISM; NORWICH POST; STAMFORD MERCURY.

bias The favouring of one side, viewpoint, argument, or disposition over another (*compare* BALANCE). Bias within journalism is sometimes a conscious and deliberate approach, as in *advocacy journalism and some forms of *alternative journalism that reject *objectivity and *impartiality and prefer to state their bias openly to enable members of the *audience to take it into consideration. Other forms of bias might be unconscious or the result of structural factors: for example, a newsroom dominated by white, middle-aged, heterosexual men who drive fast cars and are interested in football and rock music from a certain era may not surprisingly end up reporting the world through the eyes and mindset of white, middle-aged, heterosexual men who fast drive cars and are interested in football and rock music from a certain era (*see* CULTURAL BIAS). News organizations and journalists frequently find themselves accused of bias; sometimes such accusations are made simultaneously by people on opposing sides of an argument, who all think coverage is biased against them.

bigfooting The process whereby a senior journalist or star correspondent takes over a story from a more junior colleague and/or arrives on the scene after someone with local contacts and knowledge has laid the groundwork.

Bild The biggest-selling newspaper in Germany, often accused of *sensationalism and *sexism. A conservative *tabloid owned by Axel Springer, in 2012 *Bild* ended the practice it started in 1984 of running a picture of a semi-naked woman on its front page every day, but the topless picture was merely moved inside. *See also* PAGE THREE; PORNIFICATION.

bill A paper sheet or placard advertising the contents of a newspaper and displayed by newspaper vendors. The wording is typically aimed at enticing buyers without giving away precise details, such as 'Film star dies'.

bimedia journalism When a story is covered for both radio and television by the same journalist or editorial team, often using *audio for the radio version that has been *repurposed from a television *package. Bimedia journalism was seen as the future by the *BBC in the 1990s, when some distinct TV and radio newsrooms were converted to bimedia operations. Since then it has been somewhat supplanted, first by converged journalism (*see* CONVERGENCE) and today by journalism that may be delivered on multiple *platforms. *See also* MULTISKILLED JOURNALISM.

binology A semi-humorous term for the ethically questionable practice of searching through the dustbins of celebrities, lawyers, and others of interest to journalists in the hope of finding evidence of *scandal, wrongdoing, or other potentially *newsworthy events or relationships. *Compare* MUCKRAKING. *See also* DARK ARTS.

Birmingham Post A daily *broadsheet newspaper covering the major
UK city of Birmingham from 1857 to 2009, when it became a weekly
*compact plus website. It is now owned by *Trinity Mirror.

BJTC *See* BROADCAST JOURNALISM TRAINING COUNCIL.

Black Dwarf 1. A radical satirical weekly newspaper published
in London between 1817 and 1824 by Thomas Jonathan Wooler
(1786–1853). It was an unstamped publication (*see* STAMP DUTY). During
the time he published and edited *Black Dwarf,* Wooler faced trials for
seditious libel and served time in prison for conspiracy. *See also*
SATIRICAL JOURNALISM.
2. A radical newspaper published in London between 1968 and 1972 and
produced (ostensibly weekly) by a collective of socialists and feminists
that included Tariq Ali, Adrian Mitchell, and Sheila Rowbotham. Apart
from expressing opposition to the Vietnam War and support for
revolting students, its main claim to fame was that it provoked an angry
exchange of letters with John Lennon over the politics of the Beatles'
song *Revolution. See also* ALTERNATIVE MEDIA; RADICAL PRESS;
UNDERGROUND PRESS.

(((●))) SEE WEB LINKS
• John Lennon responds to criticism in *Black Dwarf*

black media Newspapers, magazines, broadcast organizations, and
other forms of media serving a largely black *audience and often
emerging from within black communities (or 'people of colour'). The
first black newspaper to emerge in the USA is generally thought to be
Freedom's Journal, published in New York between 1827 and 1829, and
by the end of the American Civil War in 1865 there were around 40 such
papers, growing to a reported 1,200 by the early years of the 20th
century. Papers tended to come and go and most had small, localized
readerships, but there were exceptions; in 1945 the ***Pittsburgh Courier***
became the largest black paper in US history, selling around 350,000
copies a week with editions covering many parts of the country. Black
newspapers in the USA began to decline in the second half of the
20th century, partly because black people began to see themselves
mentioned in—and sometimes even employed by—mainstream (white
dominated) media. However, black magazines such as *Ebony* continue
to find a niche in the 21st century. The black media in the UK never had
the reach or influence of their US counterparts, although there is a long

history of political, religious, expatriate, and community-based publications being produced by black people in the UK, dating back at least as far as *Lux* in 1892 and *Fraternity* the following year, both under the editorship of Celestine Edwards (1858–94). Almost a century later, in 1982 the *Voice* newspaper became a lively presence on the news-stands, and more recently online, reporting news, sport, and entertainment in a *tabloid style for a primarily Afro-Caribbean readership. Black radio stations operate in both the USA and UK, many of them available online, but few focusing on journalism. *See also* CALIFORNIA EAGLE; ETHNIC MINORITY MEDIA; NATIONAL ASSOCIATION OF BLACK JOURNALISTS; REPRESENTATION.

(⊕) SEE WEB LINKS
• The black press in the USA

blagging The obtaining of confidential information by using a mixture of *deception, charm, persuasion, and confidence. One of the so-called '*dark arts' of journalism, blagging is a form of *intrusion into the *privacy of an individual or possibly even an organization. It might involve a journalist making a telephone call to a bank and pretending to be a particular customer in an effort to obtain details of their personal finances, for example; or a call to a clinic purportedly from a hospital currently treating one of their patients and in urgent need of their medical records. Such blagging is generally regarded as ethically dubious, at best, and plain wrong, at worst, but some journalists justify it in cases where an investigation is deemed to be clearly in the *public interest. The *Leveson inquiry into the UK press heard evidence that some newspapers contracted out such information-gathering tasks to third parties, such as *private investigators. *See also* DATA PROTECTION; ETHICS; HACKGATE.

Bliss A best-selling monthly *magazine for teenage girls published in the UK and specializing in stories about celebrities, fashion, dating, and 'fit lads'. Since 2006 the magazine and its *MyBliss* online *brand have been owned by the Panini Group. *See also* WOMEN'S MAGAZINES.

blog An abbreviation for **web log**, an online journal that typically displays the most recent items, or blog 'posts', first and which also allows readers to post comments beneath items. Blogs can include text, *pictures, *video, and *audio. A blog is most often the work of one individual but there are some group or collectively produced blogs.

They range from confessional, personal diaries and observations on random pieces of trivia, to the obsessive detailing of hobbyist minutiae, and deranged examples of 'hate speech'. Some are works of fiction produced under a false identity. However, many blogs are of considerable use to journalists, for example if the *blogger is an expert commentator on, or participant in, something that may be *newsworthy; the blog *www.order-order.com* is required reading for political journalists in the UK and there are similar 'must-read' blogs within any specialism that are routinely monitored for *tips, *sources, and controversies. Many print and broadcast journalists also produce their own blogs, which they sometimes use to break stories, sometimes to discuss stories either before or after publication, sometimes to foster a relationship with their audience, and sometimes even to reveal elements of their personal lives (which can also be considered part of building a personal *brand). *See also* BLOGGER; BLOGOSPHERE; LIVEBLOG; ONLINE JOURNALISM; SOCIAL MEDIA; WORDPRESS.

(⊕) SEE WEB LINKS
• Technorati's list of the 100 most influential blogs

blogger Somebody who produces a *blog, which in nearly all cases is done for no pay. Some bloggers are *journalists, some journalists are bloggers, and some want nothing to do with each other despite the fact that many regard the division between blogging and journalism as becoming increasingly blurred. *Compare* BLOGGER.

Blogger Software that, when it was released on the *internet free of charge by Pyra Labs in San Francisco in 1999, allowed virtually anybody to set up their own *blog even without having technical knowledge of computer coding or online design. This led to the rapid growth of *blogging beyond its initial more 'nerdy' exponents. The popularity of Blogger (which was bought by *Google in 2003) has to some extent been supplanted by *WordPress. *See also* CITIZEN JOURNALISM; ONLINE JOURNALISM.

blogging The act of producing a *blog or *liveblog.

blogosphere The world of *blogs in which *bloggers and people who post comments on blogs talk to each other and to anyone else who takes an interest. New blogs are started all the time just as existing blogs close down, or more often are simply abandoned, dormant yet visible in *cyberspace.

Bloomberg A US-based media company, *news agency, and multimedia news organization, specializing in financial news and *business journalism since 1982 and boasting *bureaus in more than 70 countries.

Boston Globe A daily newspaper covering Boston, Massachusetts, and owned by the New York Times Company from 1993 until 2013, when it was bought by billionaire John Henry (1949–) (the owner of the Boston Red Sox baseball team and Liverpool football club). Although it is one of the top 25 best-selling newspapers in the USA, Henry is reported to have paid only around a tenth of what it had cost the NY Times Company twenty years earlier.

Boston Herald A daily newspaper and website based in Boston, Massachusetts, that is a descendant of titles that were once part of both the *Hearst and *Murdoch newspaper empires, but since 1994 it has been independently owned.

boundary maintenance A term sometimes used within *journalism studies to describe the way in which *journalists are said to create a professional and/or socio-cultural distinction between themselves and non-journalists. Such boundaries are often described as being blurred by phenomena such as *user-generated content and *citizen journalism, but arguments about who is or is not a 'proper' journalist pre-dated the advent of the *internet by at least a hundred years. *See also* AMATEUR JOURNALISM; CRAFT; FIELD; PROFESSION; TRADE.

brand An identifiable name, logo, image, or reputation that media organizations (and some individual journalists and *bloggers) try to project and protect. *See also* BRANDING.

branding A marketing exercise by media organizations aiming to extend and retain their *audience by offering more services under one *brand. For example, a *magazine and its website may also offer readers access to events such as fashion shows, *podcasts, a dedicated *YouTube channel, *apps, interaction via *social media, and other activities and branded products ranging from T-shirts to jewellery, all labelled with the magazine brand and all aimed at increasing audience loyalty.

breaking news A story that emerges or unfolds unexpectedly, as opposed to a *diary story. Breaking news may begin with an *alert and be updated as a *running story. *24-hour news channels specialize in breaking news. *See also* NEVER WRONG FOR LONG; ROLLING NEWS.

bribe 1. A financial inducement offered *to* a journalist in the hope of securing favourable coverage in the media, a practice condemned by journalists' organizations as wholly unethical.
2. A pejorative word for a financial inducement offered *by* a journalist in the hope of securing information or access that would not otherwise be forthcoming; depending on the story and the *source, this may be condemned as corruption or defended as being in the *public interest. *Compare* BUY-UP; FREEBIE.

brief 1. A note of how a particular story should be covered, typically provided to a reporter by the editor who commissions the item.
2. Background notes provided by a researcher or reporter to a *presenter who will be conducting an *interview.
3. A short news item or *nib.

British Association of Journalists (BAJ) A small journalists' trade union in the UK, centred on the *_Daily Mirror_ and *_Sunday Mirror_. The BAJ was established in 1992 as a breakaway from the *National Union of Journalists (NUJ), which was accused of being too concerned with political issues by BAJ founder Steve Turner (himself a former long-standing NUJ *Father of Chapel and shortlived NUJ general secretary). *See also* INSTITUTE OF JOURNALISTS.

British Broadcasting Corporation *See* BBC.

British Journalism Review A quarterly journal launched in 1989 with the aim of combining commentary written by reflective journalists and analysis by reader-friendly academics. *See also* REFLECTIVE PRACTICE.

broadcast ban Restrictions imposed on radio and television journalists by the UK government between 1988 and 1994 that outlawed *audio spoken by members or supporters of certain organizations involved in the Northern Ireland 'troubles'. Several republican and loyalist groups were covered by the ban but the prime target was Sinn Fein, the political wing of the IRA (Irish Republican Army). Prime Minister Margaret Thatcher had spoken of wanting to deny such groups 'the oxygen of publicity' and the broadcast ban was aimed at putting her wish into effect. However, broadcast journalists could engage actors to read aloud the words of political figures such as Sinn Fein leader Gerry Adams, even if they could not broadcast Adams and others speaking them directly. The controversial ban was met with opposition by *human rights campaigners, who argued that it contravened freedom of speech, and by the *National Union of Journalists, which pointed out that it prevented journalists from conducting effective questioning of key players on the political scene. The UK broadcast ban, similar to one imposed in the Irish Republic (*see* SECTION 31), was only lifted after the IRA announced a ceasefire in 1994. *See also* CENSORSHIP; REAL LIVES.

broadcasting The transmission of sound by radio and of audio-visual material by television. The name implies the potential for a mass audience (*compare* NARROWCASTING), although subscription-only cable, satellite, and digital channels have delivered broadcast material to more niche audiences in recent decades. *See also* BROADCAST JOURNALISM.

Broadcasting Act 1990 The piece of legislation that paved the way for the breaking up of the 'cosy' way in which commercial television (funded by *advertising) was often said to have been run since its creation in the 1950s. The Act opened the way for broadcasting franchises to go to the highest bidder and for the Independent Broadcasting Authority to be replaced by the lighter-touch Independent Television Commission. It resulted in job losses and a reduction in serious news, current affairs, and documentary programming.

broadcast journalism News and current affairs reporting using sound and/or pictures and delivered by means of radio and/or television transmission. In its early days *radio journalism often offered little more than the reading out of items taken from *news agencies or newspapers; the early days of *television journalism similarly relied upon the work of its predecessors, in its case cinema *newsreels as well as radio and print. Over time, however, broadcast journalism developed its own styles, subjects, and stars, and during the last quarter of the 20th century many newspaper editors and commentators believed that audiences got their news from TV or radio first (and consequently newspapers had to provide something else if they were to compete and survive). Then came the *internet and with it the realization that broadcasting was no longer the newest way of presenting news. This offered fresh opportunities as well as fresh challenges, and in the 21st century broadcast journalism has increasingly become part of a *multimedia approach that has incorporated *online journalism and *user-generated content. *See also* BBC; BIMEDIA JOURNALISM; CONVERGENCE; 24-HOUR NEWS.

Further reading: G. Hudson and S. Rowlands, *The Broadcast Journalism Handbook* (2012).

Broadcast Journalism Training Council (BJTC) An accrediting body for *training courses in *television journalism, *radio journalism, and *online journalism in the UK, established in the 1980s and run as a partnership by a council on which broadcasting employers, universities, and the *National Union of Journalists are all represented. In 2013 the BJTC accredited 72 different courses in 43 higher education institutions.

(((●))) SEE WEB LINKS
• Courses accredited by the BJTC

broadsheet A large-format *newspaper as opposed to a *tabloid or *compact; the standard broadsheet page size in the UK is 750 mm by 600 mm and there are variations in other countries. A broadsheet will normally be folded in half horizontally for display in shops. The broadsheet format allows for numerous stories and other items to be featured on each page, with the most eye-catching material typically placed *above-the-fold. However, the term 'broadsheet' says as much about content, readership, and *branding as it does about size or format because it is used as shorthand for the *quality press (also known as the '*heavies' in the UK: the *Daily Telegraph, The *Times, the *Guardian, the *Financial Times, the *Independent, and their Sunday equivalents, even those that are now printed in a smaller format), and their online operations. In this sense, broadsheet means privileging serious news over celebrity or entertainment-driven stories, longer and more complex stories over short and punchy ones, and text over pictures; the term also implies that the product will maintain a relatively clear separation between news and comment. *See also* BERLINER, TABLOIDIZATION.

B2B (business-to-business) A sector of the media that is aimed at other businesses rather than at a wider public audience (business-to-consumer or B2C). *See also* BUSINESS JOURNALISM; TRADE PRESS.

bulks Free or heavily discounted copies of newspapers and magazines that are used to increase *circulation figures, thereby making the publication more attractive to *advertisers.

bulletin A summary of *news items delivered on TV or radio, typically on the hour or half-hour. News bulletins (sometimes called *newscasts, news programmes, or simply 'the news') usually last anything from 30 seconds to several minutes and may be just headlines but might incorporate full reports as well. *Compare* ROLLING NEWS.

Bullivant Media Ltd A family-owned company that owns a series of local weekly newspapers (plus associated magazines and websites) in the English Midlands, which generally place it in the top twenty publishers in the UK provincial press. As of 2013 its nine *free newspapers achieved an average weekly *circulation of around 300,000 copies.

bullshit detector *See* SCEPTICISM.

bureau A news organization's base in a particular area, country, or continent. A bureau may be a fully staffed *newsroom or a lone journalist with a mobile phone.

Bureau of Investigative Journalism A London-based not-for-profit organization set up by a number of experienced print and broadcast journalists in 2010 to carry out investigations for and/or alongside major news and current affairs outlets ranging from *Al Jazeera and the *BBC to *Le Monde and the *Sunday Times. It obtained unwelcome notoriety in 2012 when an investigation for *Newsnight led to false allegations of child sex abuse being made against an innocent man (*see* POLLARD REVIEW). *See also* INVESTIGATIVE JOURNALISM.

(((●))) SEE WEB LINKS
• Some of the bureau's investigations

burning 1. Betraying the trust of a *source, for example by revealing the identity of a *confidential source or by publishing material that a source had believed to be *off the record.
2. Altering the contrast of a *photograph (*see* DODGING).

business journalism Reporting on commerce, companies, industrial matters, stock prices, and so on, whether in specialist media such as the *Financial Times, in a separate page or section of a general news outlet, or as business stories on broadcast news bulletins. Business journalists have been criticized for reporting economic stories from the perspective of shareholders and/or consumers rather than workers or citizens, and some business journalism at a local or regional level often appears to be little more than a collection of *press releases. *See also* B2B; BLOOMBERG; CITY AM; CITY SLICKERS; ECONOMIST; FORBES; WALL STREET JOURNAL.

buy-up A story that results from a financial exchange, as when a newspaper or magazine pays for the *serialization of extracts from a new book, or when somebody involved in a story is paid a fee to persuade them to tell their version of events. The other side of such a buy-up is usually that the *source undertakes not to tell their story to a rival media outlet, at least for a specified period. *See also* CHEQUEBOOK JOURNALISM; KISS-AND-TELL.

BuzzFeed A *website that, since its launch in 2006, has proved extremely popular with *users (if not always with rival media) for its non-stop *aggregation of *viral online content, especially pictures of 'cute' cats and the like. Since 2012 *BuzzFeed* has also invested in more original *reporting, including serious *long-form journalism. *See also* ONLINE JOURNALISM.

byline The attribution of the journalist who has written a particular story (or, at least, the journalist who has been deemed by a *sub-editor to have written it). A byline may include additional information after the name, such as 'crime correspondent', and on some titles will include a photograph of the journalist (a 'picture byline') and perhaps contact details. *See also* COD BYLINE; DATELINE.

byline

news outlet or as business stories on broadcast news bulletins. Journalists have been criticized for reporting corporate matters from the perspective of shareholders and/or consumers rather than workers or citizens, and some business journalism at a local or regional level often appears to be little more than a collection of *press releases. See also B2B; BLOOMBERG; CITY AM; DOW JONES; ECONOMIST; FORBES; WALL STREET JOURNAL.

buy ...

cablegate The publication in 2010 of more than 250,000 secret diplomatic messages, assessments, and cables written by US diplomats around the world. The cables were revealed by the *whistleblowing website *WikiLeaks*, which cooperated on the project with the *New York Times*, the *Guardian*, *El Pais*, *Der Spiegel*, and *Le Monde* to release the information while concealing the identity of intelligence sources whose lives could have been put at risk. The *leak of the cables made headlines around the world, embarrassing and outraging the US government in equal measure. *WikiLeaks* and its partner news organizations argued that it was in the *public interest to put diplomats' frank assessments of various countries and their rulers into the public domain. *See also* ANONYMOUS SOURCE; INVESTIGATIVE JOURNALISM.

((⊕)) SEE WEB LINKS
• The US embassy cables

Calcutt Reports Two critical assessments of the *ethics of the British press in the late 1980s and early 1990s, commissioned by the UK government and drafted by the lawyer David Calcutt (1930–2004). Following what were widely perceived to be excesses of *intrusion and unethical journalism, ministers set up an advisory Committee on Privacy and Related Matters, chaired by Calcutt and known colloquially as the Calcutt Committee. Its 1990 report recommended replacing the widely derided *Press Council with a new 'self-regulatory' body, the *Press Complaints Commission (PCC), and further recommended that if press misbehaviour had not been tackled effectively within eighteen months the PCC should in turn be replaced by some form of *statutory regulation. The PCC was duly set up and Calcutt, who had become Sir David in the meantime, was asked by John Major's government to review its performance. Although Calcutt's subsequent (1993) report was damning, his recommendation that the PCC be replaced by a statutory tribunal was rejected by the government. *See also* LAST CHANCE SALOON; LEVESON INQUIRY; SELF-REGULATION; YOUNGER COMMITTEE.

California Eagle One of the longest-running black-owned newspapers in the USA, which campaigned for civil rights, against *racism in general, and against the Ku Klux Klan in particular. Launched in Los Angeles in 1879 as the *California Owl*, it became the *California Eagle* in 1912 under the direction of Charlotta Bass (1874–1969), who went on to become the first black woman to run for national office in 1952, when she stood as the Progressive Party's candidate for US vice-president. The paper had changed ownership by then and it eventually closed in 1964. *See also* ALTERNATIVE MEDIA; BLACK MEDIA.

calls Regular checking with routine *sources to see if anything *newsworthy has happened. Such routinized inquiries to a range of agencies are a staple of *newsgathering. Minimum calls will be to the police, the fire brigade, and the ambulance service, noting down anything of interest including updates to *running stories. Weekly newspapers might do calls once a day; daily papers will make several rounds of calls a day; broadcast and online newsrooms, as well as *news agencies, typically do the calls hourly or even more frequently to ensure they miss nothing on their *patch. A final round of calls will be made just before *deadline. The calls once meant actual visits but these days tend to involve telephone calls, text messages, or the checking of websites or *Twitter feeds. The calls provide a predictable supply of unpredictable stories ranging from *nibs to *splashes and may be carried out routinely by any competent reporter even without personal knowledge of, or contacts within, the agencies being called. *See also* CRIME NEWS; INFORMATION SUBSIDY; ROUTINES.

Camillagate A scandal involving widespread publication by the international media in 1992 and 1993 of the transcript of an intimate telephone conversation (apparently recorded in 1989) between Charles, Prince of Wales, and his future wife, Camilla Parker-Bowles, when they were both married to other people. The affair is also sometimes referred to as 'tampongate' or 'tampaxgate' after the future king was recorded comparing himself to a tampon. *See also* INTRUSION; PRIVACY; SQUIDGYGATE.

campaign A coordinated and planned programme of coverage of a particular issue over a sustained period of time, usually for a defined

cause. Campaigns may range from a national newspaper's repeated 'naming and shaming' of paedophiles to a local radio station helping to raise funds for a piece of medical equipment for the community. Such campaigns often involve *features as well as *news stories, with a campaign logo or slogan used to tie the coverage together. Attempts will typically be made to involve the audience via polls, letters, phone-ins, comments, social media, photo opportunities, and petitions.
A campaign can be seen as part of a news organization's *brand image and an effort at building audience loyalty. *See also* CAMPAIGNING JOURNALISM.

Campaign for Press and Broadcasting Freedom (CPBF) A
UK-based activist group formed in 1979 that has campaigned against *bias, *censorship, and increasing *concentration of media ownership, in favour of independent journalism, and in defence of the *BBC against commercial and political attack.

(⊕) SEE WEB LINKS
• CPBF 'What we stand for'

Campaign for Real People An initiative by members of the
*National Union of Journalists in the UK during the 1970s and 1980s to raise awareness of *sexism within media output, particularly the *stereotyping and objectification of women in news stories as housewives, sex symbols, or other one-dimensional characters. The name was inspired by the popular consumer organization the Campaign for Real Ale (an issue generally thought to be particularly close to the hearts of journalists). *See also* FEMINIST MEDIA; PAGE THREE.

campaigning journalism (crusading journalism) Reporting with a
bee in its bonnet about a particular issue, when news organizations or even individual journalists repeatedly report on wrongs that, they argue, must be righted. *See also* ADVOCACY JOURNALISM; CAMPAIGN; INVESTIGATIVE JOURNALISM; OPPOSITIONAL REPORTING.

Canadian Association of Journalists (CAJ) A membership body
set up in 1978 to provide a voice for journalists in Canada and to promote ethical and investigative journalism. Until 1990 it was called the Centre for Investigative Journalism.

(⊕) SEE WEB LINKS
• CAJ magazine, *Media*

caption The explanatory words accompanying a *photograph, map, graph, or other form of graphic; and, in *television journalism, a piece of text giving the name of the person on screen, or further details, such as '*library footage'. *See also* KEYWORDS; PHOTO CAPTION.

CAR *See* COMPUTER-ASSISTED REPORTING.

cartoon A drawing that might variously contain a joke, a comment on one or more topical news stories, a caricature of a public figure, an expression of outrage or disgust, and sometimes all of the above. Cartoons in newspapers and magazines are either single frames that stand alone or regular *comic strips with familiar characters, and they help create the *brand identity of a news organization. It is not uncommon for cartoons to generate controversy; on rare occasions they can even result in death threats.

case study An individual account used to illustrate a wider story or trend.

casualization The process whereby news organizations replace staff journalists with *freelancers and/or casual staff, who work shifts of varying frequency depending on the needs of the employer. The resulting lack of employment security amongst journalists and the fear that they could be dispensed with at any moment was blamed at the *Leveson Inquiry for some journalists' willingness to cut corners ethically and for their reluctance to speak out about unethical (or even illegal) practices within *newsrooms.

catchline A one or two-word label attached to a story when it is filed, enabling it to be identified correctly during the *subbing and production process, but not included in the published version. Also sometimes known as a *slug. Jokey, obscene, or potentially defamatory catchlines are normally discouraged in case they appear by accident and cause embarrassment or worse.

CBS A major commercial entertainment, broadcasting, and news organization in the USA, which is responsible for the agenda-setting current affairs TV programme *60 Minutes. See also* MCCARTHYISM.

CCTV 1. Footage from closed-circuit television that is sometimes used by media organizations to illustrate stories both serious and humorous, either as *video or as a *screengrab.

2. China's major television and *multimedia organization, China Central Television, which runs the English language CCTV News channel among numerous other outlets targeted at domestic and international *audiences.

CDA *See* CRITICAL DISCOURSE ANALYSIS.

celebrities People in the public eye who tend to be divided by journalists into the A-list (only the very best known international stars in film, music, sport, modelling, plus the most glamorous presidents and royals); the B-list (those on their way up to, or down from, the A-list); the C-list (the best known of the rest); the D-list (winners of TV 'reality' shows); and the Z-list (losers of TV 'reality' shows). A-listers sometimes need only to turn up somewhere or have a new hairstyle to become the subject of news stories, but the threshold of *newsworthiness gets harder to cross the further down the unofficial alphabet somebody is deemed to be. If two celebs combine to become a celebrity 'golden couple' they can rapidly move up the list. *See also* CELEBRITY JOURNALISM.

celebrity The condition of being famous, sometimes just for being famous. A subject's celebrity status or lack of it will be among the factors taken into consideration when journalists consider the *newsworthiness of a potential story (*see* NEWS VALUES). *Compare* ELITE PEOPLE. *See also* CELEBRITIES; CELEBRITY JOURNALISM.

celebrity journalism Coverage of the lives, loves, and even lies of *celebrities. Such coverage of famous people has become a specialist genre, with its own magazines and other media output, in addition to being increasingly prevalent within mainstream general journalism. *See also* CELEBRITY; DUMBING DOWN; LIFESTYLE JOURNALISM; PAPARAZZI; SELFIE; TABLOIDIZATION; USIE.

censorship The prohibition and/or control of what information may be published or otherwise made public. The power to censor is normally associated with governments and states (*see* BROADCAST BAN; OFFICIAL SECRETS ACT) but forms of censorship may also be practised by media *proprietors, by the courts (*see* INJUNCTIONS; REPORTING RESTRICTIONS), and even by armed criminal gangs (*see* DEATHS OF JOURNALISTS). *See also* CHILLING EFFECT; LICENSING OF JOURNALISTS; SELF-CENSORSHIP; WHISTLEBLOWER.

centrespread An item or series of related items that are presented across the middle two pages of a magazine or a newspaper, typically making use of the larger than normal space to incorporate prominent display of *photographs and/or other graphics into the design of the spread.

Champion Newspapers A publisher of local *free newspapers, based in the north-west of England. Set up in 1994, as of 2013 it was the twentieth biggest regional press group in the UK in terms of *circulation, with 155,000 copies of its six *Champion* titles being distributed each week.

Channel 4 News The television (and online) news service of Channel 4, the UK's commercially funded *public service broadcaster that was launched in 1982 with a remit to experiment and serve diverse communities. Although provided by *ITN, *Channel 4 News* competes with the BBC's **Newsnight* and **Today* programmes at the more serious end of daily news broadcasting, often leading on its own investigations and/or with overseas stories.

(⊕) **SEE WEB LINKS**
• *Channel 4 News* blogs

chapbook A form of cheaply produced *pamphlet, popular in 17th- and 18th-century Europe, often featuring material that presaged the cultural mix to be found in later *magazines and *periodicals. Chapbooks condensed and helped popularize works of fiction such as *Robinson Crusoe*, which apparently was thought by some contemporary readers to have been a documentary account of a real-life adventure. *Compare* NEWSBOOK.

chapel A workplace branch of the *National Union of Journalists (NUJ) in the UK and Ireland, whose members will elect a shop steward (known within journalism as a *Mother or *Father of Chapel) to negotiate with management on their behalf. Print trades unions used similar terminology.

Chartered Institute of Journalists *See* INSTITUTE OF JOURNALISTS.

chequebook journalism A somewhat pejorative term for *reporting that involves paying a *source for information. Although it is often spoken of as if the practice is, by definition, unethical, payments to sources sometimes result in stories that are widely agreed to have been in the *public interest (as when the 2009 MPs' expenses scandal was revealed thanks to the *Daily Telegraph* reportedly paying a six-figure sum for the information). *See also* BRIBE; BUY-UP; ETHICS; KISS-AND-TELL.

Cherokee Phoenix Credited with being the first Native American newspaper in the USA as well as the country's first bilingual publication. It was published by members of the Cherokee nation between 1828 and 1834 and included material in both Cherokee and English. *See also* ALTERNATIVE MEDIA; INDIGENOUS MEDIA.

(⊕) SEE WEB LINKS
• *Cherokee Phoenix* digital archive

Chicago Sun-Times A US daily newspaper published in Chicago that traces its origins back to 1844, making it the longest-running paper in the city (although its current title has been used only since 1948). Since 2011 the paper and its online *brand have been owned by the technology and media company Wrapports. It is one of the top ten best-selling newspapers in the country.

Chicago Tribune A major daily newspaper published in Chicago, Illinois, that is one of the top ten best-selling newspapers in the USA. Founded in 1847, it is the flagship paper (and website) of the Tribune Company of Chicago.

chilling effect When the possibility of negative consequences is said to dissuade potential *sources of information from coming forward, or to put journalists and news organizations off covering certain subjects. If the identity of an *anonymous source is revealed, as when Sarah Tisdall was jailed for leaking information to the *Guardian* in 1983, the resulting fear among an unknown number of other potential *whistleblowers is described as a chilling effect. Similarly, the anticipation of a political, legal, or even violent backlash may dissuade some media from investigating particularly sensitive subjects or litigious individuals. Judges' rulings in *libel cases, and inquiries into media behaviour such as those by *Calcutt, *Hutton, and *Leveson, are also sometimes accused of cooling the ardour of news organizations. *See also* DEATHS OF JOURNALISTS; FLAK; McCARTHYISM; SELF-CENSORSHIP.

China Daily A state-run English-language newspaper (and website) that has presented authorized news and views about China to the English-speaking world since 1981.

Christian Science Monitor A US magazine and website owned by the First Church of Christ, Scientist, in Boston, Massachusetts, but which aims to be a mainstream news organization rather than a religious *propaganda operation. Founded as a daily newspaper in 1908, it became a weekly magazine a hundred years later.

chronology The order in which events happen, which is not necessarily the order in which they will be recounted in a piece of journalism. News stories often start with the outcome or end result rather than the beginning, and *features may begin at any point in the narrative, including the middle. Complex or long-running stories may include a chronology or *timeline in an accompanying explanatory *sidebar.

churnalism A form of journalism that relies on recycling *press releases and *agency copy and which involves little or no *independent reporting or attempt at *verification. Churnalism has been blamed on poorly staffed newsrooms and on employers' demands for journalists to produce an increasing number of stories at an increased speed for an increasing number of platforms. The term was coined by BBC business journalist Waseem Zakir, who used it to contrast 'proactive' reporting with the way that so many newsrooms had become 'reactive', whereby: 'You get copy coming in on the wires and reporters churn it out, processing stuff and maybe adding the odd local quote . . . Reporters are becoming churnalists' (Harcup, 2004). The term was later popularized by *Guardian* journalist Nick Davies (2008), since when countless academic critics of journalism have themselves engaged in a form of churnalism by recycling mistaken claims that Davies himself coined the phrase; he did not nor did he claim to. *See also* McJournalism.

Futher reading: T. Harcup, *Journalism: Principles and Practice* (2004). N. Davies, *Flat Earth News* (2008).

Cincinnati Enquirer A US daily newspaper published since 1841 and covering northern Kentucky as well as Cincinnati in the state of Ohio. It and its online *brand are part of the *Gannett empire.

circulation The number of copies of paid-for newspapers or magazines that are sold and the number of copies of free publications that are distributed. *Compare* READERSHIP. *See also* ALLIANCE FOR AUDITED MEDIA; AUDIT BUREAU OF CIRCULATION.

circulation war The direct competition for sales and/or readers by two or more rival publishers utilizing tactics such as special offers, *covermounts, *spoilers, and predatory pricing designed to damage or eliminate the competition. Heavy price cuts helped the *Murdoch empire boost *circulation of *The *Times* in the 1990s, in large part at the expense of rival *broadsheet newspapers in the UK. *See also* PRICE WAR.

City AM A UK business-oriented daily (weekday) newspaper distributed free in and around London since 2005. The upmarket *compact and its accompanying website, which both use the tagline 'business with personality', are owned by a private company. *See also* BUSINESS JOURNALISM; FREEMIUM; FREESHEET.

citizen A member of the journalistic *audience conceptualized as an active participant within the social and *public spheres rather than merely as a consumer. Journalism that aims primarily to inform a society's citizens and to act as a form of *fourth estate is often contrasted with journalism that concerns itself more with *entertainment, although in practice there can be a blurring between the two. *See also* ALTERNATIVE MEDIA; BLOGGER; CIVIC JOURNALISM; NETIZEN; PUBLIC JOURNALISM; WORDPRESS.

citizen journalism Something of a contested term for material produced by people who are not employed as journalists but whose writing or other media output appears to contain *journalistic elements. The term has most often been applied to *bloggers and people who contribute *user-generated content to mainstream media, but it has also been used to describe *alternative media and *community media, including those that predate the *internet. Triumphalist accounts of the rise and rise of citizen journalism in the digital age are countered by critics who argue that the phenomenon often has little to do with either citizenship or journalism; in the UK the *National Union of Journalists preferred the term '**witness contributors**', but it never really caught on. *See also* ALTERNATIVE JOURNALISM; AMATEUR JOURNALISM; BOUNDARY MAINTENANCE; NETIZEN; OPEN JOURNALISM.

Citizen Kane The title of the film (dir. Orson Welles, 1941) about the good and bad of journalism (*see* ETHICS), telling the dramatic story of the power and influence wielded by a newspaper *proprietor who is loosely based on the real-life US press magnate William Randolph Hearst (1863–1951). The film typically comes at or near the top of journalists' lists of 'best movies of all time'. *See* HEARST NEWSPAPERS.

City Slickers The title of a personal finance page that featured in the UK's *Daily Mirror* in the late 1990s and which resulted in the prosecution of two journalists. When the pair working on the column realized that by writing positively about a company's shares the price would go up, they took to buying shares cheaply beforehand, ramping up the price, then selling at the top of the market, and pocketing the money. Their behaviour was not only against the Financial Services Act but was widely condemned as a breach of journalistic *trust and *ethics because they were in effect fleecing their own readers. After the column was investigated by the *Daily Telegraph* the Slickers were sacked for gross misconduct in 2000 and subsequently convicted in the courts: one was imprisoned for six months and the other sentenced to a 180-hour community service order. The *Press Complaints Commission criticized the paper's editor, Piers Morgan, for allowing the case to happen on his watch. *See also* BUSINESS JOURNALISM.

civic journalism A form of reporting that emphasizes the role of journalism not merely as a *watchdog on behalf of the public, still less as something that exists merely to entertain or make money, but as a form of social intervention to encourage active citizenship and facilitate wider participation in the *public sphere. *See also* CITIZEN; PUBLIC JOURNALISM.

class A socio-economic division within society that, according to *Marxist thinkers, results in the perspective of the ruling class becoming the dominant view of the age, in part because it is the ruling class perspective that tends to become embedded within and be circulated by much mainstream journalism and other media output. However, alternative class perspectives can be found within the *radical press. *See also* HEGEMONY; OPPOSITIONAL REPORTING; POLITICAL ECONOMY; REPRESENTATION.

Cleveland Plain Dealer A daily newspaper published in Cleveland, Ohio, since 1842. Along with the website *Cleveland.com*, it is owned by Advance Publications, and it is one of the top 25 best-selling newspapers in the USA.

cliché A hackneyed or predictable phrase. News organizations' *style guides invariably instruct journalists to avoid clichés like the plague, and yet journalism remains as full of over-familiar words and phrases as it ever was, and fresh formulations can quickly become clichés: go figure. *See also* JOURNALESE.

clickstream The flow of *users to a *website and the ways in which those users navigate the site. *See also* ONLINE JOURNALISM; SEARCH ENGINE OPTIMIZATION.

clip A brief extract from a longer piece of *audio or *video, such as may be used in a short news *bulletin on TV or radio or embedded within an online story.

Clyde & Forth Press Ltd A provincial newspaper (and online) publisher in the UK. Its flagship title is the *Clydebank Post* in Scotland.

CMS *See* CONTENT MANAGEMENT SYSTEM.

CN Group Ltd A regional media company based in Cumbria in the UK, which runs a series of daily and weekly newspapers, news websites, and commercial radio stations. It is among the top twenty provincial newspaper publishers in the UK, with ten titles achieving an average weekly *circulation of more than 300,000 in 2013.

CNN A US cable television news network, founded in 1980, which pioneered the broadcasting of 24-hour *rolling news. Part of the *Time Warner media empire, CNN is available around the world either online or on TV. *See also* CNN EFFECT; 24-HOUR NEWS.

(())) SEE WEB LINKS
• CNN's Christiane Amanpour

CNN effect The phenomenon whereby governments, military strategists, and other powerful individuals or organizations have to take into consideration the fact that, following the emergence of *CNN in 1980, pictures depicting the results of their decisions and actions could be beamed instantaneously into people's homes around the world, as could reactions to and protests against their actions. The CNN effect is also said to be at play when the strength of public reaction, for example, to TV pictures of a humanitarian disaster overseas, results in politicians taking some form of action they would not otherwise have considered.

Cobbett's Political Register An influential radical weekly published by William Cobbett (1763–1835) from 1802 until his death. In 1816 he published two different editions: a full-price version and a cheaper one that avoided *stamp duty by carrying no *news, which built a large *circulation on the basis of its low price (2d) and high polemic. It was dismissed by critics as 'twopenny trash' but was probably the main periodical read by working-class people at the time. Cobbett had several brushes with the laws of *libel and sedition, and in 1819 the *Six Acts closed the stamp duty loophole. Cobbett continued with the weekly *Register* and later brought out a cheaper monthly version that adopted the name ***Twopenny Trash***. *See also* RADICAL PRESS; TAXES ON KNOWLEDGE.

cod byline The use of a fictitious name for a *byline, giving the impression that an item has been written by a member of staff when in fact it has been supplied by a *news agency. The use of cod bylines tends to be regarded as unethical because it misleads readers; it can also be awkward if a reader or potential source telephones the *newsroom and asks for the fake reporter by name.

code A system for sending, receiving, and/or understanding the messages contained within any form of *communication, including journalism, according to theories of communication (*see* SEMIOTICS). *See also* CONNOTATION; ENCODING, DECODING.

codes of conduct Sets of rules, guidelines, principles, or exhortations that are designed to promote ethical journalism—but which are not necessarily always followed to the letter. The *National Union of Journalists claims to have been the first journalists' organization in the UK to establish a code of conduct for members, in 1936. Subsequently amended several times, its code has remained a relatively brief statement of basic principles rather than an exhaustive series of specific dos and don'ts designed to cover every eventuality. In the USA the *Newspaper Guild code dates from 1934. *See also* ETHICS.

(🌐) SEE WEB LINKS

• Codes of conduct from around the world

coffee houses The locations for swapping news (both oral and in the form of newspapers, pamphlets, and other printed matter as well as letters) and the development of a public discourse independent of church and state in late 17th- and early 18th-century London and elsewhere. According to the theorist Jurgen Habermas (1929–), these coffee houses formed an almost ideal form of *public sphere, albeit one consisting almost exclusively of bourgeois men. More female-friendly public spaces could be found in the theatres of the time, while a form of *plebeian public sphere is said to have operated in taverns and inns, where stories from the working-class *radical press would be read aloud and discussed.

collaborative journalism The involvement of the *audience in the production of a piece of journalism, for example by inviting people to send in personal accounts, pictures, or other forms of *user-generated content, or by placing a large quantity of raw information online and asking readers to trawl through it and help identify potential *angles to pursue. *See also* CROWDSOURCING; LIVEBLOG; NETWORKED JOURNALISM; OPEN JOURNALISM; TRAFIGURA; WIKI.

collect pic A *photograph supplied other than by a press *photographer, such as from a *source, an interviewee, a member of the family, a school, or an employer. Also known as a *pick-up pic, such *pictures are today often taken from *Facebook, Flickr, and other forms of *social media. If allowed to look through a family's analogue photo album, an unscrupulous journalist might try to collect all prints, thereby denying them to rivals.

colour Journalistic material included more for purposes of description, atmosphere, emotion, or entertainment than because the factual content is essential for a story to be understood. Colour may be incorporated as an incidental element of a longer story, may accompany a story as a separate-but-linked item, or may be a stand-alone piece the purpose of which is to provide contrast with other unrelated material. *See also* COLOUR PIECE.

colour piece A story emphasizing the *colour of a situation; that is, one based on description, atmosphere, and emotion rather than straightforward factual reportage. A colour piece may accompany a more factual story as a separate-but-linked item or may be a stand-alone piece the purpose of which is to entertain and/or provide contrast with other unrelated material. Colour pieces may sometimes be written from the point of view of a participant rather than an observer. *See also* SKETCH.

colour supplement A *magazine printed in colour and given away with a newspaper, usually at weekends.

Columbia Journalism Review A US magazine and website that is a major forum for discussion about the state of journalism and its future, with journalists and academics taking part. The magazine, published six times a year, was launched by the journalism school at Columbia University in 1961.

(((●))) SEE WEB LINKS
• *Columbia Journalism Review* magazine archive

Columbus Dispatch A US daily newspaper published in Columbus, Ohio, since 1871 and which since 1905 has been privately owned by the Wolfe family. The *Dispatch* claims to have published the world's first 'online newspaper' when in 1980 it tested a CompuServe dial-up service by sending news stories direct to the relatively few home computers there were at the time.

column 1. A regular article that typically appears in the same place, often with its own logo and title, in which the writer (the *columnist) or team of writers tend to write from a personal, specialist, or opinionated point of view.
2. A division of a print or online story so that the text does not run across the width of a page but is split into two or more strips of type. The narrow width of most newspaper columns is one of the reasons for the typically short length of paragraphs, because a long paragraph in a thin column is thought to appear daunting to the reader.

columnist The writer of a regular *column in a newspaper, magazine, or website. Columnists are often engaged because of their expert knowledge, forthright opinions, or entertaining style of writing, and they are sometimes treated as prized assets with big picture *bylines and salaries or freelance fees to match. Some *celebrity columnists, especially sports stars, do not actually write the columns that appear under their own name; such material is often drafted by a staff journalist after a quick chat on the telephone. *See also* FEATURE WRITER.

comic strip A series of linked *cartoons, typically two to four frames next to each other, that tell a story and feature regular characters. From *Andy Capp* to *Doonesbury*, comic strips have long been a feature of newspapers, at both the popular and broadsheet ends of the market, and they are also part of many magazine and online *brands.

comment The inclusion within a piece of journalism of the journalist's or news organization's own *opinion. Since the emergence of *impartiality and *objectivity norms, comment is normally treated (or labelled) separately from *news *reporting. However, there are exceptions, for example in *advocacy journalism, *campaigning journalism, *oppositional reporting, and on *Fox News*.

commentariat A collective noun for the most high-profile and influential *columnists whose work dominates the *op-ed pages of major newspapers and current affairs magazines and who are often invited to give their views on TV and radio too. Influential bloggers and tweeters may also be part of the commentariat. *See also* TWITTERATI.

Comment is Free An online discussion forum of the *Guardian* and *Observer* newspapers, the title of which is taken from a famous sentence that editor C. P. Scott (1846–1932) included in an article marking the *Guardian*'s centenary in 1921: 'Comment is free, but facts are sacred.' Scott added that comment should also be 'subject to a self-imposed restraint', something with which not all users of *Comment Is Free* would seem to concur (*see* TROLL).

⊕ SEE WEB LINKS
• C. P. Scott's 1921 article

Committee of Concerned Journalists (CCJ) A grouping of US journalists, academics, and other citizens who came together in 1997 to highlight and combat what they saw as a crisis in journalism. The CCJ, initially based at Columbia University and then at the University of Missouri, conducted research and lobbying before folding in 2011.

⊕ SEE WEB LINKS
• CCJ legacy website

Committee to Protect Journalists A US-based organization of journalists and concerned citizens which, since its formation in 1981, has campaigned for the safety of journalists around the world, monitored the numbers of journalists imprisoned or killed, acted as an advocate for individual journalists who need its help, and issued guidelines for working in dangerous territories. *See also* DEATHS OF JOURNALISTS; SPEAK JUSTICE.

(((•))) SEE WEB LINKS

• The CPJ's *Journalist Security Guide*

commodification The process of turning journalism and journalistic products into commodities that can be bought and sold in a market place (or as ways of creating an *audience that can be sold to *advertisers) rather than as something produced primarily for the benefit of a society and its *citizens. Whether news as a commodity and news in the *public interest are mutually exclusive is the subject of much debate, as is the question of whether commodification inevitably leads to a *dumbing down of journalism. *See also* MARKET-DRIVEN NEWS; POLITICAL ECONOMY.

common sense A society's widely accepted views which, according to *Marxism, tend to emanate from its ruling class and which by definition need to be questioned and challenged by journalists and other citizens. *See also* HEGEMONY; MANUFACTURE OF CONSENT.

Commonwealth Journalists Association A networking and lobbying organization set up in 1978 to promote 'free, bold, and honest journalism' across the 54 countries of the Commonwealth.

(((•))) SEE WEB LINKS

• CJA news

communication The exchanging of messages. Journalism has traditionally been understood as following a one-way or linear model of communication, whereby messages are transmitted from sender (the journalist or news organization) to receiver (the *audience), but this has been questioned in recent decades with the emergence of concepts such as the *active audience and *user-generated content. *See also* ENCODING, DECODING.

Communications Act 2003 The piece of UK legislation that established *Ofcom and relaxed a number of restrictions on media *ownership.

Communication Workers of America *See* NEWSPAPER GUILD.

community correspondent *See* VILLAGE CORRESPONDENT.

community media Non-profit forms of media that serve as noticeboards within specific geographical communities and which may include elements of journalism and *reporting. Community newspapers, radio stations, and other forms of media often invite public participation in the production process. *See also* ALTERNATIVE MEDIA; AMATEUR JOURNALISM; LOCAL JOURNALISM.

community of interest A potential media *audience based on a shared interest (in anything from Arsenal football club to zoo-keeping) rather than on sharing the same geographical location. Communities of interest tend to have their own specialist magazines, websites, and *zines. *See also* NICHE.

compact A *newspaper published in *tabloid size but whose editor and/or proprietor wishes to distance the product from the more sensationalist (and popular) end of the market. Many *quality newspapers that once published in *broadsheet format are now compacts but remain keen to distinguish themselves from the *redtops in style, content, and target readership.

compassion fatigue The idea that media *audiences can become inured to horror and tragedy as a result of repeated exposure to human suffering via the media, especially in the form of television news coverage of wars, famines, and disasters. *Compare* CNN EFFECT.

composition The balance of a news product (or *brand) taken as a whole. Composition was one of the factors identified by the academics Johan Galtung and Mari Ruge in their influential 1960s study of *news values; they argued that some events may become *news less because of any intrinsic value or importance than because they fit into the overall balance—or composition—of the newspaper or news broadcast. A light story might be included to balance a preponderance of heavy stories, for example.

computer-assisted reporting (CAR) A form of journalism involving detailed and systematic use of computer technology, most notably the searching of databases, to research and report stories. The phenomenon emerged during the 1990s, initially in the USA where *freedom of information laws meant that a vast quantity of information was technically available to the public but was difficult for most people to access or comprehend. Journalists use computer-assisted reporting to explore and cross-reference data such as crime figures, police shootings, disease rates, and income distribution, looking for patterns, trends, and discrepancies. Skilled use of CAR goes beyond searching official databases to include inputting into computer programs information that the journalist has gathered by other means, which can then be digitally searched, analyzed, or presented in ways that would have been enormously time-consuming (and therefore virtually impossible in practice) before the arrival of computers. The labels 'computer-assisted reporting' and 'CAR' have become less popular as computers have become more ubiquitous amongst journalists and the wider public, and such reporting now tends to be referred to as *data journalism. *Compare* ALGORITHMIC JOURNALISM. *See also* INVESTIGATIVE JOURNALISM.

concentration of ownership The tendency for more and more media outlets to be owned by fewer and larger commercial organizations that, in turn, tend to seek to outdo, eliminate, or buy up rival outfits. In response, journalists' trade unions such as the *National Union of Journalists campaign for plurality of media ownership as a way of preserving journalism's diverse ecology. *See also* OWNERSHIP; HORIZONTAL INTEGRATION; VERTICAL INTEGRATION.

Condé Nast A US-based *magazine publisher, created in 1909, that today produces some of the world's best-known magazine and online *brands such as *GQ, *New Yorker, *Vanity Fair, and *Vogue. It is owned by **Advance Publications**. *See also* GLOSSIES.

conference A meeting between an *editor and senior colleagues who run various *desks—such as the news editor, features editor, and picture editor—to discuss what stories have come in or are expected to come in, and how those stories will be covered or projected. Editorial conferences might take place weekly, daily, or several times a day depending on the news organization and frequency of publication. A few newsrooms open up conference to as many editorial staff as can fit in. *See also* PROSPECTS.

confessional journalism The use of a newspaper or magazine *column to detail (some of) the ins and outs of the *columnist's personal life, or that which purports to be their personal life.

confessional mode A style of writing that centres on the journalist's personal life, thoughts, and experiences. *See also* IHTM; SUBJECTIVITY.

confidentiality *See* ANONYMOUS SOURCE.

confidential source *See* ANONYMOUS SOURCE.

conflict A disagreement, dispute, *row, or fight. Reporting on conflicts ranging from wars and terrorism to strikes and even divorces is one of the staple functions of journalism but can also be a major area of contention, with claims of *bias, *censorship, and *self-censorship flying in different directions. *See also* BROADCAST BAN; PEACE JOURNALISM; WAR REPORTING.

conflict of interest Something that might give grounds for suspicion that a journalist or news organization might be thought to have a reason to be *biased because of a possible connection to a story's subject or *source. Some organizations insist that any potential conflicts of interest be declared openly or that journalists in such a position step aside from certain stories. *See also* ETHICS; TRUST.

connotation A meaning contained within a form of communication (such as a piece of journalism) that is neither obvious nor explicit, but which may be implied, inferred, or decoded by an *active audience. *Compare* DENOTATION. *See also* CODE; ENCODING, DECODING; SEMIOTICS.

conscience clause A stipulation in a *code of ethical conduct and/or contract of employment that allows a journalist to refuse an assignment on ethical grounds, without being disciplined or dismissed as a consequence. The introduction of such a conscience clause has long been the policy of the *National Union of Journalists in the UK. The idea was repeatedly rejected by the *Press Complaints Commission but the *Leveson Report subsequently recommended just such a clause, along with a whistleblowing hotline for journalists wishing to report unethical practices by their employers. *See also* ETHICS.

consent form A means of obtaining written and signed permission if and when it is deemed necessary, as for a television item that involves filming a patient undergoing hospital treatment.

consonance A process whereby journalists might expect something *newsworthy to happen and therefore report it more in accordance with their expectations than with what in fact happens. Consonance was one of the factors identified by the Norwegian scholars Johan Galtung and Mari Ruge, whose study of *news values found that journalists may form a mental 'pre-image' of an event, which can then increase the chances of that event being covered as a news item.

constraints A range of influences, rules, and *routines that may limit the work and output of journalists. These include legal constraints and regulatory *codes of journalistic conduct as well as the often more opaque influence of a *proprietor, who hires and fires the editor, fixes the editorial budget, and establishes an organization's ethos. Other constraints on individual journalists include time pressures and *deadlines, space pressures, and adherence to a *style guide, an unwillingness of *sources to provide information, a need to cater for a particular audience, a requirement to produce advertiser-friendly material, job insecurity, and the journalist's own subjectivity and values. One constraint may be in conflict with another, as when an editor instructs a journalist to act in a way that would breach an ethical code of conduct, and journalists may be subject to conflicting loyalties and pressures. The constraints under which journalists typically work are not total or all-powerful; rather, they are a range of sometimes conflicting influences, some more powerful than others and some more powerful at certain times, with a *tendency* to influence journalists in certain ways. Constraints on journalists are subject to counter-pressures and, potentially, can be negotiated and resisted as well as accepted. *See also* AGENCY; AUTONOMY.

construction of news The creation and shaping of *news as a mediated product. To say that news is constructed, or even manufactured, is not to accuse journalists of inventing information; rather, it is to highlight the human intervention that is required for events to become news in the first place, including observation, *selection, *framing, and interpretation. *See also* MANUFACTURE OF NEWS; NEWS VALUES; STORY.

consumer magazine A *magazine that is normally sold on news-stands and which is aimed directly at a fairly broad section of the population—such as women, men, teenage girls, or 'lads'—rather than a more specialist *niche readership. Such magazines tend to promote themselves as *brands that extend far beyond the printed product to include an online presence, *tablet and smart phone editions, extensive use of Facebook and Twitter to create a sense of community, the marketing of clothing and gadgets, and invitations to special events such as roadshows. *Compare* B2B; CUSTOMER MAGAZINE; SPECIAL-INTEREST MAGAZINE. *See also* GLOSSIES.

contacts A journalist's frequent or regular *sources.

contacts book A paper or electronic record of the names and contact details of a journalist's *contacts or *sources. Reporters' reputations and careers can depend to a significant degree on the quality of the names in their contacts books.

contempt of court Publishing information in the UK that a judge has ruled should not be made public or that contravenes the standard legal *reporting restrictions that limit coverage of legal proceedings. A journalist might also risk being found in contempt of court for refusing to reveal the identity of a *confidential source despite being ordered to do so by a judge. Contempt of court is punishable by a fine and/or a prison sentence. *See also* COURT REPORTING.

content Management-speak for journalism and/or that which may look like journalism. *See also* CONTENT PROVIDER; HARVESTING CONTENT.

content analysis The systematic study of media output by categorizing, coding, counting, and tabulating various components and factors of journalism produced by particular outlets during a sample period. Such quantitative content analysis is a frequently used research methodology within *journalism studies, where it is sometimes combined (or triangulated) with more qualitative research methods such as interviewing, focus groups, newsroom observation, or *critical discourse analysis.

content management system (CMS) A computer software program that allows journalists to input and edit *copy and create pages for websites or printed publications according to a set of pre-designed *templates.

content provider The role of a journalist, as no self-respecting journalist would put it. It is a label used by some non-journalists who run large media organizations and who, in turn, tend to be derided by journalists as mere 'bean counters'. *See also* CONTENT.

continuity Continuing coverage of an event or issue once it has become *news. In their 1960s study of *news values, Johan Galtung and

Mari Ruge found that, after an event has become headline news, it may remain in the media spotlight for quite some time, even when little new is happening. *See also* FOLLOW-UP.

convergence The integration of and blurring of distinctions between different media *platforms and technologies. As a result of convergence, a newspaper reporter who was once employed essentially to write words for *print journalism may now also be expected to provide *pictures, *video, *audio, and slideshows for the news organization's *website, while broadcast journalists may also need to write text for online versions of their stories. *See also* HORIZONTAL INTEGRATION; MULTIMEDIA; MULTISKILLING.

conversation Journalism as a two-way process that invites *audience participation and is therefore often said to be more akin to a conversation than to a lecture. *See also* ACTIVE AUDIENCE; CROWDSOURCING; HASHTAG; INTERACTIVITY; 90-9-1 RULE; USER-GENERATED CONTENT.

copy The text of a story.

copy approval Allowing an interviewee or subject of a story to see it prior to publication, to suggest changes, and to withdraw cooperation or consent if they do not approve what has been written. Copy approval is typically rejected by journalists as an unethical practice that can also lead to numerous practical difficulties, but it is occasionally agreed for particularly sensitive *interviews (where a victim of crime needs to hide their identity or whereabouts, for example) or when it is the only way of persuading somebody such as an A-list *celebrity to talk.

copyleft The concept pioneered in some *alternative media that their material ought to be freely copied, reproduced, and distributed. *Compare* COPYRIGHT.

copyright A property right that prevents the reproduction without permission of journalistic and other material. Copyright resides in the form in which information or ideas are presented rather than in the information or ideas themselves. *Compare* COPYLEFT. *See also* PLAGIARISM.

copytaker Somebody who inputs *copy that is dictated over the *telephone by a reporter in the *field. Copytakers have become an endangered species in the digital age, as reporters are more likely to *file via laptop or tablet directly into a news organization's computer system.

copy taster A journalist, normally a senior *sub-editor, whose role is to examine (or taste) *copy that comes in on the *wires and make almost instant decisions about what might be used, followed-up, or *spiked. *See also* SELECTION.

corps A group of reporters covering the same *beat, as in the transport corps or the Washington corps. *See* PRESS CORPS.

correction An acknowledgement of an *inaccuracy and its replacement with what is believed to be the accurate information. Some publications have a regular column or space for corrections and clarifications, whereas websites tend to amend the copy itself and add a note at the end to highlight the fact that a change has been made since original publication (failure to do so, or 'invisible correcting', is generally frowned upon as unethical for all but the most trivial corrections). *See also* ACCURACY; APOLOGY; READERS' EDITOR.

correspondent A *reporter who specializes in a particular topic ('our tennis correspondent', for example) or who covers a particular location for a particular outlet (such as the BBC's South Asia correspondent). The name derives from the writing of *letters or 'correspondence'. *See also* FOREIGN CORRESPONDENT; SPECIALIST.

Cosmopolitan A glossy *women's magazine that, since it launched in the UK in 1972, has made its name by including more open discussion of sex and other issues that tended to be downplayed or shrouded in mystery within other commercial women's magazines. The monthly magazine (also published in the USA) and online *brand are owned by the *Hearst Corporation. *See also* GLOSSIES.

counter public spheres Multiple and overlapping *public spheres within which those excluded from or marginalized by the bourgeois public sphere can make themselves heard. *See also* ALTERNATIVE MEDIA; ALTERNATIVE PUBLIC SPHERE; BLACK MEDIA; CLASS; FEMINIST MEDIA; OPPOSITIONAL REPORTING; PLEBEIAN PUBLIC SPHERE; REPRESENTATION.

CounterPunch An independent magazine, newsletter, and website published in the USA since 1996 and specializing in investigations into and critical commentary upon the activities of the state and big business. *CounterPunch* has adopted the slogan, 'Tells the facts, names the names', and relies for its survival on donations from supporters. *See also* ALTERNATIVE JOURNALISM; OPPOSITIONAL REPORTING.

(⊕) SEE WEB LINKS
• Archived *CounterPunch* stories

court reporting The utilization of court proceedings as a regular source of *diary news stories that frequently involve *tragedy, *conflict, *human interest, and occasionally *humour. Journalists often portray themselves as the public's eyes and ears within the courtroom, ensuring that the workings of the justice system are seen to be done. Major court cases may be broadcast *live or reported virtually instantly via *Twitter, depending on rules of different jurisdictions. *See also* CRIME NEWS; PRIVILEGE; REPORTING RESTRICTIONS; SHORTHAND.

cover The front page of a printed product, the purpose of which is to grab the attention of readers and potential buyers by the strength of the *splash story, use of a striking photograph, and/or by a series of *teasers and *coverlines indicating what can be found inside. Pictures of certain A-list *celebrities on the cover can see the sales of some *magazines rise dramatically.

coverlines Brief pieces of text that appear on the covers of magazines and are designed to entice readers. Some magazines print two different covers: one for subscribers that is adorned with fewer coverlines and one for display in shops featuring many more coverlines in the hope that at least one will attract the eye of a potential buyer.

covermount An item given away free with a magazine or newspaper and which is often attached to the *cover. Typical covermounts include DVDs, CDs, software, and items of make-up; to the dismay of most journalists, sales often rise and fall more on the basis of the quality of the free gift featured on the cover than on the quality of the journalism within (*see* CIRCULATION WAR).

CPBF *See* CAMPAIGN FOR PRESS AND BROADCASTING FREEDOM.

craft A term used by many journalists to describe the occupation of journalism, to distinguish it from a more formally registered *profession. *See also* TRADE.

credit 1. Public acknowledgement of work supplied, as when the name of the *photographer is incorporated into a *photo caption.
2. Internal acknowledgement of work supplied, as when a reporter informs the *newsdesk that a story originated with a *tip from a *news agency or a *freelance journalist.

Crikey An Australian alternative website specializing in media, politics, culture, technology, and business stories. Based in Melbourne, since its launch in 2000 it has delighted in keeping an independent eye on the country's mainstream media. *See also* ALTERNATIVE JOURNALISM.

(⊕) SEE WEB LINKS
• *Crikey*'s coverage of journalism

crime news Stories concerning (alleged) criminal activity, which is one of the staples of *news reporting. Crime news is popular with news organizations because it can be dramatic but also because there tends to be a steady supply of it emanating from the police and courts. Critics argue that the operation of *news values results in unusual or horrific crimes being given disproportionate coverage in the media, which can lead to exaggerated public fear about some crimes (and some types of perpetrator), with little or no attention being paid to some other forms of criminal activity. Photogenic *victims can also receive more media attention than others. *See also* COURT REPORTING; CRIME REPORTING; MORAL PANIC; NAME AND SHAME; STEREOTYPING.

crime reporting Coverage of *crime news that is often undertaken by *specialist reporters who build up networks of *contacts and tend to pride themselves on not relying on official channels or the police *press office.

critic A journalist who reviews art and/or culture and who may or may not be an expert in their field. *See also* REVIEW.

critical discourse analysis (CDA) The study of journalism and other texts by exploring the ideological assumptions and power relations that are said to be embedded within any form of *communication. CDA is one of the research methods used within *journalism studies that requires no questioning of or interaction with actual journalists; as such, the findings of such research are often dismissed by many journalists themselves. In turn, advocates of CDA sometimes accuse journalists (and academics who adopt more quantitative research methods) of 'naïve empiricism' (*see* EMPIRICAL RESEARCH). *See also* ACADEMIZATION OF JOURNALISM; CRITICAL THEORY; IDEOLOGY; SEMIOTICS.

critical theory A way of investigating journalism and other forms of *communication by recourse to *Marxism and/or other approaches within *journalism studies that emphasize the identification, unpicking, and questioning of any implicit ideologies thought to be at work. *Compare* EMPIRICAL RESEARCH.

crop To remove any unwanted parts of a *picture above, below, or to the side of the part of the image that is wanted. *Compare* DIGITAL MANIPULATION.

cross-head A small, short heading, often consisting of just one or two words selected from the paragraph which follows. A cross-head is more likely to be used to break up text that is set in columns than it is to convey particularly useful information.

cross platform A news story or other piece of journalism that is run across more than one form of media *platform and which typically includes print, online, and broadcast versions. *See also* CONVERGENCE; MULTIMEDIA; REPURPOSING.

cross promotion When one outlet within a media organization or empire is used to publicize another part of the organization. UK newspapers owned by *News UK and *Northern & Shell are frequently accused of giving preferential coverage to media products with which they share *ownership, but cross promotion can also be seen when a *BBC news bulletin is used to promote one of the corporation's *current affairs programmes or sports broadcasts. *See also* HORIZONTAL INTEGRATION.

crowdsourcing Basing news or other forms of journalistic output on 'the wisdom of the crowd' rather than relying solely on an individual journalist's knowledge or expertise. This typically takes the form of inviting members of the *audience to contribute information, case studies, anecdotes, examples, photographs, audio, video, or tweets, to help give a story breadth as well as depth. *See also* CITIZEN JOURNALISM; COLLABORATIVE JOURNALISM; NETWORKED JOURNALISM; OPEN JOURNALISM; OPEN-SOURCE PUBLISHING; SOCIAL MEDIA EDITOR.

crusading journalism *See* CAMPAIGNING JOURNALISM.

cultural bias The reporting (or exclusion) of events from a particular perspective; for example, that of a Western male, white, middle-aged, heterosexual, middle-class, home-owner, and car driver. Whether intentionally or not, alternative perspectives may be excluded from much mainstream journalism unless such *bias is acknowledged and countered. *See also* COMMON SENSE; CULTURAL IMPERIALISM; DISCRIMINATORY LANGUAGE; HEGEMONY; McLURG'S LAW; MEANINGFULNESS; RACISM; REPRESENTATION; SEXISM; STEREOTYPING.

cultural imperialism The way in which the interests and influence of the most powerful countries and economies are said to tend to dominate or drown out voices from less powerful societies, resulting in indigenous journalism and media output adopting many of the codes, conventions, and perspectives of the more powerful societies, particularly the USA. *Compare* DEVELOPMENT JOURNALISM. *See also* ELITE NATIONS, NEWS FLOW.

curation The process of guiding users of a *website through what might otherwise appear to be an undifferentiated jumble of information and other material. *Online journalism as curation typically involves introducing and contextualizing content from a variety of sources, *aggregating and *linking to material found elsewhere, adding explanations and making connections where appropriate, and constantly updating with new developments. Public discussion being conducted on *social media, and readers' views expressed directly via a *Your Comments facility, will normally also be fed into the mix. This form of journalism, often seen in *liveblogs or on websites using *Storify, is described as being more like curating a *conversation with the *audience than the more traditional journalistic model of delivering a lecture. *See also* COLLABORATIVE JOURNALISM; HASHTAG; 90-9-1 rule; SOCIAL MEDIA EDITOR.

curiosity A desire to find things out, which is widely believed to be a prerequisite for journalism in general and *reporting in particular.

current affairs Journalism that is topical but is not necessarily restricted to coverage of the very latest *news headlines, and which typically takes a more in-depth look at issues.

customer magazine A *magazine produced on behalf of a supermarket or other form of business and given away to its customers.

Although customer magazines may have high production values, may employ journalists to create the content, and may include material of general interest, they are generally regarded as more a form of *public relations than of journalism. *Compare* B2B; CONSUMER MAGAZINE.

cuttings Copies of stories that have been previously published, which will typically be consulted by journalists working on new stories about the same subject.

cuttings job A piece of journalism containing little or no original *reporting. Although generally used as a derogatory term for a story based simply on *cuttings of previously published material, many journalists will have produced such work when up against a *deadline. *See also* CHURNALISM.

cuttings library A collection of *cuttings organized in such a way as to make it possible to find and cross-reference previously published material on a range of topics, institutions, or individuals. A cuttings library is sometimes referred to as a **morgue**. *See also* ARCHIVE.

cyberspace A rather outdated term for all things *internet-related.

daily A publication that appears once a day, either on six days (Monday to Saturday) or five days (weekdays) a week. Publications that are published on seven days a week tend to use a different title for Sunday editions even when sharing staff with the daily.

Daily A digital newspaper delivered via iPad that was launched by the *Murdoch empire in 2011 and closed in 2012 after failing to attract sufficient subscribers. *See also* NEW TECHNOLOGY; TABLET.

Daily Beast *See* NEWSWEEK. *See also* SCOOP.

Daily Courant One of the world's first daily *newspapers, published on London's *Fleet Street from 1702 until 1735.

Daily Express A *mid-market national *tabloid newspaper (and website) published in the UK that, since 2000, has been owned by Richard Desmond's *Northern & Shell, which also owns *OK! magazine and the downmarket *Daily Star. Launched as a *broadsheet in 1900 by C. Arthur Pearson (1866–1921), who wanted it to rival the already successful *Daily Mail, the *Express was unusual at the time in putting news on the front page rather than advertisements. In 1916 the paper was sold to Max Aitken, who went on to become the *press baron Lord Beaverbrook (1879–1964), and by 1936 it was selling 2.25 million copies a day, making it the biggest-selling daily in the world; twenty years later *circulation had climbed to more than 4 million. The *Daily Express* has traditionally been a right-wing newspaper, and Beaverbrook told the 1947–49 *Royal Commission on the Press that he published it chiefly for the purpose of *propaganda. The switch to a tabloid format took place in 1977, the same year that Beaverbrook Newspapers sold the title, since when a series of owners have presided over fluctuations of political allegiance and a relentlessly diminishing circulation. By 2013 it was only the sixth best-selling UK national with an average sale of around 500,000. Under Desmond's ownership in the early 21st century, the *Express* gained a reputation for repeatedly featuring a small number of issues on its front page, notably the search for missing child Madeleine McCann, theories about the death of Diana, Princess of Wales, and frequent stories warning that the UK might be about to experience an 'arctic winter'. *See also* SUNDAY EXPRESS.

Daily Herald A popular daily newspaper in the UK that, under a variety of owners between 1911 and 1964, provided a left-of-centre alternative to the rest of *Fleet Street. The paper began as the strike sheet of a group of compositors in London who had been locked out by their employers, and it retained close connections to the labour and trade union movement as well as to the campaign for women's suffrage. The *Herald* gained a substantial working-class readership but struggled to attract sufficient *advertising, and in 1964 it was revamped as a very different type of publication, renamed the *Sun*, and eventually sold to the *Murdoch empire.

Daily Mail The leading *mid-market national tabloid newspaper and online *brand (the hugely popular *Mail Online*) published in the UK. Traditionally both conservative and Conservative, the *Daily Mail* likes to portray itself as speaking for 'middle England'. The *Mail* was launched in 1896 by Alfred Harmsworth, later the *press baron the first Lord Northcliffe (1865–1922), and his younger brother Harold, later the first Lord Rothermere (1868–1940), and it is still owned by their descendants in the guise of *Associated Newspapers. When the *broadsheet format was abandoned in favour of *tabloid in 1971, the *Mail* became the first 'serious' UK national newspaper to be published in what it preferred to call a *compact size. A significant moment in *Fleet Street history occurred in 1998 when its circulation overtook that of the *redtop *Daily Mirror*, making it the second-biggest selling daily newspaper in the UK (after the *Sun*). In 2013, under long-serving editor Paul Dacre (1948–), the *Daily Mail* was selling around 1.8 million copies a day, comfortably more than the *Mirror* and almost within sight of the *Sun*. Its circulation is also significant because the *Mail* is the only UK national newspaper to be read by more women than men. *See also* MAIL ON SUNDAY.

(())) SEE WEB LINKS

• *Daily Mail* editor Paul Dacre's evidence to the Leveson Inquiry

Daily Mirror A daily *tabloid newspaper (and website) published in the UK at the popular *redtop end of the market; since 1999 it has been owned by *Trinity Mirror. When it was first published in 1903, under the direction of Alfred Harmsworth (*see* DAILY MAIL), it was targeted specifically at women, but within a few months it was relaunched as a picture-driven title with broad appeal. During the 1930s and particularly during the Second World War and its aftermath, the *Mirror* became strongly associated with speaking up for working-class communities, for rank-and-file soldiers, and for the Labour Party, which it helped win the 1945 general election. It embraced the concept of *sensationalism, and in 1949 it overtook the *Express* to become the biggest-selling daily newspaper in the UK, achieving a record daily *circulation of 5 million in 1964. It remained the country's biggest seller until 1977, when it was overtaken by Rupert Murdoch's *Sun*. For most of those years the *Mirror* was shaped by Hugh Cudlipp (1913–98), who combined tabloid populism with *investigative journalism and coverage of serious social issues. Although he was never the paper's *editor, as features editor, editorial director, and eventually chairman, Cudlipp became the towering figure of pre-Murdoch popular journalism. Following its Cudlipp-inspired heyday, the *Mirror* went through several changes of ownership, most notoriously between 1984 and 1991 when it was run almost as a personal fiefdom and megaphone for Robert 'Bob' Maxwell (1923–91). Later, under the editorship of Piers Morgan, the paper took a strongly anti-war stance in the run-up to the US-led invasion of Iraq in 2003; Morgan was sacked by Trinity Mirror the following year after publishing apparently faked photographs purporting to show British soldiers assaulting Iraqi prisoners. In 2013 a number of *Mirror* journalists were arrested when police extended *phone-hacking investigations beyond *News International titles. By then its average daily sale was just 1 million—well behind both the *Sun* and the *Mail*. *See also* CITY SLICKERS; PEOPLE; SUNDAY MIRROR.

(⊕) SEE WEB LINKS
• The Cudlipp archive

Daily Planet Probably one of the two most famous fictional newspapers in the world, featuring in the *Superman* comics and films. With a staff including Clark Kent, Lois Lane, and Jimmy Olsen, the *Daily Planet* is portrayed as a paper of record for the city of Metropolis; however, a 2012 edition of the comic saw Kent (aka Superman) quit the paper amid speculation that he was about to become a *blogger. *Compare* DAILY PROPHET.

Daily Prophet Probably one of the two most famous fictional newspapers in the world, featuring in J. K. Rowling's globally successful series of Harry Potter books and films. With its star reporter Rita Skeeter, the *Daily Prophet* is the unreliable organ of Rowling's wizarding world and features cool photographs that move like videos (*see* CONVERGENCE). In real life Rowling went on to take legal action against the *News of the World* for *intrusion during the *hackgate scandal. *Compare* DAILY PLANET.

Daily Record A popular Scottish national newspaper published since 1895. Along with its online *brand and its sister paper, the **Sunday Mail**, it is owned by *Trinity Mirror.

Daily Star A popular *tabloid newspaper in the UK launched in 1978 and now part of Richard Desmond's *Northern & Shell. The *redtop *Star*, along with its Sunday version (**Star on Sunday*) and their associated website, has frequently been criticized for relying on a diet of semi-pornographic pictures, stories that tend to show Muslims in a bad light, and wall-to-wall coverage of 'reality' TV shows. Its sales figures suggest there is a sizeable market for such fare, with *circulation in 2013 averaging more than 500,000 copies a day. An Irish edition is published jointly with Tony O'Reilly's *Independent News & Media. *See also* PORNIFICATION; SEXISM; STEREOTYPING.

Daily Telegraph 1. An Australian *tabloid daily newspaper, based in Sydney, that is part of the *Murdoch empire. Along with its *News Corp sister title, the *Australian*, the *Daily Telegraph* (and its Sunday counterpart) is often accused of playing a right-wing *agenda-setting role, with critics highlighting as an example the front-page headline that greeted news of the 2013 federal election: 'KICK THIS MOB OUT'. **2.** The UK's biggest-selling daily *quality newspaper, with an average sale in 2013 of more than half a million copies of the print edition. It launched in 1855 and since 2004 has been owned by the Barclay brothers, David and Frederick (1934–). Often described as 'the house organ of the Conservative Party', the *Telegraph* has traditionally been ultra-conservative as well as pro-Conservative, retaining its *broadsheet format long after rival quality titles had abandoned it. However, in 1994 it became the first British national paper to establish a serious online presence, known at the time as the *Electronic Telegraph*; in 2013 it introduced a metered *paywall to its *website, allowing *users up to

20 free articles per month before charges kick in. The *Telegraph* dominated the UK's political and news agenda for weeks on end in 2009 when it revealed an expenses scandal involving politicians from all major parties. *See also* SUNDAY TELEGRAPH.

(((●))) SEE WEB LINKS

• MPs' expenses: how the scandal unfolded

Daily Universal Register The forerunner of The *Times* of London that began publishing on 1 January 1785 before changing its name exactly three years later.

Daily Worker 1. In the USA, a newspaper linked to the Communist Party USA that was first published in 1924. It later became a weekly and went through several name changes before becoming the online-only radical website *peoplesworld.org.* in 2010.
2. In the UK it was the Communist Party of Great Britain's official newspaper; launched in 1930, its name was changed to the *Morning Star* in 1966. Along with *The Week*, it was suppressed between January 1941 and September 1942. Home Secretary Herbert Morrison justified *censorship on the grounds that the *Daily Worker* was trying to 'weaken the will of our people to achieve victory' in the Second World War; the newspaper tended to toe the Moscow line, only fully backing the war effort after Germany invaded the Soviet Union in June 1941. *See also* LENINIST THEORY OF THE PRESS; RADICAL PRESS.

(((●))) SEE WEB LINKS

• The Home Secretary's statement to the House of Commons about the *Daily Worker*

Dainik Jagran A Hindi language newspaper that is the biggest-selling daily paper in India. Its website proclaims that it is also 'the world's largest daily read'. Launched in 1942 amidst India's struggle for independence, *Dainik Jagran* is the flagship publication of Jagran Prakashan Ltd.

Dallas Morning News The major daily newspaper and website covering Dallas in the state of Texas. Published since 1885, today it is the flagship newspaper of the Belo Corporation, also based in Dallas, and is one of the top 25 best-selling newspapers in the USA.

DA-Notice (D-Notice, Defence Advisory Notice) A request for the UK media to ignore or downplay certain military, security, or intelligence issues that are deemed by the official Defence, Press, and Broadcasting Advisory Committee to be particularly sensitive and therefore to require restraint or *self-censorship in the cause of the national interest. Dating from 1912, the committee is an entirely voluntary collaboration between state representatives and senior media figures nominated by industry bodies. The committee's current standing DA-Notices, which date from 2000, cover:

- Military operations, plans, and capabilities
- Nuclear and non-nuclear weapons and equipment
- Ciphers and secure communications
- Sensitive installations and home addresses of individuals likely to be attacked by terrorists
- UK security services, intelligence services, and special services.

The committee has no powers of enforcement or punishment, relying on persuasion; however, any journalist who ignores its advice may be inviting prosecution under the UK's *Official Secrets Act. *See also* CENSORSHIP; INTELLIGENCE SERVICES; NEWS MANAGEMENT.

SEE WEB LINKS

- Website of the Defence, Press, and Broadcasting Advisory Committee

dark arts Information-gathering methods that may be regarded as of dubious taste at one end of the continuum and downright illegal at the other end, with the ethically questionable somewhere in the middle. So-called dark arts include *binology, *blagging, *deception, the *hacking of telephones or computers, and bribing people with access to official data to 'turn around' phone numbers or car registrations into names and home addresses. As the name implies, the dark arts tend to be shrouded in mystery, although the light shed during the *Leveson Inquiry revealed that some UK news organizations had paid tens of thousands of pounds to *private investigators to carry out such inquiries on their behalf. *Compare* ETHICAL JOURNALISM. *See also* BRIBE; DATA PROTECTION; HACKGATE; INVESTIGATIVE JOURNALISM.

Further reading: N. Davies, *Flat Earth News* (2008).

data journalism The mining of databases for trends, discrepancies, and other potential stories. This might involve accessing official information released under *freedom of information legislation or provided unofficially by a *whistleblower, but it can also include creating a searchable database by inputting into computer programs information gathered by other means. In addition to providing evidence to substantiate (or stand up) a story, data journalism may also enable such stories to be presented graphically and interactively (*see* INFOGRAPHICS). *See also* COMPUTER-ASSISTED REPORTING; INVESTIGATIVE JOURNALISM.

data protection Legislation designed to prevent unauthorized access (by journalists or others) to private information that may be stored on computers or files by government departments, hospitals, universities, and other institutions. Journalists may find a conflict between *laws that protect such material and others that promote *freedom of information; a reporter may seek to justify breaching data protection rules if it is necessary to investigate a story in the *public interest. *See also* DARK ARTS; INVESTIGATIVE JOURNALISM; PRIVACY.

dateline A line of information indicating from where a story was written and sometimes indicating the day, such as 'Mumbai, Monday'. A dateline will typically be incorporated into a *byline.

DC Thomson Publisher of newspapers, magazines, and comics based in Dundee, Scotland. Its titles include the *Dundee Courier*, the *Aberdeen Press & Journal*, and the *Beano*. Founded in 1905, the company was long famous for declining to negotiate with the *National Union of Journalists even when talks were the norm elsewhere in the UK press. As of 2013 it was the eighth biggest regional press publisher in the UK, with its six titles achieving an average weekly *circulation of 1.4 million.

dead air An unintentional period of silence on radio or a blank screen on television. A sure sign that something has gone wrong, dead air is dreaded by presenters, editors, and technical staff alike.

deadline The cut-off point for the completion of a story before it is published. The deadline is the focus of a print journalist's work but deadlines tend to be redundant in *online and *web-first journalism.

death knock The point at which a journalist attempts to *interview a bereaved family member or partner. The death knock is a standard *reporting technique following a death and, if carried out with sensitivity, it can provide *quotes, information, and pictures at least as often as it prompts a door to be slammed in the face of the reporter. The knock on the door tends to be favoured over the phone call because it is believed by most editors to produce better results. As one of the more delicate areas of journalistic practice and *ethics, death knocks are often the subject of squeamishness, macho boasting, and gallows' humour among journalists. Direct contact with bereaved relatives has to some extent been supplanted in recent years by the easy availability of material on *social media and online tribute sites (*see* DIGITAL DOORSTEPPING), but offering the family a chance to speak at such times remains a staple activity, particularly of *local journalism. *See also* DOORSTEPPING; INTRUSION; TRAGEDY.

Death on the Rock A 1988 *documentary made by Thames Television in the UK, which investigated the killing by British forces of three Irish republicans in Gibraltar. The programme caused a huge political and ethical furore before and after it was broadcast, and it was attacked by the Thatcher government and sections of the British press (notably the *Sunday Times*) for engaging in 'trial by television'. Many *Sunday Times* journalists subsequently expressed dismay at the way their own newspaper had covered the issue. The row was one of the more high profile of numerous examples of disputes about *bias, *censorship, and *ethics that broke out during the Northern Ireland 'troubles'. *See also* BROADCAST BAN; FLAK.

deaths of journalists In what can be seen as an occupational hazard in some situations, and a deliberate act of silencing and intimidation in others, dozens of journalists are killed each year in the course of their duties. Statistics are compiled by several international organizations and, although their figures may vary due to differences in definition and because of uncertainty over some incidents, they all tell a similar story of journalists being killed not just as foreigners in war zones, but often while carrying out investigations or simple reporting tasks in their own countries that are not necessarily engaged in international conflict. Local *fixers are also targeted.

International journalists' organizations are increasingly making **safety** a priority in their work, and the end of 2012 saw the launch of the *Speak Justice campaign against the apparent culture of impunity that protects many of those who target journalists around the world. The death toll for that year, according to the *International Federation of Journalists, was 121 'journalists and media staff [who] lost their lives in targeted attacks, bomb attacks, and other cross-fire incidents'. For the same year, *Reporters Without Borders listed 89 journalists, 6 'media assistants', and 47 *'netizens and citizen journalists'; the *International News Safety Institute recorded 'at least 156 journalists and other media staff killed because of their work'; and the *Committee to Protect Journalists said it had confirmed the motive for the death of 70 journalists killed that year and was investigating another 31 cases. *See also* CENSORSHIP; CHILLING EFFECT; CONSTRAINTS; SELF-CENSORSHIP.

(((⊕))) SEE WEB LINKS

• Death toll of journalists in 2012, according to the IFJ

death watch The wait by journalists and news organizations for the anticipated death of a major celebrity or figure in world politics, the announcement of which will trigger the running of instant reaction along with pre-prepared *obituaries.

deception Reporting that involves a journalist pretending to be something other than a journalist, for the purposes of gaining information or access that is deemed necessary to investigate or verify a story. Going *undercover in this way is generally justified by recourse to the *public interest defence and by arguing that the required evidence could not have been obtained by more straightforward means; it tends to be frowned upon if conducted as part of a speculative *fishing expedition. *See also* FAKE SHEIKH.

deck A line of type in a *headline. A three-deck headline would be a headline set in three lines of text, for example.

decoding *See* ENCODING, DECODING

Deep Throat The nickname given to the *confidential source who famously helped the *Washington Post* expose the *Watergate scandal in the 1970s. In 2005 he revealed himself to be Mark Felt (1913–2008), who had been the associate director of the Federal Bureau of Investigation (FBI), effectively the FBI's number two, at the time he was secretly meeting reporter Bob Woodward in a shadowy car park to leak secret information and help steer the newspaper's investigation. The name 'Deep Throat' was taken from the title of a notorious pornographic film of the time. Woodward and his colleague Carl Bernstein protected the identity of their source until the elderly Felt himself revealed his role (via his family) in an article for *Vanity Fair* magazine; Woodward then confirmed it. Felt is regarded by some as a dishonourable figure who betrayed his organization and his president, and by others as a hero who helped save *democracy in the USA. By the time of his death in 2008 at the age of 95, his motivation for becoming one of the world's most famous *whistleblowers remained unclear.

(((⊕))) SEE WEB LINKS

• *Vanity Fair*: 'I'm the guy they called Deep Throat'

defamation The publication or circulation of a statement, allegation, or other form of communication that could have the effect of destroying or diminishing somebody's reputation. Defences against allegations of defamation include that the statement can be shown to be true or that publication is protected by *privilege. The legal costs associated with defending defamation and *libel actions are often said to have a *chilling effect on *investigative journalism, particularly in the UK. *See also* REYNOLDS DEFENCE; SLANDER.

d

Defamation Act 2013 A piece of legislation that overhauled the *libel laws in England and Wales and was largely welcomed by journalists for its requirement that claimants would in future need to demonstrate that they had suffered some serious harm before being able to make a claim for *defamation. The Act also introduced a statutory defence of responsible publication on matters of the *public interest, to replace what had been the common law *Reynolds defence.

delayed drop A form of *intro that does not make it immediately obvious what the story is about or what the main *angle might be.

Delicious A US-based *social media and *social bookmarking site launched in 2004, prompting many major news *websites to feature *links to enable online *users to share stories via Delicious. *See also* ONLINE JOURNALISM; SOCIAL NETWORKING.

democracy A political system whereby *citizens can participate in decision-making, either directly or by the election of representatives, and which is said by advocates of a *free press to be impossible without vigorous, independent journalism (*compare* DEMOCRATIC DEFICIT). *See also* AREOPAGITICA; FOURTH ESTATE; PUBLIC SPHERE; PUTNEY DEBATES; WATCHDOG ROLE.

Democracy Now! An independent TV, radio, and online news and current affairs service based in the USA that has covered national and international news from an alternative perspective since 1996. *Democracy Now!* does not accept *advertising and relies for its survival on donations. *See also* ALTERNATIVE MEDIA.

(((⊕))) SEE WEB LINKS
• Topics covered by *Democracy Now!*

democratic deficit The situation that is said to result from some *citizens being deprived of *access to *public interest journalism, either as members of the *audience who require the media to keep them informed or as potential *sources with their own stories to tell. There is often said to be a democratic deficit when media outlets close or reduce coverage of certain communities or institutions, thereby reducing their effectiveness as society's *watchdogs (*compare* FOURTH ESTATE). Some *alternative media and *citizen journalism projects declare their goal explicitly as being to redress the democratic deficit caused by the limitations of *mainstream media. *See also* DEMOCRACY; DIGITAL DIVIDE; PUBLIC SPHERE.

Dennis Publishing *See* THE WEEK; OZ.

denotation The literal or most obvious meaning of a message or form of *communication (*compare* CONNOTATION). *See also* CODE; ENCODING, DECODING; SEMIOTICS.

Denver Post A daily newspaper covering Denver, Colorado, since 1892. Today it and its associated website are owned by the MediaNews Group (one of the biggest newspaper chains in the USA) and is generally one of the top ten best-selling titles in the country.

deregulation The weakening or abolition of restrictions on media *ownership and/or media content. *Compare* REGULATION; STATUTORY REGULATION.

desk The senior journalist or journalists within a news organization responsible for specific sections such as news, features, sport, and pictures. Most journalists report to their desk, while those on the desk report to the *editor. *Compare* HUB.

Detroit Free Press A US daily newspaper and online *brand covering Detroit, Michigan, that is part of the *Gannett empire.

Deutsche-Presse-Agentur (DPA) The largest *news agency in Germany, which launched in 1949 and is based in Hamburg.

(())) SEE WEB LINKS
• DPA's English-language website

development journalism A form of *reporting that places an emphasis on the perspectives of developing countries, primarily in the global south, rather than reproducing the dominant views or media practices of *elite nations. *Compare* CULTURAL IMPERIALISM; NEWS FLOW; REPRESENTATION. *See also* ADVOCACY JOURNALISM; ALTERNATIVE JOURNALISM; ASIAN VALUES IN JOURNALISM; PEACE JOURNALISM.

diary The mechanism by which news organizations plan those of their activities that are known about in advance. Whether a large physical diary or an electronic online calendar, the diary is used by the relevant *desk to log predictable events that require coverage and the names of those allocated to cover them. *See also* ROUTINES.

diary story A story that results from covering an event that was known about in advance and was therefore in a news organization's *diary. Typical diary stories include reports on court hearings, meetings, *press conferences, public inquiries, tribunals, and demonstrations. Although they account for a large proportion of journalistic output, diary stories tend to be valued less highly than *off-diary stories because they are less likely to be *exclusive. *See also* CALLS; FREQUENCY.

Digg A news *aggregation and *social media site launched in the USA in 2004 that gave *users the opportunity of voting which items ought to be featured more or less prominently ('digging' and 'burying'). Many major news *websites feature a link to enable their users to share stories via Digg and other *social bookmarking sites. *See also* ONLINE JOURNALISM; SOCIAL NETWORKING.

digital divide Inequality in access to *online journalism (and other forms of internet-based and mobile *communication). There may be a divide between classes and certain communities within one country as well as between nations and regions globally. *See also* DEMOCRATIC DEFICIT.

digital doorstepping The journalistic use of online and *social media sources to obtain the sort of information that, in *analogue days, would have required direct personal contact either face-to-face or on the telephone. The term is a broad one that tends to cover the lifting of information, comments, and pictures from profiles on *Facebook and elsewhere, following *Twitter users, and making direct requests for information or comments via social media. *Compare* DEATH KNOCK; DOORSTEPPING. *See also* DOXING; INTRUSION.

digital immigrants Journalists who began their working lives in the *analogue era before *digital media and audience members who began their consumption of media before the arrival of *online journalism and *social media. *Compare* DIGITAL NATIVES.

digital manipulation (Photoshopping) The alteration of a digital photograph before publication. Very minor adjustments to contrasts and shadows tend to be deemed acceptable, as an equivalent to the *dodging and *burning of a pre-digital image, but ethical arguments have frequently erupted over more substantial alterations, such as when somebody who was not there is added to a picture, when somebody who was there is removed or moved, or when a model is made to look even more unnaturally skinny than in real life. *Compare* PIXILATION. *See also* ETHICS; TRUTH.

digital media A broad term that encompasses news *websites, *blogs, and numerous other spaces on the *internet, *social media, the use of mobile telephony as a delivery mechanism for media output, and ways in which previously *analogue forms of media are now produced using digital technology such as computers, *content management systems, *templates, smart phones, digital editing equipment, and lightweight digital cameras and recorders. This process of digitization usually entails more work being carried out at greater speeds by fewer people. *Compare* LEGACY MEDIA. *See also* CONVERGENCE; NEW TECHNOLOGY; REUTERS INSTITUTE FOR THE STUDY OF JOURNALISM; TABLET.

digital natives Journalists and audience members alike who have grown up or always worked in an era of *online journalism and *social media, for whom it has always been as much a part of their environment as print and broadcast media. *Compare* DIGITAL IMMIGRANTS. *See also* AMBIENT JOURNALISM.

direct quote The actual words of a *source as included in a piece of journalism and placed within quotation marks. *Compare* INDIRECT QUOTE. *See also* QUOTE.

disco A *live discussion between two or more guests on a radio programme, chaired by a *presenter whose main task will be to prevent the participants talking over each other. *Compare* TWO-WAY.

discourse Discussion, speech, text, and language. Within *journalism studies, use of the word 'discourse' tends to signify that attention is being paid to the existence of *codes and to the more or less hidden ideological assumptions and/or dominant narratives found within any particular field of *communication. *See also* CRITICAL DISCOURSE ANALYSIS; ENCODING, DECODING; IDEOLOGY.

discourse analysis *See* CRITICAL DISCOURSE ANALYSIS.

discrimination Treating some people less favourably than others, either individually or collectively. In journalism this can result in many top jobs being dominated by white, middle-class men who have been educated at 'elite' universities. Discrimination and prejudice can also lead to *stereotyping and *discriminatory language within journalistic output. *See also* CLASS; CULTURAL BIAS; NEWSWEEK; RACISM; SEXISM.

discriminatory language Words and phrases that tend to stereotype individuals, groups, races, or nationalities, the use of which in news stories is said by critics to foster prejudice and even hatred, often against some of the most vulnerable sections of society. *See also* CAMPAIGN FOR REAL PEOPLE; DISCRIMINATION; POLITICAL CORRECTNESS; STEREOTYPING.

Dissent A quarterly radical magazine published in the USA since 1954. An independent, non-profit publication and website covering 'politics and ideas', its contributors have included Hannah Arendt, Norman Mailer, and Aleksandr Solzhenitsyn. *See also* ALTERNATIVE MEDIA.

Diva A glossy *magazine for lesbians published in the UK since 1994 and owned by Millivres Prowler. It sells more than 50,000 copies a month, making it reportedly the biggest selling magazine for lesbian and bisexual women in Europe. *See also* GAY MEDIA; GLOSSIES; WOMEN'S MAGAZINES.

docudrama *See* DRAMA-DOCUMENTARY.

documentary A stand-alone television or radio programme comprising a piece of *long-form journalism, typically lasting anywhere between 15 and 60 minutes (sometimes even longer), that may look back on an old story or add depth to a (relatively) topical story. *See also* CURRENT AFFAIRS; DRAMA-DOCUMENTARY.

dodging Altering the contrast of a *photograph, or part of a photograph, for visual effect. Dodging (also known as dodging and burning) is widely regarded as an ethically acceptable practice in journalism as long as it does not alter the meaning or *truth of a picture, although this can be a grey area—sometimes literally. *See also* DIGITAL MANIPULATION.

doorstepping Turning up at somebody's home or place of work to seek an *interview, at best, or a 'no comment', at worst. Doorstepping typically occurs when a person involved in a news story has rejected more formal approaches, or is the subject of a piece of *investigative journalism as a result of which a reporter wishes to confront them with allegations and invite a response just before the story is run. Doorstepping can involve a journalist hanging around for hours in the hope of a comment or even just a sighting, leading sometimes to complaints of *harassment and *intrusion. *Compare* DIGITAL DOORSTEPPING. *See also* DEATH KNOCK; MEDIA SCRUM.

doxing Investigating details of somebody's life by following the 'digital footprints' they have left on various websites, networks, databases, or documents available online; dox refers to docs, short for documents. Confusingly, the term is sometimes also extended to refer to the practice of publicizing such personal information, including home addresses and phone numbers, by internet *trolls. *See also* DARK ARTS; DATA PROTECTION; DIGITAL DOORSTEPPING; INVESTIGATIVE JOURNALISM; NAME AND SHAME; TROLLING.

drama-documentary (docudrama) A television or radio version of a factual story that, although based on journalistic research, involves the use of actors, *sound effects, music, and other dramatic devices more commonly associated with works of fiction than with traditional *documentary or *current affairs programmes. *See also* INFOTAINMENT; RECONSTRUCTION.

Drudge Report Online news *aggregation site in the USA that occasionally breaks its own stories, most notably in 1998 when it revealed the White House sex scandal involving President Bill Clinton and the intern Monica Lewinsky, an exposé of which had been pulled at the last minute by **Newsweek*. Begun as a gossip-based email newsletter in 1995–6, since its launch as a website in 1997 the *Drudge Report* has often been cited as one of the success stories of *citizen journalism that exists outside the *mainstream media structures, albeit one that relies to a large extent on *linking to the work of others. *See also* ONLINE JOURNALISM.

(⊕) SEE WEB LINKS

• The *Drudge Report*'s original Monica Lewinsky story

dumbing down The trivialization and over-simplification of news and current affairs (amongst other things). Dumbing down is a contested concept that is often countered with accusations of *elitism and snobbery. *See also* INFOTAINMENT; NEWSZAK; TABLOIDIZATION.

dummy A mocked-up version of a newspaper, magazine, or website produced either before it is launched or as part of a planned redesign. Dummies can be used to attract potential *advertisers, to discuss with *focus groups of potential readers, and to test the production process in real time.

Dunfermline Press Group A family-owned company that has published newspapers in Scotland since 1859. Its flagship title is the *Dunfermline Press*, a weekly paper plus website covering the town of Dunfermline in Fife.

East Village Other *See* VILLAGE VOICE.

Eastern Eye A weekly newspaper (and online *brand) serving the Asian community in the UK that was launched in 1989 and since 2009 has been owned by Garavi Gujarat Publications, which publishes a range of other titles including *Asian Trader*. *See also* ETHNIC MINORITY MEDIA.

Ebony A glossy magazine and digital *brand published in the USA that is aimed at what has been described as an 'aspirational' black readership, selling well over a million copies each month and claiming a readership of more than 10 million. Founded in 1945 by John H. Johnson (1918–2005), who had previously published the small circulation *Negro Digest*, the new *Ebony* magazine was modelled on *Life* magazine and placed a similar emphasis on *photojournalism. *See also* BLACK MEDIA; ETHNIC MINORITY MEDIA.

SEE WEB LINKS
• John H. Johnson oral history

economics correspondent A specialist reporter covering the business and financial *beat for a particular news organization or outlet. *See also* BUSINESS JOURNALISM.

Economist An influential UK-based international weekly *magazine and online *brand covering business, politics, and current affairs. Published since 1843, the *Economist* always describes itself as a *newspaper and famously eschews *bylines. *See also* BUSINESS JOURNALISM.

Ecquid Novi A peer-reviewed academic journal launched in 1980 to publish primarily the work of African scholars in the field of *journalism studies. *See also* ACADEMIZATION OF JOURNALISM.

editing 1. The job of an *editor in running the overall editorial operation of a news organization.
2. Commissioning, selecting, preparing, cutting, rewriting, or rearranging *copy, *video, or *audio for publication or broadcast. *See also* SUBBING.

editor 1. The journalist with overall responsibility for running and overseeing a news organization's editorial operation, staffing, and content. Editors typically have the power to hire and fire journalists within the financial constraints imposed by their employers, and in turn editors of commercial media outlets are appointed by and generally answerable to *proprietors.
2. A title given to journalists who run particular sections or departments (as in *news editor) and sometimes even to senior *correspondents who are not in charge of anybody other than themselves. *See also* EDITING.

editorial 1. A word denoting journalistic *content as distinct from other material such as *advertising, promotions, and competitions.
2. The department/s within a news organization responsible for producing journalistic content (as opposed to the advertising department, for example).
3. A *leader column that offers what purports to be the *opinion of the *editor.

editorial conference *See* CONFERENCE.

editorial independence The concept that journalists ought to be able to conduct their work without coming under undue influence to provide coverage tailored to suit the commercial interests of *proprietors or *advertisers. The *editorial and *advertising departments of commercial media organizations are sometimes said to be separated by a 'firewall', although they often cooperate in practice more than is implied by such rhetoric. *See also* ETHICAL JOURNALISM.

Editors' Code The ethical guidelines of the UK's *Press Complaints Commission, which were drafted in 1991 (and frequently amended thereafter) by a committee of *editors. The code details what is and is not deemed to be acceptable behaviour by journalists working for newspapers, magazines, and their websites. It includes a clause whereby certain practices are allowed only in pursuit of a story in the *public interest. Despite repeated requests by the *National Union of Journalists

and by journalists working on the *Daily Express*, the code has no
*conscience clause. *See also* CODES OF CONDUCT; ETHICS; LEVESON
INQUIRY; SELF-REGULATION.

(())) SEE WEB LINKS
• The Editors' Code of Practice

effects 1. A shorthand term meaning *sound effects.
2. Theories that media output including journalism can influence
individual and/or social behaviour, for example by means of *agenda-
setting or *moral panics. The extent to which journalism can be shown
to have effects, and whether any such effects might be malign or benign,
is a fiercely contested issue within *journalism studies and beyond. *See
also* HYPODERMIC MODEL; MEDIA EFFECTS.

elite nations Countries that are powerful or particularly significant on
a global or regional basis, the activities of whose governments and major
institutions tend to be seen as more consequential than those of other
nations, and which therefore are more likely to become *news. Ideas of
which are the elite nations may change over time as well as vary in
different parts of the world, and may involve considerations of power in
military, economic, political, and/or cultural spheres. The notion of elite
nations was one of the factors identified in Johan Galtung and Mari
Ruge's study of *news values. *Compare* DEVELOPMENT JOURNALISM.
See also CULTURAL IMPERIALISM.

elite people Individuals or groups of people who are seen as
powerful, influential, or even just well known, whose activities tend to be
regarded as more *newsworthy than the activities of 'ordinary' people,
or at least until ordinary people are involved in something extraordinary.
Ideas of who are the elite people change over time and place. The notion
of elite people was one of the factors identified in Johan Galtung and
Mari Ruge's 1960s work on *news values, but later scholars have tended
to draw a distinction between the *power elite on the one hand and
mere *celebrity on the other.

elite source Individuals or institutions whose every statement or
action tends to be regarded as potentially *newsworthy, who tend to
have privileged *access to the media, and who may be thought of as
playing the role of *primary definer on major issues of the day.

elitism The disdainful attitude displayed by many critics of *tabloid and other forms of popular journalism, according to many of those who produce or consume such media. *See also* DUMBING DOWN.

Elle A *glossy women's *lifestyle magazine and online *brand that was launched in France in 1945 and which is now published in numerous international editions, including in Canada, Germany, the USA, and the UK. *See also* WOMEN'S MAGAZINES.

email Electronic mail which, since the mid-1990s, has become one of the main ways in which journalists communicate with each other, with their *desks, and with their *sources. Publication of staff email addresses made it much easier for *audience members to communicate with journalists directly, which is seen by many of the latter as something of a mixed blessing.

email interview A journalist questioning a *source and receiving answers via an exchange of *emails. Conducting an *interview in this way is regarded by many journalists as a last resort because it lacks the instantaneous to-ing and fro-ing of a real-life conversation, makes it more difficult to pick up on nuance or tone, and reduces the possibility of adding *colour to the published version of the encounter.

email lists A means of distributing newsletters, circulars, and *alerts to interested people via *email. Reporters and correspondents are likely to get themselves on several lists so that they can receive useful (and not so useful) information on issues relevant to their specialism, locality, or *beat.

EMAP A UK-based publisher of *B2B and *trade magazines including *Construction News*, *Drapers*, *Local Government Chronicle*, and *Nursing Times*. Under the name East Midland Allied Press, EMAP was also a publisher of regional newspapers for much of the 20th century.

embargo A request by a *source, most often a *PR person, that news organizations refrain from publishing or broadcasting material such as that contained in a *news release until a specified time on a certain date. Similarly, the text of a speech or statement may be given to the media in advance, embargoed until the words have been spoken, and subject to being checked against delivery. Normally the only consequence of breaking such an embargo is the risk of being denied such advance information in the future and of being frowned upon by journalists from rival organizations.

embedded reporting Journalistic coverage by reporters who are allowed access to locations and/or organizations on condition that they accept certain limitations on their activities. Such embedding most frequently occurs during wars and other forms of armed conflict, when news organizations may deem it expedient and worthwhile to exchange independence for access. Although the term has become common only in recent decades, the practice itself was undertaken during many earlier wars. Some journalists reject embedding on the grounds that it can reduce reporters to propagandists, and some former embedded journalists have themselves expressed disquiet at the way they came to identify with the members of the armed forces among whom they were living and upon whom they relied for protection. *See also* CENSORSHIP; SELF-CENSORSHIP; WAR REPORTING.

embedding A system whereby journalists live and work within and alongside organizations such as the army, offering *embedded reporting within certain limitations and restrictions.

empirical research Ways of studying journalism that rely more on gathering evidence (by means of a *content analysis, for example) than on abstract theorizing. *Compare* CRITICAL DISCOURSE ANALYSIS; CRITICAL THEORY. *See also* ACADEMIZATION OF JOURNALISM; ETHNOGRAPHIC RESEARCH; JOURNALISM STUDIES.

empowerment Facilitating *citizens in taking action and/or speaking out, which is one of the avowed aims of *alternative media. *See also* AGENCY; CITIZEN JOURNALISM; FEMINIST MEDIA; REPRESENTATION.

encoding *See* ENCODING, DECODING.

encoding, decoding A model of *communication whereby the receiver does not necessarily absorb, uncritically, whatever message is intended by the sender. Cultural studies theorist Stuart Hall (1932–2014) argued that audiences may adopt a *preferred or dominant reading that essentially accepts information at face value, along with whatever *ideology has been embedded within the text; a *negotiated reading that adopts a more questioning approach; or an *oppositional reading that rejects outright any ideological assumptions thought to be implicit

within whatever is being communicated. *See also* ACTIVE AUDIENCE;
CODE; CRITICAL THEORY; HEGEMONY.

Enlightenment An intellectual and cultural movement (or range of
more or less parallel 'movements') that involved the pursuit of
knowledge based on rational thought, scientific study, the questioning
of authority, a rejection of superstition, and a belief in (relative) freedom
of expression. The development of independent journalism and of a
print culture informed by ideas of *democracy tend to be seen as
running alongside Europe's 'Age of Enlightenment' roughly from the
mid-17th century to the end of the 18th century. *See also* COFFEE
HOUSES; OBJECTIVE JOURNALISM; PRINTING; PUBLIC SPHERE.

entertainment Those elements of journalism that are designed more
to attract, amuse, or enthral *audience members rather than to convey
vital information. This would include many stories concerning *sex,
showbusiness, *human interest, animals, an unfolding drama, or stories
that offer opportunities for humorous treatment such as funny *pictures
or 'amusing' *headlines. *See also* INFOTAINMENT; NEWS VALUES;
TABLOIDIZATION.

ethical codes *See* CODES OF CONDUCT.

ethical journalism Journalistic activity conducted in accordance
with both the letter and the spirit of relevant ethical guidelines and
*codes of conduct, and which is informed more by a commitment to
*ethics and to the *public interest than to commercial or careerist
considerations. Some argue that the very notion of ethical journalism is
an oxymoron while others see it as a beacon to help illuminate a tricky
path through conflicting demands, loyalties, and *constraints. Notions of
what is and isn't ethical journalism may change over time as well as
varying between different countries and workplaces. *See also* EDITORIAL
INDEPENDENCE; REFLECTIVE PRACTICE.

(⊕) SEE WEB LINKS
• The Ethical Journalism initiative of the *IFJ

ethics The ideas of right and wrong that may inform the work of
journalists either formally or informally. Many journalists choose to
follow collective *codes of conduct, such as that of the *National Union
of Journalists in the UK and Ireland, and many are required to follow
codes, guidelines, or rules laid down by their employer and/or by

regulatory bodies covering the industry in the country in which they are working. Individual journalists may also follow their own conscience in a personal way, which may be informed by cultural, political, religious, secular, philosophical, family, community, or other influences. Ideas of ethics often align with and/or draw on *laws governing media output but this is not always the case: a journalist might defy the law to uphold the ethical principle of protecting the identity of an *anonymous source, for example, or might risk breaking the *Official Secrets Act to reveal information in the *public interest.

Major areas of ethical controversy include *privacy, *intrusion into grief, *war reporting, *bias, *censorship, *harassment, *media scrums, *stereotyping, and the use of *discriminatory language. However, ethics cannot be reduced to a list of discrete aspects or separated from other aspects of journalism, because everything journalists do has potential implications: every story selected, followed-up, or ignored; every door knocked on or every call made; every conversation with a *source or potential source; every *interview requested or conducted; every *quote or *soundbite included, excluded, or edited; every piece of evidence checked and weighed up; every piece of contextual or background information added, removed, or simplified; every *picture taken, not taken, *airbrushed, published, or *spiked; every piece of audio-visual material recorded or edited; every use of *social media to track down people or material; every question asked; and every question not asked.

Although some journalists think of ethical considerations as a set of obstacles or *constraints on their work, others see ethics as integral to good journalism, arguing that *reflective practice can encourage journalists to care more about people (as sources, *audiences, and *citizens), about *accuracy, about the public interest, and about journalism itself. *See also* BBC EDITORIAL GUIDELINES; CALCUTT REPORTS; CONSCIENCE CLAUSE; DARK ARTS; ETHICAL JOURNALISM; LEVESON INQUIRY; MEDIAWISE; PRESS COMPLAINTS COMMISSION.

Further reading: C. Frost, *Journalism Ethics and Regulation* (2011).
T. Harcup, *The Ethical Journalist* (2007).
C. Meyers (ed.), *Journalism Ethics: A Philosophical Approach* (2010).
W. Wyatt (ed.), *The Ethics of Journalism: Individual, Institutional, and Cultural Influences* (2014).

ethnic minority coverage The appearance in news stories of people from ethnic minority communities. Such coverage is often said by members of those communities to render them as stereotypes, when they are not simply invisible. Dissatisfaction with the record of mainstream media has led to the creation of *ethnic minority media. *See also* DISCRIMINATORY LANGUAGE; RACE; RACISM; REPRESENTATION; STEREOTYPING.

ethnic minority journalists News *reporters and *feature writers from minority communities who, if working for *mainstream media, may find themselves expected to act almost as representatives or spokespeople for their particular ethnic grouping in a way that members of the majority community never are, and/or to cover only those issues deemed to particularly involve people from ethnic minorities. Such pressures and expectations may come from editors, colleagues, and from members of their 'own' community; while some are happy to embrace such a role, many just want to be journalists, full stop. *See also* DISCRIMINATION; ETHNIC MINORITY MEDIA; RACE.

ethnic minority media Those newspapers, magazines, broadcast organizations or programmes, websites, and any other form of media that are produced specifically to serve an *audience primarily comprising members of an ethnic minority. Such media tend to be owned and largely staffed by people from the same ethnic grouping, but that is not always the case. Such media are occasionally referred to as 'ethnic media', which is meaningless because everybody has an ethnicity. *See also* BLACK MEDIA; INDIGENOUS MEDIA.

ethnographic research Methods of studying journalism that involve newsroom observation and engaging journalists in workplace discussions as a way of gathering qualitative evidence. *Compare* CRITICAL DISCOURSE ANALYSIS. *See also* ACADEMIZATION OF JOURNALISM; EMPIRICAL RESEARCH; JOURNALISM STUDIES.

European A weekly English language newspaper launched by Robert Maxwell (1923–91) in 1990 that was intended to sell across post-Cold War Europe but which sold very few copies anywhere, attracting limited *advertising in the process. Having been a drain on the finances both of Maxwell and subsequent owners the Barclay brothers, it died a quiet death in 1998.

European Convention on Human Rights A treaty drawn up by the Council of Europe in 1950 in the wake of Nazi Germany's defeat in the Second World War, which guarantees a series of *human rights including freedom of expression. The convention was incorporated into UK law under the *Human Rights Act 1998. Of particular interest to journalists is Article 10, which asserts the right to freedom of expression, but the Convention counterbalances this with Article 8, which seeks to protect citizens' rights to *privacy. These two rights can be weighed against each other, according to the merits of individual cases, in national courts and right up to the European Court of Human Rights. *See also* UNIVERSAL DECLARATION OF HUMAN RIGHTS.

(⊕) SEE WEB LINKS
• The European Convention on Human Rights

European Federation of Journalists (EFJ) The European arm of the *International Federation of Journalists. Its member organizations represent more than 300,000 journalists working in 36 European countries.

(⊕) SEE WEB LINKS
• EFJ member organizations

European Journalism Training Association (EJTA)
A networking organization bringing together more than 50 journalism *training centres, colleges, and universities in 24 European countries. Since its formation in 1990 it has initiated a number of Europe-wide research projects.

(⊕) SEE WEB LINKS
• EJTA events

Evening Standard A UK regional newspaper published in London on Monday to Friday that has been distributed free since 2009. First published in 1827, the *Standard* is the sole surviving evening newspaper in London, having seen off rivals such as the *Pall Mall Gazette*, the *Evening News*, and the *Evening Star*. It was owned by *Associated Newspapers until 2009, when it was sold for a reported £1 to the Russian oligarch Alexander Lebedev (1959–) and his son Evgeny (1980–). The Lebedevs later bought the *Independent* and, in 2013, won the franchise to run a new local television service in London. *See also* FREE NEWSPAPER.

Exaro A website specializing in *investigative journalism that launched in the UK in 2011. Initially subscription-only, it dropped its *paywall in August 2013. It was *Exaro* that, along with *Private Eye* and *Channel 4

News, revealed the contents of the 2013 Murdoch tape: the secret recording of a meeting between Rupert Murdoch and angry journalists on his **Sun* newspaper. *Exaro* has set up a 'secure dropbox' online for the use of *whistleblowers wishing to *leak information confidentially. *See also* DIGITAL MEDIA.

exclamation mark *See* SCREAMER.

exclusive A story that, at the time of publication or broadcast, appears in just one media outlet. At least that is its purported meaning but, whether deliberately or not, the term is frequently misapplied. It is not uncommon to see several *Fleet Street newspapers running the same story at the same time, all labelled 'world exclusive'. *See also* SCOOP; SPOILER.

Exiled Journalists' Network A lobbying and networking organization that has been supporting journalists who have fled to the UK to escape persecution in their own countries since 2005.

(⊕) SEE WEB LINKS
• Exiled Journalists' Network on Facebook

expenses Money claimed by journalists from their employers in reimbursement for a variety of real or imagined expenditure on travel, entertaining *sources, and so on. Expenses are the subject of many a *Fleet Street legend (*see* GOLDEN AGE).

exposé A piece of *investigative journalism that uncovers some form of (allegedly) *scandalous behaviour. *See also* EXCLUSIVE; SCOOP.

Express *See* DAILY EXPRESS.

Express & Star A family-owned daily newspaper published in the city of Wolverhampton that is the biggest-selling regional newspaper in the UK in the 21st century. Flagship title of the *Midland News Association, the *Express & Star* was first published in 1889 following a merger between two existing titles. *See also* GUITON GROUP.

ezine An electronic or *online form of *zine that, typically, is written (and illustrated) by and for those who share an interest, for example in a particular type of music, sport, or literary genre (*see* COMMUNITY OF INTEREST).

F

Facebook An online *social networking service that launched in 2004 and which, by the end of that decade, had become a staple way in which reporters could spot potential news stories, identify *sources, and maintain their *contacts. Media organizations and individual journalists also use Facebook to promote themselves as *brands and to 'curate' *conversations with *audiences. *See also* CURATION; DIGITAL DOORSTEPPING; INTERNET; MYSPACE; ONLINE JOURNALISM; SOCIAL MEDIA; TWITTER.

factbox A *sidebar in the form of a boxed-off piece of text containing several key *facts pertaining to the main story that it accompanies.

fact-checking 1. Establishing the veracity of the information contained within a piece of journalism before it is published or broadcast. Checking *facts is something that all journalists are expected to do as part of their job, but it is a particular responsibility of *sub-editors, where they still exist. US media have traditionally employed teams of people (often relatively junior staff) specifically as fact-checkers.
2. A practice of some *bloggers and media organizations whereby the veracity of information is investigated after it has been published or broadcast, with the results then being made public. *Compare* NEVER WRONG FOR LONG. *See also* ACCURACY; RESEARCH; TRUTH; VERIFICATION.

((⊕)) SEE WEB LINKS
• *Columbia Journalism Review* on fact-checking

facticity The factual quality of a piece of journalism. *See also* ACCURACY; FACTS; TRUTHINESS.

facts Verifiably accurate pieces of information that are included in news stories and other forms of journalism, as opposed to *comment, *colour, interpretation, or speculation. Good journalism is invariably said to involve some form of *fact-checking and *verification, although what are accepted as facts can change as fresh information is discovered. *See also* OBJECTIVE JOURNALISM; TRUTH.

factuality A piece of broadcasting based on real-life events and *facts, as in a *documentary. *Compare* ACTUALITY.

FAIR *See* FAIRNESS AND ACCURACY IN REPORTING.

fair comment *See* HONEST COMMENT.

Fairfax Media A major media company in Australia and New Zealand that competes head-on with the *Murdoch empire. Its newspapers include the *Sydney Morning Herald* and the *Age* in Melbourne, both of which erected *paywalls around their websites in 2012 and switched their print format from *broadsheet to *tabloid the following year.

Fairness and Accuracy in Reporting (FAIR) A campaigning and lobbying group in the USA that, since 1986, has been monitoring and critiquing the performance of 'corporate media' and drawing attention to under-reported stories and under-represented perspectives. FAIR produces a magazine (*Extra!*) and radio programme (*CounterSpin*) in addition to a website, blog, podcast, and email list for action alerts.

(∰) SEE WEB LINKS
• The FAIR blog

fakery The publishing or broadcasting of fake words or pictures as if they are genuine, for example by running a *reconstruction without clearly labelling it as such, thereby deceiving and betraying the *trust of the *audience. Such practices are regarded as deeply unethical and they can also be costly: in 1998 a commercial TV company in the UK was fined £2 million by the Independent Television Commission (one of the regulatory predecessors of *Ofcom) for fabricating footage in a *documentary about drug-smuggling. News organizations may run fake material unwittingly if one of their journalists submits an invented story (*see* HACK HEAVEN; LITTLE JIMMY). *Compare* DECEPTION; HOAXES. *See also* COD BYLINE; ETHICS; TRUTH.

fake sheikh The disguise of choice adopted by the *News of the World* investigative reporter Mazher Mahmood during countless *undercover reporting operations from the 1990s to the paper's closure in 2011. Typically, a *celebrity (sometimes a non-celebrity) would be recorded making unguarded remarks or engaging in questionable (sometimes illegal) activity in the presence of a man who they were tricked into believing was an Arab businessman of enormous wealth, and who might just be persuaded to put some of that wealth their way. Whenever critics questioned the *ethics of *deception involving the sheikh or a range of other personas, Mahmood and his editors would defend the method as being in the *public interest. Following the demise of the *News of the World*, Mahmood worked briefly for the *Sunday Times* before joining the *Sun on Sunday*. *See also* INVESTIGATIVE JOURNALISM; STING; SUBTERFUGE.

SEE WEB LINKS
• Mazher Mahmood's evidence to the Leveson Inquiry

fanzine A media product created, written, and illustrated by members of a *community of interest and circulating within that community; typically it is produced on a non-commercial basis and often celebrates an 'amateur' style of writing and 'do-it-yourself' production values. There were particular flowerings of UK fanzines associated with punk music in the late 1970s and football in the following decade. *See also* EZINE; SNIFFIN' GLUE; ZINE.

Father of Chapel (FoC) A male journalist in the UK or Ireland who has been elected by fellow members of the *National Union of Journalists in their workplace to be their lay representative (or shop steward) in talks with management. *See also* CHAPEL; MOTHER OF CHAPEL.

FCC *See* FEDERAL COMMUNICATIONS COMMISSION.

feature 1. An article in a newspaper or magazine that is not *hard news and which is generally written at greater length than most news stories. Features may provide more detailed, contextual information behind a topical event (*see* BACKGROUNDER) but may also stand alone in their own right. Features may include celebrity interviews, real-life stories, political analysis, thinkpieces, picture spreads, *profiles, *colour pieces, *opinion columns, and many other things.
2. A *human interest, humorous, or *soft news story broadcast on TV or radio.

features desk The features editor or member/s of staff who plan and commission *feature articles (and often other forms of editorial content that are neither sport nor news, such as *reviews, horoscopes, advice columns, and TV listings). The features desk is normally responsible for supervising a team of staff or *freelance *feature writers, and liaising with other *desks, especially over *pictures. The features editor or desk will be answerable to the *editor.

feature writer A journalist who writes *features, whether as part or all of their job. Some feature writers believe the phrase has pretensions of grandeur and prefer the description journalist or even just *reporter. Many journalists conduct extensive *research in the *field before writing their features; others never leave their desks.

feature writing The writing of *feature articles in a manner that typically allows the *feature writer to develop a more personal style as opposed to the *inverted pyramid model commonly followed in *hard news. In this sense, some features tend to be regarded as a more 'writerly' form of journalism in which style may be at least as important as substance. However, features written for certain publications may still be required to follow a required formula (such as *triumph-over-tragedy) and to adhere to conventions of *house style.

Federal Communications Commission (FCC) An independent agency of the US government that, since 1934, has licensed radio and television broadcasters, among other things. In recent decades the FCC has frequently been criticized by lobby groups such as *Fairness and Accuracy in Reporting (FAIR) for failing to resist the *concentration of ownership within commercial media. *See also* DEREGULATION.

(⊕) SEE WEB LINKS
• The FCC's Media Bureau

feminist media Newspapers, magazines, websites, and other media projects produced primarily by and for those women campaigning against *sexism and *discrimination. What is often described as the first-wave of feminism can be seen in late 19th- and early 20th-century publications such as the *Women's Suffrage Journal*, *Votes for Women, and *Woman's Dreadnought*; second-wave feminism in the late 1960s and early 1970s saw the birth of *Ms. and *Spare Rib among countless other publications; and third-wave feminism from the 1990s onwards has tended to find its voice(s) online with *blogs such as *F-Word* and *Week Woman*. A key feature of feminist media has long been to challenge *stereotyping and *discrimination within *mainstream media, and a more recent focus has been on the tendency towards

*pornification of much mainstream output. *See also* ALTERNATIVE MEDIA; CULTURAL BIAS; SHOCKING PINK; REPRESENTATION.

( ) SEE WEB LINKS
• The *F-Word* on *Spare Rib*

FHM A monthly *lads' mag published in the UK since 1985, initially as *For Him Magazine*. Owned since 2008 by *Bauer Media, the magazine now publishes in more than a dozen additional countries and also has a successful online *brand. *FHM*'s main claim to fame is its annual '100 sexiest women in the world' list, from which it derives copious amounts of picture-driven free publicity in the *tabloid press and beyond. *See also* PORNIFICATION; SEXISM.

field 1. A network of individuals, groups, and institutions that together comprise a particular domain or area of activity, in which sense individual journalists may be thought of as belonging to the journalistic field. According to cultural theorist Pierre Bourdieu (1930–2002), such a field provides the social context and *constraints within which individual activity takes place (*see* AUTONOMY), although different fields may compete with each other and/or overlap (*see also* BOUNDARY MAINTENANCE).
2. Where *reporting is said to take place if it involves leaving the *newsroom and actually going somewhere in the 'real world'.

fifth estate Citizens, journalists, *bloggers, and activists who believe that mainstream journalism has become insufficiently vigorous in its *watchdog role and that there is a need for participants in civil society to rescue the idea of a socially responsible journalism from the clutches of giant media corporations. *Compare* FOURTH ESTATE. *See also* ALTERNATIVE JOURNALISM.

( ) SEE WEB LINKS
• Ignacio Ramonet on the need for a fifth estate

file To submit a story. Failure to file by *deadline is one of the most egregious things a *reporter can do.

filler A journalistic item of no particular importance or value that may be used to fill a space but which could be discarded with no great loss. *Compare* NIB.

Financial Times An influential daily business-oriented *broadsheet newspaper and online *brand based in the UK, produced in a range of international editions, and owned by *Pearson. Published since 1888, and traditionally printed on pink-coloured paper (*see* PINK 'UN), the *FT*'s specialist content has helped it achieve one of the industry's more successful attempts at securing income via online *paywall and subscription models. Its print edition sold a daily average of around 260,000 copies in 2013, giving it a higher *circulation than either the *Guardian* or *Independent* within the *quality sector of the market. *See also* BUSINESS JOURNALISM.

(((•))) SEE WEB LINKS
• The *FT*'s 125-year anniversary slideshow

Finkelstein Report The findings of the **Australian Independent Media Inquiry** of 2011–12, chaired by former judge Raymond Finkelstein, which included a recommendation for a News Media Council to regulate print, broadcast, and online journalism. As with the UK's *Leveson Inquiry, the report proved controversial and perhaps raised more issues about *ethics, *regulation, and *press freedom than it resolved.

(((•))) SEE WEB LINKS
• The Finkelstein Report
• *Crikey* on the Finkelstein Report

FIPP *See* INTERNATIONAL FEDERATION OF THE PERIODICAL PRESS.

First Amendment A change to the constitution of the USA that formed part of the Bill of Rights, proposed in 1789 and adopted by the states in 1791. The First Amendment makes it unconstitutional for the US Congress to make any law 'abridging the freedom of speech, or of the press', among other things. This presumption in favour of freedom of expression has resulted in fewer *laws and legal *constraints on US journalists than on their counterparts in many other countries, including the UK. However, the limit of what is constitutional is often tested in the courts, and the emergence first of the *internet and then of *social media have led to a number of fresh controversies over the extent of citizens' 'First Amendment rights'. *Compare* CENSORSHIP; STATUTORY REGULATION. *See also* FREE PRESS; REPORTERS COMMITTEE FOR FREEDOM OF THE PRESS.

fishing expedition When a journalist conducts an investigation without having any particular reason to do so, in the hope of finding something interesting and preferably scandalous. *Undercover reporting and *deception are generally regarded as unethical and unacceptable if they are based on a fishing expedition rather than on at least some evidence that an investigation would be in the *public interest. *See also* ETHICAL JOURNALISM; INVESTIGATIVE JOURNALISM.

five Ws The essential *questions that need to be asked by any journalist working on virtually any story: *who?, *where?, *what?, *when?, and *why? The five Ws are normally accompanied by an additional H question: *how? Along with the *inverted pyramid model, the five Ws and an H comprise some of the basics of journalism *training. *See also* INTERVIEW.

fixer Somebody employed by journalists and news organizations to arrange or 'fix' things, most commonly by using their local knowledge, *contacts, language skills, and ingenuity to help *correspondents arriving from overseas. Fixers may help set up *interviews, get permission for filming or recording, assess safety issues in particular areas, and even bribe local officials. Many fixers have been threatened, injured, and even killed in the course of their duties (*see* DEATHS OF JOURNALISTS). *See also* FOREIGN CORRESPONDENT; FOREIGN NEWS; PARACHUTE JOURNALISM.

flak Outspoken criticism of, or even punitive action against, any journalists or news organizations that step outside the consensus, according to the *propaganda model of the media described by the critical scholars Edward Herman and Noam Chomsky. This tendency of the *mainstream media and politicians to give a hard time to journalists who question the dominant *ideology, or who seek out alternative perspectives or *sources, has the effect of limiting the extent to which informed discussion can take place within the *public sphere, argued Herman and Chomsky. *See also* ANTI-COMMUNISM; CHILLING EFFECT; DEATH ON THE ROCK; MCCARTHYISM; SELF-CENSORSHIP.

flam-up To strengthen a story in the telling almost (but not quite) beyond recognition. *See also* TOPSPIN.

flannel panel A column or box that gives a publication's readers information such as how to contact the *newsroom or *advertising department, the names and responsibilities of various members of staff, and so on. On a website, similar information will often be labelled 'Contact us'.

Fleet Street The road in central London that was synonymous with the national press of the UK from the beginning of the 18th century to the end of the 20th century because most national *newspapers (as well as many *magazines and *news agencies) were based in offices on or just off it. Fleet Street remains in use as the collective noun for the UK national press even though there are scarcely any media companies left in the vicinity following the newspaper publishers' exodus to Docklands and beyond in the 1980s. *See also* NEWSPAPER PUBLISHERS ASSOCIATION; WAPPING DISPUTE.

Further reading: D. Griffiths, *Fleet Street: Five Hundred Years of the Press* (2006).

fly-on-the-wall A style of TV or radio *documentary that (supposedly) allows the action to unfold as if the presence of the camera, microphone, or journalist can go almost entirely unnoticed by those being filmed or recorded. Many hours of *editing may be required to create a 'naturalistic' impression before the finished product is broadcast.

FoC *See* FATHER OF CHAPEL.

focus group A research method involving a small group brought together with a moderator to discuss attitudes towards issues such as media content or journalistic behaviour, either to inform news organizations about audience preferences or to inform the academic study of journalism.

FOI *See* FREEDOM OF INFORMATION.

folk devils A term used by sociologists to describe a group of people (or animals) who for a while become the subject of negative news stories and stereotyped coverage that has the tendency to blame them for some or all of a society's ills. Such folk devils in the UK are said to have included mods and rockers in the 1960s, dangerous dogs in the 1990s, asylum seekers in the 2000s, and single mothers pretty much all of the time. *See also* ARCHETYPES; MORAL PANIC; STEREOTYPING.

follow-up A story, or an idea for a story, that originates with an earlier one but which either adds additional information or moves it on with news of a fresh development. For particularly big *running stories, the *newsdesk might expect a follow-up even when there is nothing to say, just to inform the audience that nothing new has happened and to reassure them that the news organization remains on the case.

Forbes A US business magazine founded in 1917 that today specializes in lists such as 'the richest people on the planet' (Rupert Murdoch was 91st in 2013) and 'top-earning dead celebrities' (Elizabeth Taylor in 2012, apparently). In 1998 the *Forbes* website exposed a faked story that had been published in *New Republic magazine; the episode was hailed as an early success for *online journalism (*see* HACK HEAVEN). *See also* BUSINESS JOURNALISM.

foreign correspondent A reporter who is either based abroad or who travels overseas to provide coverage of a particular story, country, or region for a news organization's audience back home. Foreign correspondents often rely on local *fixers. *See also* BIGFOOTING; FOREIGN NEWS; ROOFTOP JOURNALISM.

foreign news The coverage of events taking place in a country other than that in which a news organization is based. Such news may be supplied by specialist *foreign correspondents, by *news agencies, or by local *stringers based in the country concerned. Which foreign news is deemed worthy of inclusion will depend on a range of factors including whether or not there is an *elite nation involved, the relationship between the home and overseas country, and the perceived level of interest (and/or prejudice) among members of the *audience. Sustained and serious overseas coverage is often regarded as one of the hallmarks of the *quality press (and equivalents in other media). *See also* MCLURG'S LAW.

format The medium, form, style, appearance, size, and/or length of a journalistic product, publication, or broadcast. *See also* PLATFORM.

Forum World Features A propagandistic operation that was run as a London-based *news agency between 1966 and 1975, having been established with help from agents from the US intelligence service, the Central Intelligence Agency (CIA). Forum World Features would seek to place pro-US stories in the UK and international media, but it was wound up after its CIA link was exposed by *Time Out magazine. *See also* INTELLIGENCE SERVICES; PROPAGANDA.

Four Theories of the Press The title of an early work in the field of *journalism studies by US scholars Fred Siebert, Theodore Peterson, and

Wilbur Schramm, whose influential 1956 book outlined four key explanations of the function/s of journalism: The authoritarian theory (whereby journalism is supportive of the state); the libertarian theory (in which the press acts as a check on the state); the social responsibility theory (whereby the public airing of issues can help resolve them); and the Soviet Communist theory (in which journalism is little more than *propaganda). *See also* CRITICAL THEORY.

Further reading: F. S. Siebert, T. Peterson, and W. Schramm, *Four Theories of the Press* (1963[1956]).

fourth estate The conceptualization of journalists as quasi-constitutional *watchdogs acting on behalf of a society's *citizens. This notion of the press as a fourth estate of the realm in the UK (alongside the Lords, the House of Commons, and Church) is believed to have been first articulated by the politician Edmund Burke (1729-97) in the 18th century; it was developed in the following century by the writer Thomas Carlyle (1795-1881), who equated the press explicitly with *democracy. *Compare* FIFTH ESTATE. *See also* FREE PRESS.

Foxification When a media product or outlet becomes more opinionated and shouty, after *Fox News.

Fox News A US television news network launched in 1996 and owned by the *Murdoch empire. Its official slogan is 'fair and balanced', but critics tend to dismiss it as little more than crude right-wing *propaganda.

frame A way of viewing or presenting a story that incorporates an explanation of its meaning, or at least indicates the boundaries within which such a meaning might be found. The frame may be implicit or explicit. *See also* FRAMING; NEWS FRAME.

framing The placing of events (such as those being reported within a news story) within a particular explanatory narrative or *discourse. Precisely the same event might be framed in a number of different ways, so the death of a child could be reported variously according to a *frame that essentially places blame on heartless capitalism, cuts to the health service, declining nutritional knowledge, the rise of the feckless poor, a breakdown in family values, or any number of alternative explanations. An *active audience may resist the ways in which a story has been framed and may interpret events differently (*see* ENCODING, DECODING). *Compare* AGENDA-SETTING. *See also* MANUFACTURE OF NEWS.

Frankfurt School An influential group of 20th-century scholars and intellectuals associated with the Frankfurt Institute for Social Research in Germany, founded in 1922–3. The scholars (who mostly moved to the USA during the Nazi years) sought to explain and counter the ways in which they believed that ruling class *ideology was transmitted via the mass media. *See also* CRITICAL THEORY; HEGEMONY; MARXISM; MEDIA EFFECTS.

freebie Goods or services supplied to a journalist free of charge, normally to facilitate a *review or other form of coverage. Freebies can range from CDs and concert tickets at one extreme to overseas holidays and high-performance vehicles at the other. Some news organizations have strict guidelines on what journalists may accept and/or on declaring any freebies. *See also* BRIBE; ETHICS.

freedom of information The presumption that public information ought to be in the public domain unless there are overriding reasons for secrecy. Such a presumption has been expressed to a greater or lesser extent in legislation in different countries (*see* FREEDOM OF INFORMATION ACT) as well as in campaigns by journalists, media organizations, and other concerned citizens. *Compare* CENSORSHIP. *See also* SUNSHINE WEEK.

(())) SEE WEB LINKS
• Campaign for Freedom of Information website

Freedom of Information Act The name commonly given to legislation such as that in the USA (passed in 1966) and the UK (2000) that enshrines the concept of *freedom of information and which lays down procedures for accessing such material and appealing against refusal. Although such *laws are typically available for all citizens to use, it has often been journalists who have led the way in putting them into practice. *See also* DATA JOURNALISM; DATA PROTECTION; INVESTIGATIVE JOURNALISM.

Freedom's Journal Believed to be the first newspaper in the USA owned by and serving members of the African-American community. It was published weekly in New York from 1827 to 1829. *See also* BLACK MEDIA.

(())) SEE WEB LINKS
• *Freedom's Journal* archive

freelance journalist A self-employed journalist who may sell his or her services to a variety of media organizations or who may work for just one employer on a contract or casual basis rather than as a permanent member of staff. Many journalists prefer the variety that freelance work can offer and/or the way that it allows some to have greater autonomy and control over their working arrangements; others are reluctant freelancers who would prefer the security of a staff job. The proportion of freelance to staff journalists has been increasing in both the USA and UK in recent years, partly as a result of *casualization.

freemium A publication, usually a *magazine, that is distributed free and targeted at readers with large amounts of disposable income (who are the most sought-after by upmarket *advertisers). Copies may be given out on the streets at select locations, distributed via hotels, or delivered to residential addresses in more wealthy areas. The editorial content of freemium publications tends to be, if not entirely advertising-driven, certainly advertiser-friendly. *See also* FREE NEWSPAPER.

free newspaper A newspaper that is distributed to readers without any cover charge and which depends for its income on *advertising. *See also* CIRCULATION; FREEMIUM; FREESHEET.

free press News organizations that have the freedom to report without being subject to oppressive restrictions such as the *licensing of journalists or wholesale *censorship (although they may still be covered by various *laws such as *libel). The social importance of **press freedom**, including the freedom to make mistakes, is often used as a counter-argument against those seeking some form of *statutory regulation of the media. However, some commentators dismiss the whole idea of a free press as largely a self-serving myth, arguing that in reality freedom of the press exists only for those rich enough to own their own media empire and that *proprietors treat the concept more as a property right than a *human right. *See also* FIRST AMENDMENT; FOURTH ESTATE; PUTNEY DEBATES; REPORTERS WITHOUT BORDERS; SELF-REGULATION.

freesheet A slightly derogatory phrase for a printed publication that is given away free, relying entirely on *advertising for its income. Historically implying something of little or no value, the label 'freesheet' has undergone some repositioning as more publications (including the London *Evening Standard*) have switched to free distribution. *See also* CIRCULATION; FREEMIUM; FREE NEWSPAPER.

frequency The rate or regularity with which an event or series of events unfolds, which can influence whether or not something becomes the subject of a news story. Frequency was one of the factors identified as *news values by Galtung and Ruge in their influential 1960s study. They found that an event unfolding at a similar frequency to the *routines of a news outlet is more likely to be selected for news coverage by that medium than is something such as a social trend that takes place over a more lengthy period, thereby rendering it less obvious or noticeable. *See also* CONTINUITY; DIARY STORY.

F-Word *See* FEMINIST MEDIA.

FX *See* SOUND EFFECTS.

G

gagging clause Any element of a contract of employment, redundancy agreement, 'golden handshake', settlement of a legal claim, or similar, that prevents one or more parties from disclosing certain information (sometimes even including the existence of such a clause). Journalists sometimes encourage *whistleblowers to defy such clauses and risk legal action for the sake of revealing information that is in the *public interest.

gagging order *See* INJUNCTION.

gallery 1. The vantage point within the UK's Houses of Parliament from which journalists can watch and listen to the proceedings below (*see* GALLERY REPORTING). *Compare* LOBBY.
2. The control room from which the transmission of a television broadcast is overseen.

gallery reporting Specifically the reporting of Parliament from the press benches in the *gallery but more generally a style of *reporting that incorporates lengthy verbatim accounts of speeches, debates, questions, and answers. The novelist Charles Dickens (1812–70) worked as a Parliamentary press gallery reporter in his early years as a writer. Such reporting, which relies in most cases on extremely fast and accurate *shorthand, was also traditionally used in local newspapers' coverage of local authority meetings, which tended to mirror *Fleet Street's treatment of Westminster. However, recent decades have seen a retreat from such reporting at both a local and national level in favour of more *human interest and *colour pieces, all accompanied by accusations of *dumbing down.

((⊕)) SEE WEB LINKS
• Charles Dickens in the Parliamentary press gallery

Gannett A major media company that owns more than 80 US daily newspapers and hundreds of weeklies, making it the country's largest newspaper chain as measured by *circulation; it also owns a substantial number of TV and online outlets. In a bid to combat declining print revenues, in 2012 Gannett erected *paywalls around the websites of its US newspapers with the exception of *USA Today. Overseas outposts of the Gannett empire include *Newsquest in the UK. *See also* CONCENTRATION OF OWNERSHIP.

-gate A suffix deriving from the *Watergate story that is frequently (and, many would say, lazily) appended to the end of words by journalists (and others) to denote an alleged *scandal or sometimes even just a disagreement. Examples range from Beefgate, concerning a row among Beefeaters at the Tower of London, to *hackgate, denoting the *phone-hacking activities that led to the closure of the *News of the World.

gatekeeper A role ascribed to journalists in general, and sometimes *editors in particular, according to *gatekeeping theory. The gatekeeper is said to select which events or potential stories are allowed to pass through a process of *selection to be reported as *news.

gatekeeping A theory that presents the journalist as a *gatekeeper who allows some events to pass through to become *news while shutting the gate on other events. The concept of gatekeeping is associated with a 1950 study by David Manning White into how and why a wire editor at one US newspaper selected stories for inclusion, drawing attention to the subjective elements involved in *selection. Critics have since labelled the theory too simplistic because it proceeds from an assumption that there is one given reality or set of events beyond the gate that may be admitted or excluded. Gatekeeping has also been criticized for telling only part of the story of journalistic selection by downplaying the organizational, cultural, commercial, and other *constraints that are said to limit the *agency of individual journalists, including editors. Since the arrival of *blogging, *citizen journalism, *social media, and *user-generated content, it has frequently been suggested that the gatekeeping role of mainstream journalism has been diminished if not eradicated entirely. *Compare* NETWORKED JOURNALISM.

Gawker A New York-based multimedia website and *blog, specializing in *celebrity gossip and news, which has broken many stories later picked up by other media.

gay media Newspapers, magazines, and other forms of media produced largely by and for gay men and lesbians, ranging from politically militant publications (*see* ALTERNATIVE JOURNALISM) to those for which the primary purpose is to cash in on the so-called 'pink pound' or 'pink dollar' by delivering a target audience to certain *advertisers. One of the pioneering publications in the UK was *Gay News*, a fortnightly newspaper between 1972 and 1993 that was prosecuted for blasphemous libel for running the James Kirkup poem, *The Love That Dares To Speak Its Name*. The National Lesbian and Gay Journalists Association (NLGJA) was formed in the USA in 1990. *See also* ATTITUDE; DIVA; REPRESENTATION; STEREOTYPING.

( ) SEE WEB LINKS

• Cover gallery of *My Comrade* magazine
• The NLGJA blog

Gay News See GAY MEDIA.

gender The condition of being either female or male, which can result in journalists of one gender being deemed more suitable for some roles or tasks while being excluded from others, in some media content being targeted at specifically gendered markets, and in some people who are featured in the news being treated differently according to whether they are male, female, or transgender. *See also* DISCRIMINATION; FEMINIST MEDIA; INTERNATIONAL WOMEN'S MEDIA FOUNDATION; LADS' MAGS; SEXISM; STEREOTYPING; WOMEN IN JOURNALISM; WOMEN'S MAGAZINES.

General Council of the Press The original name of the UK's *Press Council from the time of its establishment in 1953 until 1963. *See also* SELF-REGULATION.

Glasgow Media Group A group of academic media researchers and scholars centred on Glasgow University in Scotland. Since its formation in 1974, the group and its members have published numerous studies of media output that have tended to critique claims of *balance, *objectivity, and *impartiality, particularly in TV news. Their findings have not been universally embraced by the subjects of their research. *See also* MEDIA STUDIES.

( ) SEE WEB LINKS

• Glasgow Media Group publications

glasnost A policy of greater openness (or '*glasnost*' in Russian) that accompanied the period of restructuring (or **perestroika**) within the later years of the Soviet Union and its allies. As part of glasnost, the late 1980s saw some relaxation of *censorship and movement towards a more open and critical press, within limits. *See also* PRAVDA; SAMIZDAT.

Further reading: J. Riordan and S. Bridger (ed.), *Dear Comrade Editor: Readers' Letters to the Soviet Press Under Perestroika* (2002).

Global Editors Network (GEN) An international organization of *editors and senior news executives formed in 2011 to promote quality, independent journalism in the digital age.

(((()))) SEE WEB LINKS
• The GEN manifesto

glossies A collective term covering any *magazine that is printed on shiny, coated paper, although it is often used more specifically about those *women's magazines that focus on a 'glossy' lifestyle in addition to being printed on glossy paper. *See also* LIFESTYLE JOURNALISM.

goatfuck *See* MEDIA SCRUM.

go-last A sentence or two of text that may be placed after an article ends, adding additional information such as travel details (beneath a piece on holidays) or the dates of a subject's birth and death (after an *obituary). The go-last, also known as a **tailpiece**, will typically be set in a different font from the main story. *Compare* STANDFIRST.

golden age of journalism A mythical age that always seems to be thought of as having existed at least twenty years before it is invoked. *Compare* GUTTER JOURNALISM.

gonzo journalism A style of reporting incorporating a variety of literary conventions to place the journalist at the centre of the narrative. Most closely associated with the US writer Hunter S. Thompson (1937–2005), gonzo journalism involves a mixture of personal observation, verbatim transcripts of conversations, overheard dialogue, and extracts from documents or original notes, mostly delivered at great length and frequently focusing as much on the quest for information as on the information itself. Although often criticized for self-indulgence, elements of gonzo can be detected in much mainstream journalism today. *See also* IMMERSION REPORTING; LITERARY JOURNALISM; LONG-FORM JOURNALISM; NEW JOURNALISM.

good news An event or announcement that has positive connotations for (at least some of) those involved and which is deemed to be *newsworthy. Although much news is *bad news, more good news appears in the media than is often thought, including stories about rescues, cures, records, breakthroughs, inventions, and celebrations. *See also* NEWS VALUES; SOFT NEWS.

Google 1. The US-based but globally ambitious *internet, search, and digital communications giant that launched **Google News* in 2002 and bought **YouTube* in 2006.
2. A verb meaning to look up something or somebody on an online *search engine.

Google News An online *news aggregation site that constantly finds, sifts, sorts, and *links to material from thousands of different media outlets and which can deliver items to *users by a wide variety of methods including *RSS feeds and personalized email alerts. *Google News* does not employ any journalists or originate its own news and has often been accused of having a parasitic relationship with journalism. *Google counters this by pointing to the way its *aggregation service has dramatically expanded the readership and reach of countless stories.

Google+ (Google Plus) The *social networking platform of the *Google empire that, as with *Facebook and *Twitter, has rapidly become one of the numerous ways in which news organizations and other forms of media now promote themselves as *brands and seek to engage directly with their *audiences. *See also* ONLINE JOURNALISM; SOCIAL MEDIA.

Gotcha The famously gleeful one-word *headline used by the UK's biggest-selling daily newspaper, the **Sun*, to report the news that an Argentinian cruiser, the *General Belgrano*, had been hit during the Falklands War of 1982. It was replaced in later editions with the more sober 'DID 1,200 ARGIES DROWN?' The headline 'GOTCHA' was revived by **Private Eye* in 2011 when reporting the closure of the **News of the World* and other travails of the *Murdoch empire. *See also* WAR REPORTING.

GQ An upmarket men's fashion-oriented *magazine launched in the USA in 1931, initially as *Apparel Arts* and from 1958 as the *Gentlemen's Quarterly*. Today, appearing monthly under its shortened title, *GQ* has broadened its content into wider *lifestyle journalism and is also published in several international editions (including one in India and another in the UK); the magazine and its online *brand are owned by *Condé Nast.

grammar The rules and conventions about the ways in which words should be used and sentences constructed and punctuated. Rules of grammar may be incorporated into *house style but that does not prevent them being the subject of sometimes quite heated debate among journalists (or of complaint by readers). The boundary between acceptable and unacceptable grammar tends to move over time. *See also* APOSTROPHE; SCREAMER.

Granta A UK-based quarterly magazine that publishes reportage and some *long-form journalism in addition to its more regular literary fare. First published in 1889 by Cambridge University students, it was relaunched in 1979 as a journal of serious new writing. *See also* LITERARY JOURNALISM.

Grauniad The affectionate colloquial name for the *Guardian*, reportedly bestowed upon it by the satirical magazine *Private Eye*. The nickname arose because of the frequent appearance of typographical errors (*see* TYPO), although it may be that the high proportion of teachers within the newspaper's readership simply made its errors more likely to attract comment.

Grazia A weekly glossy *women's magazine and online *brand published in the UK since 2005 by *Bauer Media. *Grazia* began in 1938 in Italy and the Italian edition is today part of Silvio Berlusconi's Mondadori media group. Other international franchises include *Grazia India*, launched in 2008 by Worldwide Media. *See also* GLOSSIES.

Great Firewall of China A term referring specifically to *censorship of the *internet, *online journalism, and *social media in China that is sometimes broadened to encompass restrictions on other media and freedom of expression in the country generally.

green ink brigade A disparaging label traditionally used by journalists to refer to people who would write *letters to news organizations complaining that something or other presaged the end of civilization as we know it, or else urging a reporter to investigate a high-level scandal that was being covered up by the authorities and the rest of the media. Such letters would occasionally be written in different coloured ink and/or in capital letters, presumably to emphasize their importance; they have largely (but not entirely) been supplanted by communication via *email and *social media.

Green 'Un A special edition of a provincial newspaper published in the UK on a Saturday throughout much of the 20th century, featuring that day's football results and reports. Such papers were normally printed on green or pink newsprint (*see* PINK 'UN) and would often be on sale about 30 minutes after the end of the big local match. *See also* SPORT REPORTING; SPORTSDESK.

grip-and-grin A posed photograph of two people shaking hands, often as one of them presents an award or a giant cheque to the other. Such formulaic pictures remain a staple of many local newspapers despite the fact that most *photographers seem to detest taking them and some publications refuse to run them.

Guardian A UK-based daily newspaper and online *brand owned by a trust rather than a conventional *proprietor. The paper began in 1821 as the weekly ***Manchester Guardian***, founded by the reformer John Edward Taylor (1791–1844) to promote a liberal agenda in the wake of the state killing of protesters that became known as the Peterloo Massacre. The paper moved to twice-weekly publication in 1836 before becoming daily in 1855. Its most famous editor was C. P. Scott (1846–1932, *see* COMMENT IS FREE), and after his death the *Scott Trust was created to preserve 'the financial and editorial independence of the *Guardian* in perpetuity'. For most of its life it was a regional newspaper with a national and international agenda but it dropped 'Manchester' from its title in 1959 and moved its base to London five years later; although it retained a northern presence for some years, by 2013 it had just one staff reporter covering the entire northern half of England. It may have abandoned its northern roots but the *Guardian* has retained its role as a liberal voice within a mostly conservative national press.

Traditionally a *quality title published in *broadsheet format, it switched to the smaller *Berliner size in 2005. By that time its *website and other online offerings were beginning to attract a huge readership, notably in the USA, but income from digital *advertising has so far come nowhere near making up for declining revenues from the paper's dwindling print *circulation and advertising. In 2013 it was selling only around 190,000 copies of the print product daily, making it the worst-selling national newspaper in the UK with the sole exception of the *Independent; but its website was attracting around 5 million *users each day, making it one of the most popular newspaper sites in the world. Despite the *Guardian* haemorrhaging money (and experienced staff) at an alarming rate, under editor Alan Rusbridger it remained committed to *open journalism and resistant to the concept of online *paywalls. Financial difficulties notwithstanding, in the opening decade and a half of the 21st century it often led the agenda as a result of its *investigative journalism, perhaps most notably Nick Davies' dogged digging into *phone-hacking at the *News of the World* (see HACKGATE). The *Guardian* also exposed a series of scandals involving police misbehaviour in the UK, and gave extensive coverage to revelations of US state secrets provided first by *WikiLeaks* and later by the National Security Agency *whistleblower Edward Snowden. *See also* CABLEGATE; GRAUNIAD; OBSERVER; TRAFIGURA.

((⊕)) SEE WEB LINKS
• The *Guardian*'s history of the *Guardian*

Guild of Editors A networking organization formed by *editors of local and regional newspapers in the UK in 1946 that merged with the *Association of British Editors in 1999 to form the *Society of Editors.

Guiton Group A regional newspaper group publishing daily and weekly titles on the Channel Islands of Jersey and Guernsey. Like the *Midland News Association, it is part of the Claverley group of companies, and in 2013 it was the nineteenth-largest regional press group in the UK in terms of *circulation.

gutter journalism A derogatory term for whatever sort of journalism of which the speaker disapproves. *Compare* ETHICAL JOURNALISM; GOLDEN AGE OF JOURNALISM. *See also* INTRUSION; SENSATIONALISM; YELLOW JOURNALISM.

hack An informal term for a journalist, sometimes intended as an insult to mean a writer who produces work of little merit. Hack is also used in a spirit of self-deprecation by many journalists about themselves and colleagues. Although hack can refer to male and female journalists, the term '**hackette**' is occasionally used by the former to refer to the latter. *Compare* JOURNO.

hackademic A journalist who goes on to work in *journalism education where they combine the roles of journalist (*hack) and academic within the *hackademy. *See also* ACADEMIZATION OF JOURNALISM; PRACTITIONER; TRAINING.

hackademy The departments within academe where journalism *training meets *journalism studies, sometimes with mutual respect and insight, sometimes with mutual suspicion and hostility. *See also* ACADEMIZATION OF JOURNALISM; JOURNALISM EDUCATION.

Hacked Off A UK-based lobbying and campaign group formed in 2011 to represent some of the victims of the *hackgate scandal, to highlight what it saw as the ineffectiveness of the *Press Complaints Commission, and to push for tougher regulation of the press. Hacked Off, which was publicly backed by a number of high-profile *celebrities led by actor Hugh Grant, was condemned in much of the press for allegedly wishing to impose state control on a hitherto *free press. Following publication of the *Leveson Report, Hacked Off was involved in the talks between the UK's three main political parties about the 2013 *Royal Charter on the press. *See also* INDEPENDENT PRESS STANDARDS ORGANIZATION.

hackerazzi A slang term (after *paparazzi) for people who specialize in *hacking into the email or *social media accounts of *celebrities to access private photographs, which are then published online or offered for sale to any media outlets willing to buy them. *Compare* ETHICAL JOURNALISM. *See also* DATA PROTECTION; DOXING; INTRUSION.

hackette *See* HACK.

hackgate The *phone-hacking scandal that led to the closure of the *News of the World* in 2011, the establishment of the *Leveson Inquiry shortly afterwards, the resignations of the UK's most senior police officer and of the government's chief *spin doctor, and the demise of the *Press Complaints Commission. The scandal also resulted in the arrests of numerous journalists on suspicion of a variety of alleged offences, and compensation pay-outs totalling many millions of pounds to hundreds of people whose private communications had been accessed unlawfully in pursuit of possible stories, as well as claims that the political and police establishment had been in thrall to the *Murdoch empire. It also resulted in the division of *News Corp into two. It began with the arrests in 2006 of *News of the World* royal editor Clive Goodman and private investigator Glenn Mulcaire on suspicion of illegally hacking into the mobile phone messages of several individuals, including members of the British royal family. When Goodman and Mulcaire were sent to prison in 2007 *News International claimed Goodman had been a one-off 'rogue reporter', although *News of the World* editor Andy Coulson resigned on the grounds that the events had happened on his watch (Coulson went on to become *PR chief for Prime Minister David Cameron before stepping down in 2011). The *rogue reporter defence seemed to be accepted by both police and the Press Complaints Commission but *investigative journalism by the *Guardian* (and occasionally others, including the *New York Times*) eventually uncovered what was described as phone-hacking on an industrial scale. When the *Guardian* revealed in 2011 that the victims included murdered schoolgirl Milly Dowler, a wave of public revulsion and a threatened boycott by *advertisers prompted the Murdochs to close the paper. Although the Leveson Inquiry was set up in response to hackgate, it heard little or no evidence about phone-hacking so as not to prejudice any future trials. In June 2013 News Corp said that up to that point it had spent $270 million (US dollars) on legal and other fees relating to hackgate and had paid $27 million (US dollars) in civil settlements. Allegations of hacking eventually extended well beyond the *News of the World* and the

Murdoch empire. *See also* DARK ARTS; DATA PROTECTION; ETHICAL JOURNALISM; HACKED OFF; INTRUSION; LAWS; PRIVACY.

Further reading: T. Watson and M. Hickman, *Dial M for Murdoch: News Corporation and the Corruption of Britain* (2012).

(🌐) SEE WEB LINKS

• A chronology of hackgate
• The *New York Times*' 2010 investigation into hackgate
• The *Guardian*'s 2011 Milly Dowler story (and footnote clarification)

Hack Heaven The headline of a 1998 story about a hacker extracting pay-offs from computer companies that was published in *New Republic* magazine but was quickly exposed by the *Forbes* website as being false. The piece had been written by Stephen Glass (1972–), who went on to admit several further episodes of *fakery. Glass was dismissed, *New Republic* published a lengthy apology to its readers, and the episode was later immortalized in the film *Shattered Glass* (dir. Billy Ray, 2003). *Compare* ETHICAL JOURNALISM; TRUTH.

hacking Accessing the telephone calls, phone messages, emails, computer files, and/or private social networking activity of an individual or organization without their knowledge or permission. Hacking into such information, for example by *blagging or guessing passwords and codes, is usually illegal, although some journalists defend it as ethical if conducted in the *public interest rather than for *celebrity gossip. One of the so-called *dark arts of journalism, hacking has on occasion been outsourced to *private investigators. *See also* DATA PROTECTION; DOXING; ETHICS; HACKERAZZI; HACKGATE; INTRUSION; LAWS; PRIVACY.

harassment Persistently following somebody, staking out their home or place of work, and/or bombarding them with questions when they have made it clear they do not wish to comment (or be photographed or filmed). Such persistence may be justified by journalists and editors investigating powerful people in the *public interest, but the *Leveson Inquiry into media *ethics heard evidence of journalists harassing many 'ordinary' people, including victims of crime. *See also* DOORSTEPPING; MEDIA SCRUM; PAPARAZZI.

hard news Serious, topical, and fact-based *news stories about crime, politics, war, famine, business, industrial relations, and countless other events happening in the world. *Compare* FEATURES; SOFT NEWS. *See also* HUMAN INTEREST; NEWS VALUES; REPORTING.

Harper's The oldest surviving general interest monthly magazine in the USA, published since 1850 and specializing in *long-form journalism. At the height of the Vietnam War in 1970 it ran Seymour Hersh's investigation exposing the My Lai massacre, in which hundreds of civilians had been killed by US troops. Having been a commercial venture for most of its existence, *Harper's* is today owned by a non-profit foundation solely dedicated to preserving the magazine as an independent voice in US politics and culture.

harvesting content The future role of journalists, according to *Local World chairman David Montgomery (1948–), who told a group of MPs in May 2013 that traditional *reporting methods were 'hugely unproductive', adding: 'We will have to harvest content and publish it without human interface, which will change the role of journalists.' *See also* ALGORITHMIC JOURNALISM.

(((●))) SEE WEB LINKS

• *Press Gazette*: 'We will harvest content and publish it without human interface'

hashtag A keyboard symbol that, when added to a word or phrase within a *tweet, creates a link to other *Twitter users' contributions on the same topic. It has become common for news and current affairs media to suggest hashtags (such as '#c4news') as a way of encouraging online discussion of their stories; however, members of the audience often prefer to come up with their own, not always complimentary, hashtags (such as '#dailyfail'). *See also* CONVERSATION; CURATION; SOCIAL MEDIA; SOCIAL NETWORKING.

head and shoulders A *photograph of somebody's face that a news organization will be able to use whenever that person is mentioned in a story. A head and shoulders pic supplied by a *PR company will often depict their client in slightly younger days.

headline The text placed above a story in print or online journalism and the brief top line of an item about to be featured in a TV and radio news bulletin. Headlines are typically a combination of the big, the brief, the bold, and the dramatic, all aimed at attracting the attention of an audience. However, to meet the requirements of *search engine optimization, online headlines tend to be more explanatory and less enigmatic than those in newspaper or magazine versions even of the same story. *See also* BANNER HEADLINE; KEYWORDS; STRAP.

Hearst Corporation A US-based international media empire with extensive interests in newspapers, magazines, television, radio, and online. *See also* HEARST NEWSPAPERS.

Hearst Newspapers The press arm of the *Hearst Corporation. It was formed in 1887 when the 23-year-old William Randolph Hearst (1863–1951) first placed his name on the *masthead of the *San Francisco Examiner* as *'proprietor'. *See also* CITIZEN KANE; SEATTLE POST-INTELLIGENCER; YELLOW PRESS.

heavies An informal collective term for the *broadsheet or *quality press, referring both to their physical weight and to their serious content. Journalists on more popular titles sometimes refer to heavy newspapers as 'the unpopulars' and accuse those who produce them of *elitism. *Compare* POPS.

hegemony A theory put forward to help explain how some ideas come to dominate a society's *discourse or ways of thinking. According to the Italian Marxist intellectual, activist, and journalist Antonio Gramsci (1891–1937), hegemony is the way in which a dominant or ruling class does not merely have the power to control a society's political institutions and economy, it also exerts a form of moral and intellectual leadership that has the effect of making subservient classes acquiesce in their own domination. One key method by which dominant ideas are said to saturate society and become accepted as '*common sense', is because they are transmitted and amplified via the mass media and mainstream journalism industries, which are sometimes referred to as playing the role of '*ideological state apparatus'—a phrase associated with the French Marxist Louis Althusser (1918–90). However, hegemony does not result in total domination and it involves a constant process of struggle and contestation, not least by the 'counter-hegemonic' approach to be found within *alternative journalism, *oppositional reporting, and the *radical press. *See also* IDEOLOGY; MARXISM.

Hello! A weekly *magazine (plus online *brand) that specializes in rather fawning coverage of *celebrities. The UK version was launched in

1988 as an English-language sister publication to Spain's *Hola!*, which began in the 1940s. Its owner, Hello Ltd of Spain, has since launched editions in several more countries and languages.

Herald Sun A daily *tabloid published in Melbourne by Rupert Murdoch's *News Corp that is the biggest-selling newspaper in Australia. *See also* MURDOCH EMPIRE.

Hillsborough disaster The deaths through crushing and asphyxiation of 96 supporters of Liverpool football club at the Hillsborough stadium in the UK city of Sheffield in 1989 and subsequent attempts by senior police to cover up the force's role while pinning the blame on Liverpool fans themselves. When a local *news agency circulated comments from police sources after the tragedy, most UK media treated the material merely as unsubstantiated allegations. But the claims were reported as though fact as the *splash on the *Sun* newspaper under the soon-to-become notorious *headline 'THE TRUTH', leading to a mass readers' boycott in the Liverpool area from which the newspaper's *circulation never recovered (despite owner Rupert Murdoch ordering editor Kelvin MacKenzie to apologize). After 23 years an official independent panel of inquiry exonerated the victims and revealed the extent of the attempted cover up, prompting the *Sun* to apologize once again, splashing this time with 'THE REAL TRUTH' and running an *editorial that described its initial coverage as the 'gravest error' in the paper's history. *See also* ETHICS; MURDOCH EMPIRE; TRUST.

(⊕) SEE WEB LINKS
• Report and archive of the Hillsborough Independent Panel

Hindu An influential family-owned English-language *broadsheet newspaper published in India since 1878, initially as a weekly, becoming daily in 1889. The *Hindu* was an early adopter of the *internet, establishing its website in 1995.

Hitler diaries Faked diaries purportedly written by Adolf Hitler, for which both the *Sunday Times* and *Stern* were tricked into paying a fortune in 1983. The fact that they were a forgery was not discovered until after both publications had *splashed with revelations about the Fuhrer's supposed innermost thoughts, resulting in much embarrassment internally and much amusement among rivals. *See also* HOAXES; VERIFICATION.

hoaxes The running of an item in good faith that turns out to have been invented by a *source, whether to make money (as with the bogus *Hitler diaries), in the hope of influencing public opinion, or merely for the amusement of the hoaxer and his/her friends. *Compare* SPOOF. *See also* FACT-CHECKING; VERIFICATION.

honest comment An honestly held opinion or interpretation of events, based on the known *facts of an issue. Honest comment, known until 2010 as '**fair comment**', is a defence sometimes available to journalists under UK *libel law.

horizontal integration The process whereby a business that owns one media outlet seeks to own or otherwise become involved with other similar media outlets, thereby allowing economies of scale and/or *cross promotion. *Compare* VERTICAL INTEGRATION. *See also* CONCENTRATION OF OWNERSHIP; CONVERGENCE.

house style The choices made by a news organization when it comes to the language, *grammar, labelling, and tone of its output, typically ranging from whether President takes an upper-case 'p' to whether to use the term 'toilet', 'lavatory', or 'loo' to describe what was once called a 'water closet' or 'WC'. The house style of a particular newspaper, magazine, broadcaster, or online news provider is used to identify and promote that outlet as a *brand by distinguishing it from rivals through the adoption of a consistent voice and the elimination of presentational distractions (or 'noise'). A news organization's *style will normally be aimed at reflecting or attracting members of its target audience, or at least at not repelling them. Rules on house style may be unwritten and stored only inside the heads of senior journalists, or may be codified in the form of *style books and/or searchable electronic guides, with new recruits being required to learn and comply with house style almost immediately. *See also* STYLE GUIDE.

Houston Chronicle The biggest-selling newspaper in the state of Texas and one of the top 25 best-selling daily papers in the USA. Launched in 1901, it has been owned since 1987 by *Hearst Newspapers.

how? Along with the *five Ws, this is one of the most essential *questions in journalism. How something happened, how people reacted, how it looked, how people felt, and how the names are spelled, are just some of the basic questions asked by and recounted by journalists every day. *See also* INTERVIEW; REPORTING.

hub A way of combining and/or centralizing editorial functions that is designed to break down (some) traditional demarcations within a news organization. So, for example, a news editor, picture editor, web editor, and social media editor may work more closely together in a hub rather than each running their own separate *desks. Also, some newspaper groups have moved *subbing operations into generic hubs that serve several titles rather than each title having its own subs.

Huffington Post A news, features, *aggregation, blogging, video, and social media website that was founded in 2005 in the USA by Arianna Huffington (1950–) and which proved so popular that it was bought by *AOL in 2011 for a reported $315 million (US dollars). Since then its network of unpaid *bloggers have been augmented with teams of paid journalists and several international editions have been launched, including in the UK, Canada, and France (*see* LE MONDE). *See also* CITIZEN JOURNALISM; ONLINE JOURNALISM.

(((●))) SEE WEB LINKS
• The *Huffington Post*'s UK blog site

human interest Stories and *angles on stories that tend to emphasize the emotion, drama, tension, struggle, joy, despair, triumph, or tragedy of people's lives. Human-interest stories are not restricted to *soft news and can be used by journalists to interest an audience in *hard news, for example by finding individual *case studies to illustrate wider trends or statistics. Any perceived increase in the prevalence of human interest stories is seen by some commentators as a sure sign of *dumbing down; criticism of human-interest stories is seen by others as a sure sign of *elitism.

human rights The idea that the *citizens of the world have certain inalienable rights, as expressed in the *European Convention on Human Rights and the *Universal Declaration of Human Rights. The concept of human rights can influence the *laws under which journalists operate (*see* HUMAN RIGHTS ACT) as well as informing wider thinking about *ethical journalism. *See also* ARTICLE 19.

Human Rights Act A piece of UK legislation passed in 1998, which came into force in 2000, that incorporated the *European Convention on

Human Rights into UK law. Under the Act, UK courts can be called upon to balance the human right of freedom of expression with the human right of respect for *privacy and family life. *See also* HUMAN RIGHTS; LAWS.

humour A funny element within a potential story that increases its chances of being selected as *news, even if the subject matter is not particularly serious or important. *See also* ENTERTAINMENT; NEWS VALUES.

Hutton Report (Hutton Inquiry) A report by Lord Brian Hutton, former Lord Chief Justice of Northern Ireland, into events surrounding the death of UK weapons expert Dr David Kelly (1944–2003), who had been the *confidential source for a notorious story about the US-led invasion of Iraq, broadcast on *BBC radio's *Today* programme on 29 May 2003. Dr Kelly had met *Today*'s defence correspondent Andrew Gilligan (1968–) in the bar of a London hotel for an *off-the-record background discussion about Iraq, during which their conversation turned to the UK government's September 2002 dossier and its headline-grabbing claim that Iraq was stockpiling weapons of mass destruction that could be fired within 45 minutes of an order being given. A week after this encounter, Gilligan told *Today* listeners that a source involved in drawing up that dossier had claimed to him that the 45-minute reference had been included at the last minute at the behest of the government, even though it was of uncertain veracity, and that members of the intelligence services were unhappy at how their evidence had been 'sexed up' by removing qualifications and careful caveats to help make the case for a military intervention.

The story, in which the source was not named, was initially broken at 6.07 am in a *two-way discussion between Gilligan and presenter John Humphrys, in the course of which the reporter said the government 'probably knew that that 45-minute figure was wrong'; in subsequent more tightly scripted reports that day Gilligan used the word 'questionable' rather than 'wrong'. When the government's chief *spin doctor, Alastair Campbell, then attacked the BBC for accusing Prime Minister Tony Blair of lying and demanded a *retraction and *apology, the BBC robustly defended its journalist, his right to report the views of a credible *source, and the right of that source to remain anonymous. During the ensuing battle of wills between the corporation and Downing Street, Kelly volunteered the information to his line manager at the

Ministry of Defence that he had spoken with Gilligan, although he said he did not think he was necessarily the source quoted in the latter's story. Kelly's identity was publicly confirmed by his employers and he found himself at the centre of a political-media storm, being questioned by two committees of the House of Commons. His body was discovered in woodland near his home shortly afterwards, having told his wife he was going out for a walk.

The Hutton Inquiry was established by the UK government to examine the circumstances surrounding the death and resulted in one of the most detailed investigations ever undertaken into any piece of journalism, with Gilligan's 6.07 am *Today* two-way the focus of much of the evidence from journalists, politicians, intelligence personnel, civil servants, members of the Kelly family, and others, over three months. The resulting Hutton Report, published on 28 January 2004, concluded that Dr Kelly had taken his own life and that nobody else had been involved in his death. Although the suicide verdict has been persistently questioned by a small number of critics on medical-science grounds, it was what Lord Hutton had to say about the BBC's journalism that was to prove most contentious. Hutton found that Gilligan had insufficient evidence to have run the 'sexing up' story and that the BBC failed both to check his story thoroughly enough in advance and to investigate it once the government had complained. Hutton's findings were greeted with surprise and dismay by many journalists in the UK, who immediately declared it to be a one-sided establishment 'whitewash' that placed unrealistic demands on reporters to obtain absolute proof before running critical stories. Gilligan's story was defended by many as being more right than wrong, and in the *public interest, although others blamed him for bringing the government's wrath down on the BBC.

Within days of the Hutton Report being published the BBC had lost its chairman Gavyn Davies and Director General Greg Dyke, as well as Gilligan himself, all of whom resigned in its wake. In unprecedented scenes, hundreds of BBC staff around the country staged spontaneous walk-outs in protest at the governors' acceptance of Dyke's resignation. The BBC went on to conduct its own review of events, chaired by Ronald Neil, a former director of news and current affairs. Among other findings, the *Neil Report of June 2004 recommended setting up a BBC College of Journalism to promote better training of its journalists; it stressed the importance of accurate note-taking; it advised against making allegations via live two-ways; it reiterated the principle of protecting confidential sources; and called for the corporation's complaints procedures to be reformed. In the years since publication of the Hutton Report it has frequently been claimed that BBC journalists have been cowed by fear of attracting the sort of *flak that followed Gilligan's story; such claims are denied just as frequently. *See also* BBC GOVERNORS; BBC TRUST; CHILLING EFFECT.

Further reading: K. Marsh, *Stumbling Over Truth: The Inside Story of the Sexed-up Dossier, Hutton, and the BBC* (2012).

A. Campbell, *The Burden of Power: Countdown to Iraq—the Alastair Campbell Diaries volume 4* (2013).

(●) SEE WEB LINKS
• Archived evidence and report of the Hutton Inquiry

hybridity The combination of two (or more) elements to make a new whole, such as a television programme that combines stand-up comedy with *investigative journalism. The concept of hybridity is also used in academic discussions of *alternative media to refer to those products such as *Private Eye* that combine alternative editorial content with operating as a profitable business, and to describe journalistic practices that use mainstream techniques and styles for alternative purposes (and vice versa).

hyperlink A facility by which readers of *online journalism can click on a word or image and be directed to other material, which might be a background story, an original source document, the website of one of the participants in the story, an interactive element, or some other way of adding value to a piece of journalism.

hyperlocal journalism Local news taken to the extreme, typically focusing on just one neighbourhood or postal/zip code rather than an entire town, city, or region. The *internet has made hyperlocal journalism easier to produce and has eliminated many of the production and distribution costs associated with *print journalism, although few journalists have (so far) managed to make a living wage from it. *See also* ONLINE JOURNALISM; VILLAGE CORRESPONDENT.

hypertext An element of *online journalism that uses embedded *hyperlinks to allow *users of websites to read a story in the order of their own choosing, in a non-linear fashion, clicking back and forth if they so wish.

hypodermic model The idea that media output involves the straightforward, one-way transmission of attitudes and ideologies from producer to receiver. The image of a hypodermic needle being used to inject a passive audience has been largely abandoned as too simplistic in academic discussions about media and journalism in recent decades, although echoes of it can still be heard whenever critics of *mainstream media are gathered. *Compare* ACTIVE AUDIENCE; HEGEMONY; USES AND GRATIFICATIONS. *See also* EFFECTS; ENCODING, DECODING; FRANKFURT SCHOOL.

i A national *compact newspaper in the UK launched in 2010 as a spin-off of the *Independent* newspaper, offering a boiled down and re-edited version of the parent newspaper and sold at a fraction of the price in a bid to appeal to people who had lost (or never had) the habit of buying a daily paper. By 2013 it was selling an average of 300,000 copies a day, around four times more than its parent title. It does not have a Sunday edition. *See also* REPURPOSING.

ideological state apparatus (ISA) A role played by the mainstream journalism and media industries in supporting the status quo, according to a *critical theory associated with the French *Marxist Louis Althusser (1918–90). For Althusser, journalists join the education system and the Church in being the major disseminators and reproducers of the dominant *ideology within society, which complements the more coercive role of repressive state apparatuses such as the police, prisons, courts, and armed forces. *See also* HEGEMONY; SECONDARY DEFINERS.

ideology A set or system of beliefs that are disseminated, reinforced, and/or reproduced by means of *communication. *Marxists argue that the ruling ideas in society (that is, the dominant ideology at any one time) tend to be those that serve the interests of the ruling class, although such ideas may be challenged by alternative ideologies. The extent to which ideological perspectives are (or ought to be) embedded within the practices and products of journalism is an area of much contention, and the argument that ideology should (or can) be kept out of journalism might itself be seen as an ideological one. *Compare* IMPARTIALITY. *See also* CRITICAL DISCOURSE ANALYSIS; CRITICAL THEORY; ENCODING, DECODING; HEGEMONY; OPPOSITIONAL REPORTING.

IFJ *See* INTERNATIONAL FEDERATION OF JOURNALISTS.

I. F. Stone's Weekly An alternative newspaper produced from 1953 to 1971 by legendary US journalist I. F. (Izzy) Stone (1907–89), predicated on his belief that 'all governments are run by liars'. Stone was an implacable opponent of the so-called 'great fear' represented by *McCarthyism; the feeling was mutual. *See also* ALTERNATIVE PRESS; PM.

((⊕)) SEE WEB LINKS

• Online archive of *I. F. Stone's Weekly*

IHTM (it happened to me) A style of *feature article, particularly common in *women's magazines, whereby a personal story is recounted in the first person. Such stories tend to be either horrific or bizarre and may be based on the journalist's own experience or on a journalist writing up an interviewee's verbal account of events. Extreme IHTM stories are often selected to be used as *coverlines of magazines. *See also* CONFESSIONAL MODE.

Iliffe News & Media A UK regional newspaper group, whose titles include the *Cambridge News*. In 2012 the group was sold by the Yattendon Group to the newly formed *Local World.

imagined audience A concept in the head of a journalist as to who their audience is. Trainee journalists on local newspapers might be told to write a story as if it was going to be read by their grandmother rather than a young student, for example. *Compare* IMAGINED COMMUNITY.

imagined community A media audience conceptualized as a form of political, national, or other type of 'community', which often finds expression in journalists' use of terms such as 'us', 'we', and 'our' in copy. *Compare* IMAGINED AUDIENCE. *See also* IDEOLOGY; MEDIA AGENDA.

IMCs *See* INDYMEDIA.

immediacy A quality in a story that enables it to be reported as it is happening, or immediately afterwards. All other things being equal, an unfolding or recent event is more likely than an older one to become *news. *See also* BREAKING NEWS; FREQUENCY; NEWS VALUES; ROLLING NEWS.

immersion reporting Journalism from within, as when a journalist immerses him or herself in a story and writes from their own experience rather than as a dispassionate observer. *Compare* OBJECTIVE JOURNALISM. *See also* GONZO JOURNALISM; NATIVE REPORTING.

impartiality Neutrality, even-handedness, *balance, and fairness in dispassionately reporting news and current affairs. Political impartiality is a statutory requirement of *broadcast journalism in the UK, although many scholars and some journalists question the extent to which it is desirable or even possible. *Compare* JOURNALISM OF ATTACHMENT; OPPOSITIONAL REPORTING. *See also* BIAS; OBJECTIVE JOURNALISM.

(🌐) SEE WEB LINKS
• BBC journalists on impartiality

inaccuracy An untruth that is reported as if it were a *fact. Inaccuracies appear in journalism all the time even when journalists make efforts to check the facts of a story against the time pressures and other *constraints under which most reporting is undertaken. An inaccuracy might appear because a *source has lied or does not (yet) have the full story themselves, because a *reporter or *sub-editor has made a wrong assumption, misheard or misunderstood something, or cross-checked with an earlier erroneous story. An inaccuracy may result in the publication of a clarification or *correction, or even in an action for *defamation. *See also* ACCURACY; FACT-CHECKING; HOAXES; NEVER WRONG FOR LONG.

indentures A formal apprenticeship agreement between a trainee journalist and a news organization whereby the former agrees to stay (usually on low pay) until the end of their *training period and the latter agrees to provide such training (and offer a pay rise on completion). This was the system under which generations of UK journalists were trained during much of the 20th century, with local newspapers sending recruits on day-release or block-release *NCTJ courses, but indentures have been replaced by employers requiring most applicants to have paid for their own training at university. *Compare* ACADEMIZATION OF JOURNALISM. *See also* JOURNALISM EDUCATION; TRAINING.

Independent A UK national newspaper launched by three former *Daily Telegraph* journalists in 1986 under the slogan, 'It is, are you?' The concept dreamed up by founders Andreas Whittam Smith (1937–), Matthew Symonds, and Stephen Glover was for an unashamedly highbrow, *quality newspaper that eschewed fawning coverage of royalty, took its *ethics so seriously that it would not accept *freebies, and gave *photographs a much better showing than in rival *broadsheets. Only the third of those ideals lasted very long after the launch, under the editorship of Whittam Smith. Not the least of the commercial realities of newspaper publishing was a *price war launched by the *Murdoch empire's *Times*. The *Independent*, nicknamed the *Indy*, gradually lost its independence as it was passed around different owners until being bought by the Lebedev family from Russia in 2010 for just £1. By then it had pioneered the move of serious newspapers to the *compact format, having shifted gradually in 2003 and 2004 under editor Simon Kelner, but was suffering a decline in *circulation and income from *advertising that was not compensated for by advertising on its website; by the time of its sale, the word 'ailing' had virtually become a prefix to the paper's name. Within months of taking over, the Lebedevs launched an innovative *repurposed spin-off newspaper, *i, sales of which soon dwarfed those of the *Independent* itself. The latter had an average daily sale of only around 75,000 copies in 2013, making it easily the worst-selling of the UK's mainstream national press. *See also* EVENING STANDARD; INDEPENDENT ON SUNDAY.

Independent Media Centres *See* INDYMEDIA.

Independent News & Media A newspaper and *digital media company based in Ireland whose titles include the *Belfast Telegraph* in the north, the *Irish Independent* in Dublin, and the *Irish Daily Star* (a joint venture with Richard Desmond's UK-based *Northern & Shell). Since 1973 the group has been largely run by Tony O'Reilly (1936–) and family. Independent News & Media operates internationally, including in South Africa and Australasia, and for a few years around the turn of the millennium it also owned the *Independent* in the UK.

Independent on Sunday The Sunday version of the UK's *Independent* newspaper, launched in January 1990 apparently with the main aim of protecting its corner of the quality newspaper market from the rival **Sunday Correspondent** (an independent competitor that had launched under the editorship of Peter Cole in 1989). The *Correspondent* was duly killed off before the end of 1990. The episode somewhat dented the *Independent*'s reputation for *ethical journalism and all-round saintliness, but its Sunday title (nicknamed *Sindy*) survives, albeit with a fraction of the staff and sales it once had.

Independent Press Standards Organization (IPSO) The proposed replacement for the UK's *Press Complaints Commission, as put forward in the wake of the *Leveson Report by the *Newspaper Society, the *Newspaper Publishers Association, and the *Professional Publishers Association, led by the publishers of the *Daily Mail, *Daily

Telegraph, *Sun, and *Times. When it was announced to the world in
2013, IPSO was described as 'a complete break with the past' and as a
way of delivering Leveson's recommendations for effective and
independent *self-regulation. But it was quickly denounced by critics
such as the *Hacked Off campaign as being 'the PCC mark 2' and too
much a creature of powerful newspaper *proprietors. *See also* ROYAL
CHARTER ON THE PRESS.

((()) SEE WEB LINKS

• IPSO announcement
• Hacked Off response to IPSO announcement

Independent Radio News *See* IRN.

Indianapolis Star A US daily newspaper published in the capital of
Indiana since 1903. Since 2000 it has been part of the *Gannett empire.

indigenous media Journalism and other media output produced by
and for indigenous or native populations, such as the Aboriginal press in
Australia and numerous indigenous media projects in Latin America.
See also ALTERNATIVE MEDIA; CHEROKEE PHOENIX; ETHNIC MINORITY
MEDIA.

indirect quote A piece of reported speech that is summarized and
attributed but does not use the precise words or formulation of the
speaker, and therefore does not need quotation marks. *Compare* DIRECT
QUOTE. *See also* QUOTE.

industrial correspondent A specialist reporter working for a
particular news organization or outlet, covering stories relating to
industry, jobs, investments, closures, strikes, and redundancies. *Fleet
Street newspapers, in particular, once had a large and influential
industry *corps but their numbers declined along with many of the UK's
major industries from the late 1980s onwards. *See also* LABOUR
CORRESPONDENT.

Indymedia **(IMCs, Independent Media Centres)** An international
network of semi-autonomous, independent, *alternative media websites
that sprang from protests against a meeting of the World Trade
Organization in the US city of Seattle in 1999. *Indymedia*, which
pioneered the use of *open-source publishing on the *internet to allow

*users to upload material directly to the sites, rejects the concepts of *objectivity and *impartiality, preferring to counter openly what its teams of unpaid, activists-cum-journalists tend to regard as the inherent *bias of *mainstream media. Posts are published online without being edited or filtered, although they may subsequently be hidden or even occasionally removed if found to contravene editorial guidelines, for example by expressing racist or sexist views. Under the slogan, 'Don't hate the media—be the media', *Indymedia* sites operate in many languages on several continents, and often use *video, *audio, *pictures, and *hyperlinks in addition to text-based material. *See also* ACTIVIST MEDIA; ALTERNATIVE JOURNALISM; AMATEUR JOURNALISM; CITIZEN JOURNALISM; ONLINE JOURNALISM.

(((●))) SEE WEB LINKS
• *Indymedia UK*'s editorial guidelines

infographics A way of presenting information visually online, often involving elements of *interactivity whereby website users can click to change which information is displayed, open up videos or other ways of telling the stories contained within the data, or search for particular terms or places. *See also* DATA JOURNALISM.

information The *facts about something, which are widely said to be the very essence of journalism in general and *reporting in particular. *See also* OBJECTIVE JOURNALISM; TRUTH; VERIFICATION.

information subsidy A label sometimes applied by academics to the process whereby the *public relations industry supplies news organizations with almost ready-made stories that require minimal investment in time-consuming *reporting techniques. Such a process is said to favour resource-rich organizations that can afford to hire PR professionals and to result in some journalists being engaged more in what is known as *churnalism than in any form of *investigative journalism.

infotainment A mix of *information and *entertainment that is often dismissed by commentators as a form of so-called *dumbing down. *See also* HYBRIDITY; TABLOIDIZATION.

injunction (gagging order) A legal order issued by a court that prevents somebody or some entity (such as a news organization) doing some specified act (such as publishing certain details about whoever has obtained the injunction). In the UK, so-called 'superinjunctions' may include a clause prohibiting anyone even reporting the fact that an injunction is in place, although this has proved difficult to enforce since the emergence of *social media. *See also* CENSORSHIP; LAWS; PRIOR RESTRAINT; PRIVACY; TRAFIGURA.

Ink A short-lived but influential UK underground newspaper published weekly in London from 1971 to 1972. A more overtly political spin-off from *Oz* magazine, *Ink* saw itself as a bridge between the professionalism of *Fleet Street journalism and the politics of libertarian left social movements such as gay liberation and anti-war campaigns. *See also* ALTERNATIVE JOURNALISM; UNDERGROUND PRESS.

INSI *See* INTERNATIONAL NEWS SAFETY INSTITUTE.

Insight A small team of specifically investigative journalists established at the *Sunday Times* in 1963 that probably reached its apogee under Harold Evans, who edited the paper between 1967 and 1981. Under the later editorship of Andrew Neil, *Insight*'s investigations tended to be conducted more in support of a free-market *ideology and less in tune with the paper's 1960s social conscience. *Insight* has continued, on and off, to the present day, although at times it has appeared to be more of a label for any *investigative journalism conducted by the newspaper than signifying the work of a dedicated and properly resourced team. *See also* MURDOCH EMPIRE; THALIDOMIDE SCANDAL.

Instagram A *social media network that allows users to share *photographs. Since its launch in 2010 it has become an important resource for journalists to monitor not just for pictures but also for potential stories or supposed *scandals about what is being posted by whom, especially *celebrities posting pictures of themselves (*see* SELFIE; USIE).

Institute of Journalists (IOJ) A quasi-professional association of journalists in the UK that formed in 1884 (initially as the National Association of Journalists) and was subsequently awarded a royal charter by Queen Victoria. The IOJ included newspaper *proprietors in its ranks, which tended to limit members' efforts at improving journalists' wages and conditions, leading to the creation of a breakaway trade union (*see* NATIONAL UNION OF JOURNALISTS) in 1907. *See also* PROFESSION.

intelligence services State spying organizations that are sometimes accused of influencing the media by covert methods, including orchestrating *leaks (of information or misinformation) and issuing confidential briefings, warnings, and even threats. By its nature, the role of the intelligence services tends to be shrouded in secrecy, but it has been publicly acknowledged that, at least from the 1960s to the 1980s, the UK's domestic intelligence organization MI5 would vet potential recruits to the *BBC, checking on their backgrounds and any political affiliations or activities. *See also* DA-NOTICE; FORUM WORLD FEATURES.

interactivity A process of *communication that flows in more than one direction. Whereas most journalism has traditionally been seen as something of a one-way, linear process of *information being passed from news organization to *audience, journalism in the digital age tends to be more interactive, allowing instant feedback from audience members to journalists and also directly to other members of the audience (*see* CONVERSATION). Other interactive elements can include the submission of *user-generated content such as *pictures and *videos, invitations to participate in online *polls, the use of *crowdsourcing to generate material for informative graphics such as interactive maps, and giving website *users the power to decide in what order or format they wish material to be displayed. Journalists and audiences now often interact with each other via *social media too. *See also* ACTIVE AUDIENCE; HYPERLINKS; HYPERTEXT; INFOGRAPHICS; ONLINE JOURNALISM.

International Federation of Journalists (IFJ) A Brussels-based organization that brings together journalists and their trade unions from more than 100 countries around the world, campaigning on issues such as free speech, *ethics, media plurality, and the safety of journalists. The IFJ publishes an annual list of journalists and other media workers killed in the line of duty (*see* DEATHS OF JOURNALISTS).

(⊕) SEE WEB LINKS
• English-language version of the IFJ website

International Federation of the Periodical Press (FIPP) An international trade body for the magazine industry that represents member companies in around 60 countries which, between them, publish some 6,000 titles. In addition to networking, FIPP produces research into *magazines and their online *brands.

(⊕) SEE WEB LINKS
• FIPP's research pages

International Herald Tribune An internationally oriented offshoot of the *New York Times* that can trace its origins back to 1887, when James Gordon Bennett Jr. (1841–1918) first published a European edition of the *New York Herald*. The *International Herald Tribune* became an online *brand with multimedia website in addition to the newspaper, which sells in more than 130 countries. In 2013 its name changed to the *International New York Times*.

(⊕) SEE WEB LINKS
• The *International New York Times* website

International News Safety Institute (INSI) A charity and networking organization launched in 2003 to raise awareness of risks encountered by journalists working in dangerous environments, and to offer advice and support. The institute was a joint initiative of the *International Federation of Journalists and the *International Press Institute. *See also* DEATHS OF JOURNALISTS.

(⊕) SEE WEB LINKS
• INSI safety code

International Press Institute (IPI) An international network of *editors and news media executives formed in 1950 to lobby for a *free press. Based in Austria, the IPI has initiated a number of 'missions' to investigate media issues in specific countries, including Bangladesh, Sri Lanka, and Nepal.

(⊕) SEE WEB LINKS
• The IPI blog

International Women's Media Foundation A Washington-based networking and lobbying organization formed in 1990 to support and empower women journalists around the world. The foundation organizes two annual *awards open to women journalists: Courage in Journalism and the Lifetime Achievement. *See also* GENDER; SEXISM.

(⊕) SEE WEB LINKS
• *Global Report on the Status of Women in the News Media*

internet A worldwide computer network that had its origins in military technologies in the 1950s and academic networks in the 1970s, but which emerged publicly in the 1990s with *email, web browsers, and *websites. Since then the internet has facilitated myriad forms of *online journalism, *social media, *blogging, and *user-generated content. The internet is often blamed for the decline of so-called *legacy media (*see* TECHNOCENTRISM) although many of the challenges facing newspapers and other traditional media preceded the emergence of the internet as a popular medium. *See also* CONVERGENCE; DIGITAL MEDIA; NEW TECHNOLOGY.

internship A form of *work experience that is, or purports to be, properly organized and structured. An internship may offer someone who wants to be a journalist an opportunity to discover at first-hand what the job entails, demonstrate their talents, and possibly even step into a job at the end of it. Some internships are paid, some involve training, and some involve neither. As with less formalized forms of work experience, journalists' organizations and journalism educators warn wannabe-journalists of the risks of being exploited as free or cheap labour in the hope of a job that may never materialize. *See also* TRAINING.

intertextuality The way in which one *text may incorporate or reference another and/or may be understood by the *audience within the context of other texts. At its simplest, this can be seen in a newspaper *headline that refers implicitly to a line from a song or a film. A classic example would be when the *Sun's report of a football match between Inverness Caledonian Thistle and Glasgow Celtic was headlined: 'SUPER CALEY GO BALLISTIC, CELTIC ARE ATROCIOUS'. This depended on readers recognizing the headline as a play on the words of a song from the film *Mary Poppins*. At a more complex level, intertextuality means that no text stands in complete isolation: in this sense, journalists reporting a particular event will be aware of how similar incidents have been reported in the past and may find themselves reproducing certain familiar *angles, phrases, or *tropes. Similarly, the audience will read such stories within the context of similar stories (including fictional ones) they have read, seen, or heard previously. Scholars who research the intertextuality of journalism tend to argue that all texts necessarily retain traces of other texts.

interview A journalist asking somebody *questions for the purpose of obtaining *information and/or *quotes for a *news story or *feature. The interviewee's answers will typically be recorded in a notebook (*see* NOTE-TAKING; SHORTHAND) if they are not taped or broadcast. An interview may be a quick phone call or an exchange of emails or text messages, a long boozy afternoon in a restaurant, a set-piece studio encounter to be broadcast on TV or radio, or many other variations. Interviews can range from sympathetic conversations designed to cultivate a *source and help them tell their own story, to more combative *doorstepping of somebody about whom allegations have been made. Whoever it is with, however it is conducted, and whether it is intended to provide the story itself or merely background, interviewing has been one of the staples of *reporting since at least the 1920s. Before then it was often considered bad form to quote people directly. *See also* COPY APPROVAL; DEATH KNOCK; FIVE WS; OFF THE RECORD; ON THE RECORD.

In These Times A US alternative magazine that since its launch in 1976 has offered readers a mixture of investigative reporting and left-leaning critique. Founded by historian James Weinstein (1926–2005), *In These Times* attracted support from radical intellectuals such as Barbara Ehrenreich, Noam Chomsky, Herbert Marcuse, and E. P. Thompson. *See also* ALTERNATIVE PRESS.

intro The introduction to a story that is contained in its opening sentence or paragraph and which is typically aimed at grabbing attention and/or making the maximum impact. It is sometimes referred to as the *lead or top line, particularly in the USA. *See also* ANGLE; DELAYED DROP; INVERTED PYRAMID MODEL; KEYWORDS.

intrusion Seeking and/or publishing information that the individual or organization concerned would prefer to remain private. Intrusion into people's *privacy tends to be justified in ethical *codes of conduct only when it concerns a story in the *public interest. *See also* DATA PROTECTION; ETHICS; INVESTIGATIVE JOURNALISM.

inverted pyramid model A traditional way of visualizing the formula by which *hard news stories are often written: that is, with the most important (or intriguing) information at the top, followed by elaboration, detail, and evidence, leaving the least important elements to the end so that they may be cut without rendering what remains meaningless. *Compare* DELAYED DROP. *See also* FIVE WS; INTRO.

investigative journalism Reporting that sets out to discover something that somebody, somewhere, wishes to remain a secret, and that typically involves detailed and time-consuming work by an individual journalist or by a team of journalists inquiring into some kind of alleged wrongdoing. Methods associated with investigative journalism typically include meticulous searching and cross-referencing of documents and databases in the public domain; use of *freedom of information laws to place more material in the public domain; receiving *leaks of secret information; persuading people to talk either *on or *off the record; and, less typically, secret filming and/or recording, and using *subterfuge to obtain evidence of wrongdoing. The targets of such investigations can range from corrupt politicians and business people misusing or misappropriating public money on an international scale to local landlords or builders taking shortcuts and thereby risking the lives of workers, customers, or the general public. Alleged miscarriages of justice have been another popular subject for investigative journalists to probe, as have arms deals and alleged war crimes. At the *tabloid end of the market, investigative journalism often focuses more on exposing the alleged hypocrisy of *celebrities and so-called 'role models' by revealing their sexual behaviour and/or drug habits (*see* FAKE SHEIKH).

Classic examples of sustained investigative journalism include *Watergate in the USA and the *Thalidomide scandal in the UK, the latter being a product of the celebrated *Insight* team at the *Sunday Times* under editor Harold Evans. Such investigative journalism is often said to have begun in 1885 when William Stead (1849–1912), editor of the *Pall Mall Gazette*, exposed the scandal of child prostitution in Victorian England by 'buying' a 13-year-old girl for £5.

Compared with other forms of reporting, investigative journalism may involve a journalistic organization investing significantly more time and money on content than it would for a routine or *diary story, yet the outcome of the investigation is far less certain and may not even result in a story at all; investigations also typically entail more risk for journalists and their sources, whether in the form of legal action, revenge attacks, or even assassination, as in the cases of Anna Politkovskaya (1958–2006) in Russia and Martin O'Hagan (1950–2001) in Northern Ireland, to give just two examples (*see* CHILLING EFFECT). Investigative journalism is frequently said to have been in decline from a high point or supposed *golden age stretching, in the USA and UK particularly, from the late 1960s into the 1980s. Although there is some evidence that investigations, particularly on television, have turned away from some 'worthy' issues towards more populist subjects relating to *sex, drugs, and crime, significant amounts of identifiably investigative journalism can still be found in today's media, notwithstanding editorial cutbacks and declining revenues.

The term 'investigative journalism' can be problematic: on the one hand, it is seen as pandering to the pretensions of grandeur displayed by some of its exponents and, on the other hand, it implies that only certain types or higher forms of journalism need be investigative. However, investigative specialists are not necessarily a separate breed of journalist: elements of investigation can come into otherwise straightforward reportage and many journalists who conduct investigations also frequently find themselves reporting more simple news stories because investigative journalists and ordinary journalists not only inhabit the same newsrooms, they are sometimes the same people. In some ways the skills of the investigative specialist are essentially the same as those used by *all* *reporters; it is just that sometimes those skills will be utilized with an added dose of *scepticism and with a greater intensity. *See also* COMPUTER-ASSISTED REPORTING; DATA JOURNALISM; PRIVATE EYE; PROPUBLICA; UNDERCOVER REPORTING; WIKILEAKS.

Further reading: H. de Burgh (ed.), *Investigative Journalism* (2008).

IOJ *See* INSTITUTE OF JOURNALISTS.

IPC The major *consumer magazine publishing company in the UK, whose print titles and online *brands range from **Woman's Own* to *Nuts. Since 2001, IPC has been owned by the US-based international media giant *Time Warner.

IPI *See* INTERNATIONAL PRESS INSTITUTE.

IPSO *See* INDEPENDENT PRESS STANDARDS ORGANIZATION.

Irish News A daily newspaper published in Northern Ireland since 1891 that remains independent of the large newspaper chains.

Irish Post A weekly newspaper published in the UK since 1970 that covers news, sport, and culture involving the Irish community within the UK. The newspaper and its website were rescued from closure in 2011 when, after going into liquidation, they were bought by Elgin Loane, publisher of the classified *ads magazine *Loot*.

Irish Times Ireland's *quality daily national newspaper, published in Dublin since 1859. Since 1974 the *broadsheet has been owned by a charitable trust that was created with the objective of maintaining it as 'an independent newspaper primarily concerned with serious issues for the benefit of the community throughout the whole of Ireland, free from any form of personal or party political, commercial, religious or other sectional control'. In 1989 the *Irish Times* pioneered the concept of the *readers' editor.

IRN (Independent Radio News) A national news service that launched in 1973 to supply the UK's then new commercial radio sector with *bulletins, *packages, and *alerts on a 24-hour basis, to augment whatever material the stations produced locally (*see* RADIO JOURNALISM). Since 2010 the IRN news service has been supplied by *Sky News*.

ISA *See* IDEOLOGICAL STATE APPARATUS.

It happened to me *See* IHTM.

ITN A UK-based independent *news provider formed in 1955 to supply news to the new commercial television service and provide an alternative to the *BBC. Today ITN is one of the world's major broadcast news organizations, supplying factual material to clients around the world in addition to providing news and *current affairs programming for ITV (most famously with *News At Ten* each weekday evening), *Channel 4 News*, and Channel 5. *See also* TELEVISION JOURNALISM.

JEAA *See* JOURNALISM EDUCATION ASSOCIATION OF AUSTRALIA.

JEANZ *See* JOURNALISM EDUCATION ASSOCIATION OF NEW ZEALAND.

Jewish Chronicle A weekly newspaper first published in 1841 to report about and for the Jewish community in the UK. Many other Jewish periodicals were launched in the 19th century but the *JC* outlived them all. The paper and its online presence are owned by a trust rather than a commercial *proprietor. *See also* ETHNIC MINORITY MEDIA.

Jimmy's World *See* LITTLE JIMMY.

Johnston Press One of the UK's biggest regional newspaper and digital publishing groups, the flagship titles of which are currently the *Scotsman* and the *Yorkshire Post*. Johnston Press, which also owns titles in Ireland, was a family printing business when it began in Scotland in 1767 but eventually grew to become a profitable publisher of hundreds of newspapers. It became a public company listed on the London Stock Exchange in 1988 and expanded rapidly through takeovers during the 1990s and early 2000s. Shortly after it fell on harder times that saw it embark on successive rounds of job cuts, office closures, increases in cover price, and the transformation of a number of daily titles into weeklies. In 2013 it was the UK's fourth biggest regional newspaper publisher in terms of *circulation (at almost 5 million copies per week) and it owned the most titles at 215 (of which 152 were paid-for weeklies). *See also* CONCENTRATION OF OWNERSHIP; LOCAL JOURNALISM; REGIONAL MEDIA.

journalese Words and phrases that typically will be used by journalists to describe events or people, notwithstanding the fact that such language is rarely if ever heard in real life: 'axe', 'bid', 'clash', 'tot', 'revellers', 'slam', and 'mercy dash' are all examples of journalese (which is sometimes referred to as '*tabloidese'). *See also* CLICHÉ; STYLE.

Further reading: P. Dickson and R. Skole, *Journalese: A Dictionary for Deciphering the News* (2012).
R. Hutton, *Romps, Tots, and Boffins: The Strange Language of News* (2013).

journalism A set of practices through which *information is found out and communicated, often involving making public what would otherwise be private, and which is typically published or broadcast in a format such as a *newspaper, *magazine, *bulletin, *documentary, *website, or *blog. Journalism entails discovering or uncovering fresh, topical, factual material and making it publicly available, but it goes beyond that to include amplifying, contextualizing, or commenting on *facts and comments that have already been made public. Journalism can range from *hard news, *current affairs, and *war reporting to *soft news, *colour pieces, and *features; it can be generalist or specialist, local or international, serious or popular. It can cover everything from *investigative journalism in the *public interest to writing a description of a sporting encounter, from reviewing a play to *gallery reporting of politics. Notwithstanding the breadth of the *field, at the heart of most journalism is *reporting, which relies on a mixture of observation, inquiry, *verification, and *attribution in an attempt to produce as accurate a version of events as possible; at the same time, events are told as *stories as a way of making them entertaining as well as informative. Implicit within journalism, for many, is a commitment to objectivity, although others dismiss the concept as an impossibility, or even as something undesirable (*see* ADVOCACY JOURNALISM; JOURNALISM OF ATTACHMENT; OBJECTIVE JOURNALISM).

Journalism as we understand it is normally described as having only begun following the emergence of *printing (*see* CHAPBOOK; NEWSBOOK; PAMPHLET), but the predominantly oral forms of *communication that preceded the growth of print culture are also said to have contained journalistic elements, not the least of which were the activities of the town crier and the ballad singer. Journalism has constantly adapted to the arrival of new technologies (*see* BROADCAST JOURNALISM; NEWSREEL; ONLINE JOURNALISM; SOCIAL MEDIA) and has also responded to (and/or been a product of) the times in which it is produced, hence the emergence during certain periods of a *radical press, *black media, *feminist media, *gonzo journalism, and the *underground press. Most journalism within the USA, UK, and similar economies is produced by commercial organizations that employ *journalists fundamentally because their work will (it is hoped) attract an *audience to whom the product can be sold and/or who will in turn be used to attract *advertisers. However, there are other models of *ownership, ranging from the *BBC (funded by *licence fee) to the informal or cooperative groupings that are often responsible for *alternative journalism, and even one-person amateur or 'citizen journalists'. Journalism may be subject to *constraints, *laws, and forms of *regulation, all of which differ between countries and may change over time. Journalism is a contested concept that is variously described as writing 'the first draft of history', as producing little more than *propaganda for the ruling classes, as being essential to (or helping to undermine) *democracy, and as either nurturing or harming the health of the *public sphere. Scholarly attempts at understanding and explaining journalism saw the emergence during the late 20th century of the field of *journalism studies. *See also* ACCURACY; AMATEUR JOURNALISM; BOUNDARY MAINTENANCE; CITIZEN JOURNALISM; ETHICAL JOURNALISM; GOLDEN AGE OF JOURNALISM; GUTTER JOURNALISM; McJOURNALISM; NEWS.

Further reading: T. Harcup, *Journalism: Principles and Practice* (2009).
D. Randall, *The Universal Journalist* (2011).
L. Sheridan Burns, *Understanding Journalism* (2013).

Journalism & Mass Communication Quarterly A peer-reviewed academic journal established in the USA in 1924 and published in association with the *Association for Education in Journalism and Mass Communication. *See also* ACADEMIZATION OF JOURNALISM; JOURNALISM EDUCATION; JOURNALISM STUDIES.

journalism education The combination of the *training of journalists that takes place on vocational courses and the critical inquiry into journalism that tends to be undertaken on more academically oriented *journalism studies courses. Journalism education within higher education has a much longer history in the USA than in the UK, but the latter has been catching up in recent years with journalism in both countries now largely a graduate occupation. Journalism education can on occasion involve a blurring of the two strands of training and *critical theory, and at other times seems to provoke mutual antagonism between the two. By emphasizing education rather than (just) training, journalism education aspires to go beyond providing employers with a skilled labour force, to encourage a more independent, questioning, ethical, and reflective approach to journalism. *See also* ACADEMIZATION OF JOURNALISM; HACKADEMY; INDENTURES; JOURNALISM EDUCATION; REFLECTIVE PRACTICE.

Journalism Education A peer-reviewed open access online journal launched in 2012 by the *Association for Journalism Education to publish research, commentary, and reflection on journalism in general and *journalism education in particular.

((()) SEE WEB LINKS
• All issues of *Journalism Education*

Journalism Education Association of Australia (JEAA)
A membership and networking organization covering journalism educators working in Australia. Formed in 1975, initially as the Australian Association for Tertiary Education in Journalism, it became the JEAA in 1980 and publishes the journal, *Australian Journalism Review*. *See also* JOURNALISM EDUCATION.

((()) SEE WEB LINKS
• JEAA conference papers

Journalism Education Association of New Zealand (JEANZ)
A membership and networking organization covering journalism educators working in New Zealand. Formed in 2000, it has published the journal *Pacific Journalism Review* since 2003. *See also* JOURNALISM EDUCATION.

((()) SEE WEB LINKS
• JEANZ conference papers

journalism of attachment Reporting from a *conflict zone in a manner that eschews formal *impartiality and *balance in favour of distinguishing between and labelling victim and aggressor. The idea is closely associated with former BBC correspondent Martin Bell (1938–) who, in the late 1990s, expressed frustration that covering the conflicts in the former Yugoslavia in the traditional neutral manner of the *BBC left audiences none the wiser about what the fighting was all about. Journalism of attachment has subsequently been criticized for naivety in supposing that parties to conflict can easily be divided into 'goodies and baddies', and for confusing *reporting with *campaigning journalism. *See also* OBJECTIVITY; WAR REPORTING.

Further reading: M. Bell, 'The Journalism of Attachment', in M. Kieran (ed.), *Media Ethics* (1998).

journalism studies Academic inquiry into and attempts to explain the roles, meanings, and practices of *journalists and *journalism. Journalism studies is an eclectic, multidisciplinary, and relatively young field of scholarly intellectual activity, typically drawing on elements of history, sociology, cultural studies, *media studies, communication studies, *semiotics, *political economy, *Marxism, information studies, and other areas of academic inquiry, in an effort to explore and understand the complexities of journalism. Journalism studies research methodologies may include newsroom observation, *content analysis, *critical discourse analysis, theoretical exposition, surveys, *focus groups, or interviews, focusing variously on journalists, *sources, organizations, structures, products, *audiences, and/or the relationships between them. Located within the higher education sector and rapidly expanding internationally in recent years, journalism studies has its own publications, conferences, forums, theories, and jargon. As a discipline it often exists alongside the *training of journalists, and there can be tension between those involved with teaching journalistic skills and those more concerned with critical inquiry into journalism. *See also* ACADEMIZATION OF JOURNALISM; CRITICAL THEORY; EMPIRICAL RESEARCH; JOURNALISM EDUCATION.

Further reading: B. Franklin, M. Hamer, M. Hanna, M. Kinsey, and J. E. Richardson, *Key Concepts in Journalism Studies* (2005).
K. Wahl-Jorgensen and T. Hanitzsch (eds), *Handbook of Journalism Studies* (2009).
B. Zelizer, *Taking Journalism Seriously: News and the Academy* (2004).

Journalism Studies A peer-reviewed academic journal launched in 2000 under the editorship of Professor Bob Franklin to publish the work of international researchers in the field of *journalism studies and *journalism education. Related journals *Journalism Practice* and *Digital Journalism* were launched in 2007 and 2013 respectively. *See also* ACADEMIZATION OF JOURNALISM.

Journalism: Theory, Practice, and Criticism An international peer-reviewed academic journal edited by Professors Howard Tumber and Barbie Zelizer, sometimes referred to simply as *Journalism*. Published since 2000, it features the work of researchers in the field of *journalism studies and *journalism education. *See also* ACADEMIZATION OF JOURNALISM.

journalism training *See* TRAINING.

journalist Somebody who is engaged in the practice of *journalism and the production of *editorial content for journalistic products and outputs. Although the public's image of a journalist is perhaps most likely to be of a *reporter (either a *tabloid *hack or a noble investigator such as Woodward and Bernstein of *Watergate fame), journalism encompasses a whole range of additional activities, roles, and functions, including that of *agony aunt, *anchor, *blogger, *columnist, *copy taster, *editor, *feature writer, *foreign correspondent, *newsreader, *obituary writer, *sub-editor, and *VJ. Press *photographers are generally regarded as journalists too, although some prefer to see themselves as a breed apart. The label 'journalist' normally implies working in a paid capacity, either on staff or on a *freelance basis, but arguably anybody carrying out the role of a journalist can be described as one even if they receive no remuneration (*see* AMATEUR JOURNALISM; CITIZEN JOURNALISM). Journalism is increasingly a graduate occupation (*see* ACADEMIZATION OF JOURNALISM) but the status of the journalist is contested terrain, with journalists described alternatively as being engaged in a *profession on the one hand, and a *craft or *trade on the other. Opinion polls in the UK regularly put journalists near the bottom of lists of those occupations most trusted by the public. *See also* AUTONOMY; BOUNDARY MAINTENANCE; DEATHS OF JOURNALISTS; INTERNATIONAL FEDERATION OF JOURNALISTS; LICENSING OF JOURNALISTS; TRAINING.

journalistic 1. Anything pertaining to *journalism, as opposed to purely entertaining or artistic forms of media, for example.
2. A disparaging term sometimes used within academe to imply that a piece of work is more descriptive than analytical.

journo An informal term for a journalist, most commonly heard in the USA and Australia. *Compare* HACK.

j-school An abbreviated term for journalism school or any form of educational institution or department in which the *training of journalists takes place, especially in Australasia or North America.

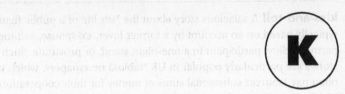

Kansas City Star A US daily newspaper published in Kansas, Missouri, since 1880, with perhaps its main claim to fame outside its home state being the fact that it employed the writer Ernest Hemingway (1899–1961) as a journalist when he was just 18 years old. Today the paper and its website are owned by the *McClatchy company.

(((🌐))) SEE WEB LINKS

• Ernest Hemingway at the *Kansas City Star*

keywords Those words and phrases that, when included in online *headlines, *intros, and *captions, increase the chances of *users finding such material via *search engines. Specific keywords—especially the names of people, places, and organizations—are thought to be more effective than more general terms. *See also* SEARCH ENGINE OPTIMIZATION.

kicker 1. An entertaining, amusing, or offbeat story that can balance a page or bulletin of otherwise serious news.
2. Confusingly, a kicker can also be the opening words of a story set in larger type, the first word or two of a *photo caption set in upper case, or even a *strap above the main headline.

kill To cancel, delete, or otherwise drop a story that has been in preparation. *See also* SPIKE.

kill-fee A payment to a *freelance journalist or *news agency when a commissioned item is no longer going to be used. Such a fee is typically much lower than it would have been if the story had been run.

KISS A slogan sometimes used in the *training of journalists, meaning both, 'Keep it short and simple' and, 'Keep it simple, stupid!' The point is to emphasize to trainee journalists the primacy of clear and uncluttered communication over decorative writing. *See also* INVERTED PYRAMID MODEL; LANGUAGE OF NEWS.

kiss-and-tell A salacious story about the *sex life of a public figure typically based on an account by a former lover, ex-spouse, estranged partner, fellow participant in a one-night stand, or prostitute. Such stories are particularly popular in UK *tabloid newspapers, which will often pay *sources substantial sums of money for their cooperation, which normally entails not speaking to rival media. *See also* CHEQUEBOOK JOURNALISM; INTRUSION; PRIVACY.

kit Whatever technical equipment is required to do the job, whether in the newsroom (e.g. computers), the studio (e.g. cameras, lighting), or on the road (e.g. digital recorder, satellite telephone). Rather like soldiers, journalists always complain about their kit, which is never as good as that in the hands of the enemy (rivals). *See also* NEW TECHNOLOGY.

kite-flying A speculative story that is run, at least in part, to test the water or to draw out a reaction. A *source close to a politician might supply a journalist (on an unattributable or *off-the-record basis) with a story about a possible new idea or policy, and then deny it if public (or political) reaction appears hostile. News organizations, especially newspapers, might also engage in kite-flying about possible campaigns of their own, to see how popular they might be with *audiences.

KM Group An independent, family-owned UK newspaper publisher, radio company, and digital media group based in the county of Kent, the flagship title of which is the weekly *Kent Messenger* newspaper. One of the top twenty regional newspaper chains in the UK, KM announced in 2013 that it was the first publishing group in Europe to have transferred its entire production system to wireless cloud computing (*see* NEW TECHNOLOGY).

labour correspondent 1. An industrial specialist whose *beat tends to be more focused on jobs, trade unions, and industrial relations than the broader issues to do with economics and investment.
2. An alternative term for an *industrial correspondent.

Ladies' Mercury Probably the first *women's magazine in the world, published for just four issues in London in 1693 and promising to answer readers' queries about love and relationships with 'the zeal and softness becoming to the sex'. Although aimed at women, it was published by a man, John Dunton (1659–1733), a bookseller, member of the Athenian Society, and publisher of the ***Athenian Mercury***, which was also based on responding to readers' questions. *See also* AGONY AUNT; LIFESTYLE JOURNALISM.

(⊕) SEE WEB LINKS
• 'Zeal and softness'

lads' mags A collective term for those weekly or monthly *magazines (and their digital *brands) that target young men by offering a hedonistic mix of entertaining *pictures and *features that are largely concerned with sport, cars, gadgets, and women's breasts—not necessarily in that order. Since their emergence in the 1990s, lads' mags have often been accused of *sexism and in the UK they are the target of campaigns by feminists and the online network *Mumsnet*, among others, seeking to persuade shops to place such publications on the top shelf, alongside pornography. Lads' mag publishers tend to accuse their critics of wishing to impose *censorship on a *free press. By the second decade of the 21st century, sales of many lads' mags had collapsed from their heyday of the late 1990s and early 2000s. *See also* PORNIFICATION.

(⊕) SEE WEB LINKS
• *Mumsnet* on lads' mags

language of news A style of writing that tends to emphasize the active rather than passive, the concrete rather than the abstract, the specific rather than the general, and the concise rather than the verbose. Despite sharing something of a common language and *grammar, journalists working for different outlets may still be required to adhere to the peculiarities of a *house style. *See also* ACTIVE WRITING; JOURNALESE; ORWELL'S SIX RULES OF WRITING.

Last Chance Saloon The metaphorical drinking den in which members of the UK national press are periodically said to be gathered, indicating that there is one final opportunity to deal voluntarily with issues of *ethics before more draconian measures (such as *statutory regulation) might be introduced. The phrase is most commonly associated with a 1989 warning by culture minister David Mellor, although it had been used in a *Guardian* *leader six years earlier and was revived around the time of publication of the *Leveson Report in 2012. *See also* ETHICAL JOURNALISM; SELF-REGULATION.

Las Vegas Review Journal A daily newspaper covering the state of Nevada, which began life as the *Clark County Review* in 1909. It is owned by Stephens Media and is one of the top 25 US daily titles in terms of *circulation. *See also* LAS VEGAS SUN.

Las Vegas Sun A US daily newspaper that launched in 1950, following a lockout of printers at the *Las Vegas Review Journal*. Founded by Hank Greenspun (1909–89), the early years of the *Sun* saw it expose and oppose *McCarthyism. It is still owned by the Greenspun family but, since 2005, it has been distributed as an insert within the *Review Journal* under an innovative joint operating agreement that allows the *Sun* to retain editorial independence, its own newsroom, and a separate online operation.

(🌐) SEE WEB LINKS

• *Las Vegas Sun* 'fighting for the little guy'

lateral thinking Considering less obvious possibilities as well as the more obvious ones, looking for possible connections, and thinking, 'What if?'—all of which are widely said to be essential to good journalism. Lateral thinking is made easier by having a good memory and/or good *archives, and it can help a journalist come up with an *angle on a story that nobody else has noticed. However, that is only the start, as any ideas produced by such lateral thinking (or 'thinking outside the box', as journalists tend not to call it) still need to be checked out to see if they stand up.

LA Times *See* LOS ANGELES TIMES.

laws The rules codified and enshrined in legislation that may impact upon journalists, whether in common with all citizens (such as laws outlawing theft, stalking, or *phone-hacking) or in the form of specific media laws that control how journalism is produced and/or regulated (such as the statutory requirement for broadcast journalism in the UK to be politically *impartial). Civil and criminal laws are among the many *constraints faced by journalists in liberal democracies and even more so in societies whose rulers are less tolerant of a *free press. *See also* CENSORSHIP; CONTEMPT OF COURT; DATA PROTECTION; DEFAMATION; FIRST AMENDMENT; LICENSING ACT; LICENSING OF JOURNALISTS; STATUTORY REGULATION.

Further reading: M. Hanna and M. Dodd, *McNae's Essential Law for Journalists* (2014).

lead 1. The main story in a news *bulletin or on a newspaper front page (*see* SPLASH).
2. A *tip or idea for a possible story that needs to be checked out.
3. An alternative term for an *intro, commonly used in the USA.

leader A column offering an opinion or *comment on behalf of a newspaper or magazine, usually on an issue of topical concern. A leader might be written or approved by the *editor or produced by one or more specialist leader writers, who may or may not help formulate the news organization's opinion in a *conference of senior colleagues. *See also* EDITORIAL.

leak The supply of confidential information by a *source without authorization and/or ahead of official publication, often resulting in an *exclusive story. *See also* ANONYMOUS SOURCE; KITE-FLYING; PENTAGON PAPERS; WATERGATE; WHISTLEBLOWER; WIKILEAKS.

legacy media A term popular amongst advocates of *new media, especially in the USA, to describe extant forms of media with longer histories such as *newspapers, *magazines, and *broadcast journalism. Presumably *Twitter will be described as legacy media one day.
See also ANALOGUE; MAINSTREAM MEDIA; TECHNOCENTRISM.

Le Monde A French quality daily newspaper and website. *Le Monde* was launched in newly liberated Paris in 1944 to provide an independent voice for the French people and its journalists have tended to pride themselves on having an independent streak ever since. In 2012 the paper teamed up with the *Huffington Post* to create the blogging site *Le Huffington Post* in addition to its standalone *lemonde.fr* news website.

Leninist theory of the press The argument put forward by Russian communist leader Vladimir Ilyich Lenin (1870–1924) that a radical political newspaper ought not merely to inform its readership but help to organize them into revolutionary activity. According to the Leninist theory, the newspaper of a political organization should follow the party line rather than be a forum for debate. Although such media provide an ideological challenge to *mainstream journalism, they tend to be less open than other forms of *alternative media. *See also* DAILY WORKER; RADICAL PRESS.

letters Written communications sent to news organizations, editors, or specific journalists, by members of the *audience. Before the emergence of *email, *text messages, and *Twitter, the posting or hand delivery of a letter was one of the few forms of audience feedback that journalists would receive. Some letters would be from those dismissed by journalists as the '*green ink brigade' of obsessives and cranks, some would contain a *tip or a statement that might result in a story, and some would be selected and edited for publication on the letters' page. The tone, content, and contributors to a letters' page used to play (and in some cases still plays) a key role in the formation of a publication's *brand image. *Compare* YOUR COMMENTS.

Leveller A socialist-feminist investigative magazine produced collectively in the UK from 1975 to 1985. Named after a group of 17th-century radicals (*see* LEVELLERS), the magazine briefly became a journalistic cause célèbre in the late 1970s when (along with the similarly alternative **Peace News** and the *National Union of Journalists journal, the *Journalist*) it was prosecuted for revealing the real identity of 'Colonel B', who had been a witness in a court case brought under the *Official Secrets Act. *See also* ALTERNATIVE PRESS.

Levellers Radical political agitators and pamphleteers who, during the English revolution (or civil war) of the 1640s, produced a nascent form of an *alternative press that spoke out against abuses of power, first by the king and then by the Commonwealth forces that replaced the monarchy. Levellers such as John Lilburne (1614–57), who earned the nickname 'Free-born John', defied severe persecution to distribute their *pamphlets and to promote the idea of a *free press. *See also* DEMOCRACY; PUTNEY DEBATES.

Leveson Inquiry (Leveson Report) An official investigation into the culture, practices, and *ethics of the UK press established in July 2011 by Prime Minister David Cameron in the wake of the *hackgate scandal at the *News of the World*. The inquiry was presided over by Sir Brian Leveson, a Lord Justice of Appeal, who pointed out that it was 'the seventh time in less than 70 years' that the government had commissioned a report into the British press (*see* CALCUTT REPORTS; ROYAL COMMISSIONS ON THE PRESS; YOUNGER COMMITTEE). The Leveson Inquiry was split into two parts. Part one, which began in November 2011 and concluded with publication of the Leveson Report in November 2012, examined *self-regulation and press behaviour towards politicians, the police, and members of the public including *celebrities and victims of *phone-hacking and other crimes. The focus was on the UK's national newspapers, although magazines, the regional press, and to a lesser extent, *online journalism were also considered. During almost nine months of public hearings streamed live on the inquiry website, oral evidence was given by more than 300 witnesses, including *proprietors, *editors, ex-editors, *reporters, victims of press intrusion, politicians, police officers, academics, and representatives of the *Press Complaints Commission. A further 300 people submitted written evidence. Witness statements along with transcripts and videos of the hearings were placed online, prompting Lord Justice Leveson to describe the inquiry as 'the most public and the most concentrated look at the press that this country has seen'. Part two of the Leveson Inquiry was intended to examine the extent of unlawful activity and corporate governance failures within the *Murdoch empire and other media organizations, and to learn lessons from the way in which such issues had been dealt with by police and other authorities; it has been delayed indefinitely so as not to prejudice any criminal proceedings.

The Leveson Report itself was 1,987 pages long and contained 92 recommendations, including a proposal for a new, independent, self-regulatory body (to replace the *PCC) with the power to investigate alleged wrongdoing and impose sanctions; the establishment of an arbitration service as a low(er)-cost way of dealing with potential legal actions against the press; and the setting up of a 'whistleblowing hotline' for the use of any journalists who feel they are being asked to do something unethical (*see also* CONSCIENCE CLAUSE). The most controversial recommendation, so far as much of the press was concerned, was that legislation was required to establish a 'recognition body' to monitor the work of the new self-regulator. This suggestion of statute was rejected outright by many in the newspaper industry, some of whom claimed that Leveson wished to return to the days of the *Licensing Act. Publication of the report was followed by several months of on-off talks, mostly conducted in private, between representatives of the main political parties and, at various points, different groups of *Fleet Street newspapers and the campaign group *Hacked Off, leading to proposals in 2013 for a *Royal Charter on the Press and for the *Independent Press Standards Organization. *See also* ETHICAL JOURNALISM; FINKELSTEIN REPORT; LAST CHANCE SALOON; STATUTORY REGULATION.

Further reading: Lord Justice Leveson, *An Inquiry into the Culture, Practices, and Ethics of the Press: Report* (2012).

J. Mair (ed.), *After Leveson? The Future of British Journalism* (2013).

(⊕) SEE WEB LINKS
- Leveson Inquiry website
- The Leveson Report

libel The publication of some statement, allegation, or piece of purported information that is claimed to have the effect of destroying or diminishing somebody's reputation and which can result in the subject suing a news organization and/or individual journalist. Libel refers to defamatory material circulated in written form whereas *slander covers spoken *defamation (apart from that spoken on TV, radio, or online, all of which comes under libel). Journalists have a number of defences against allegations of defamation, including being able to show that the statement complained of is either the *truth or an *honest comment on an issue. The publication of otherwise potentially libellous material might also be protected by *privilege in certain circumstances. The amount of money that an individual might need to take a libel action means it tends to be a recourse more open to the very wealthy than to those of more modest means; the money that a news organization might need to defend a libel action is often said to have a *chilling effect on *investigative journalism. The UK's strict libel laws were reformed in the

*Defamation Act 2013, which added a requirement that a claimant has to show they have suffered serious harm before suing, and introduced a defence of 'responsible publication on matters of public interest'. *See also* LAWS; REYNOLDS DEFENCE.

liberal theory of press freedom The argument that a free market in ideas and information is ushered in by the sweeping away of official *constraints such as the *Licensing Act and *stamp duty, resulting in a *free press that acts as a *fourth estate and plays a crucial, democratic role in monitoring the actions of the powerful on behalf of the people. The theory is expressed most forcefully in opposition to any suggestion that journalism ought to be more strictly regulated. This notion of commercial publishers leading a long and heroic march to press freedom is dismissed by many critics, including *Marxist scholars, as a simplistic reading of history that ignores contradictory tendencies within journalism and downplays the ideological role played by much *mainstream media. *Compare* HEGEMONY; POLITICAL ECONOMY. *See also* DEMOCRACY; PUBLIC SPHERE; WATCHDOG ROLE.

Libération A left-leaning national daily newspaper published in France since 1973 (when its founders included the philosopher and activist Jean-Paul Sartre). *Libération* had an *underground press forerunner, with the same name, during the years of Nazi-occupation.

Liberation News Service (LNS) An alternative *news agency that provided stories, pictures, and graphics to the US *underground press, student newspapers, community publications, and other forms of *alternative media, between 1967 and 1981. At its height in the late 1960s and early 1970s LNS supplied material to several hundred publications. Its output prioritized issues that tended to be marginalized or ridiculed in mainstream media, including the anti-war movement, feminism, homosexuality, environmentalism, and the use of psychedelic drugs. *See also* PEOPLE'S NEWS SERVICE; UNDERGROUND PRESS SYNDICATE.

(()) SEE WEB LINKS
• LNS archive

library A news organization's collection of *cuttings, *photographs, reference books, telephone directories, and maps, all of which are being replaced by digital storage and/or online resources. *See also* ARCHIVE.

library footage Television pictures from an *archive or from an earlier story that are used to illustrate a new story and which will typically be labelled as such so as not to mislead viewers.

licence fee The system by which the owners of television sets in the UK must pay an annual fee that goes to fund the *BBC as an independent entity. The licence fee is a mechanism to provide public funding for the main *public service broadcaster without drawing on direct taxation or coming under the direct control of the government of the day. However, politicians' power to set the level of the fee every few years may place limits on the BBC's independence. The existence of the licence fee is frequently attacked by the BBC's commercial rivals, especially within the *Murdoch empire, as an anti-competitive state subsidy.

Licensing Act A piece of 1662 legislation that strictly controlled *printing and publishing in what was to become the UK. Its lapse in 1695 marked the end of pre-publication *censorship and led to a rapid growth in local, regional, and national publications of all sorts. The lapsing of the Licensing Act is often harked back to in contemporary debates about the relative merits of a *free press and *statutory regulation of the media. *See also* LAWS; BERROW'S WORCESTER JOURNAL; DAILY COURANT; NORWICH POST; STAMFORD MERCURY.

(())) SEE WEB LINKS
• *History Today* on the Licensing Act

licensing of journalists A system under which people need official permission to practise journalism, as is the case in some repressive regimes around the world that do not enjoy a *free press. Journalists have traditionally opposed any form of licensing, arguing that a journalist is merely a *citizen with a notebook (and/or microphone, camera, phone, or laptop) and as such requires no special permission. Furthermore, if the state has the power to grant a licence to practise, it necessarily has the power to refuse or withdraw such a licence—and to punish any unlicensed person who commits an act of journalism. *See also* CENSORSHIP; PROFESSION; TRADE.

Life A US magazine specializing in *photojournalism that was published as a weekly between 1936 and 1972 and then monthly from 1978 to 2000. Among the numerous *photographers whose work was published in *Life* were Henri Cartier-Bresson, Robert Capa, and Lisa Larsen.

(⊕) SEE WEB LINKS
• *Life* photographers

lifestyle journalism A somewhat vague term covering *soft news and *features about topics such as cookery, fashion, travel, sex, and shopping. There is a tendency for much of it to be rather uncritical and advertiser-friendly, but that is not inevitable. The term 'lifestyle journalism' only seems to have emerged in recent decades and, although it is not a new concept (*see* LADIES' MERCURY, for example), it now appears to have greater prominence than ever, leading to accusations of *dumbing down.

link 1. A graphic or piece of text on a *website, clicking on which will open up additional material or take *users to other sites (*see* HYPERLINK). A link may stand alone and be labelled as such or may be embedded within a story, for example via a word in the text appearing in a different coloured font.
2. A sentence or two spoken by a presenter in *broadcast journalism to make a connection between two items.

LinkedIn A *social networking site aimed at professionals and wannabe-professionals that, along with *Facebook and *Google, has become one of the standard ways in which today's journalists can speedily track down people and find potential *sources without having to leave the office. Many journalists and media organizations also use LinkedIn to help promote themselves as *brands.

linking The practice within *online journalism of providing *hyperlinks to provide *users with access to further material. Some news organizations are reluctant to link to external sites, especially those of rival media (*see* STICKINESS), some are happy to link to virtually everything, and others are somewhere between. Many journalists, *bloggers, and scholars see linking as a vital component of *attribution, transparency, and *ethical journalism; they make a virtue of extensive linking to original source material as well as to other media and blogs, and will take great care to ensure that links work or will mend any 'broken' links. *See also* INTERACTIVITY; SOCIAL BOOKMARKING.

listeners The *audience for *radio journalism, *podcasts, and online *audio. *See also* IMAGINED AUDIENCE; PHONE-IN; RATINGS; USER-GENERATED CONTENT.

literal A typing error (*typo) or wrong choice of word in a piece of writing.

literary journalism A blend of journalistic *reporting with narrative forms of storytelling that are more commonly associated with fiction writing. It may range from a brief *colour piece to extensive *long-form journalism, including that published in book form such as *In Cold Blood* by Truman Capote (1924–84). Literary journalism may be produced by journalists adopting a more 'writerly' style than that allowed by the classic *inverted pyramid model of news, by novelists and other creators of fiction trying their hand at non-fiction, and by people who manage to slip back and forth between both genres. *See also* GONZO JOURNALISM; NEW JOURNALISM.

Further reading: R. Keeble and J. Tulloch (eds), *Global Literary Journalism* (2012).

Little Jimmy The name that became attached to a third-generation heroin addict who was just eight years old and the subject of a 1980 story that won a *Pulitzer Prize for a *Washington Post* reporter before it was revealed that Jimmy did not exist. The heartrending story of *Jimmy's World* caused huge public and political reaction but did not survive scrutiny as people began looking for the boy. Journalist Janet Cooke (1954–) resigned after admitting that Jimmy had been a fictitious composite character. The prize was handed back and in a 13,000-word account of the affair published in the paper itself, *Washington Post* *ombudsman Bill Green concluded: 'It was a complete systems failure, and there's no excuse for it'. Cooke left journalism, with her notorious story destined to be used in *ethics classes at US journalism schools for decades to come; however, the lesson of what happened to her failed to prevent subsequent *fakery scandals involving Jayson Blair at the *New York Times* and Stephen Glass at the *New Republic*. *See also* TOO GOOD TO CHECK.

 SEE WEB LINKS
• The original story

live Reporting in real time on radio, television, or online. *Compare* PACKAGE.

liveblog A form of *blog that is rapidly updated in real time for a certain period, typically to cover a particular event such as a major conference, a demonstration, a fashion show, or a football match. Liveblogs may have a stand-alone presence on the web or may be part of how major news organizations choose to expand their coverage and provide their online audience with added value. Displaying the most recent material first (although some liveblogs allow *users to reverse the chronological order of display), a liveblog will typically involve elements of commentary and *reporting, the introduction and contextualization of content from a variety of media and other sources, aggregating and linking to other coverage, the use of audio and video material as well as pictures, and bringing into the *conversation public reaction and comments, often drawn from *Twitter and *Facebook. *See also* CURATION; INTERACTIVITY; LINKING; STORIFY.

Liverpool Post The former *Daily Post* morning newspaper that covered the UK city of Liverpool from 1855 and which switched to weekly publication in 2012 as owner *Trinity Mirror responded to declining *circulation by cutting costs. It closed in December 2013 but its sister newspaper the *Liverpool Echo* continues to be published daily.

Loaded A monthly *lads' mag that helped define the genre. Published in the UK since 1994, it was at one point selling hundreds of thousands of copies to 'men who should know better', as its strapline put it. Once part of *IPC, *Loaded* and its digital *brand were sold in 2010, since when it has changed hands several times and *circulation has continued to decline. *See also* PORNIFICATION; SEXISM.

lobby 1. The members' area in the UK's House of Commons where, since public access was restricted in 1870, accredited journalists have been allowed in to talk to MPs, often on an *off-the-record basis.
2. The collective term for *lobby correspondents who cover politics at Westminster more by mingling with politicians and attending *lobby briefings given by official *spin doctors than by engaging in *gallery reporting on Parliamentary debates. The lobby was traditionally a secretive and rather exclusive 'club' that was boycotted for a period

in the 1980s by the *Independent, *Guardian*, and *Scotsman* newspapers; the system began to open up in the 1990s.

SEE WEB LINKS
• The Parliamentary lobby website

lobby briefing A regular event at both Westminster and Downing Street during which *lobby correspondents are able to question the *spin doctors of senior UK government politicians. Such briefings were traditionally conducted on an unattributable basis, but the UK government under Prime Minister John Major liberalized the system in the 1990s, agreeing that information could be attributed to 'Downing Street sources'. The Tony Blair government followed this by allowing briefings to be attributed to 'the prime minister's official spokesman' and then, in 2002, opening them up to specialist and overseas journalists in addition to members of the *lobby. Summaries of Downing Street briefings are now published on the government's official website.

lobby correspondent A journalist who, having been nominated by their news organization, is authorized by Parliamentary authorities to report from within the UK Parliament in London. *See also* LOBBY; LOBBY BRIEFING.

SEE WEB LINKS
• Accredited lobby correspondents

localization A media strategy based on emphasizing the benefits of the local as opposed to the regional, national, or global. This can be seen most clearly in forms of *hyperlocal journalism. *See also* LOCAL JOURNALISM; TINDLE NEWSPAPERS.

local journalism News and other journalistic output that covers events taking place in a relatively small geographical area such as a city, a town, a borough, or several villages, the *audience for which comprises mostly people living and/or working within the locality. Traditionally the local press would be owned locally, often by family firms, but by the last quarter of the 20th century a genuinely locally owned newspaper was becoming the exception rather than the norm in the UK and the USA. Increasing *concentration of ownership led to mergers, closures, economies of scale, and increasingly homogenized editorial *content. Further cutbacks within the commercial local media in the 21st century prompted fears of a *democratic deficit resulting from a decline in critical scrutiny of local authorities and institutions. However, some commentators claim that this gap may be filled to some extent by a mixture of local *bloggers and so-called 'citizen journalists'. *See also* BERROW'S WORCESTER JOURNAL; HYPERLOCAL JOURNALISM; NEWSPAPER SOCIETY; NORWICH POST; STAMFORD MERCURY.

Local World A regional newspaper and digital publisher formed in the UK from a 2012 merger of *Northcliffe Media and *Iliffe News & Media. Its more than 100 titles include the *Cambridge News*, the *Leicester Mercury*, and the *Hull Daily Mail*, and the group's total weekly *circulation of around 5 million copies place it third in the table of the UK's provincial newspaper publishers. In 2013 Local World announced plans to save money by closing some newspaper offices and replacing them with 'drop-in zones'. *See also* CONCENTRATION OF OWNERSHIP; HARVESTING CONTENT; LOCAL JOURNALISM.

long-form journalism Journalism that has been freed from conventional industry constraints of length, space, and/or time, typically drawing on some or all of the elements of *gonzo journalism, *investigative journalism, *literary journalism, and *new journalism.

Los Angeles Times (LA Times) A major daily newspaper covering the Californian city of Los Angeles and one of the top ten dailies in the USA for *circulation. First published in 1881 under the name of the *Los Angeles Daily Times*, it dropped the 'daily' from its title five years later. Since 2000 it has been owned by the Tribune company of Chicago.

McCarthyism A vociferous campaign in the early 1950s led by US Senator Joseph McCarthy (1908–57) against radicals and alleged communists in government, newspapers, the film industry, the military, and anywhere else he thought he could identify them. Many of those accused by McCarthy's House of Un-American Activities were 'blacklisted' and effectively prevented from working. At the height of the witch-hunt, *CBS journalist Ed Murrow (1908–65) famously used his *See It Now* *current affairs television programme to expose what he saw as the climate of fear and bullying that McCarthyism had spread through the USA during the Cold War; the arguments surrounding the broadcast were later the subject of the film *Good Night, and Good Luck* (dir. George Clooney, 2005). *See also* ANTI-COMMUNISM; CHILLING EFFECT; FLAK; I. F. STONE'S WEEKLY; LAS VEGAS SUN.

(⊕) SEE WEB LINKS

• Ed Murrow exposes McCarthyism: video
• Ed Murrow exposes McCarthyism: transcript

McClatchy Company One of the biggest newspaper companies in the USA, which began in California in 1857. Today it owns 30 daily newspapers plus their digital offshoots, having bought the Knight Ridder stable in 2006. Its titles include the *Kansas City Star*, the *Miami Herald*, and the *Sacramento Bee*.

McJournalism Fast and predictable journalism churned out by sections of the *mainstream media to drive down costs and boost profits (or to minimize losses), according to this analogy with the fast-food chain McDonald's (*compare* SLOW JOURNALISM). Journalism studies scholar Bob Franklin argues that McJournalism results from an increasingly corporate media *ownership structure that standardizes production and reduces investment in in-depth *reporting, *investigative journalism, *long-form journalism, *gallery reporting, *foreign news, and other forms of unpredictable and/or time-consuming journalistic activities. Critics of the thesis tend to counter that those who accuse contemporary journalism of having become more homogenous and formulaic are merely harking back to some non-existent *'golden age'. *See also* CHURNALISM; NEWSZAK.

Further reading: B. Franklin, 'McJournalism: The Local Press and the McDonaldization Thesis', in S. Allan (ed.), *Journalism: Critical Issues* (2005).

McLurg's Law A grim, semi-humorous, and possibly apocryphal way of ranking the *newsworthiness of (especially tragic) events according to the nationality and/or location of those involved, as in the UK newsroom that was said to operate on the basis of 'one European is worth 28 Chinese, or perhaps two Welsh miners worth one thousand Pakistanis'. Apparently named after a *news editor, McLurg's Law combines something of the gallows humour of a typical newsroom with what are perceived to be wider societal attitudes, leading to accusations of *racism, xenophobia, and national chauvinism. *See also* CULTURAL BIAS; MAGNITUDE; MEANINGFULNESS.

McSweeney's A quarterly journal published in the USA since 1998 that specializes in *literary journalism and *long-form journalism, among other things. The full title of the journal is *Timothy McSweeney's Quarterly Concern*. Based in San Francisco, McSweeney's is also a publishing house and has a website called *Internet Tendency*.

magazine A regular printed publication that tends to have more pages and a smaller page size than a *newspaper and which is typically published weekly, monthly, every two months, or quarterly. Magazines encompass a vast range of styles, genres, subject matter, and target markets, but they are typically more *feature-driven than *news-oriented and they often encourage readers to identify with the magazine *brand, for example by joining clubs, attending events, or conversing on *social media. Magazines may be paid for or free and usually rely to a large extent on selling *advertisements to a targeted *audience. New magazines emerge frequently and almost as frequently die, and the sector tends to be dominated by big players such as *Bauer Media, *Condé Nast, and *Time Warner. In common with other print products, magazines are seen by some commentators as a form of '*legacy media' that will eventually disappear, but the industry has not (yet?) suffered the same catastrophic decline in circulation that has hit newspapers in the USA and UK. Many magazines sell mostly to subscribers and recent years have seen the launch of subscriptions for digital replica editions of magazines that can be delivered via *tablets and other mobile devices, and there has been some experimentation with online *paywalls as publishers respond to the disruptions and opportunities of the digital age. *See also* ASSOCIATION OF MAGAZINE MEDIA; B2B; BRANDING; COLOUR SUPPLEMENT; CONSUMER MAGAZINE; COVERMOUNT; CUSTOMER MAGAZINE; FREEMIUM; GLOSSIES; INTERNATIONAL FEDERATION OF THE PERIODICAL PRESS; LADS' MAGS; PROFESSIONAL PUBLISHERS ASSOCIATION; SPECIAL-INTEREST MAGAZINE; TEENAGE MAGAZINE ARBITRATION PANEL; TRADE MAGAZINES; WOMEN'S MAGAZINES.

Further reading: T. Holmes and L. Nice, *Magazine Journalism* (2012). J. McKay, *The Magazines Handbook* (2013).

magnitude Refers to the size of some event, development, or *row that is deemed to be big enough to be regarded as a possible news story. Magnitude is one of the *news values that journalists use when considering the potential *newsworthiness of an event, and it might be measured in terms of the numbers of people involved (in a road traffic accident, for example), the size of a natural or human-made phenomenon (anything from an earthquake to the world's biggest pizza), or in potential impact (such as an announcement by a member of the *power elite). Magnitude is relative and will typically be assessed in relation to other news values as well as the perceived interests of a news organization's *audience (*see* MCLURG'S LAW). *See also* THRESHOLD.

Mail *See* DAILY MAIL; MAIL ON SUNDAY; MAIL ONLINE.

Mail Online The phenomenally popular website of the *Daily Mail* and *Mail on Sunday*. The *Mail Online* has become famous for its never-ending stream of picture-led items about *celebrities displaying their 'bikini bodies' and suffering 'wardrobe malfunctions', or teenage starlets looking 'all grown up' (*see* SIDEBAR OF SHAME). In 2012 it became the most visited English-language newspaper website in the world, with more than 100 million unique browsers per month, many of them directed to the site by *search engines and *links circulated via *social media; a year later that number topped 120 million, and *Mail Online* had around 8 million users per day. *See also* ENTERTAINMENT; ONLINE JOURNALISM; SEXISM.

Mail on Sunday A UK national *mid-market Sunday newspaper that is the sister title to the *Daily Mail*. The *Mail on Sunday* was only launched in 1982 but by the turn of the century it was the second highest-selling Sunday title, trailing only the market leader, the *News of the World* (later the *Sun on Sunday*). In 2013 it was selling an average of around 1.6 million copies each week.

mainstream journalism Any form of journalistic output produced or published by a hierarchically structured commercial media outlet, or by a major publicly funded media organization (*see* BBC; MAINSTREAM MEDIA), and which conforms to the established norms, customs, and practices of the industry. Mainstream journalism is variously said to function as society's *watchdog, a facilitator of *democracy, a nurturer of the *public sphere, an inculcator of ruling-class *ideology, and a means of *manufacturing consent. *Compare* ALTERNATIVE JOURNALISM. *See also* JOURNALISM; JOURNALISM STUDIES.

mainstream media 1. A broad term covering any form of *media produced or distributed commercially, as part of a profit-seeking industrial enterprise, or as a publicly and/or state-funded operation. *Compare* ALTERNATIVE MEDIA. *See also* MAINSTREAM JOURNALISM. **2.** A term sometimes used by *bloggers and *digital natives to refer to *newspapers and other forms of so-called '*legacy media'. In this context, mainstream media is occasionally abbreviated to '**MSM**'.

man bites dog The classic example of what makes *news, according to the journalist's adage: 'Dog bites man isn't news. Man bites dog is.' The saying underlines the importance of novelty and *surprise in the *selection of news stories but obscures the way in which dog bite stories can themselves be rendered newsworthy by other factors, such as the identity or age of the victim. *See also* NEWS VALUES.

Manchester Evening News A daily newspaper covering the Greater Manchester region of the UK and generally regarded as one of the leading titles in the country's provincial press. For much of its existence since its launch in 1868, the *Manchester Evening News* (*MEN*) shared offices and ownership with the *Manchester Guardian* (*see* SCOTT TRUST), but in 2010 it and a related stable of local weekly newspapers were sold to *Trinity Mirror for a reported £44 million.

Manchester Guardian *See* GUARDIAN.

manipulation of images The alteration of *photographs, which might once have been carried out with chemicals in a darkroom, or with scissors and paste in a newsroom, but which today is more likely to be done on a computer screen. Ethically, there can be a very fine line between acceptable and unacceptable manipulation and, although it is widely practised in glossy magazines to make cover models look 'better', it is frowned upon by many journalists. *See also* DIGITAL MANIPULATION; DODGING; ETHICAL JOURNALISM; TRUTH.

manufacture of consent The primary function of commercial mass *media within capitalism, and specifically in the USA, according to the *propaganda model of Edward Herman and Noam Chomsky. In the book *Manufacturing Consent* (1995[1988]), they argued that whatever the motivations or intentions of individual journalists, the *routines and practices of the bulk of the *mainstream media have the effect of propagating and amplifying the world view of the most wealthy and powerful within society, while at the same time ignoring or ridiculing any alternative voices that ask fundamental questions about the social order. *See also* CRITICAL THEORY; HEGEMONY.

Further reading: E. Herman and N. Chomsky, *Manufacturing Consent* (1995[1988]).

(((⊕))) SEE WEB LINKS

• Chomsky on *Manufacturing Consent*

manufacture of news The process by which events in the 'real world' become items of *news produced by journalists and news organizations. 'Manufacture' in this sense does not mean that the news is invented; rather, that producing news is a form of industrial process involving identification of potential *newsworthiness, *selection according to notions of *news values, and presentation in a way that conforms to a certain *style. In this sense, some events become *shaped* into news items while others are ignored. The ways in which such events are shaped, and which events are selected in the first place, are all influenced by journalists' awareness of how previous events have been turned into news, leading to degrees of circularity, similarity, and predictability in both subject matter and style. This process of the manufacture of news has led some scholars to argue that the news is a highly selective and hugely unreliable account of what actually takes place in the world on any given day. *See also* CONSTRUCTION OF NEWS; FRAMING.

Marie Claire A glossy *women's magazine launched in France in 1937 that has grown to become a major international *brand, under the slogan, 'Think smart, look amazing'. Editions of *Marie Claire* magazine and its extensive digital offshoots are published in more than 30 countries including the UK (where it is one of the *IPC stable), the USA (under the *Hearst Corporation banner), and in India (where it forms part of the Outlook Group). *See also* GLOSSIES.

market-driven news Journalism that is selected and tailored primarily to appeal to a particular section of the population or demographic, rather than because of considerations about inherent *newsworthiness, the *public interest, or informing the *public sphere. *See also* POLITICAL ECONOMY.

Marxism A political philosophy and mode of analysis, based on the writings of Karl Marx (1818–83) and Friedrich Engels (1820–95), which argues that the ruling ideas or dominant *ideology in a society are essentially those that serve the interests of the dominant or ruling *class. Marxist activists and commentators tend to point to the *mainstream media as one of the key ways in which such ideas are propagated and become accepted as a form of *common sense even by sections of the population whose 'real' interests might be quite different. However, early thoughts that this might be a relatively straightforward process (*see* FRANKFURT SCHOOL; HYPODERMIC MODEL) have long been rejected by most Marxist (and other) scholars who now tend to talk of *hegemony being a contested and unstable terrain. Although Marxism is not as influential as it once was, Marxists and neo-Marxists retain a significant albeit diverse presence within *journalism studies and *media studies, where they tend to emphasize issues of ideology and *political economy as opposed to the *liberal theory of press freedom. Beyond academe, some forms of *alternative media and the *radical press are also influenced by an essentially Marxist critique of society; they produce forms of counter-hegemonic journalism or *oppositional reporting to challenge, in practice, what they see as the *bias of the bulk of *mainstream journalism. *See also* CRITICAL THEORY; LENINIST THEORY OF THE PRESS; PROPAGANDA MODEL.

(((•))) SEE WEB LINKS
• 'Marxist Media Theory' by Daniel Chandler

Mashable A technology *blog launched in 2005 that is now a popular and influential site noted in particular for its news and views on developments in *social media. It is based in New York.

mashup A combination of two or more pieces of online content. Mashups have become common on *websites and *blogs, where *pictures or *audio may be mashed together to create an amusing item. However, the format is not restricted to *entertainment. More serious, journalistic use of mashups includes combining material such as the raw data on criminal offences with Google Maps and photographs of victims, to provide web *users with more detailed *information than could be contained in a text-only article or table (*see* INFOGRAPHICS).

(⊕) SEE WEB LINKS
• 'The Mashup Man'

masthead The name of a *newspaper in large print on its front page, normally incorporating an individual font or other form of graphic design to give instant recognition to the *brand, and typically remaining unchanged for many years. The top of a website homepage is also sometimes called a masthead, as is the display of the publication's name and logo above the *leader column.

MEAA *See* MEDIA ENTERTAINMENT AND ARTS ALLIANCE.

meaningfulness The perceived *relevance (or otherwise) of a potentially *newsworthy event to the interests or expectations of the *audience. Meaningfulness was one of the *news values identified by Galtung and Ruge in their seminal 1960s study of why certain events are selected to become *news. They found that the culturally familiar is most likely to be selected because it fits the frame of reference held by journalists within a news organization. The involvement of a UK citizen might make an otherwise obscure overseas event of interest to a UK audience, for example; and the UK media are more likely to run stories about the USA than about countries with which the UK audience is less culturally familiar. *See also* CULTURAL BIAS; McLURG'S LAW.

media The plural of medium (often misused as if it were singular) that encompasses journalism as part of a much broader field of public communication organizations, including *newspapers, *magazines, radio stations, TV channels, the film industry, the music industry, *websites, *advertising, and *public relations. The term may be qualified, as in *mainstream media, *alternative media, or *black media, and the most popular forms are sometimes referred to as the 'mass media'. *Compare* PRESS. *See also* MEDIUM; MULTIMEDIA; SOCIAL MEDIA.

media agenda A news organization's *selection of certain news stories, or presentation of them in a certain way, not so much because of any intrinsic qualities of *newsworthiness, but because they meet the interests of the news organization and/or its *proprietor. This might be an agenda designed to promote particular commercial or political goals, such as the frequent stories in some *Fleet Street newspapers that appear to attack the *BBC and/or to paint one political party, leader, or faction in a more positive light than others (*see* BIAS). A media agenda might also be used as part of a *branding exercise to engender a sense of *audience loyalty (*see* IMAGINED COMMUNITY), such as the *Sun*'s portrayal of itself at times of armed conflict as 'the paper that supports our boys', or the *Independent*'s launch slogan, 'It is, are you?'. *See also* AGENDA-SETTING; CAMPAIGN; CROSS PROMOTION; NEWS VALUES.

media effects The idea that exposure to *media can influence the attitudes and behaviour of individuals, groups, institutions, and even entire societies. Whether such influence exists, and if so to what extent, has long been an area of concern and contestation among media scholars. News organizations themselves sometimes claim a direct causal link between media output and people's actions, for example when the press accuses particular television programmes of encouraging teenage pregnancies or when gun crime is blamed on a certain musical genre (*see* MORAL PANIC). Early theories of the mass media, such as the *hypodermic model, now tend to be rejected in favour of more complex explanations emphasizing that potential influences or *effects can move in more than one direction and that audiences do not necessarily uncritically receive whatever message is intended by the sender. *See also* ACTIVE AUDIENCE; AGENDA-SETTING; ENCODING, DECODING; PROPAGANDA.

Media Entertainment and Arts Alliance (MEAA) The trade union that organizes workers in the Australian media, sport, and cultural industries. Formed in 1992 through a merger of the *Australian Journalists' Association with unions covering actors and others working in entertainment, it has more than 20,000 members. The media section of the alliance has a code of *ethics for journalists and will consider public complaints against members accused of breaking the code.

🌐 SEE WEB LINKS
• MEAA code of ethics

MediaLens A UK-based media watchdog group and website set up in 2001 to monitor corporate and *mainstream journalism from a perspective informed by the *propaganda model. MediaLens publishes alerts and detailed critiques of what it sees as distorted or inaccurate coverage of major issues, especially in influential 'liberal' media such as the *Guardian, *Independent, *BBC, and *Channel 4 News. Some journalists object to MediaLens' politics and/or to what they feel is a hectoring approach, but veteran journalist John Pilger has hailed the organization as 'cyber guardians of honest journalism'.

🌐 SEE WEB LINKS
• MediaLens' frequently asked questions

media mogul The *proprietor or chairman of one or more major commercial *media outlets. The term is a more contemporary version of *press baron, and both labels imply a level of power and influence that extends far beyond the particular companies that they head. *See also* MEDIA AGENDA; MURDOCH EMPIRE; OWNERSHIP.

media scrum More than a handful of journalists turning up to *doorstep somebody or to seek comment and/or *pictures when somebody in the news emerges from a meeting, court case, or similar event. Media scrums are often an unedifying spectacle involving pushing, shoving, and shouting; in the USA such a scrum is sometimes referred to as a **goatfuck**. On rare occasions a group of journalists might disperse, for example if requested by bereaved relatives; news organizations covering the aftermath of the massacre of schoolchildren in the Scottish town of Dunblane in 1996 were widely praised for holding back and allowing funerals to take place with a degree of *privacy. *See also* HARASSMENT; PACK MENTALITY.

Media Standards Trust A UK charity formed in 2006 to research and campaign for *ethical journalism and greater transparency and responsibility within the news media. It has been very critical of the *Press Complaints Commission and helped establish the campaign group *Hacked Off. The trust's other initiatives include building a searchable database of journalists' contact details and bylined articles (*journalisted.com*) and launching a website that can be used to compare news stories with the *press releases from which many originate (*churnalism.com*).

media studies Academic study of and research into the *media as institutions, industries, and forms of cultural practice. Although the role of the media absorbed some scholars for decades previously (*see* FRANKFURT SCHOOL), media studies only fully emerged as a distinct area of study in the 1970s, since when it has been widely derided by many journalists as well as academics from rival disciplines as a 'Mickey Mouse' subject. Media studies scholars tend to respond that media organizations are far too important in contemporary society to be left unexamined by academe, and that all citizens might benefit from a critical media literacy that could equip them to become a more *active audience or even producers of their own media output. Media studies is concerned with a far wider range of activities than just *journalism, from graffiti to experimental film via tattoos, drag, and even 'celebrity studies'; the more narrowly focused field of *journalism studies has since emerged in its own right, although there is some crossover. *See also* CRITICAL THEORY; GLASGOW MEDIA GROUP; MARXISM; MEDIATIZATION.

media tart An interviewee, contributor, or even a journalist who appears to be ubiquitous across news outlets. *See also* RENT-A-QUOTE.

mediatization The increasing centrality of the *media in society, as seen, for example, in the stress that political parties place on how a candidate might look on television, and in a perceived blurring between *public relations and government policy (*see* HUTTON REPORT; SPIN). It might also be seen in the increasing tendency for the media, including *social media, to be the subject of news coverage (and of other media attention such as films). *See also* MEDIA STUDIES.

MediaWise A UK-based charity formed in 1993 (originally as PressWise) to raise awareness of *ethics within the media industries in general and journalism in particular. Its activities have included producing research, reporting guidelines, and training materials on issues such as media coverage of children, refugees, health, and suicide. MediaWise also supports members of the public who believe themselves to be victims of 'inaccurate, intrusive, unfair, or irresponsible journalism'.

(((()))) SEE WEB LINKS

• MediaWise: 'Complaining about the media'

medium The singular of *media that is used to refer to the specific type of *platform, such as a *newspaper or a *website.

meme An idea, phenomenon, mode of expression, or way of thinking about something, that is transmitted, copied, and self-replicated by various means of human *communication including journalism and other media output. Memes may be identified by *journalism studies and *media studies scholars who are concerned with exploring ways in which certain ideas and explanations can suddenly gain common currency within society. *See also* COMMON SENSE; MORAL PANIC; TROPE.

methodology 1. The methods used and steps taken to produce a particular form of journalism. For example, the methodology of an *investigative journalist might include searching official records and databases, cross-referencing with other *sources, cultivating and protecting an *anonymous source, and using *freedom of information laws (*see* VERIFICATION). *See also* STRATEGIC RITUAL.
2. The methods and steps taken in a piece of scholarly research into journalism. Research methods are typically divided into quantitative methods (such as *content analysis) and qualitative methods (such as *focus groups). One form of methodology can be used to inform another; for example, the findings of a content analysis or a newsroom observation may be fed into the deliberations of a focus group or the questions asked in research interviews. *See also* JOURNALISM STUDIES.

Metro 1. The title of a series of *free newspapers published daily in more than twenty countries around the world by Metro International, which launched the first *Metro* in the Swedish city of Stockholm in 1995. It pioneered the concept of a free morning newspaper distributed by hand at major transport locations such as railway stations, giving it a readership that is attractive to many *advertisers (described by Metro International as 'a young, active, well-educated metropolitan audience of over 18.5 million daily readers in over 150 major cities in 23 countries across four continents').
2. A daily free distribution newspaper, inspired by the Swedish *Metro* concept, launched by *Associated Newspapers in 1999 and now

available in 50 cities across the UK, where the Metro International title is not available. *Metro* specializes in bite-sized stories aimed at commuters and produces little original *reporting of its own. It is also published online and is available on mobile devices. The jury is out on whether its existence hits the sales of paid-for titles or whether it encourages more people to develop a newspaper habit.

mf An abbreviated term meaning 'more follows', traditionally placed at the bottom of every page of *copy with the exception of the final page, which will be labelled 'ends'. Such messages are intended for internal consumption within the production process and do not appear in the published version (except by mistake).

Miami Herald A US daily newspaper covering Miami, in Florida, and also circulating in parts of Latin America. First published in 1903, it and its website have been owned by the *McClatchy Company since 2006.

microblogging A form of *blogging that uses *social media tools such as *Twitter and *Sina Weibo to deliver short messages to anyone who chooses to follow the microblogger. Many journalists use microblogging variously to break stories, to promote their work via *links, to seek *sources, to request information, to engage with an *audience, and/or to build a personal *brand.

Midland News Association A family-owned newspaper publishing company based in Wolverhampton in the UK, the flagship titles of which are the Wolverhampton *Express & Star* and the *Shropshire Star*. In 2013 the Midland News Association was ranked the ninth-biggest provincial press group in the UK, with its sixteen titles achieving an average weekly *circulation of around 1.3 million between them. *See also* GUITON GROUP.

mid-market That segment of the UK national newspaper market positioned between the popular *redtop end and the *quality or *broadsheet titles. The mid-market is firmly *Express* and *Mail* territory; although the former was dominant for much of the 20th century, the latter is the big beast of *Fleet Street in the 21st century. *See also* TODAY.

Milwaukee Journal Sentinel The major daily newspaper and associated website covering Milwaukee in the US state of Wisconsin since 1995, the result of a merger between two separate papers that both dated from the 19th century. The *Sentinel* was once part of the *Hearst Corporation but in the 1960s it was acquired by the locally based

Journal Communications, which published both titles until they were merged. Journal Communications still publishes the *Milwaukee Journal Sentinel* and also owns the Journal Broadcast Group, which operates TV and radio stations in twelve states.

Minneapolis Star Tribune A daily newspaper and website covering Minneapolis, in the US state of Minnesota. The result of a series of mergers between three separate titles that began life in the 19th century (the *Tribune*, the *Star*, and the *Journal*), since 2009 it has been owned by the Star Tribune Media Company, which was formed by banks and other financial institutions after the paper went bankrupt. It is one of the top 25 best-selling newspapers in the USA.

Mirror *See* DAILY MIRROR; SUNDAY MIRROR.

mobile application *See* APP.

mobile phone As essential a tool for the 21st century *reporter as the pen and the notebook were for earlier generations, as it can be used to speak to *sources, to record *interviews, to take and send *pictures, to record *video, to *tweet, to file *copy, to consult maps and other online material, and so much more. The development of the mobile phone and other mobile devices means that reporters in the *field are now rarely out of reach of their *desk, which can be irksome as well as useful. In addition to their importance for those journalists out gathering news, mobiles are also increasingly the way in which audiences choose to receive news and entertainment. *See also* PHONE-HACKING; TABLET; TELEPHONE.

MoC *See* MOTHER OF CHAPEL.

mode of address The voice or tone in which a website, magazine, or other journalistic outlet speaks to its *audience. The mode of address might be formal or informal, it might assume shared knowledge or attitudes between journalist and audience, and it might be intended to generate a sense of *brand identity. *See also* IMAGINED AUDIENCE; LANGUAGE OF NEWS; MONOGLOTTISM; POLYGLOTTISM; STYLE.

moderation The process of controlling or policing readers' comments online, whether in below-the-line *threads beneath stories or in separate discussion forums or chatrooms. Moderation is typically light touch when compared with the care traditionally taken before readers' *letters would be selected for publication in a newspaper or magazine. This is partly because of the sheer number of comments received and partly because there tends to be an expectation among website *users that contributions will appear online virtually instantly. As *online journalism has grown, a norm has developed whereby most online news organizations opt for *post-moderation, meaning that a post will normally be scrutinized only if another user flags it up as offensive or objectionable. However, some sites prefer the slower and more labour-intensive option of *pre-moderation, when everything is vetted before it appears online. A site that usually uses post-moderation might switch to pre-moderation for particularly sensitive stories: after the death of former UK Prime Minister Margaret Thatcher in 2013, moderators at the *Telegraph* website eventually turned off the comments facility on all items that mentioned her, because of the offensive nature of so many posts. *See also* CURATION; TROLLING; YOUR COMMENTS.

Modern Review A culture magazine published in the UK between 1991 and 1995 that is often said to have been more talked about than read (or purchased). Created by journalists Julie Burchill and Toby Young, among others, *Modern Review* adopted the strapline, 'Low culture for highbrows'. The magazine is remembered today as much for a succession of feuds and fallings-out as it is for its content.

monoglottism Speaking with one voice, in just one language, as opposed to allowing a multiplicity of voices. Magazines and other outlets are said to do this if they impose a strict *house style on their journalists. *Compare* POLYGLOTTISM. *See also* MODE OF ADDRESS.

Monthly Review An independent radical US magazine published in New York since 1949, the first issue of which included a controversial article by the scientist Albert Einstein (1879–1955), entitled 'Why socialism?'. Despite being targeted by *McCarthyism in the 1950s, the magazine survives, in its own words, to 'frame the issues of the day with one set of interests foremost in mind: those of the great majority of humankind, the propertyless'. *See also* ALTERNATIVE MEDIA; RADICAL PRESS.

moral panic A sociological term that has now become common parlance for an exaggerated sense of public and/or media fear over a particular social phenomenon, form of behaviour, or section of the population. A moral panic may be shortlived but while it lasts it may seem to sweep across many sections of society and dominate the *headlines for a period until gradually fading away, sometimes to return later and sometimes to vanish forever. Examples in the UK are said to include widespread public concern at one time or another over juvenile delinquents, Teddy boys, mods and rockers, football hooligans, punks, ravers, muggers, teenage mothers, single mothers, gay parents, immigrants, yardies, asylum seekers, absentee fathers, dangerous dogs, people with AIDs, people receiving welfare benefits, and paedophiles. Those targeted by such moral panics are referred to by scholars as playing the role of *folk devils and they are invariably seen by much *mainstream media as 'other'; that is, not normally part of a news organization's *imagined community. Scholars find it hard to determine whether moral panics originate with media coverage and are picked up by the *audience or vice versa (*see* MEDIA EFFECTS). *See also* AGENDA-SETTING; AMPLIFICATION; MEME; NAME AND SHAME; PACK MENTALITY; STEREOTYPING.

morgue *See* CUTTINGS LIBRARY.

Morning Star A UK daily newspaper that changed its name from the *Daily Worker* in 1966. Still associated with what remains of the Communist Party, the paper is today more broadly left-wing rather than acting as a strict party mouthpiece; it specializes in coverage of industrial and trade union issues. As it attracts very few *advertisements and sells comparatively few copies, the *Morning Star* relies for its survival on readers donating to its fighting fund. *See also* ALTERNATIVE JOURNALISM; INDUSTRIAL CORRESPONDENT; RADICAL PRESS.

Moscow Union of Journalists An organization of media employees who work in the capital of Russia. Since its formation in 1990 it has been outspoken in support of journalists who find themselves obstructed, threatened, attacked, and even killed in the course of their work. *See also* DEATHS OF JOURNALISTS; RUSSIAN UNION OF JOURNALISTS.

Mother Jones A US-based independent, non-profit magazine and website specializing in what it describes as 'investigative, political, and social justice reporting'. Launched in 1976, it is named after a legendary Irish-American trade union organizer called Mary Harris Jones (1837–1930), who was known among workers as 'Mother Jones' but was once described by a US district attorney as 'the most dangerous

woman in America'. *See also* ALTERNATIVE MEDIA; INVESTIGATIVE
JOURNALISM; RADICAL PRESS.

🌐 SEE WEB LINKS
• *Mother Jones* on Mother Jones

Mother of Chapel (MoC) The title given to a female journalist in the
UK or Ireland who acts as a workplace representative (or shop steward),
having been elected by members of the *National Union of Journalists
within the newsroom or company. *See also* CHAPEL; FATHER OF CHAPEL.

MPA *See* ASSOCIATION OF MAGAZINE MEDIA.

Ms. magazine A commercial feminist magazine produced in the
USA since 1972, having started life the previous year as an insert in the
New York magazine. Founders included writer Gloria Steinem (1934–).
Although it tends to be seen as less militant than its one-time UK
counterpart *Spare Rib*, *Ms.* set out to challenge the *stereotyping found
in much *mainstream media, including existing *women's magazines,
and over the years it has raised many issues that have subsequently been
taken up by the mainstream. *See also* FEMINIST MEDIA; GENDER; SEXISM.

MSM *See* MAINSTREAM MEDIA.

muckraking The process of making public that which somebody,
somewhere, wishes to remain private. The term may be applied equally
to the exposure of illegality and corruption in high places or to the
revelation of an individual's sexual peccadilloes. The label 'muckraker'
is sometimes levelled against journalists as a term of abuse (especially
by those whose muck has been raked) but some journalists themselves
regard it more as a badge of honour than of shame. *Compare* BINOLOGY.
See also INVESTIGATIVE JOURNALISM; PRIVACY; SCANDAL.

mugshot A straightforward, closely cropped *photograph of
somebody's face; mugshots of people frequently mentioned in stories
will normally be stored in an archive for repeat use. Police mugshots
of (alleged) criminals are often used to illustrate *crime news.

multimedia The combination of two or more forms of *media,
whether in terms of *ownership or *convergence of *platforms.
Journalists today are typically expected to have the skills necessary to
work in multimedia formats. *See also* CROSS PLATFORM; MULTISKILLED
JOURNALISM.

multiskilled journalism Journalists being required to cover stories for a variety of *platforms and/or to utilize a variety of different skills, such as writing and *subbing a story, taking *pictures, editing *audio, uploading material online, and engaging members of the *audience in a *conversation. Since the arrival of digital technology many of the traditional demarcations between different jobs and skills have been breaking down, and many employers have used this as an opportunity to cut staff numbers at the same time as increasing output. *See also* BIMEDIA JOURNALISM; CONVERGENCE; NEW TECHNOLOGY; REPURPOSING.

multiskilling The process whereby journalists are increasingly expected to have multiple skills to enable them to produce *multiskilled journalism in a converged workplace. Although some *training may be offered by employers, the expectation often seems to be that potential recruits will already have acquired the necessary skills and paid for their own training before applying for work. *See also* CONVERGENCE.

Murdoch empire The extensive interests built up, owned, and/or controlled by *media mogul Rupert Murdoch (and offspring) since 1952, when young Rupert (1931–) inherited the Adelaide *News* in Australia upon the death of his newspaper *proprietor father Keith. The Murdoch empire is an international network of companies that, despite the presence of shareholders and other directors, is essentially a family business—an extremely profitable and powerful one. Today it comprises *News Corporation (largely newspapers, magazines, and publishing interests) and *21st Century Fox (film, television, and entertainment interests including BSkyB, *Sky News*, *Fox News*, and 20th Century Fox). In 2013 *Forbes* estimated Rupert Murdoch's personal wealth to be $11.2 billion (US dollars), making him the 91st richest person in the world. As well as huge wealth, Murdoch's empire has arguably given him great influence with politicians in those countries in which he operates major news organizations. In addition to his mainstream media outlets, in 1995 he founded the *Weekly Standard* as a (loss-making) forum for supporters of a neo-conservative *ideology. Two of his former editors, Andrew Neil (*Sunday Times*) and David Yelland (*Sun*), have gone on record as saying that Murdoch appoints editors who either already think like him or end up thinking like him. This was perhaps demonstrated by the way in which the editorial line of all his 175 newspapers on three continents coincided with his own pro-war stance in the run-up to the

US-led invasion of Iraq in 2003. The issue of alleged proprietorial interference in editorial matters, as well as the nature and extent of his relationships with politicians, was scrutinized at the *Leveson Inquiry in the UK, which was itself prompted by revelations of *phone-hacking and other unethical practices within the Murdoch empire.

Murdoch evokes strong opinions. He has been celebrated by some commentators as a heroic iconoclast who invests heavily in journalism and who has created a more diverse media landscape via bold gambles such as moving his UK newspapers to Wapping and challenging the old BBC–ITV duopoly by launching pay-TV. Yet he is blamed by others for using his key media outlets to propagate a right-wing world view—coarsening public debate and diminishing *ethical journalism in the process. In some circles he is seen as a highly respectable figure: in 1990 Oxford University was happy to establish the Rupert Murdoch Professor of Language and Communication in honour of their alumnus; Murdoch has frequently been invited to wine and dine with ruling politicians; and in 2011 it was revealed that one of his young daughters has former UK prime minister Tony Blair as godfather. Again, others view Murdoch very differently: the satirical magazine *Private Eye* greeted his arrival in the UK by labelling him the 'Dirty Digger'; writer Alan Bennett rejected an honorary degree from Oxford because it had accepted his money; and in 1994 terminally-ill playwright Dennis Potter famously declared on television that he had named his cancer 'Rupert'. For friend or foe alike, the Murdoch empire is hard to ignore.

Rupert Murdoch began building his empire in 1950s and 1960s Australia, initially by adding more regional newspapers to his portfolio along with acquiring several magazines and beginning to take an interest in broadcasting. In 1960 he bought the ailing *tabloid *Daily Mirror* in Sydney and revitalized it with a trademark dose of *sensationalism (it was later merged into his *Daily Telegraph*); then in 1964 he launched the *Australian* as his flagship national *broadsheet newspaper, this time targeted at an upmarket and influential readership. Having become a big media player in his native Australia, in 1969 Murdoch began his global expansion by buying the *News of the World* in the UK, followed a few months later by his purchase of the ailing *Sun*, which he transformed into a brash, populist, and best-selling tabloid with an emphasis on entertainment, TV soaps, sport, and *Page Three girls (*see also* GOTCHA; HILLSBOROUGH DISASTER). Having established himself at the popular end of *Fleet Street, Murdoch followed his

Australian trajectory by staking ground at the quality end too by buying the *Times* and *Sunday Times* in 1981. The government of Margaret Thatcher, which was avidly supported by the Murdoch titles, controversially nodded the sale through even though it meant just one publisher would own more than a quarter of the UK national press. In 1986 production of all four Murdoch titles was moved overnight to a new non-union plant, allowing the company to shed thousands of jobs and drive costs down and profits up (*see* WAPPING DISPUTE). Three years later in 1989 he launched his subscription-based satellite television company Sky and his newspapers have been accused of going out of their way to plug what is now BSkyB ever since (*see* CROSS PROMOTION).

At the same time as it was establishing itself in the UK the empire was also making inroads into the USA, where Murdoch outlets resembled cheerleaders for President Ronald Reagan; Rupert Murdoch eventually became a US citizen so as not to fall foul of that country's ownership restrictions. In 1976 he bought the tabloid *New York Post* and, as in Australia and the UK, he eventually matched this with an upmarket title when he took over the *Wall Street Journal* in 2007. In the meantime he had built a huge TV, film, and entertainment operation in the USA, including the launch of *Fox News* in 1996. Murdoch's investments in the *internet, to which he became a late and zealous convert, have proved less profitable to date: *Myspace was offloaded at a huge loss; the iPad *Daily* closed after less than two years; and the introduction of *paywalls to newspaper websites has yet to become a moneyspinner. Murdoch companies continue to seek ways of making money from digital output, and smaller players in the media market continue to watch their every move avidly.

In the second decade of the 21st century the Murdoch empire was rocked by the *hackgate scandal in the UK. In 2011 and 2012 Rupert Murdoch had to give evidence in person, first to a group of politicians on the House of Commons culture committee, and then to the *Leveson Inquiry. Also giving evidence was his son James (1972–), the deputy chief operating officer of News Corporation and until then most observers' tip to succeed his father as head of the empire when the time comes. Facing often hostile interrogation in public was an unfamiliar experience for them both, leading to unwelcome headlines and even a rare outbreak of questioning by some of News Corps' other shareholders. Yet the Murdochs continue to run a media operation that generates great wealth, allowing for loss-making but influential outlets to be subsidized, and which arguably continues to play a powerful *agenda-setting role in the public, cultural, and political spheres of Australia, the UK, the USA, and beyond, including Italy, Germany, and parts of Asia. The empire lives on. *See also* CIRCULATION WAR; CONCENTRATION OF OWNERSHIP; FOXIFICATION; HITLER DIARIES; INSIGHT; MEDIA AGENDA; NEWS UK; OWNERSHIP; PRICE WAR.

Further reading: D. McKnight, *Murdoch's Politics* (2013).
B. Page, *The Murdoch Archipelago* (2011).

(⊕) SEE WEB LINKS
• Rupert Murdoch's evidence to the Leveson Inquiry
• James Murdoch's evidence to the Leveson Inquiry

must An item that absolutely *has* to be included, perhaps because it corrects an earlier erroneous item but sometimes just because it concerns a pet project or interest of the *editor or *proprietor. Woe betide the journalist who *spikes a 'must'.

Myspace An early form of online *social media that launched in 2003 and once had hundreds of millions of users, prompting the *Murdoch empire to buy it for a reported £361 million in 2005. Myspace was rapidly overtaken by *Facebook and in 2011 it was sold by Murdoch at a huge loss to the online *advertising company Specific Media. Today it is mostly a music-oriented site and, although now used by most journalists much less than Facebook or *Twitter, it remains useful for *specialists covering the music industry.

myth **1.** A *story that conforms to one of society's commonly accepted *archetypes such as that of the hero, the victim, the good mother, or the person transformed (as in 'rags to riches'). Many pieces of journalism are said to draw on such myths and, by doing so, to help perpetuate them.
2. A sign or act of *communication that, according to *semiotics, contains some kind of message about societal values and beliefs (such as a picture of a child that might reinforce a '*common sense' view of childhood innocence).
3. A story that is widely believed and may frequently find its way into journalism, yet upon examination turns out to be either untrue or impossible to prove (such as the statements that, in the UK, there are more rats than people and that you are never more than two metres

away from one; or the hardy perennial story about local authorities banning Christmas in favour of 'Winterval'). Journalists can debunk such myths as well as propagate them. *See also* STEREOTYPING.

(⊕) SEE WEB LINKS

- 'Are you never more than 6ft away from a rat?'
- 'Winterval: the unpalatable making of a modern myth'
- Media Myth Alert

NABJ *See* NATIONAL ASSOCIATION OF BLACK JOURNALISTS.

NAHJ *See* NATIONAL ASSOCIATION OF HISPANIC JOURNALISTS.

NAJA *See* NATIVE AMERICAN JOURNALISTS ASSOCIATION.

name and shame A news organization's *campaign to identify and expose people it deems to be miscreants (*see* FOLK DEVILS). One of the most high-profile name-and-shame initiatives was conducted in the UK by the *News of the World* (under the editorship of Rebekah Wade, later Rebekah Brooks) when it set out to publish the identities and locations of convicted paedophiles who had been released from prison. Although the campaign was supported by some victims' parents, it was condemned by others for forcing offenders into hiding where they could no longer be monitored, encouraging vigilante attacks, and prompting several cases of mistaken identity. At the height of the hysteria in 2000 a hospital registrar in paediatric medicine was forced to flee her Welsh home when the word 'paedo' was painted on her front door by somebody who had apparently confused her job as a paediatrician with the word 'paedophile'. *See also* CRIME NEWS; MORAL PANIC.

NAPA *See* NATIONAL ASSOCIATION OF PRESS AGENCIES.

narrative The structuring of a piece of journalism so as to tell it as a *story. A narrative may be as much to do with form as with content, meaning that the same event or set of facts may be used to construct very different narratives. *See also* CHRONOLOGY; CONSTRUCTION OF NEWS.

narrowcasting A form of *broadcasting that is directed at a *niche or narrowly defined target *audience rather than a general one. Targeting may be on the basis of demographics, shared interests, or a combination of the two.

National Association of Black Journalists (NABJ) A US-based networking, lobbying, and educational organization that was formed in 1975 to strengthen ties among 'journalists of colour' working in both *black media and white-dominated *mainstream media. The NABJ aims to 'sensitize all media to the importance of fairness in the workplace for black journalists' and has produced its own *style guide to advise journalists on 'terms and language usage of special interest or relevance to our membership and our community'. *See also* POLITICAL CORRECTNESS; RACISM.

(🌐) SEE WEB LINKS
• NABJ style guide

National Association of Hispanic Journalists (NAHJ) A self-help organization formed in 1984 to represent journalists of Hispanic origin working in the USA and the Caribbean. NAHJ activities include conducting research into how Latino people are represented in the news broadcasts of the major US TV networks.

(🌐) SEE WEB LINKS
• NAHJ website

National Association of Press Agencies (NAPA) A UK-based membership organization formed in 1982 to operate as a self-help association of *news agencies. NAPA, which claims that every town and city in the UK is covered by one or more of its affiliated news and/or picture agencies, has its own code of ethical conduct.

(🌐) SEE WEB LINKS
• The NAPA code of conduct

National Council for the Training of Journalists (NCTJ) An accreditation and examination body set up in 1951 to oversee the *training of newspaper journalists in the UK. Established on the recommendation of the *Royal Commission on the Press of 1947–9, and including representatives of the *National Union of Journalists as well as employers, the NCTJ assesses the basic standards that *editors, particularly on local newspapers, require of their journalists. These include skills such as *shorthand, *reporting, and news writing; knowledge of public affairs and media law; and, on some courses, the specialist skills demanded of *photographers and *sub-editors. NCTJ qualifications are divided into preliminary and final stages, the second of which traditionally marks the moment that a junior or trainee journalist becomes a senior (*see* INDENTURES). Preliminary training was once mostly provided by employers 'on the job' in newsrooms, augmented with day or block release to a local college, but is now mostly pre-entry and takes place overwhelmingly in universities at the student's own expense. The NCTJ only accredits those universities, further education colleges, and private training providers that offer students its exams. In the 21st century the NCTJ expanded beyond its newspaper base to embrace *online journalism and has even begun to move onto territory traditionally occupied by the accreditation bodies for magazines and broadcast journalism (the *PTC and the *BJTC respectively). *See also* JOURNALISM EDUCATION.

(⊕) SEE WEB LINKS
• NCTJ accredited courses

National Enquirer A weekly US *supermarket tabloid that, according to its mission statement, publishes 'the unvarnished stories about celebrities: their antics, celebrations, loves, mishaps'. Now owned by American Media Inc, it began life in 1926 as the *New York Evening Enquirer*, part of *Hearst Newspapers. Its reputation for *sensational coverage of sex, sleaze, crime, and celebs, along with its willingness to engage in *chequebook journalism, have resulted in the *Enquirer* being rather looked down upon by many journalists working for more serious news organizations. *See also* CELEBRITY JOURNALISM.

National Federation of Press Women (NFPW) A networking organization for women working in journalism and related industries in the USA, which was formed in Chicago in 1937. In addition to self-help and educational activities, NFPW is active in campaigning in defence of the *First Amendment and lobbying for effective *shield laws. *See also* GENDER; SEXISM.

(⊕) SEE WEB LINKS
• NFPW Hall of Fame

National Lesbian and Gay Journalists Association (NLGJA) An organization of US journalists, journalism educators, and students formed in 1990 to campaign against workplace discrimination and promote fair, accurate, and inclusive media coverage of issues involving homosexual, bisexual, and transgender people. The NLGJA has produced a model stylebook supplement that it encourages news organizations to incorporate into their own *style guides. *See also* GAY MEDIA; POLITICAL CORRECTNESS.

(⊕) SEE WEB LINKS
• NLGJA style

National Public Radio *See* NPR.

National Readership Survey A continuous survey conducted into the *readership (as opposed to simple *circulation) of UK *newspapers, *magazines, and their related *websites, based on questioning a large sample of the public to provide publishers and potential *advertisers with rich data on *audience demographics, reading habits, lifestyle choices, and so on. The survey is produced on a non-profit basis on behalf of the *Newspaper Publishers Association, the *Professional Publishers Association, and the Institute of Practitioners in Advertising.

National Union of Journalists (NUJ) A trade union representing journalists (plus many workers in the *public relations industry) in the UK and Ireland, which has around 30,000 members. Formed in 1907 as a breakaway from the *Institute of Journalists, the NUJ grew rapidly by taking up its members' campaigns for higher pay, shorter hours, and better working conditions; as a result, it soon overtook the IOJ in both size and influence. In 1936 the NUJ agreed its first *code of conduct for journalists and the union was instrumental in lobbying for the *Royal Commission on the Press in the 1940s which resulted in the creation of the *Press Council and the *National Council for the Training of Journalists. Members within particular workplaces are organized into *chapels (workplace branches) and elect *Fathers of Chapels or *Mothers of Chapels to represent journalists in talks with management. However, the union's power and influence were severely diminished by the victory of the *Murdoch empire in the *Wapping dispute of the 1980s (*see* REFUSENIKS), which was followed by many other *proprietors making use of the Thatcher government's anti-union legislation to withdraw from their staff the right to be represented by the NUJ. The union regained some of its influence and negotiating strength in the 21st century, although by then its members' battles tended to be more defensive ones against job losses, bullying, or attacks on pensions, rather than campaigns to improve pay or conditions. The NUJ submitted evidence to the *Leveson Inquiry about the need for journalists to have a *conscience clause to enable them to stand up for *ethical journalism. *See also* REAL LIVES.

Further reading: T. Gopsill and G. Neale, *Journalists: 100 Years of the NUJ* (2007).

(⊕) SEE WEB LINKS
• The NUJ code of conduct

Native American Journalists Association (NAJA) A self-help membership organization, based at the University of Oklahoma in the USA, that was formed in 1984 (initially under the name Native American Press Association) to empower Native American journalists, support *indigenous media, and promote greater diversity within *mainstream media. *See also* CHEROKEE PHOENIX.

((( ))) SEE WEB LINKS
• NAJA news

native reporter Somebody *reporting in the media about a story that involves them as either participant or activist, with their personal involvement normally being made explicit. *See also* AMATEUR JOURNALISM; ALTERNATIVE JOURNALISM; NATIVE REPORTING.

native reporting Journalism produced by people who are themselves involved in a story. Most commonly found within *alternative media, native reporting allows communities, groups, or individuals to speak directly on their own behalf rather than having their stories mediated by a third party. Native reporting may take the form of a first-person narrative or may adopt more of the standard techniques used by any *reporter, but in either case the fact that people are reporting their own stories tends to be highlighted (even celebrated), with no claims being made for its *objectivity or *impartiality. *Compare* NEUTRALITY. *See also* NATIVE REPORTER; REPRESENTATION.

NBC News A major commercial broadcast and digital news network in the USA. Now owned by the NBC Universal Group as part of the Comcast Corporation, it began life within the National Broadcasting Company, the first US radio network which launched in 1926. NBC's flagship shows include *Today*, the *Nightly News*, and *Meet The Press*, and it is engaged in a constant *ratings battle with rival network *ABC. *See also* NEWSVINE.

NCTJ *See* NATIONAL COUNCIL FOR THE TRAINING OF JOURNALISTS.

negativity Something in an event that can be seen as having a negative effect, at least on some people, and which thereby renders it potentially *newsworthy. Reference to something negative was one of the *news values identified by scholars Galtung and Ruge in the 1960s. They argued that negative news might be seen as relatively unambiguous (*see* UNAMBIGUITY), although that has subsequently been questioned by those who point out that even apparently straightforward events may be open to many different interpretations, and that one person's *bad news may be another's *good news.

negotiated reading When members of an *audience do not necessarily passively accept whatever ideological or other messages may be contained within media output, nor do they reject them outright. Rather, according to the *encoding, decoding model, after being sent a message will be filtered, interpreted, and understood by the receiver within the context of other information available to them. *Compare* HYPODERMIC MODEL. *See also* ACTIVE AUDIENCE; IDEOLOGY; OPPOSITIONAL READING; PREFERRED READING.

Neil Report The result of an internal review commissioned by the *BBC in 2004 in an attempt to learn lessons from the *Hutton Inquiry, which followed the death of *whistleblower Dr David Kelly. The review was conducted by a small group led by Ron Neil, a former director of news and current affairs at the BBC. The report's recommendations included: that accurate and reliable *note-taking should form part of the *training of BBC journalists; that stories based on *anonymous sources should be subjected to greater editorial scrutiny; that live *two-ways ought not normally be used to break stories containing serious allegations; and that members of the audience ought to be left in no doubt about whether it is a *source or the BBC itself that is making an allegation. The report's findings were accepted by *BBC governors, who also acted on its recommendation to establish a BBC College of Journalism. *See also* BBC EDITORIAL GUIDELINES.

(((●))) SEE WEB LINKS
• The Neil Report

netizen A *citizen who engages in forms of online *communication, especially by contributing to the *public sphere through activities such as *blogging, *citizen journalism, *networked journalism, and activist use of *social media. *See also* ACTIVE AUDIENCE; INTERNET; TECHNOCENTRISM; TRAFIGURA.

networked journalism The idea that journalism in the digital age is—and/or ought to be—an essentially collaborative process involving an *active audience as co-producers rather than as passive consumers. Networked journalism includes using *crowdsourcing, *wikis, *social media, *curation, and other forms of *communication to make the production of journalism a more fluid, interactive, and non-hierarchical process than it tended to be in the *analogue age. This can take numerous forms including *listeners tweeting or texting suggested questions that might be asked during a live radio interview, *netizens trawling through newly released databases to suggest possible *angles worth pursuing, and witnesses to events submitting mobile phone footage direct to news organizations. Although some commentators regard networked journalism as undermining the role (and employment prospects) of those who earn their living as journalists, others see the *verification skills of trained professionals remaining as an essential part of the equation. *Compare* GATEKEEPING. *See also* CITIZEN JOURNALISM; COLLABORATIVE JOURNALISM; OPEN JOURNALISM; USER-GENERATED CONTENT.

(⊕) SEE WEB LINKS
• Charlie Beckett blogs on networked journalism

neutrality Not taking sides, which in journalism is associated with ideas such as *balance, *impartiality, *objectivity, *scepticism, and keeping an open mind. Many news organizations are formally committed to neutrality, although there will normally be limits even in the most fair and balanced newsrooms, and some scholars argue that ostensibly neutral working *routines and practices may in fact play an ideological role by allowing some voices more privileged *access and/or by *framing events from their perspective. Those involved in *adversarial journalism, *campaigning journalism, or *oppositional reporting tend to reject neutrality as either impossible to achieve or as undesirable in certain circumstances. *Compare* BIAS; IMMERSION REPORTING; NATIVE REPORTING.

never wrong for long The unofficial slogan of news organizations that have a reputation among rival journalists (and sometimes their own staff) for prioritizing speed over *accuracy. Online media and *24-hour news broadcasting in particular face accusations of rushing to be first with *breaking news at the expense of checking its accuracy thoroughly beforehand, with erroneous information being corrected as more *facts become available. *Compare* FACT-CHECKING; SLOW JOURNALISM; VERIFICATION.

Newark Star-Ledger A daily newspaper published in Newark, New Jersey, since 1832. Now owned by Advance Publications, it has the largest *circulation of any newspaper in the state of New Jersey and is one of the top 25 best-selling dailies in the USA.

New Internationalist A UK-based but internationally oriented magazine that exists 'to report on issues of world poverty and inequality'. Launched in 1973, and subsidized in its early days by the charities Oxfam and Christian Aid, *New Internationalist* is published on a not-for-profit basis by an independent workers' cooperative. It is one of the few examples of a 1970s *alternative media project surviving into the 21st century, and today it has a multimedia website in addition to the monthly magazine, which itself is available in both print and digital formats. *See also* ALTERNATIVE JOURNALISM; DEVELOPMENT JOURNALISM.

new journalism A label applied both to the trend for more popular styles and subject matter in late 19th-century US and UK journalism and to the more narrative-driven *long-form and *gonzo journalism that emerged in the 1960s. Its earlier use contrasted the new, lighter style with more serious and political journalism, whereas its later use signified a more discursive style that rejected the emphasis traditionally placed on *neutrality and *facts. *See also* IMMERSION REPORTING; LITERARY JOURNALISM.

new media Emerging or relatively recent forms of *media, so labelled to distinguish them from longer established but still existing media (*see* LEGACY MEDIA). Precisely which media are regarded as new will change over time. *See also* NEW TECHNOLOGY.

New Musical Express *See* NME.

New Orleans Times-Picayune A Louisiana newspaper (and associated *nola.com* website) that, when in 2012 the print product reduced publication to Wednesdays, Fridays, and Sundays only, left New Orleans as the biggest city in the USA without its own daily newspaper (although the Baton Rouge *Advocate* swiftly increased its New Orleans coverage and sales, sparking something of a local *circulation war). Launched in 1837 as *The Picayune*, it is now owned by the New York-based **Advance Publications** (parent company of *Condé Nast), which announced plans to adopt the 'three-day week' model on several more of its print products.

New Republic An upmarket US magazine that, since its launch in 1914, has set out to give serious coverage to politics, culture, and what it terms 'the big ideas'. However, perhaps its main claim to fame among non-subscribers is that in the 1990s it was hoodwinked into publishing a number of fake stories invented by one of its associate editors, Stephen Glass (*see* HACK HEAVEN).

news Information about recent events deemed to be interesting, important, or unusual enough to be *newsworthy (or fresh information about less recent events) that is gathered, verified, and structured in accordance with *journalistic norms before being published in *media ranging from *newspapers to *liveblogs. Although news emphasizes that which is new and surprising, much of it is recurring and predictable (*see* NEWS CYCLE; NEWS FLOW). Whether it is concerned with producing *hard news or *soft news, *news journalism depends on the *routines of *reporting that involve sourcing and verifying *facts and attributing *information to *sources. Depending on the culture of the news organization, or the requirements of any regulatory regime under which it operates, news may be required to display *impartiality. Even in those *newsrooms that sometimes pursue their organization's own *media agenda, most items of news are typically relayed with formal *balance, giving both sides of any story and separating fact from *comment. Intrinsic to news is the process of *selection. Only a tiny proportion of events happening in the world every day ever become news. Even of the events of which journalists become aware, only a minority will make news. To help them decide which ones to select, journalists are said to apply criteria that are known (in academic circles, at least) as *news values. Such news values are relative because what is considered newsworthy differs over time, location, and between different media markets, with the perceived interests of the *audience a major consideration. News might be general in orientation (as on a major newspaper or the *BBC World Service), more narrowly focused (*see* LOCAL JOURNALISM; BLACK MEDIA; GAY MEDIA), or aimed at a special-interest or *niche audience (as in *trade rags, music magazines, and so on).

News can concern everything from the *tragedy of a fatal car accident to a council report revealing the number of potholes on the roads of Blackburn, Lancashire, and everything from the latest fashion craze to the outbreak of war. The context, sector, and *platform of news journalism may vary, but most news stories tend to be concerned with people doing things, including: abusing, accepting, arresting, arriving, assaulting, attacking, breaking, bullying, burning, burying, buying, campaigning, celebrating, changing, chasing, comforting, commemorating, competing, conning, crashing, creating, curing, delivering, deserting, destroying, divorcing, donating, dying, employing, escaping, failing, fighting, finding, fleeing, following, fornicating, freeing, giving birth, groping, hating, hunting, invading, inventing, investigating, jailing, judging, kidnapping, killing, kissing, leading, leaving, looting, losing, loving, making, marrying, mourning, negotiating, operating, preaching, prosecuting, quizzing, rejecting, reporting, rescuing, resigning, rioting, robbing, sacking, saving, searching, selling, stalking, stealing, striking, succeeding, suing, surviving, travelling, treating, trolling, voting, winning, and many other actions. News can also be about people saying things, whether in speeches, on *Twitter, or in a multitude of other ways. None of the above will guarantee that something will be covered as news, they are merely the raw ingredients; which ones actually become news will depend on who is involved (*see* CELEBRITIES), where, when, in what circumstances, what other potential stories are around at the same time, the interests of the audience, all filtered through the routines of and resources available to the news organization. Rather than a naturally occurring phenomenon, a neutral portrayal of daily life, or some kind of mirror reflecting the world back at itself, news is a highly selective version of events and, arguably, non-events that have been constructed to match the production requirements of the news organization with the information needs (or wants) of the audience (*see* CONSTRUCTION OF NEWS; MANUFACTURE OF NEWS). The selection and presentation of news in *mainstream media tends to play an ideological role in support of society's status quo, according to many academics and *alternative media activists alike (*see* HEGEMONY). Yet, despite its critics and its limitations, news remains the very essence of *journalism. *Compare* COLUMN; COLOUR PIECE; FEATURE. *See also* BREAKING NEWS; CRIME NEWS; FIVE Ws; GATEKEEPING; INVERTED PYRAMID MODEL; LANGUAGE OF NEWS; MAN BITES DOG; MARKET-DRIVEN NEWS; NEWSDESK; NEWS ACCESS; NEWS AGGREGATION; NEWS ANGLE; NEWS CYCLE; NEWS FLOW; NEWS FRAME; NEWS PEG; NEWSZAK; ROLLING NEWS; 24-HOUR NEWS.

Further reading: J. Harrison, *News* (2006).
H. Tumber (ed.), *News: A Reader* (1999).
B. Whitaker, *News Ltd: Why You Can't Read all About it* (1991).

news access The ability of some organizations or individuals to have their perspectives reported as part of the *news. Scholars have repeatedly found evidence of a tendency for the more powerful and resource-rich sections of society to enjoy privileged *access to news organizations, with the corollary that the least powerful or influential sections of society are comparatively rarely invited to speak for themselves in the media. *See also* NEWS FRAME; PRIMARY DEFINERS; REPRESENTATION.

news agency An organization, sometimes even a single *freelance journalist, that sells stories or pictures to the media and which carries out *reporting tasks on behalf of media clients. Not to be confused with a newsagent, which is a shop selling newspapers.

news aggregation The bringing together of *news from different news organizations and outlets and, without adding any original *reporting, making it easily available for an audience to find and navigate. *See also* AGGREGATION; GOOGLE NEWS.

news angle The element of a news story given emphasis in the *intro, and/or the *peg upon which a story is hung. The news angle will often but not always be the most recent development, and other *news values will also be taken into consideration. Also part of the equation might be what it is thought will most grab the attention of the *audience. Sometimes one news organization might opt for an unusual *angle primarily to differentiate its coverage of an event from that of its rivals.

newsbook A nascent form of *newspaper that emerged in England from around 1641 amidst the unrest that led to civil war. Newsbooks emerged as *pamphlets that began to be published with increasing frequency, in some cases becoming weekly publications containing accounts of contemporary events (*see* NEWS). *See also* CHAPBOOK; PRINTING.

Further reading: J. Raymond, *The Invention of the Newspaper: English Newsbooks 1641–1649* (2005 [1996]).

News Bunny A person wearing a rabbit costume who would signal approval or disapproval of particular stories during news *bulletins on a much-derided cable television station called *Live TV*, which briefly operated in the UK in the 1990s under the ownership of *Trinity Mirror. Reportedly the idea of station boss Kelvin MacKenzie (former editor of the *Sun*), the News Bunny would stand behind the *newsreader and give either a thumbs-up or a thumbs-down. *See also* DUMBING DOWN.

newscast A news *bulletin broadcast on radio or television, or a broadcast-style bulletin that can be viewed and/or listened to online. The term is more common in the USA than elsewhere.

News Chronicle A liberal-oriented national newspaper published in the UK between 1930 (when it emerged from a merger of the *Daily News* and the *Daily Chronicle*) and 1960, when it was taken over and killed by the *Daily Mail*. During its brief life it was notable for supporting the republican anti-Franco side in the Spanish Civil War in the 1930s and for opposing the UK invasion of Suez in the 1950s. The paper's demise was long lamented by journalists of a certain generation and a certain disposition, who never failed to point out that when it was closed by the *Mail*'s *proprietor, the second Lord Rothermere (1898–1978), the *News Chronicle* was still selling more than a million copies a day. One of its most celebrated journalists, James Cameron (1911–85), once said that the *News Chronicle* died of 'thrombosis'—that is, a 'healthy circulation impeded by clots'. *See also* CONCENTRATION OF OWNERSHIP.

news conference *See* PRESS CONFERENCE.

News Corp (News Corporation) The name of the company that *was*, in effect, the *Murdoch empire until June 2013 when News Corp was split in two as part of a rebranding exercise following the *hackgate scandal. The more profitable television, film, and entertainment side of the empire became *21st Century Fox whereas the new News Corporation retained the newspapers, digital, and publishing side, including *News UK titles in the UK, the *New York Post* and *Wall Street Journal* in the USA, Australia's major newspaper chain, and the book publisher HarperCollins. Both halves of the business are public companies in which, theoretically, the Murdoch family is merely one group among many shareholders. But media commentators noted that where the real power lay was revealed when News Corporation adopted a new 'News Corp' logo that was said to be based on Rupert Murdoch's own handwriting. Murdoch himself is executive chairman of News Corporation and chairman and chief executive of 21st Century Fox; also on both boards of directors are his sons Lachlan (1971–) and James (1972–). It remains to be seen whether or not this formal splitting of the newspapers away from the empire's bigger money-spinners will limit the Murdochs' scope for cross subsidies, *cross promotion, *price wars, political influence, and global expansion. *See also* MEDIA AGENDA; OWNERSHIP; PROPRIETORS.

news cycle The period of time that elapses before one news story or batch of stories is replaced by another. The news cycle used to last 24 hours, being based on the *deadlines of daily newspapers, but it repeatedly sped up with the arrival of radio, television, *rolling news, the *internet, and *social media, to such an extent that few scholars seem certain if there is any such thing as a news cycle any more. Journalists once tended to observe that it was only around the time that they began to tire of a story that the public even started noticing the story; this phenomenon may be less common in the digital age. However, journalists are sometimes surprised to discover that ordinary people do not always use their mobile devices to access news 24/7, and that a 24-hour news cycle still exists for those whose only consumption of news are the *headlines every breakfast time or evening.

Newsday A daily newspaper and online presence based in Long Island, New York. Published since 1940 and owned today by the Cablevision group, it is consistently one of the top 25 best-selling newspapers in the USA.

newsdesk A *newsroom's command centre from which *reporters will be given instructions and to which they must report. Presided over by a *news editor and any deputies, the newsdesk has traditionally been a physical desk located at either the head or centre of the newsroom, but the phrase can also be used for a virtual newsdesk existing only online. *See also* DIARY; HUB.

news editor A senior journalist in charge of the *newsgathering operation of a journalistic organization. The news editor runs the *diary, manages a team of *reporters, liaises with others in parallel positions in *features and *pictures, and answers to the *editor. *See also* NEWSDESK.

news flow 1. The supply of stories and potential stories on which every news organization depends and which may be supplied by a combination of staff *reporters, *freelance journalists, *news agencies, *wire services, *public relations outfits, and members of the audience via *user-generated content. The *news editor will get into difficulty if the news flow ever reduces to a trickle or dries up, hence the establishment of *newsgathering *routines such as the *calls.

2. The direction in which major news stories and their *framing tends to flow internationally, which has traditionally been from the more powerful countries in the world to developing countries (*see* CULTURAL IMPERIALISM). However, the direction of this flow is subject to challenge, for example, by forms of *development journalism.

news frame A way of *framing or presenting an item of *news in such a way that some kind of explanatory order is imposed upon the information within. Similar raw material may be framed in markedly different ways, as is demonstrated whenever the same piece of *agency *copy, containing an identical set of *facts and *quotes, is presented by rival newspapers in ways that support diametrically opposed conclusions.

newsgathering The process of obtaining *information and other material for the purpose of transforming it into items of *news. The term has echoes of a nature hunt but in most cases newsgathering is more of an industrial process carried out by *reporters organized in a *newsroom, presided over by the *newsdesk, and subject to a series of *constraints ranging from the size of the editorial budget to the *laws of the land. It might be the *off-diary stories that cause most excitement, but much newsgathering is essentially concerned with the efficient application of *routines to monitor regular *sources. *See also* CHURNALISM; HARVESTING CONTENT; REPORTING.

news in brief *See* NIB.

News International Until 2013 this was the name of the UK national newspaper arm of *News Corporation (*see* MURDOCH EMPIRE), which publishes the *Sun*, the *Times*, the *Sunday Times*, and the *Sun on Sunday*. Until 2011 it also published the *News of the World*; it was renamed *News UK in the wake of the *hackgate scandal. Between them, the four newspapers have consistently accounted for a third or more of all the UK's daily and Sunday newspaper markets, as measured by *circulation, leading to concerns about *concentration of ownership and their *agenda-setting role on political issues. In addition to the printed products, they have also adopted a range of strategies including *paywalls in an effort to 'monetize' their output online and via mobile devices. *See also* WAPPING DISPUTE.

news journalism The *reporting of events in a journalistic manner by a news organization. Although there are other forms of journalistic activity, *news is the stuff of *journalism itself because news journalists set out to inform society about itself in an accurate, comprehensible, and entertaining manner, all day, every day. *See also* NEWSGATHERING.

news management Attempts to influence, control, or even prevent coverage of an event or potential news story. News management can range from threats or violence at one extreme (*see* DEATHS OF JOURNALISTS) to mild spin-doctoring at the other (*see* PUBLIC RELATIONS; SPIN). Journalists and media organizations are sometimes accused of being complicit in news management; for example, a newspaper that is supportive of a particular political party may be more receptive to that party's version of events and overly hostile to opposing views. *See also* AGENDA-SETTING; DA-NOTICE; PREBUTTAL.

Newsnight An influential television news and *current affairs programme broadcast in the UK by the *BBC every weekday evening. Launched in 1980, *Newsnight* positions itself at the serious end of factual broadcasting, where its main competitors are the *Today* programme on radio and *Channel 4 News* on TV. Although it covers cultural as well as political and social issues, the programme is perhaps noted more for its acerbic live *interviews with politicians than for its recorded *packages. *Newsnight*'s journalistic highlights included *presenter Jeremy Paxman repeatedly asking the same question to a government minister who declined to answer (either twelve or fourteen times, depending how you count them), and the programme's unwillingness to be a mouthpiece for the UK government during armed conflicts in the Falklands and Northern Ireland. Journalistic lowlights included its dropping of a story about former BBC 'personality' Jimmy Savile (1926–2011) being a serial child-sex offender, compounded by wrongly implicating an innocent man in a later investigation into paedophiles (*see* POLLARD REVIEW).

News of the Screws A nickname for the sex-obsessed *News of the World* newspaper that was just as likely to be used by those who read it (and even those who worked for it) as by those who regarded it with disdain. The paper was also sometimes referred to simply as the *Screws*.

News of the World The biggest-selling newspaper in the UK at the time of its closure by the *Murdoch empire in 2011 as a direct result of the *hackgate scandal. It was launched as a popular Sunday newspaper in 1843 by John Browne Bell (1779–1855) and it soon attracted masses of readers along with a reputation for *sensational coverage of lurid crimes and secret sins. The paper's slogan for many years was '*all human life is there', but it was a highly selective version of human life that provided its winning formula. By the mid-20th century the *News of the Screws, as it became known, was selling more than 8 million copies per issue.

Ownership had passed to the Carr family in 1891 with Emsley Carr (1867–1941) editing the paper for 50 years, a *Fleet Street record. In 1969 the Carrs sold the News of the World to Rupert Murdoch, who gradually built on its familiar mix of sex and crime by increasing coverage of TV, sport, and *celebrities, along with a series of investigations carried out by the paper's own *fake sheikh. Along the way, despite the accusations of illegal *phone-hacking that began to emerge from 2006 onwards, the News of the World won many awards for its *scoops and retained its position as the most read newspaper in the UK, still selling around 2.8 million copies a week in 2011.

Having switched to *tabloid format in 1984, the paper later embraced *multimedia journalism by using its website to show videos of celebs who had been secretly filmed getting up to no good. However, *advertisers began withdrawing within days of the *Guardian's July 2011 revelation that among those whose private phone messages had been accessed by the paper in the quest for stories was a murdered schoolgirl. The Murdochs shocked most observers by swiftly deciding to close what they had come to see as a 'toxic brand'. The final edition of the News of the World was published on 10 July 2011, with profits donated to charity. Some of the estimated 200 people who lost their jobs with the closure eventually found work on the *Sun on Sunday or elsewhere in the Murdoch empire. The News of the World's working practices and *ethics were the subject of much scrutiny at the subsequent *Leveson Inquiry, which heard allegations of a culture of bullying there. However, detailed allegations of phone-hacking were not heard by Leveson, so as not to prejudice legal proceedings against former staff. See also CRIME NEWS; NAME AND SHAME.

News on Sunday An attempt to create a left-leaning national *tabloid newspaper in the UK that was launched into the Sunday market in 1987 with financial backing from the trade union movement and others who wished to see an alternative to what *Fleet Street had to offer. Although it sold around half a million copies of the first edition, it ran out of both money and readers and closed after a few months amid much acrimony. *See also* ALTERNATIVE JOURNALISM; ALTERNATIVE MEDIA; RADICAL PRESS.

Further reading: P. Chippindale and C. Horrie, *Disaster: The Rise and Fall of News on Sunday* (1988).

newspaper A regular printed publication, most commonly produced in either a *tabloid or *broadsheet format, that delivers *news (and much else) on a daily or weekly basis. Newspapers may be local, regional, national, or even international in coverage and *circulation; they may be paid for or free; and, with the exception of the *alternative press, they tend to be the products of profit-seeking commercial enterprises. Although they promote themselves as being a public service, most newspapers rely on income from *advertising to survive. In addition to *hard news and advertisements, newspapers typically include *soft news, *features, *sport reporting, *photographs, *cartoons, *comic strips, *colour pieces, *lifestyle coverage, *columns, *leaders, *reviews, TV listings, share prices, *agony aunts, *obituaries, readers' *letters, crosswords, competitions, horoscopes, and numerous other ingredients. As a result of this mix, a newspaper is sometimes described as a portable reading device with *serendipity.

Having been around for well over 300 years (*see* FLEET STREET; NEWSBOOK), newspapers began to be supplanted by more digital forms of portable reading devices in the 21st century, from laptops to mobile phones. Having begun with *shovelware, many publishers eventually adopted a *web-first policy for *breaking news, often filling the following issue of the newspaper with more commentary than reportage. Although newspaper sales continued to increase in some parts of the world, notably India, newspaper publishers in the USA, Australia, the UK, and elsewhere in Europe were faced with rapidly declining circulation and advertising revenues, leading to some closures or reductions in publication frequency, and significant job losses among journalists. Today newspapers tend to see themselves as converged digital and print products, although publishers are still experimenting with ways of 'monetizing' the former to compensate for the loss of income from the latter. In the UK various forms of *paywall are operating on the *websites of several national titles, and in the USA digital paywalls had already been introduced at 450 of the country's 1,380 daily newspapers according to the *Pew Research Center's 'state of the media' report for 2013. Whether delivered in print, on a *tablet, or in some other way, newspapers continue to be praised and to praise themselves for being a *free press that operates as a *watchdog and nurtures a *public sphere. However, concerns about the *ethics of newspaper journalism (and of some newspaper *proprietors) have prompted a succession of inquiries, particularly in the UK, the most recent of which was the *Leveson Inquiry in 2011–12. *See also* COLOUR SUPPLEMENT; CONCENTRATION OF OWNERSHIP; CONVERGENCE; FREE NEWSPAPER; HARVESTING CONTENT; LEGACY MEDIA; LOCAL JOURNALISM; MID-MARKET; NATIONAL READERSHIP SURVEY; NEWSPAPER PUBLISHERS ASSOCIATION; NEWSPAPER SOCIETY; POPS; PRESS BARON; QUALITY PRESS; READERS; REDTOP; SUPERMARKET TABLOIDS; VANISHING NEWSPAPER; WORLD ASSOCIATION OF NEWSPAPERS AND NEWS PUBLISHERS.

Further reading: P. Cole and T. Harcup, *Newspaper Journalism* (2010).
B. Franklin (ed.), *Pulling Newspapers Apart* (2008).
R. Greenslade, *Press Gang* (2004).

(((⊕))) SEE WEB LINKS
• Today's newspaper front pages

Newspaper Guild (TNG-CWA) The major trade union for journalists in the USA, Canada, and Puerto Rico. It was formed in 1933 by US newspaper journalists who decided to combine mostly in an effort to increase wages, and it subsequently expanded into other sectors and territories. In addition to representing members on employment issues, the guild's constitution states its mission is to 'raise the standards of journalism and ethics of the industry'. In 1997 it was absorbed into the much larger (and broader) Communication Workers of America, of which it is an industry sector organization. Today it is sometimes referred to as the TNG-CWA.

(((⊕))) SEE WEB LINKS
• The Newspaper Guild's 80th anniversary video

Newspaper Publishers Association The trade organization of the major national newspaper publishers in the UK, formed in 1906 on the initiative of *proprietors *Northcliffe and *Pearson primarily to negotiate collectively with the print unions on behalf of *Fleet Street titles. *See also* INDEPENDENT PRESS STANDARDS ORGANIZATION; ROYAL CHARTER ON THE PRESS.

Newspaper Society The trade organization of the UK's commercial regional and local press. Formed in 1836, it is the oldest newspaper

publishers' association in the world. The Newspaper Society provides a lobbying voice for the industry's *owners on issues such as legislation and *regulation, collects data on topics such as *circulation, and runs an annual Local Newspaper Week to promote the value to society of the 1,100 weekly and daily titles published by its members.
See also INDEPENDENT PRESS STANDARDS ORGANIZATION.

news peg An event, statement, anniversary, or some other reason for running a particular *news story at a particular time. *See also* ANGLE; PEG.

Newsquest One of the major publishers of provincial newspapers in the UK today, although it was only formed in the mid-1990s amid a blizzard of newspaper sell-offs and takeovers. Since 1999 Newsquest has been the UK arm of the US-based *Gannett empire and it has continued to acquire other businesses including the *advertising vehicles *Exchange & Mart* and *Auto Exchange*. Rankings by the *Newspaper Society in 2013 place Newsquest second only to *Trinity Mirror for local newspaper *circulation (at 5.7 million copies a week) and second only to *Johnston Press in the number of titles owned (186), which include the *Northern Echo*, the *Swindon Advertiser*, the *Oxford Mail*, and their online versions. *See also* CONCENTRATION OF OWNERSHIP; LOCAL JOURNALISM.

newsreader Someone who reads aloud a *script on a radio or TV news *bulletin. Newsreaders may themselves be *journalists who contribute to the process of gathering and writing the *news. *See also* ANCHOR; AUTOCUE; AUTOCUTIE; PRESENTER.

newsreel Short news and *current affairs films that were shown in cinemas from the early 20th century onwards, initially in silent format but as 'talkies' from the 1920s—often with voiceovers derided by later generations as extremely cheesy. Although newsreels began to be supplanted by *television journalism from the 1950s onwards, they continued to be produced and screened until the 1970s. *See also* PATHÉ NEWS.

(((●))) SEE WEB LINKS
• News on Screen
• Newsreel archive on *YouTube*

news release *See* PRESS RELEASE.

newsroom The editorial floor or office of a news organization, which is presided over by a *news editor (and deputies and assistants) who runs the *newsdesk. The term refers as much to the collection of journalists who work for a particular organization as to the physical infrastructure, and as such, a newsroom is generally taken to include any *reporters working remotely from home, in satellite offices, or out in the *field. *See also* HUB.

news subsidy The provision of *news stories to media outlets by the *public relations industry, allowing space and airtime to be filled with little expenditure on original *reporting. *See also* CHURNALISM; INFORMATION SUBSIDY.

New Statesman A left-of-centre *current affairs, cultural, and political magazine published weekly in the UK since 1913, when it was founded by the Fabian socialists Beatrice and Sidney Webb (1858–1943 and 1859–1947, respectively). Among its contributors have been many famous names ranging from George Bernard Shaw (1856–1950) and John Maynard Keynes (1883–1946) to Christopher Hitchens (1949–2011) and John Pilger (1939–). Recurrent financial difficulties have resulted in the *New Statesman* being known by friend and foe alike as the *Staggers*, a nickname the magazine has embraced as the title of one of many *blogs on its website. *See also* LITERARY JOURNALISM.

News UK The *Murdoch empire's national newspaper arm in the UK, known until 2013 as *News International. It publishes the **Sun*, **Sun on Sunday*, **Times*, and **Sunday Times*. *See also* NEWS CORP.

news values The factors that journalists consider when deciding the *newsworthiness of any event, statement, or other potential story. Although academics are more likely than journalists to use the actual term 'news values', practitioners and scholars alike seem to agree that some things are more likely to become *news than others, and that the process of *selection involves a range of factors. Journalists might learn to make such choices within a matter of seconds, in a way that appears to observers to be merely instinctive, but it can involve a complex intellectual process of weighing up issues such as the *public interest, the appetite of the *audience, the reliability of the *source, and the number of resources required to cover the event. Scholars have made repeated attempts over the decades to analyze the selections made by news organizations, most notably when Norwegians Johan Galtung (1930–) and Mari Ruge (1934–) produced the following taxonomy of news values in the 1960s: *frequency; *threshold; *unambiguity; *meaningfulness; *consonance; *unexpectedness; *continuity; *composition; reference to *elite nations; reference to *elite people; reference to *persons; reference to *negativity. Subsequent generations have amended or added to this list (*see* BAD NEWS; GOOD NEWS; CELEBRITY; ENTERTAINMENT) and/or critiqued it, but it remains influential and frequently cited despite the passage of time since it was first published in 1965 (and despite the fact that the original study was restricted to coverage of foreign news in the Norwegian press). Less frequently cited is the fact that Galtung and Ruge themselves suggested that journalists ought to be prepared to counteract the news values that are dominant within *mainstream media by reporting more on long-term issues than on short-term 'events', by including more contextualizing information within stories, by being prepared to tackle complex, ambiguous, and difficult issues, and by paying more attention to non-elite nations and people (*see* ALTERNATIVE JOURNALISM; DEVELOPMENT JOURNALISM; PEACE JOURNALISM).

Further reading: J. Galtung and M. Ruge, 'The structure of foreign news: the presentation of the Congo, Cuba, and Cyprus crises in four Norwegian newspapers', in *Journal of International Peace Research* (Vol. 1, 1965). D. O'Neill and T. Harcup, 'News Values and Selectivity', in K. Wahl-Jorgensen and T. Hanitzsch (eds), *The Handbook of Journalism Studies* (2009).

Newsvine A US-based *website that combines news *aggregation with original *user-generated content and the sharing of material via *social bookmarking. Since 2007 *Newsvine* has been owned by *NBC News.

Newsweek Once one of the most influential *current affairs magazines in the USA. Launched in 1933 as a slightly edgier rival to the already-established *Time* magazine, *Newsweek* went on to better capture the spirit of the age according to many commentators, especially in the 1960s with its coverage of the civil rights movement, anti-war protests, the so-called 'sexual revolution', and the rebirth of feminism. In 1970 more then 40 women employees sued the magazine for sex *discrimination. But in 2013 it abandoned print to become a digital-only publication under new owners IAC (InterActive Corp). A declining *advertising income meant that it had already merged with the **Daily Beast** website in 2010, when it was sold by the *Washington Post* for a reported $1 (one US dollar) plus liabilities. *See also* DRUDGE REPORT.

newsworthiness The extent to which some event, occurrence, statement, or observation has the potential to become *news. Many journalists talk of having an instinct, or a 'nose', that allows them to recognize news intuitively. However, *news values may be picked up from colleagues, learned through *training, and absorbed by being an observant member of the *audience. Notions of what is **newsworthy** can differ markedly between *mainstream journalism and *alternative journalism, with much of the latter predicated on an explicit rejection of established news values.

newszak A derogatory term for formulaic, unchallenging, and frequently inconsequential journalism. The label echoes 'muzak', the uniform version of background music that provides a bland soundtrack in many lifts, shopping centres, and hotel foyers. *See also* CHURNALISM; DUMBING DOWN; McJOURNALISM.

new technology Recent or emerging forms of technology used within media, often with the effect of speeding-up output, offering new creative possibilities, and cutting jobs. The switch in newsrooms from typewriters to computers, which mostly occurred in the 1980s in the UK and USA, is an example of the adoption of new technology within journalism, as are the development of *data journalism and the growth of *social media strategies in more recent years. *See also* NEW MEDIA; WAPPING DISPUTE.

New York Daily News One of the top ten biggest-selling daily newspapers in the USA since its launch in 1919 as an experimental pioneer of the *tabloid format. In March 1991, following a series of disputes with print unions, it was sold by the Tribune Company of Chicago to the UK-based *media mogul Robert Maxwell (1923–91). After Maxwell drowned just eight months later, the *New York Daily News* was acquired by Mortimer Zuckerman (1937–). As of 2013, its online presence was second only to that of the *New York Times* for the number of unique visitors to a US metropolitan newspaper website.

New Yorker A US politics, culture, literature, and humour magazine that has been published more or less weekly since 1925 and which, despite its title, circulates nationally. Famous for its *cartoon covers, the *New Yorker* is also an advocate of *long-form, *literary, and *investigative journalism: over four issues in 1965 it published Truman

Capote's account of multiple murders in a small Kansas town, which became the book *In Cold Blood*; and three issues in 2004 carried Seymour Hersh's investigation into the Abu Ghraib prison scandal in Iraq. Since 1999 the magazine and its digital offshoots have been part of the *Condé Nast stable.

New York Journal *See* YELLOW PRESS.

New York Post A popular US daily *tabloid newspaper, plus website, described as one of the two most authentic mouthpieces of *media mogul Rupert Murdoch (the other being the *Sun* in the UK). However, the *New York Post* long predated the *Murdoch empire. It began life as the *broadsheet *New York Evening Post* in 1801 and was associated with liberal views for much of its life; the name was shortened to the *New York Post* in 1934. In the 1970s it was bought by Rupert Murdoch's *News Corporation, which transformed it into a paper famed for *sensational coverage of sex, crime, and celebrities, *headlines such as 'Headless body in topless bar', and cheerleading for Republican politicians, notably Ronald Reagan. Murdoch has owned the *Post* since 1976, apart from a gap between 1988 and 1993 when restrictions on media *ownership required its disposal for a while. In addition to classic tabloid fare, the paper has also been notable for pushing the News Corp *media agenda, devoting considerable space to neo-conservative *op-ed material, and launching attacks on its 'liberal' media rivals, notably the *New York Times*. However, the paper does not always take itself too seriously: in 2013 the *New York Post* teamed up with a sightseeing company to offer regular coach trips around some of the city locations that prompted its famous headlines, with the warning: 'This tour is not for the squeamish or faint of heart'. Something similar might be said of the newspaper itself.

New York Times An upmarket quality daily newspaper published in *broadsheet format since 1851 and priding itself on being regarded as one of the two main papers of record in the USA (the other being the *Washington Post*). Nicknamed *The Grey Lady*, its claims to fame include publication of the *Pentagon Papers about the Vietnam War and the fact that it has won more *Pulitzer prizes than any other newspaper. It also helped expose the *hackgate scandal and worked with *WikiLeaks and a number of European newspapers on *cablegate. Less welcome notoriety arrived in the first decade of the 21st century, with the revelation of widespread *plagiarism by *Times* reporter Jayson Blair (1976–), and the newspaper's *mea culpa* that its reporting of the US government's case for the invasion of Iraq was 'not as rigorous as it should have been'. The newspaper and its range of digital offshoots are owned by the New York Times Company, which also publishes the **Boston Globe* and the **International Herald Tribune*. The *Times* produces the most popular US-based news website and in 2013 it overtook **USA Today* to become the US newspaper with the second highest total *readership (print and digital combined), trailing only the **Wall Street Journal*. *See also* ALL THE NEWS THAT'S FIT TO PRINT.

(((●))) SEE WEB LINKS

• From the editors: 'The *Times* and Iraq'
• Correcting the record re Jayson Blair

New York World *See* YELLOW PRESS; UNDERCOVER REPORTING.

NFPW *See* NATIONAL FEDERATION OF PRESS WOMEN.

nib (news in brief) A short *news item, often just one paragraph, that can be useful for filling a hole when designing the pages as well as for giving readers some bite-sized chunks or nibbles. Unlike a *filler, a nib may be regarded as an important story despite its brevity.

niche A magazine, website, or other form of journalistic product that is targeted at a specialized or special-interest readership, and which in turn delivers a target *audience to niche *advertisers. *See also* COMMUNITY OF INTEREST; NARROWCASTING; ULTRA-NICHE.

Night and Day The Tom Stoppard play, first performed in 1978, which contains the often quoted line: 'I'm with you on the free press, it's the newspapers I can't stand'. In a 2005 interview with **British Journalism Review*, Stoppard said people were wrong if they felt it summed up his entire view of journalism. 'The good stuff is still good', he explained in a line much less likely to be quoted ad nauseam. *See also* FREE PRESS.

90-9-1 rule (one per cent rule), The observation or rule of thumb (as articulated by web guru Jakob Nielsen in 2006) that, in the online world, roughly 90 per cent of *users never contribute actively, 9 per cent contribute a little, and the remaining 1 per cent are responsible for almost all comments and participation. *See also* CURATION; ONLINE

JOURNALISM; PUBLIC OPINION; USER-GENERATED CONTENT; YOUR COMMENTS.

(((•))) SEE WEB LINKS

• Jakob Nielsen on participation inequality

NLGJA *See* NATIONAL LESBIAN AND GAY JOURNALISTS ASSOCIATION.

***NME* (*New Musical Express*)** A UK-based music weekly launched in 1952 that has since been much mythologized as representing various *'golden ages' of music criticism in general and rock music journalism in particular. Its heyday was probably the 1970s when, even more than its rivals such as *Melody Maker* and *Sounds*, it became associated with forms of *gonzo journalism, *immersion reporting, and the publication of politico-cultural essays that on occasions scarcely seemed to mention music. Once printed on very inky newsprint in newspaper format, today it is a magazine available in various digital formats as well as print. The *NME* is owned by *IPC.

Further reading: P. Long, *The History of the NME* (2012).

noddy A practice in *television journalism whereby an interviewer is filmed nodding their head or displaying other signs of intent listening. Noddies are typically filmed at the end of an *interview and then inserted during editing.

North Briton A shortlived but ground-breaking radical weekly newspaper launched by John Wilkes (1725–97) in 1762 as an alternative to *The Briton*, which was seen as a mouthpiece for the British government. In contrast, the *North Briton* declared 'the liberty of the press' to be 'the birthright of a Briton' as it set about embarrassing the ruling aristocracy, which responded with legal persecution that led to the '*Wilkes and liberty' agitation in 18th-century London. *See also* FREE PRESS; RADICAL PRESS.

Northcliffe One of the UK's major regional newspaper groups until it was sold by the Daily Mail and General Trust in 2012 to form part of the newly formed *Local World group. *See also* ASSOCIATED NEWSPAPERS.

Northern & Shell A UK-based media company owned by Richard Desmond (1951–). Northern & Shell began life in the 1970s and initially built a profitable portfolio of 'adult' magazines before buying the *Daily Express* and *Daily Star* newspapers in 2000 and taking over Channel 5 television in 2010. Northern & Shell's other interests include *OK!* magazine.

Northern Echo A daily newspaper based in Darlington and covering north-east England. It was launched in 1870 as a liberal-leaning regional publication and the editor between 1871 and 1880 was a young W. T. Stead (1849–1912) (*see* PALL MALL GAZETTE). Today it is part of the *Newsquest stable.

(((∰))) SEE WEB LINKS

• W. T. Stead's obituary from the *Northern Echo*

Northern Star A radical weekly newspaper published in the UK between 1837 and 1852, initially in Leeds and later in London. The *Northern Star* supported the working class pro-democracy Chartist movement and achieved sales of up to 48,000 copies a week, making it one of the most popular newspapers in the world at the time. The title was revived briefly in the 1990s as a new name for the alternative weekly *Leeds Other Paper*. *See also* ALTERNATIVE PRESS; RADICAL PRESS.

(((∰))) SEE WEB LINKS

• British Library digital archive of the 19th-century *Northern Star*

Norwich Post One of the first provincial newspapers in England (some say the very first) that was launched by the commercial printer Francis Burges (*c.*1675–1706) in Norwich in September 1701, following the lapsing of the *Licensing Act six years earlier. Although Burges died in 1706 and his weekly paper folded in 1713, by that stage Norwich itself had several other newspapers and *local journalism was becoming established in many parts of the country. *See also* BERROW'S WORCESTER JOURNAL; STAMFORD MERCURY.

notes A *reporter's contemporaneous written record of an *interview, court case, meeting, *press conference, sporting contest, or some other event. A journalist's notes will inform the writing of the story and will then be kept in case its veracity is challenged, in which case they may ultimately need to be produced as evidence in a *libel case. Notes are typically handwritten in *shorthand, longhand, or a mixture of the two, but they may also be typed directly into an electronic device. *See also* ACCURACY; NOTE-TAKING.

note-taking The process of writing down what people are saying and/ or what a journalist is observing, for the purpose of writing a subsequent story. Reporters write notes contemporaneously to aid their memories and to provide some form of evidence in case their version of what was said is later questioned. Although the ability to make audio recordings on mobile devices has replaced note-taking for some journalists in some circumstances, taking an accurate note that can be retrieved within seconds remains one of the *reporter's key skills. *See also* GALLERY REPORTING; NEIL REPORT; NOTES; SHORTHAND.

Novaya Gazeta A small-circulation Moscow-based newspaper, with associated website, known for *investigative journalism and critical independence from the state and other powerful forces in post-Soviet Russia. *Novaya Gazeta* was founded in 1993 by journalists who previously worked on *Pravda*. Members of staff have repeatedly suffered threats and intimidation, and investigative reporter Anna Politkovskaya (1958–2006) was assassinated in 2006. *See also* DEATHS OF JOURNALISTS.

(⊕) SEE WEB LINKS

• English-language version of *Novaya Gazeta*

NPR (National Public Radio) A network of independent radio stations across the USA that see themselves as providing an alternative to more corporate media outlets and decided to work together in 1971. Today NPR provides its affiliates with domestic and international news for a range of digital platforms in addition to radio. *See also* RADIO JOURNALISM.

NUJ *See* NATIONAL UNION OF JOURNALISTS.

Nuts The UK's biggest-selling weekly *lads' mag (plus online *brand) that, since 2004, has successfully targeted a young male readership interested in gadgets, entertainment, and pictures of female flesh. It is owned by *IPC. *See also* SEXISM; PORNIFICATION.

NWN Media Ltd A provincial newspaper company covering north Wales and parts of the north-west of England, the flagship title of which is the *Leader*. NWN Media Ltd was ranked fourteenth in the *Newspaper Society's list of the top regional press publishers in the UK in 2013, based on its fourteen titles' average weekly *circulation of around 400,000 between them.

Oakland Tribune A US daily newspaper launched in 1874 to cover the city of Oakland in California. Together with its associated website, *Inside Bay Area*, it is now owned by the Bay Area News Group.

obit An abbreviated term for *obituary that is more likely to be heard within newsrooms than in public.

obituary A profile of the life of somebody who has recently died. Obituaries are typically about people in the public eye, or whose lives are thought to have particular relevance to the audience, and combine detailing notable successes and failures with the telling of more personal traits and anecdotes to help bring the subject to life. Once the location for code or innuendo ('He was a confirmed bachelor...', 'She did not suffer fools gladly...', and so on), obituaries have tended to become more 'warts and all' over the years, and there has also been something of a trend towards featuring more 'ordinary' people. *Obits of famous people who are old and/or ill are often prepared in advance and have even been published prematurely on occasions when rumours of somebody's death have been greatly exaggerated. Journalists working on *cuttings-job obituaries have been caught out reproducing fake information planted on *Wikipedia. *See also* DEATH WATCH; SOCIETY OF PROFESSIONAL OBITUARY WRITERS.

Further reading: M. Johnson, *The Dead Beat: The Perverse Pleasures of Obituaries* (2007).

N. Starck, *Life After Death: The Art of the Obituary* (2006).

objective journalism Journalism that separates the *reporting of *facts from the journalist's (or news organization's) own *comment or *opinion. **Objectivity** is often spoken of in the same breath as *impartiality, although the two concepts are not necessarily the same: impartial reporting is more concerned with fairness, neutrality, and *balance, whereas objective reporting is taken to mean an attempt at establishing *accuracy (or even completeness). Objectivity is associated with the *Enlightenment, which involved the rational and systematic pursuit of knowledge based on observation, evidence, and testing rather than on emotion, expectation, or prejudice. Within journalism, objectivity is often held up as an ideal, particularly in the USA, even amongst many who believe that absolute objectivity is impossible to achieve because any form of *selection and mediation necessarily has the effect of simplifying (and distorting) the complex and often messy realities of life. Notwithstanding such difficulties with the concept, a commitment to objective journalism is often seen as a promise to be as fair and as accurate as possible given the *constraints of time, space, and available resources. It involves examining two (or more) sides of a story, looking for evidence, assessing the credibility of *sources and their conflicting versions of events, running a story only if it stands up, and attributing information appropriately. In this context, the concept of *pragmatic objectivity has emerged in recent years as a way of explaining how newsrooms go about assessing the accuracy and credibility of a story before publication. Such measures are seen by some commentators as amounting to little more than a formula (a *strategic ritual) designed more to avoid accusations of *bias than to establish the *truth about something. Some journalists and some media organizations (*see* ADVOCACY JOURNALISM; ALTERNATIVE MEDIA; GONZO JOURNALISM; OPPOSITIONAL REPORTING; RADICAL PRESS) reject the very idea of objective journalism as a sham and make a point of stating their involvement or *bias openly, arguing that such a stance is more honest than pretending to be objective as it allows the audience to take it into consideration. Opinionated journalism was the norm in early newspapers, with objectivity only gradually adopted from the second half of the 19th century onwards. *See also* ETHICS; JOURNALISM OF ATTACHMENT; SUBJECTIVITY; VERIFICATION.

Observer The oldest surviving Sunday newspaper in the world, published at the *quality end of the UK market since 1791. Usually associated with liberal values, the *Observer* condemned the British government over the Suez crisis of 1956 (seen by many as its finest hour), although it surprised many readers by backing the 2003 invasion of Iraq. Since 1993 it has been owned by the Guardian Media Group (*see* SCOTT TRUST), leading to suggestions that it has become a poor relation of the *Guardian*.

Ofcom (Office of Communications) The UK's regulatory body for television, radio, telecommunications, and (since 2011) postal services. Ofcom issues licences to commercial broadcasting organizations and has the power to revoke licences and/or issue fines for breaches of its broadcasting code (which covers issues such as taste and decency, fairness, *accuracy, and *impartiality). Although Ofcom has no responsibility for licensing the non-commercial *BBC, it does deal with some complaints about BBC programming (although not on the issue of impartiality). Beyond its licensing function, Ofcom has a role in investigating whether major media mergers, deals, and takeovers might damage plurality, and this can even involve blocking a newspaper takeover if it is deemed to be against the public interest. Answerable to Parliament, Ofcom was created by the *Communications Act 2003, which involved merging the powers of predecessor bodies: the Broadcasting Standards Commission; the Independent Television Commission; the Radio Authority; the Radiocommunications Agency; and the Office of Telecommunications. *See also* STATUTORY REGULATION.

(⊕) SEE WEB LINKS
• The Ofcom broadcasting code

off-diary A story or item discovered by a journalist's own observation, initiative, investigation, or communication with *contacts. In contrast with more predictable *diary stories, off-diary ones tend to be highly prized as they help to distinguish one news organization or *brand from another. If resources allow for investment in *investigative journalism, one or more journalists may be taken 'off-diary' for a period and relieved of responsibility for covering routine stories.

Office of Communications *See* OFCOM.

Official Secrets Act Laws that apply in many countries, including the UK, India, and New Zealand, by which revealing information designated as a state secret becomes a criminal offence. Although aimed primarily at spies or traitors working on behalf of foreign powers, Official Secrets legislation has also been used to prosecute or threaten with prosecution journalists (and/or their *sources, or *whistleblowers) who investigate stories about the confidential workings of state departments, particularly in the fields of intelligence, nuclear weapons, and armed conflict. Although prosecutions are rare, *freedom of information campaigners argue that the possibility has a *chilling effect on *investigative journalism even into matters that have nothing to do with national security. The UK's first Official Secrets Act was passed in 1911 and its most recent became law in 1989, which tightened the definition of secret information but did not include what many journalists had called for, namely, a defence that revealing certain information may be in the *public interest. *See also* DA-NOTICES; LEVELLER.

off the record Information that a *source gives to a journalist on the understanding that the information will not be attributed to the source. *See also* ON THE RECORD.

OhmyNews A website launched in South Korea in 2000 that is largely (but not entirely) written by amateur contributors using *open-source publishing software and working on the principle that 'every citizen is a reporter'. The site offers alternative perspectives to those found in mainstream media, acts as a form of *watchdog on the powerful, and is incredibly popular. *See also* ALTERNATIVE MEDIA; CITIZEN JOURNALISM; NETIZEN.

(((⊕))) SEE WEB LINKS
• *OhmyNews* on citizen journalism

OK! 1. A weekly *magazine (plus online *brand) published in the UK and specializing in *celebrity coverage. Along with the *Daily Express* newspaper and Channel 5 television, it is owned by Richard Desmond's *Northern & Shell Media.
2. A weekly magazine and online brand published in the USA and specializing in celebrity coverage, owned by American Media Ltd.

ombudsperson (ombudsman, ombudswoman) 1. Somebody within a news organization whose job (or role) it is to receive, investigate, and respond to complaints or issues raised by members of the audience or by people or organizations featured in stories. Some ombudspeople are more independent than others (*see* IRISH TIMES; ORGANIZATION OF NEWS OMBUDSMEN; READERS' EDITOR; WASHINGTON POST).
2. A role carried out by representatives of some *self-regulatory media bodies whereby they receive, investigate, mediate, and sometimes adjudicate on complaints by members of the public about the activities of one or more of the news organizations.

(((⊕))) SEE WEB LINKS
• The Office of the Press Council of Ireland's Press Ombudsman

one per cent rule *See* 90-9-1 RULE.

Onion A US-based humorous magazine and website that has built a large audience for its spoof journalism since its creation in 1988 by students at the University of Wisconsin. The *Onion* now includes TV and radio output in addition to print and online material. Every now and then one of its invented news items gets picked up and reproduced in an overseas media outlet that fails to check it, or to realize the joke. *See also* SATIRICAL JOURNALISM.

online journalism News and other forms of journalistic output that is distributed via *websites, *social media, *RSS feeds, *email newsletters, and other forms of online communication. Online journalism is associated with the creation and growth of the *internet, and can range along a continuum from amateur *blogging or *ezines at one end, to commercial media websites behind *paywalls at the other. The term 'online journalism' tends to imply something more than merely the digital distribution of journalism created for print or other offline media (*see* SHOVELWARE), and it typically incorporates *multimedia and/or interactive elements that might include text, *pictures, *audio, *video, *hyperlinks, users' *comments, and the use of *Facebook and *Twitter to help deliver audiences (or 'drive traffic', in the corporate jargon) and foster *brand loyalty. Online journalism allows for stories to be presented in different, non-linear ways, with members of the *audience having an element of choice as to how and when they wish to receive it. As more and more journalists (along with an increasing proportion of the population) have grown up in the digital age, online journalism is increasingly referred to simply as journalism. However, although online journalism is widely seen as the future of journalism, few news organizations have yet managed to find a way of making any money out of it (or 'monetizing' it, in corporate-speak). *See also* AMBIENT JOURNALISM; CITIZEN JOURNALISM; CONVERGENCE; DIGITAL MEDIA; INFOGRAPHICS; INTERACTIVITY; KEYWORDS; NETWORKED JOURNALISM; 90-9-1 RULE; OPEN JOURNALISM; OPEN-SOURCE PUBLISHING; PROPUBLICA; SOCIAL BOOKMARKING; STORIFY; USER-GENERATED CONTENT; WORDPRESS; YOUTUBE.

Further reading: J. Jones and L. Salter, *Digital Journalism* (2012).
P. Bradshaw and L. Rohumaa, *The Online Journalism Handbook* (2011).

Online Journalism Review A US-based online discussion forum about *online journalism, hosted by the University of Southern California, that includes journalists, academics, and journalism educators amongst its contributors.

on spec The speculative supply of an item to a media organization by a *freelance journalist. Unlike with material that has been specifically commissioned by an *editor or section editor, material sent in on spec is normally only paid for if it is actually used. *See also* ALL-ROUNDER.

on the record Information and comments that an interviewee provides to a journalist on the understanding that the material can be published and openly attributed to the *source, as opposed to being *off the record or unattributable

op-ed A newspaper page or section that carries *opinion and *leader columns.

open journalism The idea that journalism is at its best if it involves interaction and two-way *conversations between journalist and audience, and therefore that *online journalism ought not to be hidden behind *paywalls. Perhaps most associated with the **Guardian*'s online *brand, it has been described by some critics as a failed business model. *See also* COLLABORATIVE JOURNALISM; CROWDSOURCING; INTERACTIVITY; NETWORKED JOURNALISM.

open-source publishing The opportunity for contributors to upload material directly to public-facing *websites without it passing through any form of *editing, *moderation, or *gatekeeping process in advance of publication (although it may subsequently be removed if it is found to contravene the site's rules or policies). Open-source publishing was pioneered in online *alternative media such as **Indymedia* and **OhmyNews* long before most *mainstream media began accepting *user-generated content. *See also* CROWDSOURCING.

opinion A personal, collective, or organizational viewpoint, the expression of which is traditionally eschewed in news reporting unless it is attributed to a *source or the subject of the story. While *news sticks to the *facts plus *attribution, *editorial columns exist to give the editor's official opinion on an issue, and personal *features or columns are free to state the opinions of their named writers. Journalism *training and ethical *codes emphasize this separation between fact and opinion, but in practice the line is often blurred, not only in forms of *advocacy journalism or *oppositional reporting that reject ideas of *impartiality, but also in *tabloid newspapers that frequently incorporate unattributed *comment into the text of news stories.

opportunity to reply Giving a chance for a person or organization about whom allegations are being made to respond, normally prior to publication or broadcast. This is generally regarded as good practice within journalism, even as essential. However, there are exceptions: if proof of wrongdoing is legally watertight, for example; or if there is a fear that alerting the subject might result in them giving the story to rival news organizations or seeking an *injunction to prevent publication. *Compare* RIGHT OF REPLY.

oppositional reading When members of an *audience reject whatever interpretation or *ideology may implicitly or explicitly be present within any piece of *communication. According to the *encoding, decoding model, an oppositional reading is one of the possible responses available to an audience; others are a *preferred reading and a *negotiated reading. *See also* CODE; HEGEMONY.

oppositional reporting A form of *alternative journalism that aims to speak up for the powerless in society, to allow the powerless to speak directly on their own behalf, and to inspire democratic participation and social action amongst citizens. Oppositional reporting strives for *accuracy by adopting journalistic techniques such as *interviewing, *attribution, and investigation, but it rejects *objectivity and incorporates within it an ideological critique of mainstream discourse. *See also* ACTIVIST JOURNALISM; ALTERNATIVE MEDIA; BIAS; REPRESENTATION.

Organization of News Ombudsmen An international organization of *readers' editors and internal ombudspeople within news organizations, which holds regular gatherings in various countries and runs a website to exchange information about accuracy and fairness in the media. *See also* OMBUDSPERSON.

(⊕) SEE WEB LINKS
• Homepage of the Organization of News Ombudsmen

Orlando Sentinel A US daily newspaper covering the city of Orlando in the state of Florida since 1876. Along with its websites in English and Spanish (*El Sentinel*), it is owned by the Tribune Company of Chicago.

Orwell's six rules of writing Guidelines for good writing as set out in 1946 by the journalist, essayist, and novelist George Orwell (1903–1950), which have subsequently been passed on to generations of journalists who have been urged to follow the '**plain style**' he advocated. His six rules are:

- Never use a metaphor, simile, or other figure of speech which you are used to seeing in print.
- Never use a long word where a short one will do.
- If it is possible to cut out a word, always cut it out.
- Never use the passive where you can use the active.
- Never use a foreign phrase, a scientific word, or a jargon word, if you can think of an everyday English equivalent.
- Break any of these rules sooner than say anything outright barbarous.

See also ACTIVE WRITING; LANGUAGE OF NEWS; STYLE.

Further reading: G. Orwell, *Politics and the English Language* (2013 [1946]).

ownership The proprietorship and control of media organizations, which influences the journalism produced by such organizations because ultimately it is the owners who decide issues such as financial investments and cutbacks, which markets to target, which products to launch, merge, or close, what editors to hire and fire, and in many cases, what political and/or ethical ethos their *newsrooms should follow. In capitalist economies such as the USA, UK, and Australia, most journalists work for news organizations that are owned by commercial companies or corporations with the pursuit of profit as the primary organizational goal; producing journalism is just the way (or one of the ways) in which that goal is pursued. There is a tendency in such economies for the ownership of media organizations to become increasingly concentrated in fewer yet larger entities that are likely to use their economic muscle to seek to damage, eliminate, or buy up the competition. Some *proprietors are also accused of using their perceived political influence over audiences to persuade governments to change political or economic policies, and the *Leveson Inquiry heard evidence of intensive lobbying on behalf of some media companies, notably the *Murdoch empire, much of it conducted in secret.

Concentration of media ownership has been a key area of concern for journalists' trade unions as well as for media activists such as the *Campaign for Press and Broadcasting Freedom (in the UK) and *Fairness and Accuracy in Reporting (in the USA). Other models of media ownership include the *licence fee (*see* BBC), direct state control (*see* CHINA DAILY, for example), and cooperative or collective ownership (as in many examples of *alternative media). *See also* CONCENTRATION OF OWNERSHIP; HORIZONTAL INTEGRATION; MEDIA AGENDA; POLITICAL ECONOMY; VERTICAL INTEGRATION.

Oz An *underground magazine published in Australia between 1963 and 1969 and in the UK from 1967 to 1973, *Oz*'s main claim to fame was the prison sentences handed down to its three *editors Richard Neville (1941–), Felix Dennis (1947–), and Jim Anderson (1937–) at an Old Bailey obscenity trial in 1971. The case concerned an issue of the magazine that had been guest-edited by a group of readers who were still at school, and it became something of a celebrated cause for the liberal intelligentsia, many of whom gave evidence in defence of freedom of expression. The three editors were later cleared on appeal; Dennis went on to become the multi-millionaire publisher of less risky *magazines such as *Auto Express*, *Kung-Fu Monthly*, and *The Week*. *See also* ALTERNATIVE MEDIA; SPARE RIB.

(((●))) SEE WEB LINKS
• Archive of *Oz* covers

PA *See* PRESS ASSOCIATION.

package Treatment of a *news item or *feature on TV or radio that comprises several pre-recorded and edited elements such as *interviews, commentary, and relevant pictures and/or sound.
A package will typically last between one and three minutes. A staple of *broadcast journalism, packages can also be part of the audio-video offering of *online journalism, although audience research suggests that most web *users tend to prefer much shorter clips.

pack mentality When a number of journalists and/or their news organizations reinforce each other's views, approach, and/or actions on a particular story. Although such a pack can work together positively to track down villains and uncover *scandals, a pack mentality can also lead to the *harassment and vilification of innocent people who unwittingly find themselves the focus of media attention. *See also* MEDIA SCRUM; MORAL PANIC.

page furniture A phrase covering those elements of a *newspaper, *magazine, or online page that are used to present and project an item, including the *headline, *standfirst, *caption, *cross-heads, *pull quotes, boxes, panels, and graphics.

Page Three The phenomenon of soft-porn photographs of topless young women that appear in some popular *tabloid newspapers, most famously dominating the prime third page of the UK's biggest-selling daily paper, the *Sun. Introduced in 1970, the year after the paper became part of the *Murdoch empire, the semi-naked 'pin-up' has ever since provoked affection and hostility in roughly equal measure. Supporters portray it as a piece of harmless fun, a cheerful ray of sunlight amid the overwhelmingly gloomy news, while critics see it as an insulting objectification of women. Opponents of Page Three are typically labelled by the newspaper itself as 'killjoys', most notably when the Member of Parliament Clare Short expressed concern about the impact on women of routine exposure to sexualized images in a 'family newspaper' and the *Sun* labelled her 'fat, jealous Clare' in an infamous 2004 headline. That headline appeared under the editorship of Rebekah Wade (later Brooks), the *Sun*'s first female editor. Despite speculation that Wade might drop it, she not only retained Page Three when she became editor in 2003, the first day's picture was captioned, 'Rebekah from Wapping'; the model was a different Rebekah. *See also* BILD; PORNIFICATION; SEXISM.

Pall Mall Gazette A London-based evening newspaper that was published between 1865 and 1923, when it was absorbed into the *Evening Standard*. For part of its existence the paper was associated with a populist form of *new journalism, most notably between 1883 and 1890 when it was edited by W. T. Stead (1849–1912, *see* NORTHERN ECHO). Stead described editing the *Pall Mall Gazette* as 'a glorious opportunity of attacking the devil'. His most famous journalistic exploit came in 1885 when, in a series of shocking articles headlined, 'The Maiden Tribute of Modern Babylon', the paper exposed child prostitution in the UK's capital city. The story had a dramatic impact in Victorian England: Stead served three months in prison for technically abducting a girl while researching the story, but sales of the paper rocketed, new legislation raised the age of consent from 13 to 16, and the episode has been credited with effectively beginning *investigative journalism as we know it today. After he died in 1912 (as a passenger on the ill-fated *Titanic*), a memorial to W. T. Stead was commissioned 'by journalists of many lands' and placed on London's Embankment, near to the location of the *Pall Mall Gazette*'s offices.

(⊕) SEE WEB LINKS
• W.T. Stead and the *Pall Mall Gazette*

pamphlets One-off printed products that are shorter than books yet do not feature the variety of material (or regularity of publication) of newspapers or periodicals. A pamphlet typically contains just one essay or piece of polemical writing. Pamphlets are particularly prevalent during periods of social unrest, perhaps most notably the English revolution (or civil war) of the 1640s when both the Royalist and Parliamentarian sides used them to communicate their arguments to a wider public. Such pamphlets helped inspire the *newsbook, a forerunner of the *newspaper. *See also* CHAPBOOK; LEVELLERS; PRINTING.

Panorama A *current affairs programme that has been broadcast on
*BBC television since 1953. Its high reputation is based on *investigative
journalism and a willingness to probe the BBC itself, including the
corporation's role in events leading to the *Hutton Inquiry and the
*Pollard Review. However, its record audience of 22.8 million people
was achieved for a 1995 interview with Diana, Princess of Wales, about
her disintegrating marriage.

(((()))) SEE WEB LINKS

• The *Panorama* decades

pap An abbreviation of the noun *paparazzi that is also used as a verb
meaning 'to take a paparazzi-style photograph'.

paparazzi An unofficial collective term for freelance *photographers
who take pictures of *celebrities out and about in public, typically
entering or leaving clubs, restaurants, hotels, casinos, shops, airports,
cars, or taxis, or in a location such as a beach. Such *pictures may result
from a *tip by a member of the public but they can also come about by
members of the paparazzi following targets or simply hanging around
celebrities' regular haunts. Some celebrities and/or their agents are said
to be complicit in informing the paparazzi of their movements in the
hope of attracting media coverage. *Pap photographs tend to be bought
by media organizations more on the basis of their novelty or candid
nature than because of any particular journalistic or photographic
quality. Members of the paparazzi were widely condemned for following
Diana, Princess of Wales, at the time of her death in a Paris car accident
in 1997. *See also* CELEBRITY; FREELANCE JOURNALIST; PRIVACY.

papped To be photographed by a member of the *paparazzi, often but
not always without any prior arrangement being made or permission
being sought. *See also* PRIVACY.

parachute journalism National or international news organizations
suddenly descending on a location to cover a story rather than having a
permanent presence or engaging local journalists. The phrase is often
used to imply an absence of understanding, contextualizing
information, and/or respect for locals. *See also* BIGFOOTING; FIXER.

passive audience A conceptualization of people uncritically reading,
watching, and listening to journalism, simply absorbing whatever
messages may be contained within. The counter-argument that real-life

audiences tend to be more complicated than that had gained ground within *journalism studies and *media studies long before audiences were invited to take a more active role via *UGC and *social media. *Compare* ACTIVE AUDIENCE; COLLABORATIVE JOURNALISM; ENCODING, DECODING. *See also* HYPODERMIC MODEL.

patch A geographical area covered by a *reporter in the UK. A patch tends to be known in the USA as a *beat.

Pathé News A pioneering provider of *newsreels that was founded in Paris, France, by Charles Pathé (1863–1957) in 1896. Pathé News stopped making newsreels in 1970 but the company continues (under the name British Pathé) to provide historic *clips to television news and current affairs programmes.

(((●))) SEE WEB LINKS
• Pathé News newsreels

payoff An ending to a story that offers a new twist, a summing up, a quip, or some other way of rewarding members of the audience for staying until the end. A payoff is more often found in *features or other longer items than in standard news stories.

paywall A system whereby *online journalism content is made available only to those *users who pay for it. Since the advent of the *internet, different media companies have experimented with different ways of 'monetizing' *content, including digital subscriptions, complete paywalls, and metered payments. Paywalls operate on the principle that, as the production of journalism costs money and somebody has to pay for it, why should that somebody not include members of the *audience? For a long time conventional wisdom among publishers was that paywalls were likely to be successful only for more specialist titles (such as the *Financial Times* and *Wall Street Journal*), but the *Murdoch empire challenged this view when it placed the websites of many of its general titles (including the *Times* and *Sun*) behind paywalls; many newspaper *websites in the USA had introduced some form of payment model by 2012. Some publishers have adopted hybrid systems whereby users may have free access to a certain quantity of stories online, or to certain sections of the website, after which further access requires payment. However, in many circles, especially among adherents of *open journalism, the term 'paywall' tends to have negative connotations in a way that 'cover price' does not.

PBS (Public Broadcasting Service) A US *public service broadcasting organization supplying local TV channels with programmes including the *PBS Newshour*, a serious *newscast that is broadcast each weekday evening on more than 300 stations across the USA. It is also available to view online. *See also* TELEVISION JOURNALISM.

(⊕) SEE WEB LINKS
• *PBS Newshour*

PCC *See* PRESS COMPLAINTS COMMISSION.

peace journalism A form of *reporting that questions the narrative of the inevitability of war while emphasizing long-term causes of, and possible solutions to, *conflict. Peace journalism also tends to advocate a *human rights approach to global issues and to allow civilians caught up in conflict zones to speak for themselves. It can be seen as an example of *advocacy and/or *development journalism, and it is often found within forms of *alternative media. Scholarly work in the area of peace journalism also operates as a critique of the 'war journalism' and *stereotyping that is sometimes said to dominate much of the *mainstream media's coverage of international conflict. *See also* ALTERNATIVE JOURNALISM; WAR REPORTING.

(⊕) SEE WEB LINKS
• Peace Journalism website

Peace News *See* LEVELLER.

Pearson A UK-based media company that owns the **Financial Times* and Penguin Books, and has a 50 per cent stake in the **Economist* among other interests. Pearson owned the *Westminster Press stable of provincial newspapers until 1996, when they were sold to *Newsquest.

peg The reason (or excuse) for running a particular *news story or *feature at a particular time. Such a peg might be an event, a fresh development, the release of new information, an anniversary, or merely somebody speaking anew about a story. *See also* ANGLE; NEWS PEG.

penny press Cheaply priced newspapers and periodicals that emerged in the USA and UK during the 19th century and were aimed at a mass, predominantly working-class, readership. *See also* DEMOCRACY; POPS; PRINTING.

Pentagon Papers A secret US government document about the conduct of the Vietnam War that was leaked to the *New York Times*, the *Washington Post*, and 17 other newspapers in 1971. Its 7,000 pages were photocopied and leaked by the military analyst turned *whistleblower, Daniel Ellsberg (1931–). When the Nixon administration tried to suppress publication the US Supreme Court ruled that such *prior restraint would be unconstitutional (*see* FIRST AMENDMENT). Ellsberg was subsequently tried for espionage but charges against him were eventually dismissed. Four decades later he became an outspoken supporter of whistleblowers Bradley Manning (*see* WIKILEAKS) and Edward Snowden (*see* GUARDIAN), both of whom were also pursued by the US government for revealing state secrets. *See also* LEAK; WATERGATE.

Further reading: D. Ellsberg, *Secrets: A Memoir of Vietnam and the Pentagon Papers* (2003).

(((🌐))) SEE WEB LINKS

• The battle over the Pentagon Papers

People A Sunday newspaper, sometimes calling itself the **Sunday People**, published in the UK since 1881 and which had a record for populist investigations for much of the 20th century. In the 1960s the *People* exposed a betting scandal that resulted in the jailing of several footballers, for example. Owned by *Trinity Mirror, today it competes with the *Sun on Sunday* at the *redtop end of the market with a staple fare of stories about sex, crime, and celebs. It also competes against Trinity Mirror's own *Sunday Mirror*, prompting frequent reports of the *People*'s impending demise.

People's Daily A newspaper published in China since 1946 and widely regarded as representing the views of the Central Committee of the ruling Chinese Communist Party (*see* NEWS MANAGEMENT; PROPAGANDA). Its *People's Daily Online* website, launched in 1997, also has international versions in foreign languages including English, Spanish, and Arabic.

People's News Service A cooperative organization that operated as a form of non-commercial *news agency for the UK's *alternative press during the 1970s and early 1980s. The People's News Service would send alternative publications a regular duplicated digest of stories selected from the alternative press as a whole, allowing subscribers to share material freely amongst themselves. *See also* ALTERNATIVE JOURNALISM; LIBERATION NEWS SERVICE; UNDERGROUND PRESS SYNDICATE.

perestroika *See* GLASNOST.

periodical A newspaper, magazine, or journal published on a regular cycle at intervals of one week or longer. In the UK the term is sometimes used as an alternative to *magazine.

Periodical Publishers Association (PPA) *See* PROFESSIONAL PUBLISHERS ASSOCIATION.

Periodicals Training Council (PTC) An industry body that accredits *magazine journalism *training courses in the UK on behalf of the *Professional Publishers Association. The PTC also runs *awards for student journalists. *See also* JOURNALISM EDUCATION.

(((⊕))) SEE WEB LINKS
• PTC accredited courses

persons, reference to Events that concern people, preferably named individuals, which renders such events more *newsworthy, according to the list of *news values identified by scholars Galtung and Ruge (*see also* HUMAN INTEREST). News journalism tends to present stories as the actions of specific people rather than as the result of wider trends, social forces, or structural conditions.

Pew Research Center for the People and the Press An organization based in Washington that measures public attitudes to the media, news stories, and public issues in the USA. It publishes a weekly index of *audience interest (or otherwise) in major *news stories and also runs an 'excellence in journalism' project that reports on the 'state of the media' (specifically, US journalism) each year.

(((⊕))) SEE WEB LINKS
• Annual reports on American journalism from the Pew Center

Philadelphia Inquirer A daily newspaper (and website) published in Pennsylvania and owned by the Philadelphia Media Network. Dating from 1829, the *Philadelphia Inquirer* is one of the oldest surviving newspapers in the USA and is consistently in the top 25 in terms of *circulation.

phone-hacking Unauthorized access to private telephone calls or messages for the purpose of investigating a story, checking a *tip, or merely embarking on a journalistic *fishing expedition. Phone-hacking, which has been described as one of the *dark arts of journalism, led to the closure of the *News of the World in the UK. The *hackgate scandal resulted from journalists and *private investigators dialling in and listening to voicemail messages that had been left on mobile phone numbers belonging to people in the news including royals, *celebrities, politicians, victims of crime, and their families and associates. Private messages were accessed by hackers who either guessed or blagged the required code or password, which was often simply a factory default setting. The *Leveson Inquiry heard evidence that such phone-hacking extended beyond the *News of the World* and, despite being illegal, was regarded casually, even as a source of mirth, in some *Fleet Street newsrooms during the early days of mobile and cell phones. In the wake of Leveson, and the numerous arrests that eventually resulted from hackgate, it is doubtful if there are many journalists who would still defend the hacking of telephones as a legitimate tool of the trade. *Compare* ETHICAL JOURNALISM. *See also* BLAGGING; CAMILLAGATE; HACKED OFF; PRIVACY; SQUIDGYGATE.

phone-in A common form of radio programming, also sometimes used on TV, in which members of the *audience call up to offer their views or experiences on whatever topic is being discussed. Phone-ins are popular with those who run broadcasting organizations because they are an extremely cheap way of filling airtime and, on rare occasions, they can bring extraordinary testimony to light. They also extend the range of voices and accents that are broadcast although, as with later forms of *user-generated content, they run the risk of journalists and others conflating the opinions expressed by a vocal minority on air with the views of the wider public (*see* PUBLIC OPINION).

photocall An event staged primarily to encourage, facilitate, or placate press *photographers and picture editors. News organizations may be invited to attend a photocall on the implicit (or even explicit) understanding that, in return for the opportunity, they might refrain from *intrusion at other times. A photocall is likely to exclude *reporters, or at least discourage them from asking questions. *See also* NEWS MANAGEMENT; PSEUDO-EVENTS; PUBLIC RELATIONS.

photo caption Words accompanying a *photograph, typically stating where and when the picture was taken and who it features, often in the form of a left-to-right list. The caption may also include the name of the *photographer.

photographer Somebody who takes *photographs for news organizations either as a member of staff or, increasingly, on a *freelance or casual basis. Also known as a *snapper (and sometimes in the past as a lensman), a press photographer should be considered as much a journalist as the person who writes or edits the words that accompany their pictures, and is expected to operate in accordance with the same *laws and *codes of conduct. *See also* GRIP-AND-GRIN; PAPARAZZI; PHOTOCALL; PHOTOJOURNALIST; PHOTO OPPORTUNITY; SNATCH PIC.

(⊕) SEE WEB LINKS
• Press photographers' showcase

photographs Still images taken with a camera or, increasingly these days, with a mobile phone, tablet, or other such device. Photography can be as crucial to reporting the *news (and to *sport reporting) as are the words, but photographs are also used in many other areas of journalism, ranging from *Page Three pin-ups to their *broadsheet equivalents—models in bikinis used to illustrate business page stories about the share prices of a retail chain, for example (*see* SEXISM). Today, journalism in print or online is hard to imagine without photographs, but newspapers and periodicals long pre-dated photography; even when photographs became available they were not immediately embraced by the press, initially because they were difficult to reproduce but also because many older readers were not too keen at such use of *new technology. When fresh pictures are not available, *websites will normally attach a *library or stock photograph to each story as it tends to improve *search engine rankings (*see* SEARCH ENGINE OPTIMIZATION). *See also* CROP; DIGITAL MANIPULATION; GRIP-AND-GRIN; HEAD AND SHOULDERS; PHOTO CAPTION; PHOTOGRAPHER; PHOTOJOURNALISM; PICK-UP PIC.

Further reading: H. Evans, *Pictures on a Page* (1987).

photojournalism A term associated mostly with *long-form journalism, often from a personal perspective, that combines text and *photographs produced by a team working together or more typically by a single *photojournalist. *See also* EBONY; LIFE; PICTURE POST.

(⊕) SEE WEB LINKS
• Photojournalism

photojournalist A *photographer who also writes the *news stories or *features that are illustrated by their own *photographs, or a *reporter who also takes *pictures. *See also* PHOTOJOURNALISM.

photo opportunity An occasion on which it will be possible for a press *photographer to take a photograph of a subject, location, or event. A photo opportunity may, or may not, be part of a *photocall or *press conference. Opportunities can range from being tipped off that a certain *celebrity will be leaving a certain restaurant at a certain time, to the annual tradition of the UK chancellor posing in Downing Street with a red case containing details of the budget speech that he or she is about to deliver.

Photoshopping *See* DIGITAL MANIPULATION.

pic An abbreviation of *picture, meaning *photograph.

pick-up pic A *photograph supplied by somebody other than a press *photographer, such as a *source, an interviewee, a member of the family, a school, an employer, or the police. Today such pictures are often lifted from *Facebook or Flickr but, in the days before digital photography and *social media, some journalists might try to collect all available prints or an entire family photo album, thereby denying such pictures to rivals. A pick-up pic is also known as a *collect pic, and the terminology has survived the shift to electronic delivery.

picture byline *See* BYLINE.

Picture Post A pioneering magazine of *photojournalism and *long-form journalism that was published weekly in the UK between 1938 and 1957. Its contributors included *photographers such as Bert Hardy, Grace Robertson, and Thurston Hopkins, as well as writers James Cameron and J. B. Priestley. Under its most influential editor, Tom Hopkinson (1905–90), *Picture Post* developed a reputation for having a social conscience: Hopkinson left the magazine, along with Hardy and Cameron, after a photo-essay on the Korean War was *spiked on political grounds by owner Edward Hulton (1906–1988) (*see* EDITORIAL INDEPENDENCE; ETHICS).

(((●))) SEE WEB LINKS

• Thurston Hopkins audio slideshow

pictures A cover-all word that can mean both still *photographs and *video footage or other moving images. For some news organizations, and for some stories, pictures are regarded as essential: no pic, no story.

piece to camera A technique within *television journalism whereby a *reporter is recorded (or broadcast live) talking directly to the camera and thereby the viewer, often while standing on location with an ostensibly relevant or symbolic location visible in the background. *See also* ROOFTOP JOURNALISM; VIDEOBOMBING.

Pink 'Un **1.** A special edition of a local or regional newspaper published in the UK on Saturdays, featuring that day's football results together with hastily compiled reports from fixtures involving local teams. Such papers were normally printed on pink or green newsprint (*see also* GREEN 'UN) and would be available for sale within minutes of the final whistle being blown. Faced with the growth of the internet and sports broadcasting (*see* SPORT REPORTING), combined with an increasingly irregular schedule of kick-offs, few such print titles survived into the 21st century.
2. A nickname used by journalists to refer to the *Financial Times* newspaper in the UK on account of its traditional use of pink (actually, 'salmon-pink') newsprint.

PIs *See* PRIVATE INVESTIGATORS.

pitch To attempt to convince an *editor, commissioning editor, or section editor of the merits of a particular story or idea, typically in very few words. Pitch is both the noun (the pitch) and the verb (to pitch).

Pittsburgh Courier *See* BLACK MEDIA.

Pittsburgh Post-Gazette A daily newspaper published in Pittsburgh, Pennsylvania, which can trace its heritage as far back as 1786, making it one of the oldest in the USA. The paper and its online operations are today owned by Block Communications, which also has extensive interests in television and other media.

pix An abbreviation for *pictures and/or *photographs.

pixilation The deliberate altering of the resolution of a still or moving image so as to hide the identity of a subject (often a child) or to obscure anything that might be deemed offensive or too gruesome. Pixilation is normally done in such a way as to make it obvious. *Compare* DIGITAL MANIPULATION.

plagiarism Passing off another's work as one's own, which in journalism often means taking *quotes, descriptions, and other material published in one media outlet and republishing them without *attribution. One of the most infamous plagiarism cases of recent decades occurred at the *New York Times* in 2003, when reporter Jayson Blair (1976–) was found to have constructed a whole series of stories in which he purported to be reporting from the scene but was in fact often at home, lifting information from local newspapers and embellishing it with details and local *colour gleaned from online picture archives. Journalists in the USA, Australia, and elsewhere tend to take a harder line on plagiarism than do many UK newspapers, where a little bit of lifting of stories, quotes, and the wholesale use of *news agency copy without attribution, are all more likely to be accepted as simply part of the job and not thought of as plagiarism. However, even in the UK there can be consequences if it is seen as going too far, as when Johann Hari (1979–) left the *Independent* in 2012 following a plagiarism scandal. *See also* COPYRIGHT; ETHICS.

(⊕) SEE WEB LINKS
• The Jayson Blair case

plain style *See* ORWELL'S SIX RULES OF WRITING.

platform The specific form of *media or technology for which a piece of journalism is being produced, such as print, radio, television, or online. *See also* CROSS PLATFORM; FORMAT.

plebeian public sphere A space in which working-class people can exchange information and opinions. The idea of a plebeian public sphere is a development of the Habermasian *public sphere, which was largely a bourgeois (and very male) space in which early forms of *public opinion could be arrived at independently of Church and State. Although the public sphere can to some extent be seen as a conceptual space that today incorporates the *media, historically it has also had physical manifestations: if the bourgeois public sphere is associated with *coffee houses and the circulation of certain forms of news and correspondence, then the plebeian equivalent might be the inns and taverns frequented by workers, where stories from the *radical press would have been read aloud at times of social unrest during the 18th and

19th centuries. *See also* ALTERNATIVE MEDIA; CLASS; COUNTER PUBLIC SPHERES.

PM A radical daily US newspaper published in New York between 1940 and 1948 that was something of a highbrow *tabloid. *PM* has been credited with pioneering a form of journalistic writing that rejected rigid newspaper formulas in favour of a more colourful, magazine-style; the large-format display of *photographs and satirical cartoons; the introduction of complete radio listings; and with launching a media criticism column that examined the press itself. Founded by former *New Yorker* and *Time* managing editor Ralph Ingersoll (1900–85), *PM* rejected *advertising and tried to make up the lost income by charging a higher cover price than its commercial rivals; this was to avoid what Ingersoll saw as the 'spiritual degradation' of *reporters toeing an advertiser's line. The paper also rejected many other newspaper conventions, including *neutrality, and was openly pro-labour, pro-civil rights, and anti-fascist in its editorial line. Among those who contributed to *PM* during its brief life were I. F. Stone, Dashiell Hammett, Dorothy Parker, James Baldwin, Ben Hecht, and Dr Seuss. *See also* ALTERNATIVE JOURNALISM; I. F. STONE'S WEEKLY.

podcast A digital *audio recording that can be downloaded by the *user who can then listen to it, at their own convenience, on a computer or mobile device. Podcasts may contain radio programmes (either in their entirety or as edited highlights) but they are also used by newspapers and magazines to add a *multimedia element to their *brand (even if some are basically just a bunch of journalists chatting to each other).

political correctness A dismissive and disparaging term for the use of non-discriminatory language about women, ethnic minorities, gay people, transgender people, people with disabilities, and others who may be seen as socially disadvantaged in one way or another. However, even in most of those news organizations that publicly attack so-called political correctness (which is invariably described as having 'gone mad'), the casual use of sexist, racist, and other forms of *discriminatory language tends to be less prevalent today than it was during the 20th century. *See also* CAMPAIGN FOR REAL PEOPLE; GENDER; RACE; RACISM; REPRESENTATION; SEXISM; STEREOTYPING; STYLE GUIDE.

political correspondent A *reporter who specializes in covering politics, usually of the party political and central government kind. *See also* LOBBY CORRESPONDENT.

political economy A method of analyzing journalism and other media output not as stand-alone cultural activities but as a part (and a product) of the political and economic structures of a society. Associated with academic critiques influenced by *Marxism, a political economy approach highlights how, within capitalist countries such as the UK and USA, commercial imperatives impact on journalists in a variety of ways, ranging from decisions about how many staff to employ to which market segments will be targeted to boost sales or attract *advertisers. Emphasizing the fact that most journalists work for such commercial employers, political economists argue that the other functions frequently claimed for journalism (such as its *watchdog role) are incidental to its primary function of being part of a commercial enterprise within a capitalist marketplace. Critics of the political economy school argue that it is far too crude a way of explaining diverse media activity; adherents counter with the argument that economic power relations remain fundamental to our understanding of journalism, notwithstanding apparent diversity and nuance between and within media. *See also* OWNERSHIP; PROPAGANDA MODEL.

Politico A Washington-based *website (and sometime newspaper) that focuses on US politics and was launched in 2007 by a number of former *Washington Post* journalists. *See also* DIGITAL MEDIA.

Pollard Review An independent inquiry commissioned by the *BBC and carried out by Nick Pollard (a former head of *Sky News*) into the circumstances surrounding the dropping of a *Newsnight* investigation into allegations of child sex abuse by former BBC presenter Jimmy Savile. Pollard's report of 2012 found that the decision to drop the original story had been 'seriously flawed', as was an explanation of the decision placed on a BBC editors' blog, and that senior BBC management had reacted to unfolding events with 'chaos and confusion', resulting in Director-General George Entwistle standing down after only 54 days in office. Pollard's recommendations included the observation that: 'Challenging decisions is good. No one has a monopoly on wisdom.' In 2013 the BBC went much further than most media organizations in washing its dirty linen in public by publishing on its website the transcripts and statements of (almost all) the evidence considered by Pollard. In a separate process, BBC Scotland Director Ken MacQuarrie investigated how a different *Newsnight* story managed to accuse an innocent man of child sex abuse (*see* BUREAU OF INVESTIGATIVE JOURNALISM); he concluded there had been a number of editorial failings and that 'some of the basic journalistic checks were not completed' before the erroneous item was broadcast.

(⊕) SEE WEB LINKS
- The Pollard Review transcripts
- The MacQuarrie findings

polls 1. A means by which a media outlet gauges opinion by asking members of its *audience to vote online or over the telephone on a particular issue that is typically linked to a topical story. The result of the poll is sometimes used as a *follow-up story. Polls are also used by news organizations to help foster a sense of involvement and loyalty among the audience (*see* BRANDING), although some have been accused of using these more as a way of generating income via charges for telephone voting.
2. Professionally conducted opinion polls commissioned by news organizations for the purpose of generating stories about *public opinion and support for political parties or policies.

polyglottism Speaking in many voices and/or in many languages or registers as opposed to one uniform voice (*compare* MONOGLOTTISM). Whereas some news organizations impose a strict *house style on contributors, others make a virtue of featuring a multiplicity of styles and voices. *See also* MODE OF ADDRESS.

pool The agreed sharing of content between news organizations whereby just one report is pooled. A pool is most commonly used to prevent a mass media presence at sombre occasions such as funerals or to allow a much-sought interviewee to give just one *interview.

Poor Man's Guardian A radical working-class newspaper, published weekly in the UK between 1831 and 1835, that refused to pay *stamp duty. This allowed it to be sold for just one penny but resulted in hundreds of people being prosecuted and imprisoned for distributing copies. The *Poor Man's Guardian*, edited by the defiant Henry Hetherington (1792–1849), incorporated into its *masthead the motto 'knowledge is power', which became something of a rallying cry for the unstamped *radical press. *See also* TAXES ON KNOWLEDGE.

pops A shortened term for popular *newspapers. Although the term is associated with titles published in the *tabloid format these days, the popular press goes back a long way (*see* PENNY PRESS) and many pops began as *broadsheets in size if not style.

Further reading: M. Engel, *Tickle the Public: One Hundred Years of the Popular Press* (1997).

pornification The process whereby increasingly sexualized and semi-naked images of women become the norm in much *mainstream media, arguably desensitizing people to their pornographic nature. This normalization of pornified imagery can be seen most obviously in *lads' mags and some *tabloid newspapers but, according to critics, its impact is felt on media and culture much more widely. *See also* PAGE THREE; SEXISM.

(((⊕))) SEE WEB LINKS
• End Violence Against Women website

Portland Oregonian A US daily newspaper and website published in Portland, Oregon, and owned by Advance Publications. Launched in 1850, the paper was the scene of a long and bitter labour dispute that began with a strike by production workers in 1959. Supported by many journalists who refused to cross a picket line, the dispute lasted until 1965.

post-moderation The *moderation of readers' comments only after they have been published online. The system relies on other users complaining about offensive or inappropriate posts, whereupon a moderator will consider if the comment ought to be removed and the poster warned or even banned. *Compare* PRE-MODERATION. *See also* TROLLING; YOUR COMMENTS.

POV An abbreviation for point-of-view, as in *TV journalism or an online video diary, when the *pictures are shot as if through the eyes of the person directly involved in a story.

power elite Those politically, economically, or culturally powerful individuals, organizations, or institutions whose every action or utterance seems virtually guaranteed to become *news. Presidents, prime ministers, and other senior politicians all form part of the power elite as far as most news organizations are concerned, as will institutions such as the Pentagon, the Vatican, NATO, and even the exclusive private school Eton. Not only are their own initiatives and announcements more likely to be deemed *newsworthy than those of others with less power, influence, or status, but some connection with them will render any story more likely to be selected—including ones that might show them in a bad light. *See also* ELITE PEOPLE; NEWS VALUES.

PPA *See* PROFESSIONAL PUBLISHERS ASSOCIATION.

PR *See* PUBLIC RELATIONS.

practitioner Somebody who practises journalism as opposed to somebody who simply studies it. Within *journalism education the term has been known to be used in a faintly derogatory way to describe those *hackademics who teach journalistic skills.

pragmatic objectivity An approach that stresses the possibility and importance of checking the veracity of stories, notwithstanding the difficulty—some would argue the impossibility—of ever achieving absolute *objectivity. Pragmatic objectivity advocates the incorporation into newsroom practice of criteria for testing the *accuracy of evidence, explanations, and assumptions, as far as it is possible to do so, and of placing critical distance between a journalist and their story. *See also* TRUTH; STRATEGIC RITUAL; VERIFICATION.

Further reading: S. Ward, 'Inventing Objectivity: New Philosophical Foundations', in C. Meyers (ed.), *Journalism Ethics: A Philosophical Approach* (2010).

Pravda The main Russian newspaper during the 20th-century Soviet era. *Pravda* means 'truth' but it tended to be associated more with *propaganda and *spin than with unburnished truth. This has resulted in occasional use of the term 'Pravda' as a synonym for any publication containing uncritical journalism. *See also* GLASNOST; NOVAYA GAZETA.

prebuttal An attempt by the subject of a potential story (or by a *spin doctor acting on their behalf) to pre-empt, rebut, deny, derail, and/or deflect attention away from the story before it appears. *See also* NEWS MANAGEMENT.

preferred reading When members of an *audience accept information at face value and/or absorb whatever message or *ideology may be contained within a piece of *communication. According to the *encoding, decoding model, a preferred (or dominant) reading is only one possible response open to audience members; others are a *negotiated reading and an *oppositional reading. *See also* CODE; HEGEMONY.

pre-moderation A system of moderating readers' comments before they are published online, to check if they are acceptable. Although pre-moderation reduces the risk of offensive or legally dangerous material appearing, it also has the effect of slowing the speed of discussion among *users. *Compare* POST-MODERATION. *See also* MODERATION; TROLLING; YOUR COMMENTS.

presenter A UK term for the *anchor of a broadcast news programme. *See also* NEWSREADER.

press A generic term variously applied to *newspapers alone, to newspapers and *magazines combined, to all news organizations including *broadcast and *online journalism, and to their journalists (who are still occasionally referred to on formal occasions as 'the ladies and gentlemen of the press'). *See also* MEDIA.

Press Association (PA) The UK's major *news agency supplying the media with *news, *features, *sports journalism, *pictures, *videos, *audio, listings, weather forecasts, page-ready material, *subbing, and a range of related editorial services. Founded in 1868 by a group of provincial newspaper proprietors, PA developed a reputation for providing subscribers with a steady supply of accurate coverage delivered in a neutral tone. Many reporters and news organizations 'take in PA'; that is, incorporate PA *copy into their own, often without *attribution. Today PA is a *multimedia operation. A private company, its major shareholders are the UK's big newspaper publishers.

press baron 1. An owner of a major UK newspaper who is knighted, such as the Lords Beaverbrook, Northcliffe, and Rothermere. Press barons were criticized by Prime Minister Stanley Baldwin in the 1930s for wanting 'power without responsibility, the prerogative of the harlot throughout the ages'.
2. The owner of one or more news organizations who is seen as wielding or seeking significant power and influence. *See* MEDIA MOGUL; PROPRIETORS.

PressBof *See* PCC.

press card A personal ID card identifying the bearer as a *journalist.
Press cards are typically issued to bone fide journalists by media
employers and/or journalists' trade unions. Although a card is not
guaranteed to get a journalist into events or out of scrapes, it can
sometimes help.

Press Complaints Commission (PCC) A complaints handling
organization established by the UK newspaper and magazine industries
to replace the *Press Council in 1991. Having spent most of its existence
describing itself as the press 'self-regulator', the PCC retreated from this
claim during the *Leveson Inquiry, which followed the PCC's failure to
get to the bottom of the *hackgate scandal. Funded by the industry itself
through the Press Standards Board of Finance (**PressBof**), and normally
chaired by one Conservative peer or another, the PCC was widely seen
as being too much the creature of the *proprietors and senior *editors,
having been established primarily to ward off any threat of *statutory
regulation (*see* CALCUTT REPORTS; LAST CHANCE SALOON). The PCC
established the *Editors' Code of ethical practice and this, together with
the commission's verdicts on public complaints about alleged breaches
of the code, provided journalists with guidance on what is deemed to be
ethical behaviour by newspapers, magazines, and their online versions
(including new issues such as the use of *user-generated content and
of audio-visual material on websites). The PCC also advised members
of the public who complained of suffering *harassment at the hands of
the press. However, signing up to the PCC and its code was voluntary
(with Richard Desmond's *Northern & Shell titles among those opting
out) and the fact that the PCC had no power to impose punishments on
any publication found to have broken the code prompted accusations
that it was a watchdog with no teeth. Having acknowledged that it
had never in fact been any sort of regulator, the PCC announced its
own demise in 2012, although it carried on with business as usual
for some time pending the establishment of a post-Leveson
self-regulator (*see* INDEPENDENT PRESS STANDARDS ORGANIZATION;
ROYAL CHARTER ON THE PRESS). *See also* CONSCIENCE CLAUSE; ETHICS;
SELF-REGULATION.

(⊕) SEE WEB LINKS
• PCC archive of complaints

press conference (news conference) An invitation-only event for journalists at which a formal announcement or statement is made by (or on behalf of) an organization or individual, usually followed by *questions. Press conferences traditionally take place in the flesh but they can also be held remotely via telephone conference calls or online communications technology such as Skype. *See also* PSEUDO-EVENT; PUBLIC RELATIONS.

press corps A number of journalists from various news organizations covering a particular story, topic, *patch, or *beat. The term 'corps' is most commonly heard in the USA; in the UK a collection of journalists tends to be referred to as a 'pack'.

Press Council An organization established by the UK press in 1953, on the recommendation of the *Royal Commission on the Press, to deal with complaints about unethical behaviour on the part of newspaper and magazine journalists. Until 1963 its name was the **General Council of the Press**. Described as a form of *self-regulation, it came to be regarded even by many of its own members as cosy, slow, and largely ineffective. After newspaper *proprietors were warned they were drinking in the *Last Chance Saloon following a fresh series of scandals, the Press Council was disbanded in 1990 to be replaced by the *Press Complaints Commission. *See also* CALCUTT REPORTS; ETHICS; YOUNGER COMMITTEE.

presser A term sometimes used among journalists to refer to a *press conference, *photocall, *press trip, or some other kind of *public relations event staged in the hope of persuading the media to attend.

press freedom *See* FREE PRESS.

Press Gazette The UK journalists' *trade rag that launched as a weekly magazine in 1965; following several changes of owner and format and one or two near-death experiences, it became online-only in 2013. *Press Gazette* (originally known as *UK Press Gazette* or *UKPG*) has always prided itself on being independent from the major media companies, which have been known to cancel subscriptions or withdraw *advertising in pique at stories about them or at rivals winning press *awards ceremonies that the mag has often helped organize.

(((🌐))) SEE WEB LINKS
• *Press Gazette*

press kit *See* PRESS PACK.

press officer Somebody who carries out a *public relations function on behalf of an organization and who may or may not be a full-time PR professional. Governments, local authorities, the police, and big companies all employ teams of press officers, and even local charities, sports clubs, and campaign groups are likely to have a member who operates as a press officer, liaising with local journalists and acting as a spokesperson when required.

press pack (press kit) 1. Material supplied to journalists as part of a *public relations operation, often including a *press release, the text of a statement or speech, background information, and *pictures. Press packs in the past were physical products, normally placed in a cardboard folder, and often handed out at a *press conference, but now press kits are more likely to be delivered electronically or simply made available to download from a website.
2. An alternative term for *press corps.

press release Information sent to the media by or on behalf of individuals or organizations seeking to publicize an announcement, product, event, policy, campaign, or anything for which they hope to attract coverage. A press release (also known as a handout or **news release**) will often be written in the form of a ready-made news *story, complete with *quotes, but journalists are trained to treat such material as merely the start of a potential story rather than the end (*see* SCEPTICISM). *See also* CHURNALISM; PUBLIC RELATIONS; VIDEO NEWS RELEASE.

press trip A visit somewhere by one or more journalists at the behest of a *press officer or *public relations company in what amounts to an organized outing. This can vary from junkets such as free holidays for the purpose of facilitating the writing of travel pieces to accompanying a senior politician to a war zone or on a trade mission to an overseas country. *See also* FREEBIE.

price war A *circulation war between two or more commercial media outlets when one or more of the participants engages in 'predatory pricing' with the intention of inflicting damage on its rivals. Boosting sales by reducing the cover price and often selling at a loss is a tactic available only to *proprietors with very deep pockets or with the ability to subsidize costs from other parts of a media empire.

primary definers Those powerful and influential voices who tend to be afforded disproportionate *access to the media. In the book *Policing the Crisis* (1978), cultural studies theorist Stuart Hall (1932–2014) and colleagues argued that by enjoying privileged access to the media in general and to news organizations in particular, a society's more powerful sectors and individuals can to a large extent establish the parameters of debate on many social and political issues. In this way, senior politicians, business leaders, judges, lawyers, and 'experts' become the primary definers of the meaning and significance of events and of what are considered to be appropriate responses to such events. According to this analysis, journalists play the role of *secondary definers, transmitting the interpretations of the powerful who are almost by definition seen as credible and authoritative *sources. Although definitions are not fixed, and can be contested, the theory of primary and secondary definition is put forward to help explain the tendency for the dominant forces within society to have their interpretations disproportionately circulated and amplified by journalists. The theory is sometimes dismissed or criticized for downplaying the potential of powerful media organizations such as the *Murdoch empire to become primary definers that, according to some commentators, may be even more powerful than elected politicians. *See also* HEGEMONY.

Further reading: S. Hall et al, *Policing the Crisis* (1978).

printing The mechanical or digital reproduction of text and pictures on paper, as in *print journalism in the form of *newspapers and *magazines. Although earlier forms of printing had been around for hundreds of years, notably in China and Korea, it was Johann Gutenberg's (c.1395–1468) development of a system of printing involving moveable metal type around 1450 that paved the way for the (relative) mass production of *chapbooks, *newsbooks, *pamphlets, and other nascent forms of journalism in Europe. Gutenberg's innovations also contributed to the *Enlightenment and the growth of democratic thought. William Caxton (c.1422–92) is credited with taking printing to England when he established a press at Westminster in 1476. As with many later examples of *new technology, printing inspired fear in some (notably the powerful) and hope in others (mostly the powerless).

History suggests that attempts at suppressing printing usually prove hopeless in the end. *See also* AREOPAGITICA; DEMOCRACY; FREE PRESS; LEVELLERS; LICENSING ACT; SAMIZDAT; UNDERGROUND PRESS.

print journalism A generic term for *journalism produced to be published as a series of collated pages in a printed format such as a *newspaper or a *magazine. Many but not all of the practices established initially in print journalism have subsequently been incorporated into or adapted for *broadcast journalism and *online journalism. In the digital age, print-style journalism may also be produced without the actual *printing element, with pages placed online or delivered directly to readers' mobile devices. *See also* PRESS.

print run The number of copies produced of an issue of a printed publication such as a newspaper, magazine, or fanzine. The print run might be temporarily increased if a particular boost in *circulation is anticipated, for example because of a major story or *scoop.

prior restraint A form of *censorship that involves the use of *laws to prevent certain information or material being revealed or published. In the UK such restraint is normally imposed only in the form of an *injunction, usually in *privacy cases. The threat of an injunction or of subsequent legal action for *defamation may act as a de facto form of prior restraint (*see* SELF-CENSORSHIP).

privacy The state of being free from the attention of the public in general and of journalists in particular. Because much journalism involves making public that which would otherwise be private, the issue of privacy is a constant consideration for news organizations and is one of the most contentious issues as regards the *laws and ethical *codes of conduct that can operate as *constraints on journalists' activities. Journalistic *intrusion into people's private lives is normally justified by reference to an overriding *public interest and/or to *human rights such as freedom of expression. However, media outlets particularly at the more popular end of the market are often accused of infringing privacy merely to satisfy their audience's fascination with prurient and entertaining stories. Reporters and those upon whom they report can have very different concepts of what is legitimately private or when there might be a reasonable expectation of privacy; even within the media there can be widely divergent attitudes. In one of the most jaw-dropping exchanges at the *Leveson Inquiry, former *tabloid journalist Paul

McMullan declared that 'privacy is the space bad people need to do bad things in', adding: 'Privacy is for paedos'. *See also* DATA PROTECTION; ETHICS; INJUNCTION; KISS-AND-TELL; PHONE-HACKING; PRIVATE INVESTIGATORS; YOUNGER COMMITTEE.

Private Eye A fortnightly satirical, humorous, and investigative current affairs magazine published in the UK since 1961. It is probably the most-read periodical among journalists themselves, not least for its *Street of Shame* gossip pages about shenanigans in the newsrooms and boardrooms of the Fleet Street diaspora. Curiously old-fashioned in design, the *Eye* has steadfastly refused to give away most of its content for free online, preferring to use its website largely to promote the printed product. One of *Private Eye*'s most celebrated journalists was Paul Foot (1937–2004), in whose name a prize for *investigative journalism is awarded each year. *See also* ALTERNATIVE MEDIA; THE WEEK; SATIRICAL JOURNALISM.

private investigators (PIs) Individuals or companies that conduct inquiries and investigations on a commercial basis and who are sometimes hired by some of the wealthier news organizations to undertake the so-called *dark arts of information-gathering. Although many investigators' activities are perfectly legal, a light was shone on a more shady trade in private information when the UK's official *data protection watchdog, the Information Commissioner's Office, published a report in 2006 entitled *What Price Privacy?* The *hackgate scandal and the subsequent *Leveson Inquiry focused further attention on the allegedly unethical and unlawful duties that some investigators have sometimes been paid to perform at the behest of news organizations. *See also* ETHICAL JOURNALISM; INVESTIGATIVE JOURNALISM; PRIVACY.

(((⊕))) SEE WEB LINKS
• *What Price Privacy?*

privilege The term used in the UK to refer to situations when the law allows journalists to report certain material (even though it might be untrue), the publication of which could result in legal action for *defamation were it not for such privilege. The law recognizes that there is a *public interest in the media being free to provide an accurate account of court cases, Parliamentary debates, and council meetings, without journalists themselves being required to demonstrate the *truth

of the allegations, comments, or speeches they report. *See also*
ABSOLUTE PRIVILEGE; QUALIFIED PRIVILEGE.

Further reading: M. Hanna and M. Dodd, *McNae's Essential Law for Journalists*
(2014).

profession A contentious term used by a minority of journalists to
describe the occupation of journalism but rejected by most on the
grounds that, unlike regulated professions such as medicine and the
law, entry to journalism is not restricted, and journalists cannot be
'struck off' a register. *Compare* CRAFT; TRADE. *See also* BOUNDARY
MAINTENANCE; LICENSING OF JOURNALISTS.

Professional Publishers Association (PPA) The trade body of the
UK's commercial *magazine industry, known until 2010 as the
Periodical Publishers Association. The name change was designed to
reflect publication across a variety of *platforms, and in 2013 the PPA
began publishing a chart giving the combined *circulation of magazines'
print and digital editions. *See also* INDEPENDENT PRESS STANDARDS
ORGANIZATION; PERIODICALS TRAINING COUNCIL.

(((●))) SEE WEB LINKS
• PPA combined circulation chart

profile An account of the life and/or activities of a particular person,
usually while they are still alive (*compare* OBITUARY), or of an
organization, location, or community. Profiles are *features that typically
run when people or places have suddenly become *news, or have
returned to the limelight, to provide background for other coverage.
A profile may be based on an *interview with the subject, on interviews
with others, or merely on *cuttings.

Progressive A radical US magazine and website specializing in
*investigative journalism, political commentary, *literary journalism,
and the like. It emerged from *La Follette's Weekly*, which launched in
1909, and it is now published monthly. Its current writers include the
veteran feminist and socialist commentator Barbara Ehrenreich.

Project Censored An annual compilation of the 25 biggest stories
that have been either ignored or downplayed by the bulk of the
*mainstream media. The list has been compiled since 1976 by social
science staff and students at Sonoma State University in the USA.

Captioned 'The news that didn't make the news', many of the items on the list each year are taken from *alternative media.

propaganda Information, misinformation, ideas, and arguments that are published or broadcast primarily for the purpose of influencing *public opinion in one way or another. *See also* ADVERTISING; ADVOCACY JOURNALISM; AGENDA-SETTING; MEDIA EFFECTS; NEWS MANAGEMENT; PUBLIC RELATIONS; SPIN.

propaganda model The theory offered by academics Edward Herman (1925–) and Noam Chomsky (1928–) as a way of explaining how (US) media routinely circulate and amplify the world view of the wealthy and powerful while marginalizing dissenting perspectives, notwithstanding the views or intentions of the individuals involved in media production. In their influential 1988 book *Manufacturing Consent*, Herman and Chomsky identified five 'filters' that, when applied in combination, have the effect of ensuring privileged media *access for government and big business interests. The filters are:

- The wealth and concentrated *ownership of dominant commercial media firms.
- The influence of *advertising.
- A reliance on accessing information from the most powerful elements within society.
- Punitive action or *flak unleashed against journalists who transgress.
- An ideological backdrop (in the USA in particular) characterized as *anti-communism.

Since the end of the Cold War, and particularly since the 11 September 2001 attacks on the World Trade Centre in New York, a prevailing anti-communist ideology is said by some to have been replaced by an ethos that is more likely to be anti-Islam or at least anti-militant Islam. The propaganda model has been dismissed by critics as a conspiracy theory and/or as too mechanistic, but Herman and Chomsky counter that their model describes a market system with a *tendency* towards certain consequences rather than an omnipotent system that controls and explains everything. *Compare* WATCHDOG ROLE. *See also* POLITICAL ECONOMY.

Further reading: E. Herman and N. Chomsky, *Manufacturing Consent: The Political Economy of the Media* (1995[1988]).

((()) SEE WEB LINKS

- Herman on the propaganda model

proprietors The owners of commercial media organizations, who may range from small local family firms to giant multinational corporations, and whose motivation may be to serve the *public interest, to disseminate *propaganda, to maximize profits, or some combination thereof. *See also* CONCENTRATION OF OWNERSHIP; EDITORIAL INDEPENDENCE; MEDIA MOGUL; OWNERSHIP; PRESS BARON.

ProPublica A US-based non-profit *website that, since its first appearance in 2008, has specialized in *investigative journalism, especially that which 'shines a light on exploitation of the weak by the strong'. *ProPublica* broke new ground for *online journalism when its stories outshone those of print rivals to win *Pulitzer prizes in 2010 and 2011. Although it accepts *advertising, *ProPublica* relies on philanthropic donations to survive.

(((●))) SEE WEB LINKS

• 'How *ProPublica* changed investigative reporting'

prospects Potential news items and story ideas that are presented, discussed, commissioned, or abandoned at editorial planning meetings (or *conferences).

Providence Journal-Bulletin A US daily newspaper published in Providence, the capital of Rhode Island. Launched in 1829, it claims the title of the longest continuously published daily newspaper in the USA because some other even older titles have had gaps in publication. The newspaper and its associated website are both owned by the A. H. Belo Corporation of Dallas.

PSB *See* PUBLIC SERVICE BROADCASTING.

pseudo-event Anything that has been arranged primarily for the purpose of generating media coverage and which would have no independent existence in its own right. Such pseudo-events might include *photocalls, *press conferences, and even *interviews. *See also* NEWS MANAGEMENT; PUBLIC RELATIONS.

Public Broadcasting Service *See* PBS.

public interest The way in which society as a whole is said to benefit from the reporting of something that, without such a public interest justification, might be regarded as an unethical or even unlawful piece of journalism (*see* PUBLIC INTEREST DEFENCE). Definitions of the public interest vary from country to country and organization to organization, but they are typically based on the following points: detecting or exposing criminal, corrupt, or other wrongful behaviour; protecting public health and safety; preventing the public from being seriously misled; and revealing conflicts of interest or acts of hypocrisy by those in positions of power. Serving the public interest is central to journalists' image of themselves as *watchdogs and as a *fourth estate serving *citizens in a *democracy. As is frequently pointed out, however, what is in the public interest is not necessarily that which most interests individual members of the public; and vice versa. *See also* CODES OF CONDUCT; ETHICS; INVESTIGATIVE JOURNALISM.

public interest defence The argument that a journalistic activity or story that might be deemed unethical or even unlawful in normal circumstances is justified because it is in the *public interest for certain allegations to be investigated or for certain information to be revealed. The public interest defence might be used, for example, to justify a reporter going *undercover or a newspaper publishing leaked information. Journalists' *codes of conduct typically allow for some methods to be used only in cases that are clearly in the public interest. *See also* ETHICAL JOURNALISM; REYNOLDS DEFENCE.

public journalism A term used in the USA from the 1990s to describe a form of journalism that seeks to promote civic engagement and *citizens' participation in democratic structures, and/or to bemoan the absence of such journalism from much commercial media. *See also* CIVIC JOURNALISM; DEMOCRACY; PUBLIC SPHERE.

public opinion The views of citizens as measured by *polls and less rigorous methods such as readers' *letters, *voxpops, *Your Comments, and *Twitter. Public opinion may be drawn on by news organizations to help inform their *selection decisions and editorial positions, and shifts of public opinion may be used as the basis for stories in their own right. *See also* 90-9-1 RULE; PUBLIC SPHERE.

public relations (PR) The management of information and access on behalf of an organization or individual in the public eye. Organizations ranging from local charities to multinational corporations, and individuals ranging from talent show contestants to ruling politicians, now typically engage public relations personnel and adopt PR strategies. Journalists are often supplied with potential stories, comments, background briefings, and picture opportunities by those engaged in PR in a process that has been described as a form of *information subsidy favouring those who can afford extensive PR operations at the expense of independent inquiry. The PR professionals, *press officers, and *spin doctors who promote a particular individual or organization do not simply supply information to the media, they also play a role in controlling journalists' *access to people or events, which critics say gives them the potential power to reward or punish more or less 'helpful' journalists (*see* NEWS MANAGEMENT). Although journalists often speak of having a healthily antagonistic relationship with the PR industry, academic research suggests that, on a day-to-day basis, journalists and press officers cooperate on numerous stories. Many journalists go on to be employed in PR where their inside knowledge of how journalism operates is valued by clients. *See also* CHURNALISM; PSEUDO-EVENT.

public service broadcasting (PSB) Radio and television services with a remit to provide for the needs of *citizens, including the provision of *news, rather than considering purely commercial interests. *See also* AUSTRALIAN BROADCASTING CORPORATION; BBC; CHANNEL 4 NEWS; PBS; REITHIAN PRINCIPLES.

public sphere A space in which informed *citizens can engage with one another in rational debate and critical reflection, helping to form *public opinion (or opinions plural). German sociologist and philosopher Jurgen Habermas (1929–) located the initial emergence of such a conceptual sphere, independent of Church and State, in the physical space of London *coffee houses in the late 17th century. Subsequently, the *press and later forms of media are said to have played a similar role for the bulk of the population, although Habermas has argued that the public sphere declined in the 20th century as a result of increasing commercialisation and commodification of journalism (and other methods of mass communication). Habermas has been accused of *elitism and of idealizing an exclusionary *golden age that may never have existed, but the concept of the public sphere remains influential in *journalism studies where it is often used as a yardstick against which to measure the performance of various news media. *See also* COUNTER PUBLIC SPHERES; DEMOCRACY; ENLIGHTENMENT; PLEBEIAN PUBLIC SPHERE.

publish and be damned The reported response of the Duke of Wellington when he was informed, in what appeared to be at attempt at blackmail, that some salacious details of his private life were about to be published in 1824. The phrase is generally used to mean, 'Go ahead and publish if you like because people will draw their own conclusions'. Editors sometimes use the phrase themselves when they decide to publish something that is likely to be unpopular or controversial.

puff A derogatory term for an overly positive and/or uncritical item of journalism that comes across like a glorified *press release, *advertisement, or advertorial.

Pulitzer Prize One of the premier *awards in the world of journalism, being awarded each year for excellence in newspaper (and now online) journalism in the USA. The prize was established in 1917 by the Columbia School of Journalism and named after the journalist and press proprietor Joseph Pulitzer (1847–1911, *see* YELLOW PRESS). *See also* LITTLE JIMMY.

(((●))) SEE WEB LINKS
• Pulitzer Prize winners

pull quote A section of the text of an article, usually just a sentence or partial sentence, that is reproduced in a larger font as a design device to help break up a page at the same time as giving the reader a further clue about the story's contents. Pull quotes are especially common in *features and *long-form journalism but are also used in news.

p

Punch A satirical and literary magazine famous for its *cartoons that published weekly in the UK between 1841 and 2002 (apart from a gap between 1992 and 1996). Once regarded as something of a radical publication, *Punch* gradually came to be seen as a rather safe humorous periodical, more often flicked through in dentists' waiting rooms than purchased on the news-stands. *See also* SATIRICAL JOURNALISM.

(((●))) SEE WEB LINKS
• *Punch* cartoon galleries

Punk A seminal alternative US music magazine published in New York between 1976 and 1979 that probably had more influence on the subsequent *fanzine scene than it had actual readers during the time of its brief life. *Punk* has subsequently been revived from time to time. *See also* ALTERNATIVE MEDIA; AMATEUR JOURNALISM.

(((●))) SEE WEB LINKS
• *Punk* archive

Putney debates Discussions held in 1647 under the chairmanship of Oliver Cromwell concerning the future direction of England, which was then in the midst of civil war and revolution. The radical *Levellers used the Putney debates to articulate the case for a *free press. *See also* Areopagitica; democracy; newsbook; pamphlets; printing.

(((●))) SEE WEB LINKS
• The Putney debates website

Q&A (question and answer) 1. A way of presenting an *interview in a
printed publication (especially popular in *magazines) that purports to
allow both the *questions and the answers to speak for themselves,
rather than embedding and contextualizing them within a longer
*feature or narrative account. The Q&A format may give the impression
that it is presenting an unvarnished interview in its entirety but in reality
it is likely to be a heavily edited version of the encounter. Readers may
be invited to suggest questions in advance, and some Q&As may be
based on *questionnaires.
2. A broadcast *presenter interviewing a reporter or specialist
correspondent in the form of a *two-way.
3. A guest interviewee answering *audience questions live online via the
*internet and/or *social media.

qualified privilege The term used in the UK law whereby journalists
in certain circumstances cannot be sued for *defamation providing that
various conditions are met. Qualified privilege is of most use to
journalists covering court cases, parliament, and council meetings, and
applies to reports that are fair, accurate, and published without malice.
Reports and other publications published by parliament, government,
and some other official bodies can also be reported under the protection
of qualified privilege. *See also* ABSOLUTE PRIVILEGE; PRIVILEGE;
REYNOLDS DEFENCE.

quality press Serious newspapers, magazines, and their digital
offerings, that are more likely to offer in-depth coverage of politics,
economics, and foreign affairs than they are to focus on *celebrity or
*sensational news (*compare* MID-MARKET; TABLOID; POPS). Also known
as the *heavies, the quality press tends to be targeted at a smaller but
more upmarket readership than are titles positioned at the more
popular end of the market. *See also* BROADSHEET; TABLOIDIZATION.

questionnaires A *Q&A format of *interview, popular with *magazines, whereby the interviewee is sent a standard series of personal questions, such as, 'When did you last cry?' and 'Who would you most like to be stuck in a lift with?'.

questions The essence of journalism in general and of *reporting in particular. The series of questions commonly known as the *five Ws (*who?, *where?, *what?, *when, *why?, plus *how?) form the basis of most *interviews and of other inquiries conducted by journalists, but good journalism is said to also require a self-questioning approach (*see* ETHICS; REFLECTIVE PRACTICE; REFLEXIVE PRACTICE) that challenges the journalist's own assumptions and ethical approach. During broadcast and online interviews that are conducted in real time, members of the *audience may suggest (via email, text, or Twitter) particular questions they would like the interviewee to answer. Broadcast journalists occasionally repeat a question if they feel it has not been answered (*see* NEWSNIGHT).

quote A verbatim account of words spoken or written by interviewees, *sources, or other participants in an event, that is included within a *news story or *feature, and is attributed to the speaker. Quotes are typically used to add authority to a story by telling the reader whose version of events has been sought, to add strong or emotional language spoken by somebody directly involved in a story, or to incorporate a sense of *colour or a change of tone into a text. *Direct quotes placed within quotation marks will comprise the speaker's actual words whereas *indirect quotes (or reported speech) will contain the gist of their meaning in paraphrased form. Most written forms of journalism, even stories based on a lengthy *interview with a source, will consist of a mixture of indirect and direct quotation, with the latter often used relatively sparingly and for effect rather than to convey simple statements of fact. *See also* ATTRIBUTION; SOUNDBITE.

q

race The ethnicity of individuals and groups of people, pejorative reference to which was once common in much journalism. Today it is generally regarded as unethical to draw attention to somebody's race unless it is relevant to the story. *See also* ETHNIC MINORITY MEDIA; POLITICAL CORRECTNESS; RACISM; REPRESENTATION.

racism A belief in the superiority of one *race, prejudicial attitudes towards people of other races, and/or actions that have the effect of disadvantaging one or more racial groups. Much of the *mainstream media has long been accused of racism and *stereotyping in the way that people from some ethnic minority communities are—or are not— covered; however, much journalism has also challenged and exposed racist attitudes and policies. Material likely to encourage hatred on racial grounds is contrary to most journalists' *codes of conduct, and the most blatant examples of racist language that could be found in some of the UK *redtops in the 1970s are generally believed to be far less prevalent today. *See also* DISCRIMINATORY LANGUAGE; ETHNIC MINORITY JOURNALISTS; McLURG'S LAW.

radical journalism Forms of journalism that can be found in *alternative media, *feminist media, the *radical press, the *underground press, and occasionally in odd corners of the *mainstream media, that might articulate a critical perspective on society or eschew the established conventions of journalism—or both. *See also* OPPOSITIONAL REPORTING.

radical press Although the term may be used in association with forms of *alternative media produced in the 20th and 21st centuries, it is more commonly associated with the politically radical newspapers that appeared during the 18th and 19th centuries such as the *Sheffield Register*, the *Northern Star*, the *Red Republican*, and the *Poor Man's Guardian*, all of which offered a counter-narrative to that found in more commercial public prints. This radical press typically combined reports of demonstrations, verbatim accounts of speeches and meetings, analytical or polemical articles, readers' letters, poetry, and the lyrics of ballads, all serving (and helping to form) what the German sociologist and philosopher Jurgen Habermas (1929–) termed a *plebeian public sphere. The contents of such publications would often be read aloud in taverns and other public gatherings, meaning that their impact could be far wider than just the number of copies sold. Many titles were short-lived and the radical press tended to ebb and flow along with the fortunes of the radical movements, such as Chartism, with which it was often associated. The numbers and sales of radical newspapers declined in the second half of the 19th century as the better-resourced commercial newspaper industry began targeting cheap titles at a working-class readership (*see* POPS). *See also* STAMP DUTY; TAXES ON KNOWLEDGE.

Further reading: S. Harrison, *Poor Men's Guardians: A Survey of the Struggles for a Democratic Newspaper Press 1763–1973* (1974).

radio journalism News and current affairs reporting that uses *audio and is broadcast over radio frequencies and/or digitally. As the first form of *broadcast journalism, radio journalism began slowly in the 1920s, with early *bulletins largely featuring the reading aloud of items culled from newspapers and news agencies. However, as radio journalists were allowed more freedom to develop original stories and techniques, radio journalism came into its own for its immediacy, intimacy, and—eventually—for allowing a range of regional and class accents to be heard. It is a common observation among broadcast journalists that radio has better pictures than television. *See also* BBC; BIMEDIA JOURNALISM; DOCUMENTARY; LISTENERS; PACKAGE; PHONE-IN; PODCAST; RATINGS; RIP AND READ; ROLLING NEWS; SCRIPT; TWO-WAY.

rag A colloquial term for a printed publication, usually a *newspaper, as in the 'local rag' or a *trade rag.

rag-out The reproduction of a section of a previous story, usually comprising the *headline and *intro, as a graphic alongside a *follow-up item, thereby reminding readers of the earlier coverage. A rag-out is often encased in a jagged border to give the impression of it having been torn from the original page.

ratings The industry term for *audience figures in broadcasting, which inform most decisions about TV and radio output.

rat-like cunning One of only three qualities essential for success in journalism, according to a much-cited 1969 article in the *Sunday Times* magazine by Nick Tomalin (1931–73). The other two qualities were a 'plausible manner' and a 'little literary ability'. The 'rat-like cunning' quote is particularly beloved of old-school journalists who dismiss the value of *journalism education and reject the idea that journalism skills can be taught. Tomalin was killed in 1973 while covering the Arab-Israeli War. *Compare* REFLECTIVE PRACTICE; TRAINING.

raw footage *Video pictures before they have been edited in any way.

readers The *audience for *print journalism and text-based forms of *online journalism, although the latter are often referred to as *users. *See also* IMAGINED AUDIENCE; LETTERS; NATIONAL READERSHIP SURVEY.

readers' editor A member of staff on some newspapers and magazines whose role is to receive complaints from members of the public, get to the bottom of the issue, and, where appropriate, arrange for a *correction or clarification to be published. Readers' editors often have a regular column in which they may discuss wider issues as well as dealing with readers' criticisms of specific items. Where they are seen as combining independence from the *editor with a willingness to be critical of their own publication, readers' editors are said to have the effect of increasing readers' *trust in the news organization. *See also* IRISH TIMES; ORGANIZATION OF NEWS OMBUDSMEN; WASHINGTON POST.

readership The total number of people who read a particular newspaper or magazine. Readership figures are much higher than the simple number of copies sold or distributed because each printed copy may have multiple readers: 2.7 readers per copy of the *Sun* newspaper, for example, or nine readers per copy of *What Car?* magazine, according to the UK's *National Readership Survey, which counts everyone who spends at least two minutes reading or looking at a publication. The fact that so much *print journalism is now available to read for free online has further increased the total readership of some journalists' work at the same time as *circulation of printed products has declined. Many publications target particular readerships and/or encourage readers to identify with a publication's *brand identity. *See also* AUDIENCE; BRANDING; USERS.

Real Lives The title of a 1985 television *documentary about the conflict in Northern Ireland, which led to one of the biggest journalists' strikes ever seen in the UK. Members of the *National Union of Journalists at the *BBC, supported by some colleagues at *ITN and elsewhere, walked out in protest at what they saw as *censorship when the BBC initially refused to broadcast the programme because of government pressure. The journalists' action blacked out BBC TV news programmes for 24 hours and made headlines around the world. *Real Lives* was subsequently shown, with only minor alterations, but three years later the British government introduced its controversial *broadcast ban. *See also* NEWS MANAGEMENT.

(((⊕))) SEE WEB LINKS

• The BBC on *Real Lives*

Really Simple Syndication *See* RSS.

reconstruction A technique used in *television journalism whereby actors are used to play the part of real people and to act out one or more scenes to illustrate a story. Reconstructions are more common in *current affairs and *documentaries than in news bulletins, and their frequent use in some programmes (often augmented with dramatic music, lighting, and camera angles) has prompted complaints of *dumbing down. Broadcast regulations and *codes of conduct stipulate that a reconstruction must be clearly labelled as such, so as not to mislead viewers (*see* FAKERY).

recording A piece of *broadcast journalism that has been made in advance and will not be broadcast *live.

Reddit A *social media site built on *user-generated content that calls itself 'the front page of the internet' and is often monitored by journalists looking for potential stories to follow up. Reddit was at the centre of a storm of controversy in 2013 when, in the wake of the Boston Marathon bombings in the USA, its *users wrongly identified a number of innocent people as suspects.

(((⊕))) SEE WEB LINKS

• *Reddit*: 'Reflections on the recent Boston crisis'

Red Pepper An independent left-wing magazine and website published in the UK since 1995. *Red Pepper*'s *alternative journalism is informed by what its editorial charter refers to as a 'fusion of red, green, feminist, and other radical traditions'.

redtop An industry term for those *tabloid newspapers in the UK that are at the more popular end of the market (*see* POPS) and which have traditionally had their name printed in large white letters on a red box at the top of the front page. The *Sun* and the *Daily Mirror* are examples of redtops. *Compare* MID-MARKET; QUALITY PRESS.

Reed Business Information *See* REED ELSEVIER.

Reed Elsevier A major publishing and information company that was formed in 1993 as a result of a merger between the UK-based newspaper and magazine publisher Reed International and a Dutch publisher of scientific journals, Elsevier. Reed Elsevier's operations include the LexisNexis legal and news database and, through **Reed Business Information**, a range of specialist magazines (and digital *brands) such as *Estates Gazette*, *Farmers Weekly*, and *New Scientist*.

reflective practice Journalists thinking about and reflecting upon the job that they are doing while they are doing it. Reflective practice involves critical thinking about *ethics and a questioning approach to how and why certain stories tend to be covered in certain ways. Although few journalists are themselves likely to embrace the phrase itself to describe their work, and many prefer to celebrate *rat-like cunning, reflective practice can be seen as informing countless decisions taken by journalists every day. Increasingly, *journalism education promotes the idea of reflective practice and seeks to encourage journalists to be reflective practitioners. *Compare* REFLEXIVE PRACTICE. *See also* ETHICAL JOURNALISM; ETHICS.

reflexive practice 1. A process in which a journalist self-consciously questions and scrutinizes their own personal assumptions and predispositions in the course of carrying out their work (*compare* REFLECTIVE PRACTICE).
2. The foregrounding of subjective experience (*see* SUBJECTIVITY), often placing the journalist as the main subject in a story. *Compare* OBJECTIVE JOURNALISM.

refuseniks More than 50 journalists working on the *Murdoch empire's UK newspapers who refused to cross the picket lines of sacked production and clerical staff during the *Wapping dispute of 1986–7. Although many of their fellow *National Union of Journalists members did go in, the refuseniks chose to sacrifice their jobs (and the large pay rises that they were offered) rather than move to what was to become a non-union plant at Wapping.

regional media The news and other journalistic output produced and consumed within a particular regional area that, typically, is larger than one specific locality but is still small enough to allow for a sense of regional identification among the target *audience (often with consequent attempts at using the region itself in *branding exercises). As with *local journalism, there has been a *concentration of ownership within regional media, leading to the growth of large chains with consequent consolidation, cutbacks, and closures.

regulation The system of media-related rules and/or *laws that may limit how news organizations conduct themselves, both in relation to issues of *ownership and in terms of journalistic behaviour and content. Regulation may provide the public with some means of redress against an organization found to have breached the rules. Regulatory regimes vary between different countries, market systems, and media *platforms. In the UK, for example, *broadcast journalism is subject to a system of *statutory regulation that can result in a fine or even, in an extreme case, in the withdrawal of a licence; *print journalism operates under a much lighter touch form of *self-regulation that involves no penalties; and, to date, *online journalism has scarcely been regulated at all beyond the strictures of laws that apply to everyone, such as *defamation, *contempt of court, and incitement to racial hatred. *See also* DEREGULATION.

Reithian principles Information, education, and entertainment—the three principles of *public service broadcasting in the UK as established by John Reith (1889–1971), the guiding light of the *BBC in its early years. A Scot who is invariably described as 'dour', it is probably fair to say that Reith placed less emphasis on entertainment than on the other two.

relevance A journalistic consideration of the extent to which potential news items may be of interest to or may impact upon the lives of members of the *audience. On the whole it is those stories about issues, groups, and nations perceived by journalists to be most relevant to their audience (or target audience) that are more likely to be selected as *newsworthy. *See also* CULTURAL BIAS; McLURG'S LAW; MEANINGFULNESS; NEWS VALUES.

rent-a-quote A mildly derogatory phrase used by journalists among themselves to describe somebody in public life who can be relied upon to provide a quotable comment if contacted about virtually any story. Politicians, lawyers, authors, religious figures, and self-styled 'community leaders' are particularly likely to fall into this category. Although journalists tend to belittle those seen as rent-a-quotes, they usually keep their phone numbers just in case. *See also* MEDIA TART.

reporter A journalist who finds things out rather than one who merely processes, polishes, and presents the work of others. Reporters may be generalists or specialists, staff or freelance, and they may bring in their own *stories or be sent out by the *newsdesk to cover a particular event (*see* DIARY STORY). Their role is, essentially, to discover and/or verify fresh information about topical and *newsworthy events, to turn such information into stories appropriate to their news organization's outlets, and—just as important—to discard information that does not stand up to scrutiny. To help them in this task, reporters will build a network of *contacts and *sources and will be capable of working at great speed, usually on several stories at once. Some employers have reduced the number of reporters employed and have stated their intention of filling the gap with more *user-generated content (or '*harvesting content'). *See also* NEWSGATHERING; REPORTING; SHORTHAND; VERIFICATION.

Further reading: D. Randall, *The Great Reporters* (2005).

Reporters Committee for Freedom of the Press A non-profit self-help organization launched by US journalists in 1970 to provide legal and other support to those defending their *First Amendment rights. The committee has a 24-hour hotline that provides emergency advice and a website that monitors threats to *press freedom. *See also* SUNSHINE WEEK.

(⊕) SEE WEB LINKS

• Reporters Committee for Freedom of the Press in the news

Reporters Sans Frontières *See* REPORTERS WITHOUT BORDERS.

Reporters Without Borders (Reporters Sans Frontières) An international organization founded in France in 1985 with a remit to monitor attacks on freedom of information and to help persecuted journalists and their families. Reporters Without Borders publishes an annual Press Freedom Index: in 2013, Finland was top and Eritrea was bottom. *See also* CENSORSHIP; DEATHS OF JOURNALISTS; FREE PRESS.

(⊕) SEE WEB LINKS
• Press Freedom Index

reporting The process of discovering, recording, and/or verifying fresh information about topical and *newsworthy events, and turning such information into *stories in a timely, accurate, and appropriate manner. Reporting involves *research and the asking of *questions, recording the answers via *note-taking or digital recording methods, subjecting material to basic *fact-checking before filing *copy, and eliminating anything that cannot be verified or, at the very least, attributed. Reporting typically entails separating *facts from *comment, and adopting a tone of *neutrality, but this is not always the case (*see* OPPOSITIONAL REPORTING). Technologies and market conditions may change, but reporting remains the central activity of most *journalism. *See also* REPORTER; VERIFICATION.

reporting restrictions Legal limitations on which elements of a particular court case may be reported and at what stage of proceedings. In particular, UK law treats as *contempt of court the publication of material that may prejudice the fair trial of somebody who has been charged with an offence. *See also* COURT REPORTING.

representation The portrayal of people in *news stories and other media output which, according to many commentators, often relies on *stereotyping and *cultural bias. *Feminist media, *black media, and other forms of *alternative media are often set up with the intention of providing direct representation for social groups that are less likely to have *access to *mainstream media. *See also* ARCHETYPES; CLASS; COUNTER PUBLIC SPHERES; DEVELOPMENT JOURNALISM; GENDER; NATIVE REPORTING; OPPOSITIONAL REPORTING; RACE.

repurposing The process of taking a piece of journalism that has been produced for one outlet or medium and making it suitable for a different outlet or medium, for example by translating *copy into a different *house style or simply by rewriting the *intro (also known as 'giving it a new nose'). *Compare* SHOVELWARE. *See also* VERSIONING.

research 1. The collection and assessment of *information for the purposes of journalistic *reporting, which may involve attending events such as meetings and hearings, conducting *interviews with *sources, accessing databases, and studying documents (*see* DATA JOURNALISM; FACT-CHECKING; NEWSGATHERING; VERIFICATION).
2. The collection and assessment of information for the purposes of academic scholarship within the field of *journalism studies, which may involve methods such as *content analysis, *critical discourse analysis, newsroom observation, and interviewing (*see* CRITICAL THEORY; EMPIRICAL RESEARCH; ETHNOGRAPHIC RESEARCH).
3. The collection and assessment of information about *audiences for the purpose of informing news organizations and *advertisers. *See also* ALLIANCE FOR AUDITED MEDIA; AUDIT BUREAU OF CIRCULATION; NATIONAL READERSHIP SURVEY.

retraction A form of *correction that withdraws the offending piece of journalism and/or states that it was untrue. *See also* APOLOGIES.

Reuters The world's biggest international *news agency that was founded in London in 1851 by Paul Julius Reuter (1816–99). Now fully *multimedia and employing more than 2,800 journalists in almost 200 bureaus, Reuters has been owned by the Thomson Corporation (renamed **Thomson Reuters**) since 2008. *See also* REUTERS INSTITUTE FOR THE STUDY OF JOURNALISM.

Reuters Institute for the Study of Journalism A research centre based at Oxford University in the UK with financial backing from Thomson Reuters (*see* REUTERS). Its publications include an annual *Digital News Report*, a survey of the consumption of *digital news media.

(((●))) SEE WEB LINKS

• The *Digital News Report*

review A critical evaluation or assessment of a cultural artefact such as a book or a film, or of an event such as a concert. Reviews include the personal opinions of the reviewer or *critic and therefore are not normally required to demonstrate *impartiality, although they are nonetheless expected to be accurate.

Reynolds defence An argument developed in the UK courts to protect news organizations even if they publish potentially defamatory information that cannot be proved to be true, as long as the story can be defended as responsible journalism that was conducted in the *public interest. Named after a *libel case between Albert Reynolds, a former Taoiseach (prime minister) of Ireland, and the *Sunday Times*, the Reynolds defence was outlined in a Law Lords' ruling in 1999 setting out ten factors to be taken into consideration when courts decide if there might be a public interest defence to a claim for *defamation. The ten factors are:

- The seriousness of the allegation.
- The nature of the information and the extent to which the subject matter is of public concern.
- The source of the information.
- The steps taken to verify the information.
- The status of the information.
- The urgency of the matter.
- Whether comment was sought from the claimant.
- Whether the item contained the gist of the claimant's side of the story.
- The tone of the story.
- The circumstances of publication, including timing.

Although the *Defamation Act of 2013 abolished the common-law Reynolds defence and replaced it with a statutory defence of publication on a matter of public interest, the courts continue to be guided by case law that was developed in relation to Reynolds, and many journalists continue to treat the ten points as something of a checklist for *investigative journalism.

right of reply 1. The standard journalistic practice whereby anybody about whom allegations of wrongdoing are going to be published is normally offered the chance to comment in advance of publication (*see* OPPORTUNITY TO REPLY).
2. A formal arrangement whereby anybody criticized or inaccurately reported in the media is, on request, subsequently granted space to respond. Such a right of reply, which operates in some European countries, has been a longstanding demand of many media reform campaigns in the UK and was recommended by the 1974-7 *Royal Commission on the Press, to no avail.

rip and read *Copy for radio news *bulletins *syndicated from a central source, or supplied by a *news agency or *wire service, that can simply be read aloud without any additional editorial input. *See also* SCRIPT.

risk assessment Weighing up the potential dangers of a reporter, photographer, or TV crew going out on a particular job, with the aim of ensuring that nobody goes into a dangerous or volatile situation without knowing how they will be able to get away safely if the need should arise. *See also* DEATHS OF JOURNALISTS.

rogue reporter defence An argument sometimes put forward by a news organization accused of unethical practices: that one 'bad apple' is to blame rather than any wider systems failure (*see* HACKGATE).

rolling news News that is broadcast on a continuous basis rather than being confined to specific *bulletins. *See also* NEVER WRONG FOR LONG.

Rolling Stone A music and culture magazine published in the USA since 1967 that has been best known at various points for *gonzo journalism, *immersion reporting, in-depth *interviews, 'greatest album of all time' lists, and the perceived boost to the career of anyone featured on its cover. *Rolling Stone* was founded in San Francisco by Jann Wenner (1946–) and Ralph Gleason (1917–75), and some of its most celebrated contributors have been Hunter S. Thompson, Tom Wolfe, and Greil Marcus. Wenner remains editor and publisher of both the magazine and its digital offshoots.

Romanes Media Group A regional media group based in Scotland, whose titles include the *Clydebank Post* and the *Greenock Telegraph*. In 2013 the group was the thirteenth largest publisher in the UK regional press, with an average weekly *circulation of more than 400,000 copies.

rooftop journalism A television journalist reporting from overseas, often during times of *conflict, who rarely gets the opportunity to see things for him- or herself out in the *field because it is too dangerous or because of the demands placed upon them to appear frequently on screen. Rooftop journalism is so named because a *foreign correspondent may spend most of his or her time standing on the roof of a hotel or other building on which it is possible to get a satellite signal and also be filmed with a panoramic backdrop in spite of the fact that they are required to file endless reports about the mood on the streets or other things of which they may have had no opportunity to experience at first-hand. *See also* TELEVISION JOURNALISM; WAR REPORTING.

routines Recurrent journalistic practices designed to ensure that each edition or news bulletin has exactly the right amount of material, produced in accordance with *house style, with all *deadlines met. Routines typically include making regular *calls, allocating *diary jobs, monitoring the *wires, and checking the output of rival news organizations.

row A disagreement or dispute between two or more people, the reporting of which is one of the staples of journalism.

Royal Charter on the Press A system for overseeing *self-regulation of the UK press proposed in 2013 in response to the previous year's *Leveson Report. The charter would empower a recognition body to assess periodically whether or not any successor to the *Press Complaints Commission that applied for official recognition was sufficiently independent and effective. Publishers opting-in to such a system would in effect be protected from the threat of having punitive exemplary damages and costs awarded against them in any *libel cases that ended up in court. An initial charter was drafted by representatives of the three biggest political parties at Westminster; a counter draft was put forward by the major press publishers who also announced plans to establish their *Independent Press Standards Organization with or without any formal recognition. The draft all-party charter was subsequently amended in response to press hostility but the major newspaper groups continued to oppose it as unwarranted and unacceptable political interference in a hitherto *free press.

(🌐) SEE WEB LINKS
- Royal Charter on the Press
- The *Mail* on the Royal Charter

Royal Commissions on the Press Government-initiated official inquiries into the state of the UK press, which took place in 1947–9, 1961–2, and 1974–7. Although all three inquiries heard some evidence of unethical journalism, each accepted the role of a *free press as a *fourth estate and backed the concept of the *self-regulation of newspapers and magazines rather than introducing broadcast-style *statutory regulation. The first commission was established by the post-war Attlee administration following lobbying by the *National Union of Journalists, amid concern at the power of the *press barons and increasing *concentration of ownership. It led to the establishment of both the *General Council of the Press and the *National Council for the Training of Journalists. The second commission resulted in the General Council of the Press changing its name to the *Press Council and extending membership beyond the newspaper industry to include a number of lay members. The third commission recommended that the Press Council should have an equal number of lay and industry members and be chaired independently, plus a number of other reforms including the establishment of a *code of conduct and a *right of reply. Before its eventual abolition, the Press Council adopted the suggested change in membership and the independent chairperson but rejected a code and a right of reply. Many of the issues raised during the three Royal Commissions were later revisited in the *Calcutt and *Leveson Reports.

RSS (Really Simple Syndication) An online system whereby people can click to be alerted on updates to websites, for example by signing up to receive a daily email containing the latest headlines from a newspaper's website, together with links to the stories online.

running order A list from first to last of which stories will feature in a broadcast news *bulletin. Changes may be made up to the last minute (and even beyond, once the bulletin has started). *See also* SCRIPT.

running story An event or item that continues and develops over a period of time.

Russian Union of Journalists A trade union representing journalists and other media workers across Russia. The Russian Union of Journalists, which is affiliated to the *International Federation of Journalists, runs a defence hotline to support members who are attacked for doing their jobs. *See also* MOSCOW UNION OF JOURNALISTS.

Sacramento Bee A US daily newspaper and website published in Sacramento, California, and the flagship title of the *McClatchy Company. In its first issue, published in 1857, the newspaper informed readers: 'The name of the *Bee* has been adopted as being different from that of any other paper in the state and as also being emblematic of the industry which is to prevail in its every department.'

safety *See* DEATHS OF JOURNALISTS.

Saga The UK's biggest-selling monthly magazine, a subscription-only publication aimed at people aged 50 years or over, selling more than half a million copies each month in 2013.

St Louis Post-Dispatch A US daily newspaper published in St Louis, Missouri. Originally founded by Joseph Pulitzer (1847–1911), the newspaper and its digital brand are today owned by the Iowa-based Lee Entreprises.

Salon A pioneering US website that has specialized in news, politics, culture, and technology stories since its launch in 1995.

((⊕)) SEE WEB LINKS

- About *Salon*

Salt Lake Tribune A US daily newspaper and online brand published in Salt Lake City, the capital of Utah. First published in 1870, initially as the weekly *Mormon Tribune*, today it is owned by the MediaNews Group of Denver.

samizdat A term covering the *underground press as well as the circulation of other forms of unofficial and/or clandestine communication in defiance of the regime of *censorship that operated in the Soviet Union and some of its allies for much of the 20th century. *See also* ALTERNATIVE MEDIA; GLASNOST.

San Diego Union-Tribune A daily newspaper with digital offshoots, published in the Californian city of San Diego, that was created by a 1992 merger of two titles dating from 1928. Since 2011 it has been owned by real-estate company MLIM, which in 2012 rebranded it *U-T San Diego*. It is one of the top 25 dailies in the USA in terms of *circulation.

San Francisco Chronicle A formerly independent US daily newspaper and website covering the San Francisco Bay area of California that, in 2000, was bought by *Hearst Newspapers—the owner of its major rival for more than a century, the *San Francisco Examiner*.

San Francisco Examiner Once a flagship *Hearst newspaper that was sold to comply with ownership regulations when Hearst took over the rival *San Francisco Chronicle* in 2000. The *Examiner* subsequently switched to become a free distribution *tabloid and is now owned by a private company, the San Francisco Newspaper Company.

San Jose Mercury News A US daily newspaper and digital *brand published in San Jose, California, that is today part of MediaNews' Bay Area News Group. As the major newspaper covering Silicon Valley, the *San Jose Mercury News* has been a keen chronicler of the *internet and between 1994 and 2005 it employed the influential media and technology journalist Dan Gillmor, who was an early evangelist for *blogging and *collaborative journalism.

(((🌐))) SEE WEB LINKS
- The *San Jose Mercury News*' Silicon Beat

satirical journalism Forms of journalism that incorporate a humorous approach and/or forms of humour that incorporate a journalistic approach. Satirical journalism sets out to mock or ridicule its targets, which are often powerful individuals or institutions. *See also* BLACK DWARF; ONION; PRIVATE EYE; PUNCH.

scandal Something that causes public outrage and is therefore seen as being *newsworthy, and/or something that is reported with a view to provoking public outrage.

scepticism A questioning approach to statements, evidence, received opinions, *common sense, and anything that initially appears to be blindingly obvious. Some journalists refer to their sense of scepticism as a built-in '**bullshit detector**'. It is often said to be the best starting point for good journalism, with a heightened dose of scepticism regarded as

essential to *investigative journalism. *Compare* TOO GOOD TO CHECK.
See also VERIFICATION.

scoop An *exclusive story, which can mean either a story that no other
news organization knows of, or one that nobody else has yet published.
Individual journalists are occasionally given the nickname 'Scoop',
sometimes in recognition of their ability to bring in stories and
sometimes as an ironic comment on their inability to do so.

Scoop A satirical novel by Evelyn Waugh (1903–1966) that introduced
the world to Lord Copper, proprietor of the *Daily Beast*. Since
publication in 1938, *Scoop* has invariably been described as one of the
best books about journalism ever. Up to a point, Lord Copper.

Further reading: E. Waugh, *Scoop* (2003 [1938]).

Scotsman A Scottish national daily newspaper that was founded in
Edinburgh in 1817, initially as a weekly. Traditionally a *broadsheet, the
Scotsman switched to what it terms the *compact format in 2004 while
under the ownership of the Barclay Brothers (owners of the *Daily
Telegraph*, among other media interests). Since 2006 the newspaper and
the associated *scotsman.com* website have been owned by *Johnston Press.

Scott Trust The organization established to protect and preserve the
existence and independence of the UK's *Guardian*, giving the
newspaper (and now its digital offshoots) what is virtually a unique
structure of *ownership. Named after the *Guardian*'s most famous
editor, C. P. Scott (1846–1932), the trust was set up in 1936, since when
the newspaper has been free from the influence of *proprietors, *press
barons, and shareholders demanding higher dividends. Instead, any
profits can be reinvested in journalism and/or used to subsidize
loss-making elements of the operation, in accordance with the trust's
central purpose, which is: 'To secure the financial and editorial
independence of the *Guardian* in perpetuity: as a quality national
newspaper without party affiliation; remaining faithful to its liberal
tradition; as a profit-seeking exercise managed in an efficient and cost-
effective manner'. To this end, other parts of the trust's Guardian Media
Group such as the *Manchester Evening News* (along with its associated
local weekly newspapers) have been disposed of when they stopped
bringing in sufficient income. *See also* COMMENT IS FREE; OBSERVER.

screamer Journalistic jargon for an exclamation mark, emphasizing the point that this particular form of punctuation is generally frowned upon except when used in a *quote of somebody actually exclaiming. Any *copy containing a preponderance of screamers tends to be regarded by journalists as a sure sign that it is the work of an amateur. *See also* GRAMMAR; STYLE.

screengrab 1. A still picture taken by freezing the footage from a television programme, a televised event, or a piece of online video, such as may be used to illustrate a story about the programme or the event itself.
2. An image of a web page or other online display, such as may be used to illustrate a story about the site itself.

script The words to be spoken by a *newsreader or presenter on a radio or TV *bulletin, a reporter presenting a *package, a narrator on a *documentary, or the participants in a planned and scripted *two-way. The production of an accurate and clear script is as integral to *broadcast journalism as writing with accuracy and clarity is to *print journalism. Scripts will typically be divided vertically, with one side containing the text for reading aloud and the other containing technical information about items, including their duration. As with the *running order, a script may be altered even while a bulletin is on air. *See also* LANGUAGE OF NEWS.

search engine A website that searches public areas of the *internet on behalf of users who type in what it is they wish to search for. Search engines have become an important way of driving traffic towards the websites of news providers, hence the development of *search engine optimization techniques. *See also* GOOGLE; KEYWORDS; SERPs.

search engine optimization (SEO) Writing *copy and selecting *photographs for *online journalism in such a way as to increase the likelihood of items being found by and ranked highly in search engine results pages (*see* SERPs). This typically includes ensuring that *headlines, *photo captions, and the first page of text (*above-the-fold) include several keywords that are likely to be searched for by both human readers and by the digital 'spiders' that scour the web on behalf of *search engines. *See also* KEYWORDS.

Seattle Post-Intelligencer A US online-only newspaper covering Seattle in Washington state and owned by *Hearst Newspapers. The print edition ceased in 2009 after 146 years, when the *Seattle P-I* became the first major metropolitan daily newspaper in the USA to switch to online-only publication.

(((⊕))) SEE WEB LINKS
• 'Seattle P-I to publish last edition'

Seattle Times The only daily newspaper in the US city of Seattle since the rival *Seattle Post-Intelligencer* abandoned print in 2009. The biggest-selling daily in the state of Washington, the *Seattle Times* is one of the few remaining family-owned metropolitan newspapers in the USA.

secondary definers Journalists (and others) who, in effect, help to spread the world view of a society's '*primary definers'. When it comes to determining how social and political issues of the day are defined and discussed, a journalist normally plays the role of a secondary definer, argues a strand of cultural analysis associated with the academic Stuart Hall (1932–2014). According to the theory of primary and secondary definition, journalists tend to privilege and circulate the interpretations of the more dominant forces in society who thereby become the primary definers of events and issues. Journalists tend to fulfil this function not necessarily because of any form of deliberate conspiracy, it is argued, but because the most powerful institutions and individuals within society are those most likely to be seen as authoritative and credible *sources of information and interpretation. The theory is criticized for taking insufficient account of the possibility that journalistic products such as the *Daily Mail* or the *Sun*, and media organizations such as the *Murdoch empire, may have the power to become primary definers in their own right. *See also* ACCESS; HEGEMONY.

Section 31 A provision within the Broadcasting Act in the Irish Republic that allowed the government in Dublin to issue orders preventing *broadcast journalists from using the voices of people who were deemed likely to incite crime or undermine the authority of the state. Most controversially, from the 1970s to the 1990s, TV and radio journalists in Ireland were banned from broadcasting the spoken words of members or supporters of the republican movement, among others, including elected representatives of Sinn Fein. The *National Union of Journalists and other opponents of *censorship argued that Section 31 prevented journalists doing their jobs of asking questions and informing the public. *See also* BROADCAST BAN.

selection Making choices about which of all the world's potentially *newsworthy events might be reported, then choosing which of the available reports will actually be published or broadcast, and what *angles, *information, *quotes, and other material will be included within each story. News, features, sports, and other items will typically be selected in accordance with established *news values in conjunction with considerations such as the perceived interests of the *audience, the logistics of providing coverage, and the availability of *pictures. This role in selection has led to journalists, especially those with editorial responsibility, being described as playing *gatekeeping and *agenda-setting roles within society.

self-censorship A process whereby journalists are said to avoid reporting certain stories, sources, allegations, arguments, or opinions for fear that to do so might land them in some kind of trouble or difficulty with their *editor, *proprietor, the law, or even criminal elements. Journalists adopting the approach known as self-censorship do not need to be told what to do and what not to do because they anticipate what is required and act accordingly. *Compare* CENSORSHIP. *See also* CHILLING EFFECT; EDITORIAL INDEPENDENCE; FLAK.

selfie A *photograph taken by the person featured in the picture who then makes it publicly available via *social media such as *Instagram, *Twitter, or *Facebook. Such pictures, which are usually taken with the use of outstretched arms or reflections in mirrors, seem to be irresistible to some publications and websites if the self in question is a *celebrity, scantily clad, or preferably both. *See also* USIE.

self-regulation A system under which journalists or, more often, their employers establish the rules and conventions that govern the culture, practices, and *ethics of news organizations. This has been compared to schoolchildren marking their own homework, and contrasts with *statutory regulation whereby rules are imposed upon the media by force of law. *See also* CALCUTT REPORTS; INDEPENDENT PRESS STANDARDS ORGANIZATION; LAST CHANCE SALOON; LEVESON INQUIRY; PRESS COMPLAINTS COMMISSION; PRESS COUNCIL.

semiotics (semiology) The study of signs, systems of signs, ways in which such signs are communicated, and what they may mean. Semiotics has been used by some scholars in the field of *journalism studies (as well as in wider media and communication studies) to explore the possible ideological and other meanings that may be contained within journalistic *texts. A text in this sense can include visual and audio *communication in addition to the written form, and semiologist scholars tend to put as much emphasis on the ways in which any text can be 'read' by the receiver as on whatever message was intended by the sender (*see* ENCODING, DECODING). *See also* ACTIVE AUDIENCE; CODE; CONNOTATION; CRITICAL THEORY; DENOTATION.

sensationalism A contested term that, to some, means an exaggerated story or the overhyped presentation of a supposed *scandal, yet to others means the powerful communication of important information that urgently needs to be brought to the attention of the public. In a signed front page article in 1949, *Daily Mirror* editor Silvester Bolam (1905–53) famously defended his newspaper's sensationalism as the 'vivid and dramatic presentation of events', adding: 'Every great problem facing us ... will only be understood by the ordinary man busy with his daily tasks if he is hit hard and hit often with the facts. Sensational treatment is the answer, whatever the sober and "superior" readers of some other journals may prefer.' *See also* ELITISM; POPS; TABLOIDIZATION.

SEO *See* SEARCH ENGINE OPTIMIZATION.

serendipity The unexpected discovery of interesting and/or entertaining items of information. Serendipitous exposure to material of which the reader was previously unaware, and for which they were not searching, has long been regarded as one of the joys of browsing printed media in general and newspapers in particular. Such serendipity is sometimes said to be undermined online by the tendency for users to access only material that they have specifically looked for or that has been provided by sources they have chosen to follow or 'like'. However, the ease with which material can be shared via *social media has led some commentators to counter that the digital age may provide even greater opportunities for serendipity than did the heyday of the printed press.

serialization The publication of extracts of a book, such as the diary of a retired politician or the autobiography of a celebrity, over two or more editions of a newspaper or magazine. In most cases the publication will have paid for the rights and, in addition to running the extracts, might also use the contents as the basis for front page news. *See also* BUY-UP.

SERPs An industry abbreviation for 'search engine results page', meaning what appears on somebody's screen after searching for a word or phrase on *Google or other online *search engines. Studies suggest that many internet users never look beyond the first page of results or even delve beneath the top of the first page, so media organizations are keen to feature as high up the SERPs rankings as possible (hence *search engine optimization). Journalists searching for information might be expected to dig more deeply and/or to refine their searching to produce fewer, more targeted results.

sex A sexual element to potential stories, which—all other things being equal—tends to make them appear more *newsworthy than similar stories with no sexual element. Many media organizations, by no means just the *tabloid press, look favourably on stories about sex or containing some kind of sex angle that can be emphasized as much for the purpose of *entertainment as providing information in the *public interest. *See also* NEWS VALUES.

sexism Discriminatory attitudes or prejudices based on *gender that may find expression in journalistic output or in job allocation and career progression within news organizations. Generations of women journalists have resisted the assumption that they are innately suited to writing *human interest features or covering *'soft' news. Female journalists and other women in the public eye are sometimes subjected to sexist and misogynist abuse (including threats of death and sexual assault) by online *trolls. *See also* CAMPAIGN FOR REAL PEOPLE; DISCRIMINATORY LANGUAGE; FEMINIST MEDIA; INTERNATIONAL WOMEN'S MEDIA FOUNDATION; PAGE THREE; PORNIFICATION; SIDEBAR OF SHAME; STEREOTYPING; WOMEN IN JOURNALISM.

Further reading: D. Chambers, L. Steiner, and C. Fleming, *Women and Journalism* (2004).

(((●))) SEE WEB LINKS

• Report by Women in Journalism: *Seen But Not Heard: How women make front page news*

shield law Legislation that may prevent a journalist from being compelled to reveal the identity of a *source who has been promised confidentiality. Such shield laws operate in most US states. *See also* ANONYMOUS SOURCE; WHISTLEBLOWER.

Shocking Pink An influential feminist magazine produced in the UK by and for teenage girls and young women from the late 1970s to early 1980s, with occasional short-lived revivals in later years. *Shocking Pink* set out to challenge the *sexism and *stereotyping found in much *mainstream media, including commercial *women's and teen magazines. *See also* ALTERNATIVE MEDIA; FEMINIST MEDIA; REPRESENTATION.

(🌐) SEE WEB LINKS
• 'A shocking shade of pink'

shorthand A system of fast and accurate *note-taking, such as Pitman and Teeline, that is based on abbreviations and symbols. A shorthand speed of at least 100 words per minute is required for *reporters on most local and regional newspapers in the UK; some other employers in the digital age see it more as an added bonus than as a prerequisite.

(🌐) SEE WEB LINKS
• NCTJ shorthand video

shovelware Taking material created for another platform, typically a news story written for a newspaper, and placing it online without any attempt at making it more web-friendly. The process has begun to reverse in recent years, whereby media outlets with a *web-first policy might include one day's online stories in the following day's newspaper with the story wrongly stating 'today' rather than 'yesterday'. *Compare* REPURPOSING.

sidebar A smaller item linked to the longer story that it accompanies. A sidebar could be a *factbox containing several key facts, a chronology or *timeline of events, a personal *case study to illustrate a wider issue, advice provided by an expert, or some other way of adding value to the main piece.

Sidebar of Shame Unofficial nickname for the *Femail Today* column on the *Mail Online* website, which specializes in picture-led items about female *celebrities and the state of their bodies and/or relationships. *See also* SEXISM.

Sigma Delta Chi *See* SOCIETY OF PROFESSIONAL JOURNALISTS.

silly season A period during which major *news is said not to happen (because politicians, judges, and other providers of serious news are on holiday), resulting in the media covering more trivial or flimsy news items than normal.

Sina Weibo The Chinese equivalent of *Twitter that is hugely popular despite the fact that, from time to time, it is subjected to official *censorship. *See also* GREAT FIREWALL OF CHINA; SOCIAL MEDIA; SOCIAL NETWORKING.

Six Acts A series of laws hastily passed by the British government (following the Peterloo Massacre of 1819) that were aimed at curtailing the activities of the *radical press, among other things. One of the six pieces of legislation was the Newspaper and Stamp Duties Act 1819, which increased *stamp duty and extended it beyond publications that carried *news to include those featuring *opinion (such as the popular cheap version of *Cobbett's Political Register*). *See also* TAXES ON KNOWLEDGE.

60 Minutes A US *current affairs television programme broadcast weekly by *CBS since 1968 and which has often set the agenda with its *investigative journalism into major issues of the day.

(⊕) SEE WEB LINKS

• 60 Minutes

sketch 1. A *colour piece about an event that, although intended to be accurate, will incorporate jokes, allusions, and comments to create a piece of journalism that is at least as much about *entertainment as it is about information.
2. A drawing, typically of somebody in a courtroom (*see* ARTIST'S IMPRESSION).

sketch writer A journalist who covers events such as political debates, public inquiries, or major court cases, by focusing more on apparently incidental elements than on reporting the most important *facts. Arguably, however, skilled Parliamentary sketch writers such as Simon Hoggart of the *Guardian* and Ann Treneman of the *Times* can capture something of the essence of events and contribute in their idiosyncratic way towards journalism's *watchdog role. *Compare* GALLERY REPORTING. *See also* SKETCH.

Sky News A *24-hour satellite television (and online) news channel launched in the UK by the *Murdoch empire in 1989. In contrast to *Fox News* in the USA, *Sky News* has a reputation for reporting the news in a relatively straightforward way, and it has broken many stories. However, critics argue that its determination to be first with *breaking news has occasionally led to the broadcasting of erroneous information (*see* NEVER WRONG FOR LONG). Although the Murdochs actually own only around 39 per cent of BSkyB (which runs *Sky News*), it is still seen as a key and hugely profitable part of the family's media interests. Controversial plans to take 100 per cent control of BSkyB were abandoned in 2011 in the wake of the *hackgate scandal, but seasoned observers have not ruled it out in the future. In 2013 *News Corporation's stake in BSkyB became part of *21st Century Fox, following the division of the Murdoch empire into two.

slander A form of *defamation that is spoken rather than written. However, defamatory material spoken on TV, radio, or online, comes under *libel rather than slander.

slow journalism A concept of journalism that puts quality, depth, and *accuracy above speed. Inspired by the 'slow food' movement, adherents of slow journalism argue that journalists need the time and space to do their jobs properly by getting out of the office, nurturing a range of *contacts, building *trust, reading documents, and generally engaging in *reflective practice. *Compare* AMBIENT JOURNALISM; McJOURNALISM; NEVER WRONG FOR LONG; ROLLING NEWS. *See also* LONG-FORM JOURNALISM.

(((●))) SEE WEB LINKS
• 'Slow journalism' by Susan Greenberg

slug The working title given to a story as it proceeds through the production process. Normally just one word, it is strictly for internal consumption only. *See also* CATCHLINE.

snapper A colloquial term for a press *photographer, most likely to be used by non-photographers.

snatch pic A photograph taken by a press *photographer without the subject's knowledge and/or in a fleeting situation such as a momentary appearance in a doorway.

Sniffin' Glue The UK's first and most famous punk *fanzine, which emerged in London in the summer of 1976. Photocopied with an initial print run reported to be only 50 copies, and lasting just twelve issues, *Sniffin' Glue* used a form of what might be described as '*native reporting' or *immersion reporting to record the punk music scene from down below, inspiring hundreds of others to create their own fanzines and become do-it-yourself journalists (for a while, at least). *See also* ALTERNATIVE MEDIA; AMATEUR JOURNALISM; PUNK.

Further reading: M. Perry, *Sniffin' Glue: And Other Rock 'n' Roll Habits* (2009).

social bookmarking The sharing of *links to online items, including news stories and videos, via third-party *social networking services such as *Facebook, *Twitter, *Delicious, *Digg, *StumbleUpon, or *Reddit. News organizations typically encourage such sharing because it drives traffic to their *websites. *See also* LINKING; ONLINE JOURNALISM; SOCIAL MEDIA.

social media A broad term covering a growing range of peer-to-peer and many-to-many forms of *communication conducted via computers and, increasingly, mobile devices. Social media include *Facebook, *Twitter, *YouTube, and countless other forums, and in just a few years they have become as important a way for journalists to find *stories and *sources as they are for news organizations to promote their *brands. Social media have allowed for more direct communication and interaction between journalist and *audience, with information and comment flowing in both directions. *See also* COLLABORATIVE JOURNALISM; CROWDSOURCING; DIGITAL MEDIA; INTERACTIVITY; MASHABLE; NETWORKED JOURNALISM; ONLINE JOURNALISM; SOCIAL BOOKMARKING; SOCIAL MEDIA EDITOR; SOCIAL NETWORKING; TROLLING.

Further reading: M. Knight and C. Cook, *Social Media for Journalists: Principles & Practice* (2013).

social media editor A journalist with specific responsibility for utilizing *social media technologies and engaging with *users to help tell *stories in new ways. News organizations only began to create such posts around 2010 but already by 2013 there were declarations that 'the social media editor is dead' on the grounds that all journalists ought now to be undertaking such activities. *See also* COLLABORATIVE JOURNALISM; CROWDSOURCING; CURATION; STORIFY; USER-GENERATED CONTENT.

((∰)) SEE WEB LINKS
• 'The social media editor is dead'

social networking Horizontal, peer-to-peer *communication online and/or via mobile devices, making use of *social media such as *Facebook, *Twitter, and *Sina Weibo (a sort of Chinese Twitter). Journalists routinely engage in social networking to research *stories and find *sources as well as to promote themselves and their work. *See also* NETWORKED JOURNALISM; SOCIAL BOOKMARKING.

Society of Editors An organization of *editors in all sectors of the UK media that was created in 1999 as the result of a merger between the *Guild of Editors and the *Association of British Editors. The society, which organizes an annual conference with high-powered speakers, lobbies in support of a *free press.

Society of Professional Journalists A membership organization of journalists in the USA formed in 1909, initially as the **Sigma Delta Chi** journalistic fraternity at DePauw University, Indiana, and dedicated to the perpetuation of a *free press as the cornerstone of liberty. It has allowed women to join since 1969.

Society of Professional Obituary Writers A membership organization for journalists who write obituaries for the US and Canadian media. The society holds the annual Grimmies Awards to celebrate the art of writing an *obituary, and its website hosts the illuminating *Obituary Forum*.

(((●))) SEE WEB LINKS
• The society's *Obituary Forum*

soft news The opposite of *hard news. Soft news tends to be regarded as inconsequential and is included more for its *entertainment value and to balance otherwise gloomy content than because of its importance to society. *See also* NEWS VALUES.

soundbite A brief piece of *audio, often from a longer *interview or statement, that contains a comment deemed to be worth broadcasting. Experienced interviewees often speak in pre-prepared soundbites and experienced interviewers often try to get beyond them. *See also* BROADCAST JOURNALISM; QUOTE.

sound effects Pieces of *audio added to *broadcast journalism to help illustrate a story, such as the sound of a dentist's drill to go with an item about dental health. Sound effects (often referred to simply as 'effects' or in written form as '**FX**') may be taken from library recordings or, on occasions, be recorded especially on location.

source An individual or organization from whom potential *news stories and *features originate, and to whom a journalist will turn to help check potential stories. Sources are central to journalism, especially *reporting. Journalists typically insist that potential sources are everywhere, but academic research suggests that in practice many journalists tend to use a relatively narrow range of sources most of the time and that the sources most likely to be used are from the resource-rich worlds of *public relations, local government, central government, the police, business, academe, the law, and the entertainment industry, including sport. An individual who becomes a frequent source of information for a journalist, and whose record suggests their information can be trusted, becomes one of that journalist's *contacts. Although the majority of journalist-source encounters are routine and *on the record, some sources provide information only on an unattributable basis: one example would be a *spin doctor who wishes his or her role in a story to be kept in the background, and another would be a *whistleblower who seeks to expose some wrongdoing but who fears repercussions if their identity were to be revealed. *See also* ACCESS; ANONYMOUS SOURCE; ATTRIBUTION; TRUST.

Southern Weekly A Chinese newspaper, also known as the *Southern Weekend*, that gained some global notoriety early in 2013 when its journalists staged a strike against *censorship. The incident at the Guandong-based newspaper was seen by many commentators as a sign of a growing assertiveness and sense of independence among some journalists in China.

(((●))) SEE WEB LINKS

• 'The *Southern Weekly* controversy'

Spare Rib A pioneering feminist magazine produced in the UK between 1972 and 1993 that was born when some women involved in the post-1968 *underground press objected to what they saw as its *sexism and *stereotyping of women. Initially edited by founders Marsha Rowe (1944–) and Rosie Boycott (1951–), *Spare Rib* was soon produced collectively, and its journalism often challenged distinctions between the personal and political spheres. The fact that the magazine was available in many mainstream newsagents' shops, and that it sold between 20,000 and 30,000 copies a month at its height, meant that it was the first exposure many women had to feminist thinking or the women's liberation movement. *See also* ALTERNATIVE MEDIA; FEMINIST MEDIA; Ms. MAGAZINE.

Speak Justice An initiative of the *Committee to Protect Journalists and others to challenge the culture of impunity that is said to protect many of those around the world who threaten, assault, kidnap, or murder journalists. *See also* DEATHS OF JOURNALISTS.

(()) SEE WEB LINKS
• Speak Justice online toolkit

special-interest magazine A niche *magazine covering a specialist topic, which could be anything from adult-oriented rock to zydeco music. Normally having a circulation that is much smaller and much more targeted than more general *consumer magazines, special-interest magazines tend to be sold mostly via subscription although some are available on news-stands; their targeted readership makes them attractive to specialist *advertisers. Many also promote themselves as *brands through use of *podcasts, websites, *social media, events, online shops, and discussion forums. *Compare* FANZINE. *See also* NICHE, ULTRA-NICHE.

specialist A journalist who covers a specific field such as health, education, technology, or countless other specialisms.

Spectator A UK-based weekly magazine of politics and culture that tends to be both conservative and Conservative. Launched in 1828, although there had been a brief earlier incarnation in the 18th century, it now describes itself as 'the oldest continuously published magazine in the English-speaking world'. Today the *Spectator* has a lively online presence and is owned by the Barclay brothers, who also own the *Daily Telegraph.*

(()) SEE WEB LINKS
• The *Spectator* archive

spike Once literally a sharp metal on an editor's desk onto which discarded stories would be impaled, the term retains its use in the digital age when 'to spike' a story means to decide not to run it.

spin The practice of pushing a particular *angle or interpretation on events with a view to influencing journalistic coverage and therefore, it is hoped, *public opinion. The term 'spin' is mostly applied to the efforts of *press officers working for politicians but it is also used more widely to cover *public relations as a whole (*see* SPIN DOCTOR). *Compare* TOPSPIN. *See also* AGENDA-SETTING; NEWS MANAGEMENT.

spin doctor An individual who engages in *spin and who may or may not be a full-time *PR professional. In public, spin doctors tend to dismiss the importance or even the existence of spin; such apparent self-deprecation has itself been described as a form of spin.

( ) SEE WEB LINKS
• Nicholas Jones: 'The role of spin doctors'

splash A newspaper's main front-page story, the one with the biggest *headline. The term may also sometimes be used to indicate the lead item in broadcast and online media

spoiler A story produced to pre-empt, rubbish, or divert attention away from a *scoop or other big story produced by a rival media organization.

spoof An item that looks and/or sounds like a genuine piece of journalism but which is a parody produced as a form of *satirical journalism or to entertain the audience (*see* APRIL FOOL SPOOFS). *Compare* HOAXES.

sport reporting Coverage of sporting events and related stories that can range from the local, the schools' level, and the amateur, to the global, the elite level, and the professional. Sport reporting typically covers the build-up to and fallout from major events in addition to coverage of the event itself, and often also includes the presentation of relevant data in the form of league tables, player statistics, and so on. Sports pages and bulletins include match reports but also draw on many of the standard elements of journalism such as the *news story, the *feature, the *profile, the *colour piece, *investigative journalism, and so on. Mainstream sports coverage is often accused of *sexism for paying far more attention to male sportspeople than to female, and for the way in which coverage of sportswomen (and the wives and girlfriends, or 'WAGs', of male sports stars) is sometimes as much about their appearance as about their prowess. Recent decades have seen something of a blurring of distinctions between news and sport, with sport stories often being given huge prominence; this phenomenon tends to be regarded by non-fans as a sure sign of *dumbing down and *tabloidization. *See also* GREEN 'UN; PINK 'UN; SPORTSDESK.

sportsdesk The *desk from which the coverage of sports is coordinated by a sports editor (and deputies). The sportsdesk will also liaise with the *editor and other desks, most notably the picture desk. *See also* SPORT REPORTING.

Squidgygate A scandal involving publication of the transcript of a telephone conversation between Diana, Princess of Wales, and an alleged lover. Explanations vary as to how and why the call was recorded, and by whom, but the *Sun* newspaper obtained a copy and ran the story in 1992, even putting sections of the tape on a telephone hotline so that readers could listen to it for themselves. In the recording, the Princess was repeatedly referred to by her admirer as 'Squidgy'. *See also* CAMILLAGATE; PRIVACY.

Stamford Mercury A weekly published in Lincolnshire that claims to be the UK's oldest surviving newspaper, dating from 1695; however, British Library records date it from only 1713, which would make it the second-longest survivor after *Berrow's Worcester Journal*. Today it is owned by Johnston Press. See also LOCAL JOURNALISM; NORWICH POST.

(((●))) SEE WEB LINKS
• *Stamford Mercury* archives

stamp duty A tax imposed by the British government from 1712 that forced up the price of *newspapers, thereby making them too expensive for the mass of the population to be able to purchase. Stamp duty was imposed on the cover price of each newspaper sold as well as on the cost of *advertising within newspapers and on the price of newsprint. Such duties were increased after the French Revolution (1789) and several times during the early years of the 19th century (*see* SIX ACTS). Many unstamped newspapers defied what they saw as '*taxes on knowledge' and refused to pay, giving their cheaper titles a large readership but at the expense of the repeated arrest, trial, and imprisonment of anyone involved in their production or distribution. The various duties began to be reduced from the mid-1830s and were finally abolished altogether in 1861, partly because of the defiance of the unstamped *radical press and partly because of pressure from a commercial newspaper industry that was eager to target cheap papers (*pops) at a mass readership, nationally and regionally.

standby story An item that can be used if a planned story falls through.

standfirst A sentence or two of text that is typically placed beneath a *headline but before the main body of an article, which introduces or contextualizes what follows. More often used for *features than news, a standfirst may also incorporate the writer's *byline. *See also* GO-LAST.

Star on Sunday The Sunday sister title of the *Daily Star*, one of the UK's *redtop newspapers. Although the daily version began publishing in 1978, the *Star on Sunday* was launched only in 2002 under the ownership of *Northern & Shell.

statutory regulation The system under which journalists are required to work in accordance with rules governing the culture, practices, and *ethics of news organizations that are imposed upon the media by force of law. This has been described by critics as inimical to the very concept of a *free press, although many journalists covered by statutory regulation (such as those working in *broadcast journalism in the UK) point out that it does not prevent them producing critical, independent journalism. Statutory *regulation contrasts with *self-regulation, which is when the journalism industry is allowed in some senses to police itself. *See also* CALCUTT REPORTS; LAST CHANCE SALOON; LEVESON INQUIRY; OFCOM.

stereotyping Coverage of certain individuals, groups, and/or communities in a clichéd manner that conforms to pre-existing images of such groups. Examples of stereotyping can range from the bulk of today's teenagers being regarded as if they are all 'feral youths' to welfare recipients being thought of as mostly workshy 'scroungers'. Stereotypes might be widely regarded as a form of *common sense within much of society, but their use in journalism is decried by critics as the lazy and uncritical reproduction of prejudice. Much *alternative journalism is a conscious effort at challenging stereotypes and *cultural bias by offering more direct media *representation to the 'real people' behind the stereotype. *See also* ARCHETYPES; CAMPAIGN FOR REAL PEOPLE; DISCRIMINATORY LANGUAGE; POLITICAL CORRECTNESS; RACISM; SEXISM.

Stern A major weekly current affairs magazine published in Germany since 1948 and which, along with the *Sunday Times* in the UK, was deeply embarrassed by its publication of the fake *Hitler diaries in 1983.

stickiness The extent to which a website encourages its *users to remain on the site. Within *online journalism a desire to create sticky content can conflict with transparent sourcing that links to external content and original source material.

sting The moment in *undercover reporting when the target of an investigation says or does something damaging while unwittingly being in the presence of a journalist who is using *subterfuge. There can sometimes be a very fine line between a sting operation conducted to serve the *public interest and entrapment in the cause of a *sensational headline. *See also* ETHICS; INVESTIGATIVE JOURNALISM.

Storify A website that since 2011 has facilitated its users in telling stories primarily through the *curation of other people's material posted on *social media, including videos on *YouTube. In this way, Storify's users (who range from individuals to major news organizations) can relatively easily construct a story drawing on multiple sources, and incorporating audio-visual material, in ways that are entirely different to the linear presentation of traditional journalism. *See also* LIVEBLOG; SOCIAL MEDIA EDITOR.

(((⊕))) SEE WEB LINKS
• Storify for journalists

story The way that an item of *news or other piece of journalism is conveyed, which tends to be in the form of a *narrative designed to hold the attention of an *audience in addition (and as a prerequisite) to providing them with *information. Although journalists tend to see themselves as story-tellers, journalistic stories do not necessarily follow all the conventions of traditional story-telling such as starting at the beginning and resolving issues at the end. In contrast, a news story might start in the middle with the most dramatic piece of action, or might open with the end result. Also, news items are often left unresolved, not least because events might still be unfolding as the story is being written. *See also* CONSTRUCTION OF NEWS; MYTH.

strap A subsidiary *headline that may give additional details or explanation about the story.

strategic ritual The steps taken by journalists to reduce the possibility of being accused of *bias or a lack of professionalism, according to the sociologist Gaye Tuchman. In her influential 1972 research paper, 'Objectivity as strategic ritual', Tuchman identified four routine procedures that, taken together, work as a form of journalistic defence mechanism, allowing journalists to claim their work as being objective. The procedures are:

- Presentation of conflicting possibilities.
- Presentation of supporting evidence.
- Judicious use of quotation marks.
- Structuring of information in an appropriate sequence.

By following such a ritual, with careful *attribution, a journalist is said to be absolved from having to decide between competing versions of the *truth. *Compare* ADVOCACY JOURNALISM; JOURNALISM OF ATTACHMENT; OPPOSITIONAL REPORTING. *See also* OBJECTIVE JOURNALISM; ROUTINES; VERIFICATION.

Further reading: G. Tuchman, 'Objectivity as strategic ritual: an examination of newsmen's notions of objectivity', in *American Journal of Sociology* (77 (4) 1972).

streeter *See* VOXPOP.

Street of Shame A semi-derogatory yet partly affectionate nickname for *Fleet Street, used as the title of *Private Eye*'s long-running column of revelations from the newsrooms of the UK national press. Perhaps coincidentally, *Street of Shame* is also the English translation of the title of a 1956 Japanese film (*Akasen Chitai*) about life in a brothel.

stringer A *freelance contributor to a news organization. The term is most often associated with contributors based in other countries who can provide coverage on commission as well as a supply of *tips.

StumbleUpon A *social bookmarking site launched in 2001 that allows users to share *links and rate content by indicating an online thumbs-up or thumbs-down. The *BBC is one of many major news organizations to include a link to StumbleUpon and similar services on its *website.

style The language, *grammar, labelling, and tone of a news organization's output. A newsroom's *house style is aimed at achieving internal consistency and a form of *brand identity. Although many elements of style may be seen as the relatively trivial or even whimsical banning of certain words or phrases, declarations of punctuation wars, and the highlighting of common confusions, rules on style can also be seen as having more ideological implications. Whether a particular group operating in a particular country at a particular time ought to be labelled 'rebels', 'resistance fighters', 'guerrillas', or 'terrorists' would be one of the more obvious examples of the ideological implications of style; other examples might be whether women ought to be given the title 'Miss', 'Mrs', 'Ms', or no title at all, and in what circumstances journalists might use the phrases 'we' and 'us' in their *copy. Concepts of acceptable and unacceptable style change over time and differ between markets, even between different organizations serving similar markets. *See also* CLICHÉ; JOURNALESE; LANGUAGE OF NEWS; ORWELL'S SIX RULES OF WRITING; STYLE GUIDE.

style book *See* STYLE GUIDE.

style guide A document or database codifying a news organization's rules on acceptable and unacceptable *house style. Style guides, some of which have been made available to a wider public either online or in book format, can be didactic, amusing, and idiosyncratic. *See also* STYLE.

(((⊕))) SEE WEB LINKS

• Style guide of the *Guardian*
• Style guide of the *Telegraph*

sub 1. An abbreviation for the noun *sub-editor.
2. An abbreviation for the verb sub-edit (*see* SUBBING).

subbing Transforming raw *copy into a publishable finished product by *editing and/or rewriting, cutting for length, correcting any misspellings, checking for factual or grammatical errors, removing anything that might be *defamatory or in *contempt of court, and ensuring consistency with *house style. Some *sub-editors will also have responsibility for design, writing *headlines, selecting and captioning *photographs, and generating *page furniture. Subbing is traditionally undertaken by teams of subs overseen by a chief sub-editor; the chief sub will liaise with the *news editor and other *desks and will be answerable to the *editor. Increasingly, however, *reporters are being expected to sub their own copy. *See also* FACT-CHECKING; HUB.

sub-editor A journalist whose job is the *subbing of other journalists' *copy. During the 21st century subs have become something of an endangered species as many media companies have sought to cut costs by reducing or abolishing the role altogether, often requiring *reporters to file stories directly into pre-designed *templates. However, some titles—notably the *Sun in the UK—remain very much subs' papers with the work of reporters, news agencies, and photographers merely providing the raw ingredients.

subjectivity Approaching issues from a perspective informed more by personal thoughts and feelings than observable evidence and verifiable *facts. A subjective approach tends to be frowned upon in most news *reporting but it might be celebrated in the writers of *opinion columns and the exponents of genres such as *gonzo journalism and *immersion reporting. *Compare* OBJECTIVE JOURNALISM; VERIFICATION. *See also* CONFESSIONAL MODE; REFLEXIVE PRACTICE.

subterfuge A *reporting tactic whereby a journalist is not open or transparent about being a journalist. Subterfuge is generally regarded as being unethical unless it is deemed necessary for an investigation that is in the *public interest. *See also* BLAGGING; DECEPTION; FAKE SHEIKH; STING; UNDERCOVER REPORTING.

Sun The biggest-selling newspaper in the UK with a print *circulation of more than 2.2 million copies each day in 2013. When the *Sun* introduced a *paywall to its digital *brand in 2013 (bringing it into line with other *News UK titles) it became the first UK redtop to charge for online content, which included football *video clips. In another innovative move it printed special codes to allow readers of the print edition to gain free access to the web version. In many ways the *Sun* is the archetypal product of the *Murdoch empire: popular, populist, and profitable. It began life as the left-leaning *Daily Herald* before changing its name to the *Sun* in 1964 and being bought and transformed by Rupert Murdoch in 1969. Murdoch reinvented the *tabloid as a confident, brash, and entertaining *redtop that rapidly overtook its rivals and complemented its trumpeting of neo-conservative economics by becoming a political cheerleader first for Conservative leader Margaret Thatcher and later for Labour leader Tony Blair (both of whom were accused by critics of returning the favour). Murdoch has stated that anybody wishing to know his personal political views need only read the *Sun*. The paper's commercial success has not been without its critics, most persistently over its coverage of the *Hillsborough disaster, its *Page Three soft-porn pictures, its alleged *stereotyping of many social groupings, and its gung-ho approach to war (*see* GOTCHA). Following the *hackgate scandal at sister paper, the *News of the World*, many *Sun* journalists were arrested by police investigating alleged offences such as the corruption of public officials (as in allegedly paying police and prison officers for *tips), leading to bitterness at the way *News International had apparently compromised its journalists and *sources alike by handing the police a huge quantity of internal emails and related material. When Murdoch himself addressed some of the journalists in 2013, in an effort to calm tempers, a tape of the meeting was leaked to *Private Eye and *Exaro. See also SUN ON SUNDAY: WAPPING DISPUTE.

Further reading: P. Chippindale and C. Horrie, *Stick it up your Punter! The Uncut Story of the* Sun *Newspaper* (2013).

Sunday Correspondent *See* INDEPENDENT ON SUNDAY.

Sunday Express A *mid-market Sunday newspaper in the UK that was launched in 1918 as a sister title to the *Daily Express. Rather like its daily version, the *Sunday Express* exists today in the shadow of the giant *Mail on Sunday.

Sunday Mail *See* DAILY RECORD.

Sunday Mirror The Sunday version of the *Daily Mirror that is in the somewhat peculiar position of competing against its *Trinity Mirror stablemate, the *People, in addition to commercial rivals, notably the *Sun on Sunday. The *Sunday Mirror* began life as the *Sunday Pictorial* in 1915, adopting its current title only in 1963.

Sunday People *See* PEOPLE.

Sunday Sport A UK weekly title launched in 1986 that, although it takes some of the form of a *tabloid newspaper, is more of a collection of soft-porn pics interspersed with *advertisements for premium-rate telephone sex lines and the occasional news item with a sexual angle. Apart from its ability to make other *redtops appear highbrow, its main claims to fame are the bizarre *headlines of its early years ('World War 2 bomber found on Moon', for example) and its invasion of the *privacy of a critically ill actor's hospital room—an action that was condemned by the *Press Council and other newspapers. For some years there was also a *Daily Sport* and later a *Midweek Sport. See also* PORNIFICATION; SUPERMARKET TABLOIDS.

Sunday Telegraph The Sunday version of the UK's *Daily Telegraph. The *Sunday Telegraph* tends to be much more *features-driven than its daily counterpart and is also a relatively recent arrival, dating only from 1961.

Sunday Times 1. A weekly *tabloid newspaper in western Australia that is owned by *News Corp and based in Perth.
2. A *broadsheet newspaper that is the biggest-selling Sunday title in the UK *quality press, at more than 800,000 copies per issue in 2013. Launched in 1822 in direct opposition to the *Observer, the Sunday Times passed through many hands during the 19th and 20th centuries before being bought by Lord Thomson (1894–1976) in 1959. Innovations included a *colour supplement and the launch of the *Insight investigative journalism team, which achieved its greatest prominence by uncovering the *Thalidomide scandal under editor Harold Evans (1928–). Only in 1966 did the Sunday Times become a sister paper to the daily *Times for the first time, when Thomson bought the latter. In 1981 both titles were sold to the *Murdoch empire in a deal that was controversially nodded through by the British government despite the significantly increased *concentration of ownership that it represented; as part of the deal, *News International had to agree to keep the two titles separate. Once in the Murdoch fold, the Sunday title lost much of its former liberal social conscience and shifted more in the direction of Thatcherite neo-conservatism and advertiser-friendly, aspirational *lifestyle journalism, produced in seemingly ever more bulky sections. If its ethical high point had been Thalidomide, its low point was its embarrassment over publishing the fake *Hitler diaries in 1983. However, from time to time it has continued to produce *agenda-setting *investigative journalism, as with its 2013 exposure of a lobbying scandal involving UK politicians and its long-running campaign to expose seven-times Tour de France winner Lance Armstrong as a drugs cheat. See also DEATH ON THE ROCK; WAPPING DISPUTE.

Sun on Sunday The Sunday version of the *Sun newspaper that was launched by the *Murdoch empire in February 2012, little more than six months after the closure of the *News of the World. Several former News of the World staff, including the *fake sheikh, ended up on the new paper which, although it quickly became the UK's biggest-selling Sunday title (selling an average of 1.9 million copies each week in 2013), has not (yet) re-established the pre-eminence of its predecessor.

Sunshine Week An annual week in which US journalists, news organizations, and journalism educators take part in a range of initiatives and events in support of *freedom of information and the public's right to know about the activities of governments and other powerful institutions. After earlier events concentrated in Florida, Sunshine Week has run nationally since 2005 with its main organizers being the *American Society of News Editors and the *Reporters Committee for Freedom of the Press. *See also* WATCHDOG ROLE.

⊕ SEE WEB LINKS
• Sunshine Week examples of FOI in action

supermarket tabloids The US *tabloid newspapers such as the *National Enquirer* that are published weekly and tend to be known not so much for serious *public interest journalism as for *sensationalism, salaciousness, and *headlines such as 'Half-man half-dog baffles doctors' or 'Dinosaurs found on Mars' (both from the **Weekly World News**, which switched to online-only publication in 2007). The nearest UK equivalent might be the *Sunday Sport*.

supplement A separately printed section of a newspaper or magazine. *See also* COLOUR SUPPLEMENT.

surprise An unexpected or unusual event or statement that may be regarded as newsworthy because of the element of surprise and/or shock. *See also* MAN BITES DOG; NEWS VALUES.

Sydney Morning Herald A daily newspaper that is the oldest continuously published paper in Australia, dating from 1831 (when it was the weekly *Sydney Herald* until 1840). Traditionally a *broadsheet, the *Herald* switched to become a *compact in 2013. The newspaper and its website are owned by *Fairfax Media.

syndication The supply of *copy or other material to more than one outlet by a *news agency, or the sharing of material between different titles owned by one publisher.

tablet A mobile computer that is smaller, flatter, and lighter than a laptop, with a screen significantly larger than that on a *mobile phone, leading many producers of so-called *legacy media to believe it might offer them a digital route to survival. Newspapers and magazines in particular have been pushing subscriptions to the tablet versions of their products since around 2010, with mixed results. *See also* DAILY; DIGITAL MEDIA; NEW TECHNOLOGY.

(⊕) SEE WEB LINKS
• *Guardian* editor Alan Rusbridger introduces the iPad edition

Tablet A religious weekly newspaper published by and for the British Roman Catholic community since 1840, making it the UK's second-oldest weekly journal (after the *Spectator*).

tabloid A small-format *newspaper, as opposed to a *broadsheet or *Berliner: the standard tabloid page size is 430 mm by 280 mm. Traditionally, the tabloid press has been associated with popular and/or *mid-market journalism, focusing on *sensationalism, *scandal, sport, and *sex (*see* POPS; REDTOPS), although many serious newspapers are now also published in tabloid size (which they like to refer to as *compact). Popular tabloid journalism tends to privilege celebrity or entertainment-driven material over more serious news, big headlines over background analysis, and pictures over text; all of which contributes to them selling more copies than the so-called *quality press, but none of which means they are not just as much part of the *fourth estate in their own way. After being relatively slow to embrace the *internet—which was initially regarded with suspicion in many tabloid newsrooms as essentially the preserve of a few highbrow nerds and/or pornographers—recent years have seen the tabloid press going digital with a vengeance, perhaps most spectacularly in the case of *Mail Online*. In 2013 the *Sun* became the first UK national tabloid to introduce a *paywall. *See also* SUPERMARKET TABLOIDS; TABLOID WATCH; TABLOIDESE; TABLOIDIZATION.

tabloidese An extreme form of *journalese in which every philanderer is a love-rat, every assault is brutal, and anybody unlucky enough to suffer with cancer is described as brave. *See also* CLICHÉ; STYLE.

Further reading: K. Waterhouse, *Waterhouse on Newspaper Style* (2010 [1993]).

tabloidization The process by which more serious media such as the *quality press and *public service broadcasting organizations are said to adopt some of the popular and *entertainment-driven formats, styles, methods, and *selection criteria that are more traditionally associated with the *tabloid press. *See also* DUMBING DOWN; ELITISM; FOXIFICATION.

Tabloid Watch An independent *blog that, since 2009, has been scrutinising, critiquing, and mocking the output and obsessions of the UK's *tabloid newspapers. *See also* ALTERNATIVE MEDIA.

(⊕) SEE WEB LINKS
• *Tabloid Watch* blog

tag One of a series of labels used to describe a piece of content online; clicking on a tag takes the user to similar or related items.

tag cloud A graphic representation of the frequency with which certain *tags are used on a website, or in a particular document on a site, with the frequency of mentions signified by the size or colour of the font. *Compare* WORD CLOUD.

tailpiece *See* GO-LAST.

Take a Break The biggest-selling *women's magazine in the UK, selling more than 700,000 copies each week in 2013. Launched as a cheap and not very cheerful weekly in 1990, *Take a Break* specializes in 'real-life' stories, telling readers on its website: 'It's your magazine and we're interested in your lives: love and betrayal, loss and sin'. It is part of the *Bauer Media empire.

talking head A device in *television journalism whereby one person is filmed speaking either directly to the camera or to an interviewer. More serious broadcasting tends to favour talking heads over *reconstructions. A familiar or regular interviewee may themselves be referred to as a talking head (or even as a *media tart).

Tampa Bay Times A daily newspaper, with online offshoots, published in the Tampa Bay area of Florida, and one of the top 25 best-selling dailies in the USA. Begun in 1884 as the *West Hillsborough Times*, for most of its life it was known as the *St Petersburg Times*, adopting its current name only in 2012. Since 1978 it has been owned by the Poynter Institute *j-school, and today it also runs the *Pulitzer-winning *PolitiFact* *fact-checking website, which scrutinizes claims made by politicians and others and rates them on its 'truth-o-meter'.

(((•))) SEE WEB LINKS

• The *Tampa Bay Times*' fact-checking site

Tampa Tribune The second-biggest newspaper in the Tampa Bay area of Florida, after the *Tampa Bay Times*. Since 2012 it has been owned by the Revolution Capital Group, Los Angeles-based finance and acquisitions specialists.

taxes on knowledge The label attached by opponents and critical commentators to the various forms of duty imposed on newspapers by the British government from the late 18th to the mid-19th centuries. The imposition of *stamp duty and advertising duty on newspapers inflated their cover price, making them unaffordable for the majority of the population. This had the twin effect of delaying the entry of commercial newspapers into the mass market and of hampering the growth of a *radical press aimed at a working-class readership. However, many radical publications refused to pay such taxes, making their papers much cheaper than their commercial rivals but rendering producers and distributors alike liable to frequent prosecution and severe punishment for their defiance of the law. One such unstamped paper was the *Poor Man's Guardian*, which on 20 August 1831 told its readers: 'Of all the taxes levied (or attempted to be levied) upon the poor man, the most odious and the most inexcusable is the tax upon political knowledge'. *See also* SIX ACTS.

teaser 1. An enticing hint of a story that can be found later in a news bulletin or in a forthcoming edition of a publication.
2. A *headline, *caption, or *coverline that is aimed more at intriguing readers rather than informing them.

technocentrism A perspective that places technology in general, and *new technology in particular, at the centre of everything. For example, a technocentric view might blame the decline in newspaper sales in the

UK on the emergence of online news, thereby disregarding evidence that falling *circulation pre-dated the *internet and may have many contributing factors. Similarly, technocentrism places technology at the heart of proposed solutions, as seen in enthusiasm for delivering news via devices such as *mobile phone and *tablets. *See also* NETIZEN; TECHNOLOGICAL DETERMINISM.

technological determinism A form of *technocentrism that is sometimes found in *journalism studies and other forms of scholarship, whereby it is argued that social change (including developments within journalism) is largely determined by the invention, development, and application of technology. Technological determinism highlights how technological developments ranging from the *telegraph to the *text message have made new things possible, and the ways in which journalists have responded to such emerging possibilities. This perspective is challenged both by critics who point out that the creation and application of any *new technology is dependent upon human *agency in the first place, and by scholars from the *political economy school who emphasize the primacy of political and economic factors in creating the context in which journalism (and pretty much everything else, including technology) is produced. *Compare* MARXISM.

technology correspondent A specialist *reporter who covers technological developments, whether they be gadgets aimed at the consumer market, innovative methods of producing products, or ways in which technology is (said to be) about to transform our lives. In recent years the technology *beat has tended to supplant longer-established specialisms such as the *industrial correspondent.

Teenage Magazine Arbitration Panel (TMAP) An organization established by the UK *magazine industry in 1996 in response to concerns that some publications aimed at teenage girls were including inappropriate and irresponsible material about sexual issues. TMAP is a form of *self-regulation that considers public complaints about alleged breaches of its guidelines.

(⊕) SEE WEB LINKS
• The TMAP guidelines

Telegraph *See* DAILY TELEGRAPH.

telegraph A system for the speedy transmission of messages over long distances by means of an electrical connection carried by a wire, the development of which from the mid-19th century helped newspapers publish news much more speedily. In 1844 the *Times* was the first to report news of a royal birth thanks to a telegraph link between Windsor and London, and within less than 30 years links had been established between Europe and both America and India (and between India and Australia). News organizations' use of the telegraph, in which brevity was required, is often highlighted as one of the factors behind the emergence of the terse writing style with an emphasis on *facts that became the journalistic norm. The later development of wireless telegraph speeded things up even more and covered much greater distances. This led to the execution for murder of Dr Hawley Crippen in 1910 after the captain of the transatlantic ship on which he was fleeing the UK recognized him from newspaper photographs and telegraphed ahead, allowing the police to be waiting to arrest Crippen as the ship arrived in Canada—leading to yet more newspaper headlines. *See also* ASSOCIATED PRESS; NEW TECHNOLOGY.

telephone An electronic system of instantaneous peer-to-peer communication using voices. By the last quarter of the 20th century, the telephone had become so widely adopted that it had become the most frequent way in which journalists contacted their *sources and obtained material for stories (*see* CALLS). Reporters chasing major stories in the *field would often be reliant on using public telephone boxes to file their *copy, leading some to resort to unethical practices such as pulling out a wire or removing a vital component, thereby slowing down their rivals. By the beginning of the 21st century the usefulness of the landline telephone, and the very existence of public call boxes in many areas, was already giving way to the ubiquity of *mobile phones. *See also* COPYTAKER; PHONE-HACKING; PHONE-IN.

television journalism News and current affairs reporting that uses moving pictures as well as audio and is broadcast on TV sets or, increasingly, viewed online and/or via mobile devices. In its early days television journalism drew on the techniques and *platforms that preceded it—notably *print journalism, *radio journalism, and cinema *newsreels—before developing its own styles and genres. As *kit got lighter, less cumbersome, and faster, so TV news *bulletins were able to report directly from the field into viewers' homes, as happened during the Vietnam War in the 1960s and early 1970s, for example. Later developments in television journalism included the launch of *24-hour news channels, which can report entire unfolding events ranging from *press conferences to shooting incidents *live and unedited, to incorporating greater involvement by the *audience via *social media feedback or the submission of *user-generated content. *See also* BBC; BIMEDIA JOURNALISM; BROADCAST JOURNALISM; CONVERGENCE; DOCUMENTARY; PUBLIC SERVICE BROADCASTING; RATINGS; RECONSTRUCTION; ROOFTOP JOURNALISM; TALKING HEAD; VIEWERS.

templates Pre-designed pages for *print or *online journalism into which *subs or *reporters insert *copy and *page furniture to fit the allocated spaces. Templates tend to be favoured by managements as tools for increasing efficiency, but they are derided by many working in *newsrooms for making journalism the servant of design rather than the other way round. *See also* ATEX; CMS; SUBBING.

text 1. The words contained in any piece of journalism when written down in the form of a *story or *script.
2. Any piece of *communication, whether or not it is written or indeed contains any words at all, which is subjected to scrutiny by scholars in *journalism studies or related academic disciplines. In this sense, a text may be interpreted differently by different members of the *audience, and differently from the way in which whoever originated the text may have intended (*see* ENCODING, DECODING). *See also* CRITICAL DISCOURSE ANALYSIS; SEMIOTICS; TEXTUAL ANALYSIS.

text message *See* TXT MSG.

text service Written pieces of news and information that are available to access via televisions, such as the UK's now defunct Ceefax service that was delivered for many years by analogue TV, and the digital text services that are available on some digital TV channels today.

textual analysis Scholarly scrutiny of a piece of journalism (or other form of *communication or *text) in an effort to explore its possible meanings, *connotations, and the various ways in which the text may be interpreted. *See also* CRITICAL DISCOURSE ANALYSIS; SEMIOTICS.

Thalidomide scandal A long-running campaign of *investigative journalism by the *Insight* team on the *Sunday Times* in the 1970s, which revealed the way in which hundreds of children in the UK had been born with missing limbs after their mothers had taken Thalidomide pills while pregnant. Faced with the threat of legal action by the drug manufacturer Distillers, *Insight* probed the moral issues involved even when it was prevented by the risk of *injunctions or *contempt of court from publishing specific details of individual cases. The *Sunday Times* itself used the courts, right up to the European Court of Human Rights, to win the right to reveal the full story. The coverage created a public outcry and eventually persuaded the government under Edward Heath to establish a trust fund to provide financial support for children affected by Thalidomide. The investigation required a huge investment of time and resources over several years, as well as a willingness to risk legal action, and is widely seen as the high point of Harold Evans' fourteen-year tenure as editor of the *Sunday Times* (between 1967 and 1981). *See also* CAMPAIGNING JOURNALISM.

The *Australian* *See* AUSTRALIAN.

The *Economist* *See* ECONOMIST.

The *European* *See* EUROPEAN.

The *Hindu* *See* HINDU.

The *Independent* *See* INDEPENDENT.

The *People* *See* PEOPLE.

The *Spectator* *See* SPECTATOR.

The *Sun* *See* SUN.

The *Times* *See* TIMES.

The *Vanishing Newspaper* The title of an influential book by US journalism professor Philip Meyer, in which he postulated that if current trends continued the last printed *newspaper might roll off the presses in April 2043. When Meyer's book was first published, his hypothesis was widely seen as overly pessimistic, but within a few years it began to be seen by many as wildly optimistic. *See also* LEGACY MEDIA.

Further reading: P. Meyer, *The Vanishing Newspaper* (2004).

(🌐) SEE WEB LINKS
• Philip Meyer on the future of newspapers

The *Week* 1. An influential duplicated news-sheet published independently in the UK between 1933 and 1941 by the former *Times*

journalist Claud Cockburn (1904–81), which was suppressed (along with the *Daily Worker*) under the official *censorship that was imposed during the Second World War. Several decades later Cockburn accepted an invitation to become a contributor to *Private Eye*, which began to model its own journalistic approach on that of the long defunct *The Week*. The *Eye*'s Paul Foot (1937–2004) particularly liked to quote Cockburn's line: 'Never believe anything until it is officially denied' (*see* ALTERNATIVE JOURNALISM; INVESTIGATIVE JOURNALISM).
2. A weekly magazine (and website) published in the UK since 1995 to present a digest of the week's *news and *features, credited to the various outlets whose work it boils down. Today it is owned by **Dennis Publishing** (*see* Oz).

Thomson Reuters *See* REUTERS.

threads A more sophisticated version of an online *Your Comments facility whereby, rather than appearing one after another in (reverse) chronological order, *users' comments are grouped together in a series of threads so that replies to others' comments can form more of a *conversation than a series of random contributions. *See also* INTERACTIVITY; MODERATION; USER-GENERATED CONTENT.

three-source rule A guideline developed at the *Washington Post during its reporting of the *Watergate scandal, whereby two additional reliable *sources had to confirm any serious allegation before it would be published. This standard of seeking three independent sources has since become an unofficial rule-of-thumb for many exponents of *investigative journalism. *See also* VERIFICATION.

threshold An invisible line that events have to cross before they are likely to be regarded as being big or important enough to warrant coverage. Threshold is one of the *news values identified in a 1960s study by Galtung and Ruge, who found that events had to pass a certain threshold before being recorded, or even noticed, by news organizations; after that, the greater the size, intensity, or impact, the more likely was an event to be selected to become *news. *See also* MAGNITUDE; McLURG'S LAW.

Time Influential US weekly *current affairs magazine published since 1923 that is part of the *Time Warner empire. The magazine, which is today published digitally as well as in print, is noted for occasional 'iconic' covers and for the annual announcement of its 'person of the year' (usually a famous individual, but in 2011 it was 'The Protester' and in 2006, in recognition of the growth of *user-generated content and *social media, it was 'You'). In 2013 it was described by the *Pew Research Center as 'the only major print news weekly left standing'.

timeline A *sidebar on a page or website that gives a list of dates and events (usually selective and brief) in chronological order, so as to provide background to a story without overloading the story itself with too much information. An online timeline may include *links to take *users to coverage of the earlier events listed. *See also* CHRONOLOGY.

Time Out A weekly entertainment and listings magazine published in London since 1968 that subsequently expanded to many cities beyond the UK and which, since 2012, has been a *freesheet, relying for its income entirely on *advertising. In its early days, *Time Out* was seen as an example of *alternative media with links to the *underground press and a commitment to radical politics and *investigative journalism (*see* FORUM WORLD FEATURES). However, much of the reporting of London life disappeared along with most of the magazine's radicalism as it became more of an advertising-driven commercial enterprise. Along the way, in the 1980s, an unsuccessful strike by staff seeking to maintain equality of wages led to the publication of a cooperatively run radical rival, *City Limits*, which managed to survive for around a decade.

Times A UK *quality daily newspaper that, since 1981, has been part of the *Murdoch empire, becoming a *compact in 2003; abroad, it is often referred to as *The Times of London*, as if that were its actual title. The paper began in 1785 as the *Daily Universal Register*, becoming *The Times* in 1788, and for some years its founder, printer John Walter (1739–1812), reportedly received an annual government subsidy of £300 in return for the newspaper's political backing. *The Times* gradually became more independent in outlook and it invested heavily in reporting from overseas, including coverage of the Crimean War by pioneering war correspondent William Howard Russell (1820–1907). *The Times* earned the nickname 'The Thunderer' for its reputed ability to make the powerful quake on occasions, although when it spoke it was as part of the Establishment within the bourgeois *public sphere rather than as a voice of opposition (*compare* RADICAL PRESS); indeed, it once promoted itself as the paper for 'top people'. It was only in 1966 that the paper put *news rather than *advertisements on its front page. That same year ownership passed from one Lord (Astor) to another (Thomson, who already owned the *Sunday Times*), but in 1981 both titles were sold to *News International. Murdoch's *Times* initiated a *price war that increased daily sales from 354,000 in 1993 to 670,000 just two years later. Its circulation war, the later switch from broadsheet to compact format, a reduction in *gallery reporting in favour of *colour pieces and *sketches, increasing coverage of sport and other forms of popular culture, and the greater prominence of pictures, all led to accusations of *dumbing down and *tabloidization; in that, The Times is hardly alone among the *quality press. It has also found room for *investigative journalism, including an award-winning campaign to expose the grooming and sexual exploitation of teenage girls, and the failure of the authorities to listen to or protect the victims. By 2013 it was selling just under 400,000 copies a day, making it the UK's seventh biggest national daily newspaper in terms of print *circulation, and the second biggest quality title (after the *Daily Telegraph*). *See also* NEWS UK; PAYWALL; WAPPING DISPUTE.

Times of India A quality English-language newspaper published daily in India since 1851 (having begun life in 1838 as the twice-weekly *Bombay Times and Journal of Commerce*) and which is today one of the most widely read newspapers in English across all platforms anywhere in the world.

Time Warner A US-based media and entertainment giant that, among many other international interests, owns *CNN cable news, the UK's *IPC stable of consumer magazines, *Time* magazine, and many other print and digital titles ranging from *Sports Illustrated* to *InStyle*. *See also* CONCENTRATION OF OWNERSHIP.

Tindle Newspapers A UK regional press group set up by Ray Tindle (1926–), who reportedly moved into newspaper publishing with the £300 'demob' money that was given to British soldiers at the end of the Second World War. In contrast to most rivals, Tindle has pursued a strategy of making his titles more and more local, adding new editions even as other publishers have been retrenching. By 2013 the group was ranked the tenth-biggest regional newspaper publisher in the UK in terms of circulation (with weekly circulation of over 1 million) and fifth for the number of titles with 78, many of them being *freesheets. *See also* LOCAL JOURNALISM; LOCALIZATION.

tip (tip-off) A journalist or news organization being alerted to a potential story by a *source, a member of the public, a *stringer, or a *freelance journalist. The last two will normally expect to be paid a tip fee if the story is subsequently used.

TMAP *See* TEENAGE MAGAZINE ARBITRATION PANEL.

TNG-CWA *See* NEWSPAPER GUILD.

Today 1. A news and current affairs programme broadcast six mornings a week on *BBC Radio Four that is widely seen as one of the UK's key *agenda-setting outlets, particularly as regards political and economic issues. *Today* sees itself as competing with *Newsnight* and *Channel 4 News* at the more serious end of daily factual broadcasting, with *soundbites from its *interviews frequently being replayed in news *bulletins across the BBC during the rest of the day. The *Today* programme itself sometimes makes the news, perhaps most famously during events that led to the *Hutton Report. *See also* AUDIOBOO.
2. A *mid-market national newspaper published in the UK between 1986 and 1995. It was launched by proprietor Eddy Shah (1944–) as a non-union *tabloid, using *new technology and printed in colour, following his victory in the *Warrington Messenger* dispute. The *Today* newspaper was later bought by the *Murdoch empire which eventually closed it down, thereby abandoning the mid-market once more to the *Daily Mail* and *Daily Express*.

too good to check A semi-humorous phrase sometimes used among journalists about a story they really wish to be true but which they fear may not withstand rigorous *fact-checking. Even while making such a joke, in reality journalists will still be expected to check. *Compare* VERIFICATION.

Topper Newspapers A UK *freesheet publisher formed in 1994 that was bought by *Northcliffe in 2012, thereby becoming part of the *Local World stable that same year.

topspin An intangible quality that journalists are sometimes said to apply to stories to make them appear a bit bigger and more significant than they really are. *Compare* SPIN. *See also* FLAM-UP.

TOT *See* TRIUMPH-OVER-TRAGEDY.

town crier An individual who communicates news, proclamations, and other forms of information by means of shouting it out in the street. Dating back at least as far as the Middle Ages, the town crier may be seen as a form of pre-print *media and to presage *public service broadcasting by many hundreds of years.

trade The term preferred by many journalists, particularly in the UK, to describe the type of job that journalism is, thereby distinguishing it from more regulated *professions such as the law and medicine. *See also* CRAFT.

trade press Publications in the *B2B sector; that is, newspapers, magazines, and websites that report news and developments about (and for) those working in particular industries, occupations, or trades.

trade rag Colloquial name for a newspaper or other publication that covers a particular industry. *See also* B2B; TRADE PRESS.

Trafigura An oil company that in 2009 sought to prevent the UK media publishing allegations about the dumping of toxic waste but which dropped its *gagging order after it began trending on *Twitter. The case is often highlighted as an example of how one *tweet (in this instance by the *Guardian* editor) can rapidly lead to a Twitterstorm that draws ever more public attention to whatever it is that somebody wishes to be kept secret, thereby—it is argued—allowing journalists and online citizens (*see* NETIZENS) to collaborate in revealing information in the *public interest. *See also* COLLABORATIVE JOURNALISM; FREEDOM OF INFORMATION; NETWORKED JOURNALISM.

(((●))) SEE WEB LINKS
• The *Guardian*'s Trafigura coverage

tragedy An example of *bad news involving death and/or disaster and, as such, an event that is likely to pass the test of *newsworthiness, although other *news values will also come into play (*see* McLURG'S LAW). *See also* TRIUMPH-OVER-TRAGEDY.

training 1. A form of *journalism education that aims to prepare students and trainees with the skills and knowledge regarded as essential for working journalists, ranging from technical skills such as *shorthand to knowledge of the various *laws that impinge on

journalists' activities (*see* BJTC; NCTJ; PTC). Training is described by some critics as the uncritical reproduction of almost mechanical skills, in contrast to the more critical approach associated with *journalism studies (*see* ACADEMIZATION OF JOURNALISM); however, such a characterization is countered by those who argue that, as journalism itself necessarily entails complex intellectual processes in support of *reflective practice and *ethical journalism, so therefore does good journalism training. *Compare* RAT-LIKE CUNNING. *See also* INDENTURES.
2. Instruction and education of people who are already working as journalists and which is aimed at expanding, updating, or refreshing their skills and/or knowledge. Such training is offered by some, but by no means all, employers.

Trinity Mirror One of the UK's major newspaper publishers, the flagship title of which is the *Daily Mirror*. Trinity Mirror was formed in the 1990s from the merger of the Mirror Group and Trinity, which owned a chain of regional newspapers including the *Liverpool Post* and *Echo*, and in 2010 it bought the *Manchester Evening News* and other local titles from the Guardian Media Group. As of 2013 Trinity Mirror topped the regional press league table for *circulation, at more than 9 million copies per week, and was third in the number of regional titles owned, with 132. *See also* CONCENTRATION OF OWNERSHIP; NEWS BUNNY.

triumph-over-tragedy (TOT) A familiar *trope within journalism, particularly prevalent in many *women's magazines as well as much *sport reporting, whereby an individual is presented as having faced almost insurmountable obstacles yet emerges victorious (or simply survives) against the odds. *See also* ARCHETYPES; CLICHÉ; MYTH.

troll Somebody who disrupts an online or *social media community by posting abusive or irrelevant material, normally while hiding their identity behind one or more user-names. Outspoken women in the public eye, including journalists, are particularly likely to be targeted by trolls (*see* SEXISM). *See also* TROLLING.

trolling The practice of intervening in, dominating, and often disrupting online discussion *threads, forums, comments facilities, and *social media by posting abusive or irrelevant posts. A *troll typically operates under a user-name, or even multiple user-names, rather than contributing under their own name. Dealing with trolling is one of the responsibilities of moderators (*see* MODERATION) and, at the more extreme end of the scale, the responsibility of the police.

trope A familiar, metaphorical, and/or rhetorical figure of speech or way of telling a story (including visually), the detection of which in media output forms part of *journalism studies and *media studies scholarship. *See also* ARCHETYPES; CONSTRUCTION OF NEWS; MEME; MYTH; NARRATIVE; STEREOTYPING.

trust A belief in the reliability and truthfulness of somebody or some organization, which is generally regarded as an essential component of most relationships in journalism, perhaps most obviously and mutually between *reporters and *sources, especially *confidential sources. News organizations also rely to a large extent on being trusted by members of the *audience, and if trust is lost it may never be recovered (*see* HILLSBOROUGH DISASTER). Some publications have appointed independent *readers' editors specifically to increase levels of trust among their audience, and the wider media's greater willingness to run *corrections and clarifications is also seen as part of this effort. *See also* ETHICS.

truth Reality as it really is, which is what journalism claims to uncover and make public. Journalists aim to get as close to the truth as possible within the *constraints under which they work and in as far as the *facts of the matter under consideration are known to anyone. In pursuit of the truth journalists use a range of techniques such as asking *questions, assessing evidence, and seeking *verification; the resulting material will then be reported accurately, with careful *attribution, to produce what *Watergate reporter Carl Bernstein once described as 'the best obtainable version of the truth'. However, all the potential facts will be subjected to a process of *selection and *construction of news that is often said to simplify the messiness of reality into neat narratives. Also, exactly what the best obtainable version of the truth is may change over time as more information becomes available and/or more *sources speak out. Furthermore, what is regarded as being true may also depend on the background and predispositions of journalists, sources, and members of the *audience (*see* CULTURAL BIAS), and the advent of *social media has, arguably, greatly increased the circulation of (and amplified) competing 'truths'. *See also* ACCURACY; ETHICS;

INVESTIGATIVE JOURNALISM; OBJECTIVE JOURNALISM; PRAGMATIC OBJECTIVITY; REFLEXIVE PRACTICE; REPORTING; TRUTHINESS.

truthiness 1. The quality of truthfulness and of being in accordance with the *facts, as far as they are known. Scholars and critics sometimes attempt to measure the truthiness of a piece of journalism although, as with the *truth itself, it can be difficult to know if the full story has been told.
2. A satirical term referring to something that feels as if it might be true, or that somebody (even a journalist) wishes to be true, regardless of the evidence.

((()) SEE WEB LINKS
• 'Truthiness'

tumblr A multimedia *microblogging and *social networking site formed in the USA in 2007 and which, as with many other forms of *social media, has since been adopted by journalists as yet another online location in which to find potential stories and contacts, and as a forum in which to promote the *brand and/or engage directly with the *audience.

TV *See* TELEVISION JOURNALISM.

tweet A message of no more than 140 characters that is sent to followers via *Twitter and which, if deemed newsworthy, may end up being the subject of a news story and/or being incorporated into forms of *online journalism such as a *liveblog. Journalists' own tweets may contain *links to fuller coverage online. Tweets are now also sometimes used as part of the live coverage of events such as major court cases. *See also* HASHTAG; STORIFY.

21st Century Fox The television, film, and entertainment side of the *Murdoch empire that was separated from *News Corp in 2013 in the wake of the *hackgate scandal, but which remains a key part of the Murdoch family's media interests—not least because it provides most of the profits. Although 21st Century Fox is primarily focused on entertainment, its portfolio also includes *Fox News and a major share of BSkyB, the company behind *Sky News.

24-hour news Radio, TV, and/or online news output that is produced on a continuous basis (*see* ROLLING NEWS) rather than delivered for specific *bulletins or to set *deadlines. Critics point out that much of the output of such channels tends to be extremely repetitive as well as, on occasions, speculative (*see* NEVER WRONG FOR LONG).

Twitter A *microblogging form of *social networking allowing users to post brief *tweets, sometimes with *links to other material, that may be seen (and retweeted) by whoever follows them. Although it emerged in 2006 and was quickly adopted by some *bloggers and technology-savvy journalists, Twitter only began to be taken seriously by most news organizations from around 2009 onwards. Since then it has become ubiquitous as a way for journalists to find information and *sources, promote individual and company *brands, encourage *interactivity and feedback, monitor trends, and make instant assessments of (a portion of) *public opinion. Arguably, Twitter has accelerated the process by which *news has become more about what somebody has said and less about what they have done, but it has also made it harder to keep information secret (*see* TRAFIGURA). Some commentators have hailed Twitter as a voice of the people ('warts and all') that has reinvigorated and democratized the *public sphere; others remain to be convinced. Either way, for most journalists in the second decade of the 21st century, using Twitter has become as much a part of the job as *shorthand and the *telephone once were (and still are); as with other forms of *new technology, Twitter complements existing forms of *newsgathering rather than replacing them. *See also* AMBIENT JOURNALISM; CITIZEN JOURNALISM; HASHTAG; INSTAGRAM; SINA WEIBO; SOCIAL MEDIA; STORIFY; TROLLING; TWITTERATI.

Twitterati A term for the twittering classes of prolific *Twitter users, especially those in the public eye, whose individual output may become the basis for news stories and whose collective output is often used as an instant (albeit extremely unscientific) measure of *public opinion.

Twopenny Trash *See* COBBETT'S POLITICAL REGISTER.

two-way A commonly used format in *broadcast journalism whereby a *presenter or *anchor in the studio discusses a story with another journalist, who is often on location in the *field. A two-way will often take the form of a semi-scripted interview. In the wake of the *Hutton Report in the UK the *BBC warned its journalists against breaking controversial stories via unscripted two-ways.

txt msg A brief **text message** that can be sent via a *mobile phone and has become yet another way in which today's journalists keep in touch with their *contacts. Members of the *audience, particularly for *broadcast journalism, may also be invited to contribute questions or contributions by texting in.

typo A typing error that appears in the text of a journalistic item. *See also* LITERAL; SUBBING.

UGC *See* USER-GENERATED CONTENT.

ultra-niche A publication or other form of journalistic product aimed at an extremely small and specialized audience. *See also* NICHE.

unambiguity The characterization of an event that appears to journalists to be easy to understand, label, or describe. Unambiguity is one of a list of twelve factors devised in the 1960s by Norwegian academics Johan Galtung and Mari Ruge to help explain why some types of event tend to be selected to become *news while others are not. In their influential study of the *news values used by journalists, Galtung and Ruge argued that the more ambiguous or complex an event appeared to be, the less chance there was of it becoming news. Conversely, the more clearly and simply an event can be observed, understood, and interpreted, the greater the chance of it being selected. As with each item on their list of news values, unambiguity is not considered in isolation but in conjunction with other factors; an ambiguous event might still become news if it is deemed of sufficient *relevance to the audience and/or involves *elite people, for example. In any event, as other academics have pointed out, a lack of ambiguity within the news may owe more to the way journalists are said to simplify stories in the telling of them than to any inherent quality in events themselves. *See also* CONSTRUCTION OF NEWS; NEWSWORTHINESS; SELECTION.

unattributed source A person or organization who supplies information (or other material) to a journalist but whose role in doing so is not acknowledged within the resulting journalistic output. The *attribution of information and opinions to *sources is one of the accepted norms of journalism, so unattributed sources are generally frowned upon unless there is a strong *public interest justification for withholding the identity (or even the existence) of a *confidential source or *whistleblower. Journalists who fail to acknowledge and attribute their use of *cuttings and material originated by others run the risk of being accused of *plagiarism.

undercover reporting A form of *investigative journalism that involves the journalist pretending to be somebody other than a journalist. Undercover reporting typically involves investigating matters of public concern (or curiosity) or the behaviour of powerful (or famous) people or organizations, whereby the details could not be obtained by more straightforward means. *Codes of conduct for journalists generally regard *subterfuge as a last resort that must be justified by reference to the *public interest. In addition to finding things out that might not be discovered without such *deception, undercover reporting can also facilitate the gathering of evidence through secret filming and taping of those who would not speak (or who would not speak candidly) to a journalist. Undercover reporting can range from making a phone call while purporting to be a customer, for the purpose of exposing a dodgy business practice, to gaining a job with fake references to investigate alleged vetting and security flaws. Ryan Parry, a reporter with the UK's *Daily Mirror, famously managed the latter twice in 2003, first at the Wimbledon tennis championships and then by spending eight weeks working at Buckingham Palace as footman to the Queen. He was far from being the first: Nellie Bly (1864–1922) has been described as the best undercover *reporter in history for a series of exploits that included pretending to be mentally ill so that she could expose conditions within an insane asylum (for Joseph Pulitzer's New York World in 1887). Journalists and news organizations that use undercover reporting are likely to be accused, by those they have duped, of engaging in stunts and *stings that have more to do with creating news than reporting it. Rival journalists and news organizations often make the same criticisms, but just as often they follow up the initial *scoop and begin planning their own exposés. See also FAKE SHEIKH.

(()) SEE WEB LINKS
• Nellie Bly: a resource website

underground press A label that is today most commonly applied to alternative youth-oriented magazines and newspapers produced from the mid-1960s to the mid-1970s, among them *Oz, *Ink, and IT. This underground press, which originated in Australia, the USA, and the UK, was associated with a counter-culture that focused on rock music and was broadly in favour of a liberal approach to drugs, sexual relations, and civil rights, and against *censorship, materialism, and the Vietnam War. However, despite their alternative ethos, many self-styled radical publications were criticized for reproducing old-fashioned *sexism towards women both within their pages and in their working methods. They took the label 'underground press' from those oppositional publications produced in conditions of secrecy and fear in military states and other forms of oppressive society, most notably in Nazi-occupied Europe during the Second World War, when those involved risked almost certain death for the sake of spreading counter-messages amongst the population. *See also* ALTERNATIVE MEDIA; SAMIZDAT; UNDERGROUND PRESS SYNDICATE.

Underground Press Syndicate (UPS) A loose grouping of alternative newspapers and magazines that identified themselves as being part of the *underground press between 1966 and the mid-1970s. Based in the USA and initiated by Allan Katzman of the *East Village Other* in New York, the UPS linked the underground press on an international basis. Although it held occasional gatherings, its main function was to allow member publications to reprint each other's material (including cartoons and graphics by Robert Crumb and others) without either payment or hassle. *See also* ALTERNATIVE PRESS; LIBERATION NEWS SERVICE; PEOPLE'S NEWS SERVICE.

unexpectedness A surprising event, statement, or juxtaposition. Unexpectedness is one of twelve factors identified by Johan Galtung and Mari Ruge as helping to explain why some types of event tend to be selected to become *news while others are not. In their 1960s study of *news values, the Norwegian academics argued that, all other things being equal, it will be unexpected or rare events that are the most likely to become news. However, precisely what counts as unexpected or rare will vary over time and in different contexts (*see* CONSONANCE). *See also* MAN BITES DOG; NEWSWORTHINESS; SELECTION; SURPRISE.

Universal Declaration of Human Rights A statement agreed by the United Nations General Assembly meeting in Paris, France, in 1948, Article 19 of which reads: 'Everyone has the right to freedom of opinion and expression; this right includes freedom to hold opinions without interference and to seek, receive, and impart information and ideas through any media and regardless of frontiers'. The declaration of *human rights is often cited by journalists and others seeking to defend *press freedom and *freedom of information against *censorship and from those who seek to silence journalism by violence (*see* DEATHS OF JOURNALISTS). *See also* ARTICLE 19; EUROPEAN CONVENTION ON HUMAN RIGHTS.

(((●))) SEE WEB LINKS
• Full text of the Universal Declaration of Human Rights

UPI (United Press International) A US-based international agency offering news (and pictures) in Arabic and Spanish as well as English, founded in 1907. *See also* NEWS AGENCY.

USA Today A daily national newspaper (and website) owned by *Gannett and published from McLean in the state of Virginia. As of 2013 its combined print and digital readership placed it third in the list of dailies in the USA. Since its launch in 1982, *USA Today* has become one of the biggest selling newspapers in the USA. Described as the country's first real national newspaper (most titles are regional), *USA Today* drew on ideas from *television journalism (such as the importance of graphics, weather reports, and sport) and was an early adopter of colour printing.

user-generated content (UGC) Contributions submitted to a media organization by members of its *audience or other people not employed as media professionals. UGC can consist of video footage, photographs, comments, blog posts, tweets, emails, text messages, and other types of material produced not by the organization's employees or professional freelancers but by amateurs and other citizens. Material may be supplied directly to a news organization or to a site such as *YouTube* that will be monitored by other media. *Letters published in printed publications and calls to radio phone-in shows could be seen as *analogue forms of user-generated content, as could the amateur home cine film of the assassination of US President Kennedy in 1963. However, the phrase 'user-generated content' (or UGC) has only gained currency in the digital age, and amongst the pioneers were the alternative *Indymedia* websites, created in 1999. It was with the Indian Ocean tsunami on 26 December 2004 and the London bombings on 7 July 2005 that mainstream media began to make extensive use of such material, which included dramatic pictures captured on phones by witnesses and survivors. Large news organizations today devote considerable resources to soliciting, monitoring, verifying, curating,

selecting, and/or moderating the flow of UGC they receive. *See also*
ACTIVE AUDIENCE; AMATEUR JOURNALISM; CITIZEN JOURNALISM;
CROWDSOURCING; 90-9-1 RULE; OPEN-SOURCE PUBLISHING; SOCIAL
MEDIA EDITOR; USERS; YOUR COMMENTS.

users People who visit, read, watch, listen to, contribute to, share, and/
or in other ways interact with material on *websites. Website users are
an *audience in the sense that *readers of print journalism and *viewers
and *listeners of broadcast journalism are an audience, but *online
journalism typically works on the assumption that users of a particular
website are likely to be both more active (clicking on items in the order
of their choice rather than following a linear, pre-ordained order) and
more promiscuous (being only a click away from going elsewhere).
Users are often invited to become producers as well as consumers of
journalism by contributing *user-generated content. *See also*
STICKINESS.

uses and gratifications A theory of an *active audience for
journalism and other forms of media output, whereby *readers,
*listeners, *viewers, and other *users take from media what they want for
their own purposes and to meet their own needs, rather than simply
absorbing media messages in a passive way. Uses and gratifications
theory emerged as a reaction to the *hypodermic model and other
variants of *effects arguments that seemed to critics to be so concerned
with how the media used people that the possibility of people using the
media tended to be little explored. Potential *audience uses of media
might include a conscious diversion from everyday concerns; the
sharing of experiences with other audience members; for personal
identification, for example as 'a Radio 4 listener' or 'a *Sun* reader'; and
for obtaining information about society beyond that which can be
obtained directly by personal experience. Although the theory
originated as a corrective to simplistic assertions about media effects, it
has in turn been criticized for simplifying complex relationships, not
least by downplaying the possibility that the media help create the
perceived 'needs' that the same media then purport to meet.

usie A *selfie picture that shows two people rather than one, such as
might be used by two *celebrities wishing to inform the world that they
are now a couple.

Utne Reader A digest of the US *alternative press that was launched by Eric Utne as a bi-monthly magazine in 1984 and which now also incorporates a website and a series of blogs on issues such as the media, the environment, politics, and culture.

 SEE WEB LINKS

• *Utne Reader* on media

Vanishing Newspaper *See* The Vanishing Newspaper.

Vanity Fair A monthly US upmarket consumer and cultural magazine (plus online and social media *brands) owned by *Condé Nast and published in its present form since 1983. Several earlier incarnations of *Vanity Fair* were published in the USA and the UK between the mid-19th and mid-20th centuries, all apparently named after the novel by William Makepeace Thackeray (1811–63). *See also* Deep Throat.

verification The process of establishing the veracity or otherwise of information before it is used in a piece of journalism. Verification might be as simple as making a telephone call to check the *accuracy of a claim made in a *press release, following links to the original *sources of a *Wikipedia entry, or checking with a celebrity's agent to see if a *Twitter account in their name is genuine. *Compare* Hitler diaries; never wrong for long; too good to check. *See also* attribution; fact-checking; hoaxes; investigative journalism; scepticism; three-source rule; truth.

versioning Making stories suitable for multiple media outlets, *platforms, or editions by producing them in various styles or formats, by emphasizing different *angles, or just by rewriting *intros. This is in contrast to *shovelware, whereby the same story is reproduced unaltered. *See also* repurposing.

vertical integration The process whereby a business involved in the production of a product (such as a newspaper) also seeks to control other links in the industrial chain (such as the supply of newsprint, the operation of the printing plant, and the distribution network). *Compare* horizontal integration. *See also* ownership.

victim Somebody whose misfortune becomes a news story, either individually or as a way of personalizing some wider trend or *tragedy. Victims are familiar characters in journalism but the operation of *news

values means that not all victims are afforded equal status
(*see* McLurg's Law). Some academic critics of journalism see the
media's emphasis on victims (as on heroes and villains) as part of the
manufacture and/or perpetuation of *myths, whereby complex
humanity is often reduced to a limited number of stereotypes or familiar
*tropes. *See also* Anyone Here Been Raped and Speaks English?;
archetypes; death knock.

video Moving pictures that are used in *television journalism, *online
journalism, and on *social media and other websites, most notably
the video-sharing site *YouTube*. Today the term is used generically to
refer to any moving images whereas in previous decades it specifically
denoted material shot on videotape as opposed to film; video typically
involved more lightweight equipment and speedier processing and
editing. *See also* video journalism; VJ; vlog.

videobombing A member of the public getting in shot and waving,
pulling a silly face, or making a rude gesture behind a TV reporter who
is doing a *piece to camera. This has become an occupational hazard
of *television journalism and only occasionally results in a reporter
losing their cool (which will inevitably end up on *YouTube*).

video journalism Reporting that incorporates moving pictures (and
sound) of *actuality. The advent of lightweight *video equipment
towards the end of the 20th century enabled broadcast news
organizations to acquire pictures in situations where it might not have
been feasible to do so previously. The arrival of the *internet meant
that newspapers and magazines could expand into broadcast-style video
journalism on their websites, with traditional print journalists often
expected to become multiskilled video journalists (or *VJs).

video journalist *See* VJ.

video news release Moving pictures supplied to news organizations
for the purpose of *public relations. As with a text-based *press release,
the video version is produced with the aim of getting a particular
organization's message across to the public, via the media; therefore,
even when it is produced to high professional standards, a video news
release remains PR rather than independent reporting, and any pictures
used are generally labelled as having been supplied by the *source.
Video news releases are most likely to be featured on poorly resourced

television and online news outlets (where they can be seen as a form of *information subsidy), or in circumstances where independent filming has not been possible (for example, of an environmental campaign group engaging in an act of sabotage while filming it themselves). *See also* PROPAGANDA.

viewers The collective noun for the *audience of *television journalism. TV viewing was traditionally seen as a passive activity but in the age of the *internet and *social media viewers are more often invited to engage interactively with producers of media output, including providing feedback and supplying *user-generated content. *See also* ACTIVE AUDIENCE; LISTENERS; READERS; USERS.

viewspaper A *newspaper that focuses more on *comment and interpretation than on reporting the latest *news. Since the arrival of broadcast and then online forms of journalism, some newspaper publishers and editors have argued that, because much of the audience will already have heard some news *headlines by the time a printed product appears, the survival of the press depends less on retelling the news than on newspapers building their own *brand identity through distinctive *features, *opinion pieces, *backgrounders, and *campaigns.

village correspondent An amateur and unpaid contributor who regularly supplies a local newspaper or website with the sort of 'parish pump' information that is deemed too insignificant to warrant a *news story or *feature article but which people living in a small area might find of interest, ranging from the times of religious services to details of a forthcoming jumble sale. Such correspondents are most likely to be found in rural areas where local newspapers might cover several villages; those more urban newspapers that use these correspondents sometimes call them '**community correspondents**'. *See also* AMATEUR JOURNALISM; HYPERLOCAL JOURNALISM; LOCAL JOURNALISM.

Village Voice An alternative news weekly founded in New York in 1955 by Norman Mailer, Dan Wolf, and Ed Fancher with a focus on the city's cultural events and political news. Despite being one of the pioneer publications of the US *alternative press, the *Village Voice* was not alternative enough for some in Greenwich Village, and the mid-1960s saw the launch of a short-lived *underground rival, the ***East Village Other***. Today, in addition to the weekly print product, the *Village Voice* has a website that claims to be 'the authoritative source on all that New York has to offer'. *See also* ALTERNATIVE MEDIA; UNDERGROUND PRESS; UNDERGROUND PRESS SYNDICATE.

viral The word used to describe the phenomenon whereby a piece of online content, such as a *video, is circulated via email and *social media to such an extent that it almost seems to take on a life of its own. Journalists look out for examples of *user-generated content that have gone viral because they can make entertaining news items. Clips from broadcast news, including mistakes, can themselves go viral if sufficient people share them.

((⊕)) SEE WEB LINKS
• The year in viral videos

VJ (video journalist) A journalist who shoots and edits moving images as part of their own reporting, whose work may appear on TV or online. *See also* VIDEO JOURNALISM.

vlog A *blog that includes *video content.

vlogger A *blogger who uses *video on their *blog (or *vlog). The name has not achieved universal acceptance, even among video bloggers themselves.

Vogue A glossy monthly US fashion magazine (plus online and social media *brands, and around twenty national and regional editions) owned by *Condé Nast and first published in 1892. Long-standing editor-in-chief Anna Wintour (1949–) was widely reported to have been the inspiration behind the fearsome magazine *editor portrayed by Meryl Streep in the film *The Devil Wears Prada* (dir. David Frankel, 2006). *See also* GLOSSIES; WOMEN'S MAGAZINES.

Voice *See* BLACK MEDIA.

Voice of America (VOA) A broadcast organization created by the US government in 1942, shortly after the USA entered the Second World War. Voice of America transmits news and views to the rest of the world with output in more than 40 languages, now available online and through mobile devices and *social media as well as via traditional broadcasting. Although Voice of America has been accused of producing pro-US *propaganda, its charter (signed into law by President Ford in 1976) commits VOA journalists to produce 'accurate, objective, and comprehensive' news that presents 'a balanced and comprehensive projection of significant American thought and institutions'. *See also* BBC World Service.

voiceover A narration or commentary that accompanies moving pictures in television or online journalism. A voiceover will typically be tightly scripted and recorded in advance by a *reporter who will not be seen on screen except perhaps for a brief *piece to camera at the beginning and/or end. Professional voiceover artists, actors, or celebrity presenters may sometimes be used in the place of reporters.

Votes for Women A Suffragette newspaper published in the UK between 1907 and 1918, variously weekly and monthly, that countered *Fleet Street's tendency to portray pro-democracy women as hysterics or harridans. Just one of numerous publications to emerge during what has been described as the first wave of feminism (*see* FEMINIST MEDIA), for several years *Votes for Women* was also the official organ of the Women's Social and Political Union, one of the leading organizations campaigning for women to have the right to vote. *See also* ACTIVIST MEDIA; ADVOCACY JOURNALISM; GENDER; WOMAN'S DREADNOUGHT.

voxpop A series of brief *interviews with random people who are stopped in public places and asked to comment on some topical issue or other. Meaning 'voice of the people', voxpops are particularly prevalent in local newspapers and on regional television news. A voxpop (known for short as a 'vox') is occasionally referred to as a '**streeter**', as in reporting the views of the man or woman in the street.

VT Videotape, by which can be meant any form of moving pictures for use in *television journalism or online.

Wall Street Journal A business and finance oriented daily title that is the biggest-selling newspaper in the USA and which, since 2007, has been part of the *Murdoch empire. It was founded in New York in 1889 by Charles Dow (1851–1902), of the Dow Jones financial news service, who was its first editor. The *Wall Street Journal* responded to the advent of the *internet by setting up a *paywall in 1997, becoming the first major newspaper to do so, and perhaps the most successful: by 2013 it had around 890,000 digital subscribers, giving it a total daily circulation (print and digital combined) of almost 2.4 million. Since the Murdoch takeover the *Journal* has accelerated its already existing tendency to cover a wider range of stories beyond *business journalism.

WAN-IFRA *See* WORLD ASSOCIATION OF NEWSPAPERS AND NEWS PUBLISHERS.

Wapping dispute The battle in 1986 that resulted as a consequence of *News International secretly moving production of its UK newspapers overnight to a purpose-built plant on former dockland in east London, shedding more than 5,000 production and clerical workers in the process. As a bitter year-long dispute played out on the streets, often involving serious violence between police and pickets, on the other side of the razor wire that surrounded the Wapping complex the Murdoch newspapers were being produced with *new technology, fewer staff, and no place for the traditional print unions, which had been excluded along with their sacked members. During the dispute former workers produced their own *alternative media, the **Wapping Post** newspaper. Although some journalists supported those who had lost their jobs and declined to move to Wapping (*see* REFUSENIKS), the majority went along with the switch, having been promised that journalists rather than printers would henceforth be in control. Before Wapping, *Fleet Street printers had a reputation for relatively high wages and staffing levels, along with a willingness to threaten to down tools; the dispute changed that and other newspaper publishers took note. Long before the dispute ended in total victory for the *Murdoch empire, the 'Wapping revolution' (which had been partially inspired by the *_Warrington Messenger_ dispute) was said by many commentators to have heralded a low-cost and hi-tech future that would see the launch of many more national newspapers. However, of the few titles that did start up in the wake of Wapping, only the *_Independent_ and the *_Sunday Sport_ survive. *News UK has announced that it plans to leave Wapping and move into a new plant across the River Thames, probably in 2014. See also NATIONAL UNION OF JOURNALISTS.

Further reading: L. Melvern, _The End of the Street_ (1986).

Wapping Post See WAPPING DISPUTE.

war reporting The coverage of armed *conflict and warfare, which will typically be provided by *foreign correspondents, defence correspondents, or specialist war correspondents. War reporting can mean technical challenges, physical discomfort, and danger (see DEATHS OF JOURNALISTS), but it also typically raises a range of ethical issues, particularly for those reporting for news organizations based in a country directly involved in the conflict. Such issues can include *objectivity and *impartiality (whether to report 'us' in the same way as 'them'), government attempts at *news management and *propaganda, the restrictions involved in *embedded reporting, *intrusion into grief, and risking the wrath of *public opinion (and adverse audience reaction). _Compare_ PEACE JOURNALISM. _See also_ BROADCAST BAN; CENSORSHIP; GOTCHA; HUTTON REPORT; JOURNALISM OF ATTACHMENT; PENTAGON PAPERS; REAL LIVES; ROOFTOP JOURNALISM; TIMES; WIKILEAKS.

Further reading: P. Knightley, _The First Casualty: The War Correspondent as Hero and Myth-Maker from the Crimea to Iraq_ (2004 [1975]).

Warrington Messenger dispute A forerunner of *Wapping, in which newspaper owner Eddy Shah began hiring non-union labour in 1983 to print his _Messenger_ series of local *freesheets in the north-west of England, prompting mass picketing by members of the print union NGA (National Graphical Association). The printworks in Stockport was blockaded but Shah eventually won after the NGA's actions were declared unlawful by the courts. Shah, who was hailed as a hero by fellow *proprietor Rupert Murdoch and Prime Minister Margaret

w

Thatcher, later sold the *Messenger* series. He went on to launch *Today* as a non-union national title (before selling it to Murdoch), and in 1988 he founded a new national daily newspaper, the *Post*, which closed after just five weeks. Shah then left the newspaper industry and became a novelist, among other things.

Washington Post An upmarket quality daily *broadsheet newspaper published in Washington DC since 1877. Its reputation as one of the USA's major papers of record long pre-dated its leading role in exposing the *Watergate scandal in the 1970s, but since then all its journalists have worked in the shadows of Woodward and Bernstein. If Watergate was its high point, the handing back of a *Pulitzer Prize over the *Little Jimmy fakery scandal a few years later was an extremely low point. In 2013 the *Post* raised a few eyebrows when, after 43 years, it replaced its independent *ombudsperson with a 'reader representative' who reports to the editor. It raised a lot more eyebrows when, later that same year, the *Washington Post* was bought by the billionaire Jeff Bezos (founder of the online retailer Amazon) for $250 million (US dollars), thereby ending 80 years of control by the Graham family. At the time of the sale the paper had a daily print sale of more than 400,000 copies, making it one of the top ten best-selling dailies in the USA. *See also* NEWSWEEK; PENTAGON PAPERS; POLITICO; WASHINGTON TIMES.

Washington Times A right-wing daily newspaper launched in the US capital in 1982 by followers of the Unification Church (popularly known as the 'Moonies') who felt the *Washington Post* was biased against the religion. In 2013 the *Washington Times* newspaper and website announced plans to launch a conservative national cable news network to be called *One America News*. *See also* ADVOCACY JOURNALISM; PROPAGANDA.

watchdog role A conceptualization of journalism as the eyes and ears of a society's citizens, checking for and warning of potential danger. This idea of the journalist as watchdog is inextricably linked to concepts such as *democracy, the *fourth estate, the *public interest, and a *free press, and it can apply as much to a *blogger revealing how much a local council spends on tea and biscuits as it does to the *Watergate scandal. The watchdog role is most often claimed for *investigative journalism but it is implicit in any form of *reporting that records events or statements and makes such information available to the public. However, *mainstream media organizations are frequently accused of failing to fulfil the role effectively, and/or of revealing only individual abuses in society while ignoring or downplaying more systemic social issues. *Compare* PROPAGANDA MODEL.

Watergate A political *scandal in the USA that was exposed by the *Washington Post* and which is widely regarded as one of the greatest *scoops ever. The Watergate story is seen as an exemplar of sustained *investigative journalism on the grounds that not only did it reveal corruption and illegal practices at the highest possible level, but it eventually helped bring down arguably the most powerful person in the world, the US president. The story began on 17 June 1972 when five suspected burglars were arrested in Washington, apparently while trying to place a listening device in a Democratic party office within the hotel and business complex called Watergate. When one of the arrested men claimed that he used to work for the Central Intelligence Agency (CIA), it prompted the *Washington Post* to investigate further and deeper into what had initially been thought to be a routine burglary. Over the next two years the newspaper's journalists Bob Woodward (1943–) and Carl Bernstein (1944–) conducted a painstaking investigation that gradually uncovered a political conspiracy to smear and hobble the Democrats, tracing the plot and attempted cover-up all the way to the White House of Republican president, Richard Nixon. As a result, in August 1974 Nixon became the first US president to resign. How Woodward and Bernstein conducted their investigation is detailed in their 1974 book *All the President's Men* and the 1976 film of the same name, both of which deal as much with the journalistic process as with the political scandals of the Nixon presidency. During their time-consuming investigation the two reporters filled several filing cabinets with notes of interviews with *sources and other documentation, memos to each other and their *editor, and early drafts of stories, all of which they kept for cross-referencing purposes and to enable them to go back to the material, pursue previously unexplored *angles, and reinterview sources and potential sources. They were helped enormously by a highly placed and trusted *confidential source, known as *Deep Throat, whose identity they protected. Deep Throat pointed them in certain directions, suggested leads they might pursue more vigorously, and confirmed or denied stories that other sources had told them. Woodward, Bernstein, and their executive editor Ben Bradlee (1921–), followed what became known as the *three-source rule, whereby they would not publish any allegation made by their secret source himself unless it could be independently verified by two additional sources (*see* VERIFICATION). The identity of Deep Throat remained a secret until 2005 when Mark Felt (1913–2008), a long-retired senior officer with the Federal Bureau of Investigation (FBI), 'outed' himself.

The two key journalists working on Watergate were both in the relatively early stages of their careers at the beginning of the investigation: Bernstein had joined the *Washington Post* in 1966 to cover the local police and courts *beat, and Woodward began work on the *Metro* section of the paper only in 1970, after serving in the US Navy. The two hardly knew each other when they began working on the story that was to define their careers, but their names soon became indelibly linked and together they won the *Pulitzer Prize in 1973. As with the earlier *Pentagon Papers leak concerning the Vietnam War, the Watergate stories were run in defiance of pressure from the White House (*see* FLAK). Although the Watergate investigation subsequently achieved iconic status as an exemplar of journalists carrying out their role as vigilant watchdogs and fearlessly speaking truth to power, at the time it was largely ignored, downplayed, or rubbished by most of the rest of the *mainstream media; Nixon was re-elected by a landslide margin at the end of 1972 despite months of revelations in the *Washington Post*. In the decades since, Watergate has been held up variously as the high-water mark of investigative journalism since when the tide has gone out on such expensive, labour-intensive, and politically risky reporting; as an overblown myth used to disguise the fact that most journalism serves rather than challenges the powerful; and as a textbook example of independent and fearless journalism in the *public interest that ought to be emulated by journalists today and in the future. Another impact of Watergate is that the suffix *-gate has long been added to a vast range of other words to signify some kind of supposed scandal, most of which bear little comparison to the gravity of the original revelations. *See also* WATCHDOG ROLE.

 SEE WEB LINKS

• The *Washington Post*'s multimedia account of Watergate including archive material

webcast A form of *broadcast journalism conveyed via a *website, typically comprising live audio and/or video streaming, possibly accompanied by text and still pictures.

web-first The policy of a *multimedia news organization that breaks news online as soon as a story is ready, rather than saving it for the next print edition or broadcast *bulletin. As soon as the material is uploaded to the news organization's *website it will typically be publicized and linked to via *social media. *Compare* DEADLINE. *See also* ONLINE JOURNALISM.

web log *See* BLOG.

website An online location and digital space for journalism and public relations, among countless other things, that can be found on the World Wide Web. Public websites date from 1994, although some elements of the *internet were operational earlier. Initial websites tended to involve one-way communication but the development of so-called 'Web 2.0' from around 2004 introduced more *interactivity, leading to the development of *social networking and *social media, both of which have subsequently been embraced by the journalism industries. Rare indeed is the 21st-century organization that does not have its own website. *See also* DIGITAL MEDIA; ONLINE JOURNALISM; PAYWALL; SEARCH ENGINE; USERS; WEB-FIRST.

Week *See* THE WEEK.

Weekly Standard A neo-conservative magazine launched in Washington DC in 1995 with the financial and political backing of Rupert Murdoch (*see* MURDOCH EMPIRE). Its relatively small circulation includes copies being delivered to what it describes as 'an exclusive list of the most powerful men and women in government, politics, and the media'. Dismissed by some as a loss-making vanity project, the *Weekly Standard* is seen by others as an *agenda-setter for the right wing of US politics, perhaps best exemplified by its lengthy campaign for a military attack on Iraq. In 2009 it was sold to the Clarity Media Group of Denver, which is owned by conservative billionaire Philip Anschutz (1939–). *See also* ADVOCACY JOURNALISM.

Weekly World News *See* SUPERMARKET TABLOIDS.

Weibo *See* SINA WEIBO.

Western Mail A daily newspaper, published in Cardiff, that calls itself 'the national newspaper of Wales' even though it sells relatively few papers in northern parts of the country. Launched in 1869, the

w

Western Mail was a *broadsheet until 2004 when it switched to *tabloid format. Along with sister titles *Wales on Sunday* and the *South Wales Echo*, and the website *Wales Online*, it is part of the *Trinity Mirror chain. Trinity Mirror's commitment to Welsh journalism has been questioned by staff and readers alike following its decision to *syndicate some content from group operations elsewhere in the UK.

West Highland Free Press An independently owned campaigning local weekly newspaper (and now website) that has been published on the Isle of Skye since 1972, covering the Western Highlands and Islands of Scotland. Part alternative newspaper and part traditional local rag, the *West Highland Free Press* has often been held up as example of an alternative way of doing things, and in 2009 it became a cooperative when staff bought out the founders (who had included a Labour Member of Parliament, Brian Wilson). As a community-based, local, and now employee-owned media project, it has flourished even as many commercial publishers have been retrenching and/or centralizing their operations. *See also* ALTERNATIVE MEDIA; LOCAL JOURNALISM.

Westminster Press Once one of the major regional newspaper chains in the UK whose titles included the *Northern Echo*. Westminster Press was owned by the *Pearson group until 1996, when it was sold to (and absorbed into) the newly formed *Newsquest.

what? Along with the rest of the *five Ws—who, what, when, where, why (and *how)—this is one of the most essential *questions in journalism. What happened, what was seen or heard, and what is likely to happen next, are just some of the basic questions that are asked countless times by *reporters every day, answers to which will form the basis of *news stories and *features. *See also* INTERVIEW.

when? One of the *five Ws and, as such, an essential *question to be asked during any form of *reporting. Discovering when something happened is key to understanding and writing many stories, and knowing when something is scheduled to happen is also crucial for arranging coverage of *diary stories. *See also* INTERVIEW.

where? Another of the *five Ws that provide the basis of most *reporting, designed to find out where something happened or will happen, where a witness was standing, where the sniper was, where the prisoner is being held, and so on. *See also* INTERVIEW; QUESTIONS.

whistleblower A *source who makes public information about alleged wrongdoing, typically by or within the organization in which they are employed. A person blowing the whistle to journalists may be willing to go *on the record or may insist on being an *anonymous source. Perhaps the most famous whistleblower in history was *Deep Throat, the source in the *Watergate investigation. One of the most famous whistleblowers in the UK was the Foreign Office clerk Sarah Tisdall, who in 1984 was jailed under the *Official Secrets Act for leaking a secret memo to the *Guardian about the imminent arrival of controversial nuclear missiles at the Greenham Common airbase. In 2013 the same newspaper took the lead in publishing revelations about the extent of the US National Security Agency's surveillance of citizens' digital communications; the secret material was supplied by NSA contractor-turned-whistleblower Edward Snowden, who eventually sought sanctuary in Russia. The website *WikiLeaks presents itself as the whistleblowers' site, offering an alternative way of leaking information that does not (necessarily) require direct human contact with or placing *trust in any individual journalist. US soldier Bradley (later Chelsea) Manning was sentenced to 35 years in prison under the Espionage Act in 2013 for supplying information to *WikiLeaks*, having revealed him/herself as the source. Despite the tendency to associate whistleblowing with such high-profile cases involving state secrecy, many whistleblowers are concerned with more everyday issues: hospital cleaners exposing how staff cuts are endangering patients, for example, or staff revealing management bullying. *See also* EXARO; HUTTON REPORT; INVESTIGATIVE JOURNALISM; LEAK; PENTAGON PAPERS.

who? Along with the remainder of the *five Ws, this is regarded as one of the most essential *questions in journalism. Who was involved, who might be involved in the future, who won, who lost, and who they really are, are just some of the basic questions that are asked by *reporters every day and, in turn, explained to the audience. *See also* INTERVIEW.

why? Perhaps the least factual of the *five Ws (and *how?) of *reporting, as it often requires some degree of background analysis or *opinion. However, in news reporting, explanations of why something might have happened will typically be attributed to other *sources rather than stated as *fact; more specialist correspondents may on occasions be allowed to speculate on the 'why'. *See also* QUESTIONS; INTERVIEW.

wiki A website or part of a website that allows its *users to contribute, discuss, and edit material in an open, collaborative, and transparent way, the most famous example of which is *Wikipedia*. *See also* COLLABORATIVE JOURNALISM.

WikiLeaks A website and organization created in 2006 by the *freedom of information activist Julian Assange (1971–) with the intention of providing a secure way for *whistleblowers to *leak information that they believe is in the *public interest to know. Despite its name, it is not really a *wiki. The site first came to public prominence in 2010 when it published *Collateral Murder*, the title it gave to leaked video footage of a deadly US helicopter attack on a group of unarmed civilians (including two *Reuters staff) in Iraq. It then released nearly 400,000 secret US military 'war logs' concerning the conflicts in Afghanistan and Iraq, quickly followed by what became known as *cablegate: the publication of more than 250,000 secret diplomatic cables. The cables were published in cooperation with a number of mainstream but liberal media outlets, including the *Guardian* and the *New York Times*, which removed material they felt it might be dangerous to release. Most of its mainstream partners eventually fell out with *WikiLeaks* as it focused increasingly on defending Assange himself, who in the meantime had been accused of sexual assault in Sweden. US soldier Bradley Manning (1987–) was arrested in 2010 and accused of leaking material to *WikiLeaks*; at his trial in 2013 Manning was sentenced to 35 years in prison for multiple breaches of the Espionage Act but cleared of the most serious charge of 'aiding the enemy'. *WikiLeaks* has tended to divide journalistic (and other) opinion, with some commentators hailing it as the most powerful tool for *democracy and global citizens' right to know that the world has ever seen, even as *investigative journalism in the purest form possible; some others see it more as a potential tool for journalism rather than itself being a form of journalism; and still others regard the whole business as the irresponsible placing in the public domain of material that the public has no right to know. By 2013, as Assange himself was holed up in the Ecuadorian Embassy in London (to avoid being extradited to Sweden and subsequently, he feared, the USA), *WikiLeaks* was still publishing fresh revelations on its website and was also reported to be offering advice to the whistleblower Edward

Snowden (1983–) (*see* GUARDIAN) as he sought to find asylum away
from the USA. *See also* ACTIVIST MEDIA; ALTERNATIVE MEDIA.

Further reading: D. Leigh and L. Harding, *WikiLeaks: Inside Julian Assange's
War on Secrecy* (2011).
C. Beckett and J. Ball, *WikiLeaks: News in the Networked Era* (2012).

(⊕) SEE WEB LINKS
- The *Collateral Murder* video
- Private Manning Support Network
- John Pilger defends *WikiLeaks*

Wikinews A series of volunteer-run websites in different languages
that publish news stories and other material that has been produced
collaboratively via a *wiki. Since its launch in 2004, *Wikinews* has
promoted the idea of participatory journalism, and stories in progress
can be seen in its virtual *newsroom. *See also* ALTERNATIVE MEDIA;
AMATEUR JOURNALISM; CITIZEN JOURNALISM.

(⊕) SEE WEB LINKS
- The *Wikinews* newsroom

Wikipedia A searchable encyclopaedia available online since 2001
that is researched, written, and edited by tens of thousands of unpaid
volunteers who can range from international experts to hoaxers, and all
points between. *Wikipedia* is frequently consulted (although rarely
attributed) by journalists working on stories, and is generally regarded
as a good starting point for research. However, journalists (and
academics) relying on its information without conducting further
*fact-checking have sometimes been caught out and published
erroneous material, often to their own embarrassment (and their rivals'
amusement). A healthy dose of *scepticism is advised when using
Wikipedia, but that also applies to other *sources of information, and
its supporters point to the way it links to external sites and to the
transparency of its editing process as examples of how *crowdsourcing
can be more open and therefore trustworthy than traditional publishing
methods. *See also* VERIFICATION.

(⊕) SEE WEB LINKS
- '*Wikipedia* in the newsroom' by Donna Shaw, *American Journalism Review*

wildtrack *See* ATMOS.

Wilkes and liberty The cry of the London 'mob' in opposition to the British government's attempted suppression of the radical *North Briton* newspaper and persecution of publisher John Wilkes (1725-97). Such street protests against *censorship are credited with helping demonstrate public support for the concept of a *free press. *See also* RADICAL PRESS.

wire service A *news agency that supplies material to media organizations. The generic description dates from when copy would be sent via *telegraph wires but retains its usage even in an age of online and satellite technology.

witness contributors *See* CITIZEN JOURNALISM.

Woman's Dreadnought A weekly newspaper produced in London between 1914 and 1924 by militant anti-war Suffragettes led by Sylvia Pankhurst (1882-1960). Women factory workers were encouraged to become volunteer journalists, and the paper's working-class perspective eventually prompted a name change to the *Workers' Dreadnought*. *See also* ALTERNATIVE PRESS; CLASS; FEMINIST MEDIA; OPPOSITIONAL REPORTING; RADICAL PRESS; VOTES FOR WOMEN.

Woman's Own A UK weekly *women's magazine and digital *brand that is aimed at women aged 40 years or more and is part of the *IPC stable. Launched in 1932, *Woman's Own* has gone down in history as the publication whose interviewer Douglas Keay was told by UK Prime Minister Margaret Thatcher in 1987 that 'there is no such thing as society'.

(⊕) SEE WEB LINKS
• *Woman's Own* interview with Margaret Thatcher

Women in Journalism A networking and campaigning organization for female journalists working in the UK that has been running since 1994. In addition to holding a range of formal and informal events, Women in Journalism also publishes research on topics ranging from media coverage of teenage girls to employers' discrimination against 'older' women journalists aged 45 or more. *See also* GENDER; SEXISM; STEREOTYPING.

(⊕) SEE WEB LINKS
• Research by Women in Journalism

women's magazines A catch-all term for *magazines aimed at a predominantly female readership but which may range from upmarket lifestyle *glossies to the 'real life' horror stories that some downmarket titles specialize in. Women's magazines tend to be aimed at narrowly defined target readerships based on age, class, interests, and/or levels of aspiration. Despite their differences, they mostly tend to be *feature-driven and *advertiser-friendly, and particularly prevalent are stories that follow one, other, or both of the formulas known in the trade as *IHTM and *TOT: that is, 'it happened to me' and 'triumph-over-tragedy'. Women who reject mainstream thinking about romance, weddings, fashion, and dieting, may turn to alternative women's magazines (*see* FEMINIST MEDIA). In recent years women's magazines have made extensive use of *websites, *tablets, and *social media to promote themselves as *brands. *See also* AGONY AUNT; CONSUMER MAGAZINE; LADIES' MERCURY; TEENAGE MAGAZINE ARBITRATION PANEL.

Women's Suffrage Journal *See* FEMINIST MEDIA.

Worcester Journal *See* BERROW'S WORCESTER JOURNAL.

word cloud A graphic representation of the frequency with which certain words are used in a speech, statement, document, judgement, or similar. The higher the frequency, the bigger the depiction. *Compare* TAG CLOUD.

WordPress Free open-source *blogging software, web-hosting service, and *content management system that, since its creation in 2003, has facilitated an exponential increase in the number of *blogs and personal *websites on the *internet. Conceived by Houston University student Matt Mullenweg (1984–), WordPress describes its aim as allowing the 'non-technically minded' to be able to be 'up and running and fully functional in no longer than five minutes'. Many journalists and quasi-journalists now use WordPress to self-publish their own work online. *Compare* BLOGGER. *See also* CITIZEN JOURNALISM; ONLINE JOURNALISM.

work experience An opportunity for somebody who thinks they might want to become a journalist to discover at first-hand what the job entails by working (typically on an unpaid basis) for a news organization for anything from a few days to several months. Depending on the organization and the individual involved, work experience may mean getting the coffees, shadowing an experienced member of staff, or even—on rare occasions—writing the *splash. Journalists' organizations and journalism educators tend to warn students and recent graduates against providing free labour for extended periods. *See also* INTERNSHIP.

World Association of Newspapers and News Publishers (WAN-IFRA) A networking and information-sharing organization that claims the membership of more than 18,000 newspapers and other news publications and around 15,000 online sites in more than 120 countries. Among many other activities, WAN-IFRA publishes research, holds regular conferences, and hosts the *World Editors' Forum* on its website.

(((⊕))) SEE WEB LINKS
• *World Editors' Forum*

World in Action A pioneering *current affairs programme specializing in *investigative journalism that ran on primetime commercial television in the UK between 1963 and 1998. It was killed off as part of the quest for higher *ratings by Granada Television, the company that created it. *See also* TELEVISION JOURNALISM.

World Service *See* BBC WORLD SERVICE.

writing *See* ORWELL'S SIX RULES OF WRITING.

xerox A shorthand term meaning both the act of photocopying and the resulting piece of paper photocopied. It was in widespread use in the *fanzine scene of the late 1970s and early 1980s, when copies of many *zines would often be run off on the quiet by sympathetic office workers using photocopiers that may or may not have been manufactured by the company Xerox. *See also* AMATEUR JOURNALISM; ALTERNATIVE MEDIA; NEW TECHNOLOGY.

xhead Slang for a *cross-head; that is, a small heading used to break up the text of an article that is set in *columns.

Xinhua News Agency China's official state-backed news and information agency. Based in Beijing, Xinhua is a huge organization with around 13,000 employees operating in many languages. As well as supplying news to media outlets, it runs a series of websites for Chinese government departments, aimed at both home and international audiences.

xoJane A women's lifestyle website that launched in 2011 in the USA and the following year in the UK. It is a digital-only *brand that specializes in advice columns, *IHTM stories, and *features that celebrate 'what makes you feel good'. *See also* DIGITAL MEDIA; LIFESTYLE JOURNALISM; WOMEN'S MAGAZINES.

yellow journalism A disparaging term for a form of journalism that focuses on *sensationalism, prurience, and exaggerated coverage of crime as a way of gaining an *audience, implying little regard for *ethics. The phrase 'yellow journalism', derived from the so-called *yellow press of the late 19th century, has lived on (especially in the USA) as a term of rebuke directed by other journalists and high-minded citizens towards any reporting that they feel is driven more by commercial considerations than by a commitment to *truth and serving the *public sphere. However, others have pointed out that, by extending the readership of newspapers beyond educated people with an interest in the serious affairs of state, such journalism may in fact have played a role in informing a wider public and nurturing the public sphere, even if the intention of those publishing it was more nakedly commercial. *See also* DUMBING DOWN; GUTTER JOURNALISM; TABLOIDIZATION.

(⊕) SEE WEB LINKS
• W. Joseph Campbell's yellow journalism online resource

yellow press A derogatory term applied to those US newspapers such as the *New York Journal* that, in the 1890s, combined *sensationalism, *campaigning, big pictures, lively design, and huge *headlines with sometimes questionable *ethics as weapons in *circulation wars against rivals. The label is widely believed to have originated as a result of a popular 'yellow kid' newspaper cartoon strip that moved in 1896 from the populist *New York World*, owned by Joseph Pulitzer (1847–1911), to the even more racy *New York Journal*, owned by William Randolph Hearst (1863–1951). *Compare* ALL THE NEWS THAT'S FIT TO PRINT. *See also* HEARST NEWSPAPERS; YELLOW JOURNALISM.

(⊕) SEE WEB LINKS
• Timeline of the yellow press

Yorkshire Post A daily Conservative-leaning *broadsheet newspaper covering the county of Yorkshire in the north of England, widely regarded as one of the leading titles in the UK's regional press. The *Yorkshire Post* began life as the *Leeds Intelligencer* in 1754, adopting its current title in 1866 when it switched from weekly to daily publication under the ownership of Yorkshire Conservative Newspapers Ltd. Its editorial base has been in Leeds ever since, although printing of the newspaper was moved out of the city in 2012 after more than 250 years. That decision was made by *Johnston Press, the latest of a succession of owners, which acquired the title at the start of the 21st century (*see* CONCENTRATION OF OWNERSHIP). The year 2012 also saw the merging of *Yorkshire Post* editorial functions (including the post of *editor) with those of its traditionally distinct sister paper, the *Yorkshire Evening Post*.

Younger Committee An inquiry established by the UK government and chaired by the former MP and lawyer Kenneth Younger, whose resulting 1972 report on *privacy did not recommend any new general privacy law, arguing that it would not be possible to define privacy in a way that would satisfy everybody. A minority report was published by some members of the committee who felt there ought to be a new privacy law to protect people from press *intrusion. Although he did not recommend a new law, Kenneth Younger's report was critical of the effectiveness of the *Press Council; such issues were revisited shortly afterwards by the third *Royal Commission on the Press and, later, in the *Calcutt Reports. *See also* LEVESON INQUIRY.

Your Comments The online facility whereby readers may post comments beneath stories or comment on posts already made by other readers (or *users). Usernames tend to be used rather than real names, although many websites require users to be registered before being allowed to comment. Comments will typically be subject to some form of *moderation but very little checking, editing, or selection is normally undertaken when compared with traditional *letters' pages of newspapers or magazines, leading to the publication (for a short period at least) of some untruthful, defamatory, abusive, and often misogynist or racist comments. However, the audience's ability to enter the *conversation about media output in such a way is hailed by many as strengthening the *public sphere as the site of rational public discussion amongst *citizens. Some journalists claim never to read comments on their stories while others see these as forming a vital part of a feedback loop. Many news organizations encourage their journalists to take an active and constructive part in such below-the-line conversations, but some instruct members of staff not to engage. *See also* ACTIVE AUDIENCE; ASTROTURFING; 90-9-1 RULE; THREADS; TROLLING.

YouTube A video-sharing website that launched in 2005, was bought by *Google in 2006, and which was already having around 24 hours of *video uploaded every minute by 2010. Just two years later that had doubled to 48 hours of video uploaded every minute of every day and that doubled again to around 100 hours every minute in 2013. *YouTube* has become a method of distributing *broadcast journalism and extending audience reach, as mainstream and alternative media outlets upload clips, circulate links, and have established their own branded channels within the overall *YouTube* site. But perhaps more significantly for journalists, *YouTube* has quickly become a major *source of information, news stories, and especially *video as members of the public upload footage often shot on mobile phones on occasions where no journalists are present. Stories sourced via *YouTube* can range from quirky ones about something funny going *viral to harrowing evidence of atrocities filmed in conflict zones, although broadcast journalists will normally warn viewers if any footage from *YouTube* has not been independently verified. Relevant *YouTube* videos will often be embedded directly into stories or posts on online news sites and blogs, allowing website users to view them without having to click away. *See also* ONLINE JOURNALISM; STORIFY; SOCIAL MEDIA; USER-GENERATED CONTENT.

zine A media product written and produced by and for enthusiasts. Also known as a *fanzine, a zine may be printed or published online in the form of an *ezine. *See also* ALTERNATIVE MEDIA.

Zoo A weekly magazine aimed at young men, specializing in entertainment, humour, and the gratuitous display of female breasts. Owned by *Bauer Media, *Zoo* launched in the UK in 2004 and in Australia two years later, since when it and similar *lads' mags have frequently been accused of *sexism and tastelessness. *See also* PORNIFICATION.

Chronology

Below is a chronology showing the approximate order in which some of the major events and developments featured in the dictionary took place. Terms highlighted in bold refer to specific entries, which may in turn be cross-referenced with further entries.

Up to and including 16th century: Oral forms of **communication** and nascent forms of **journalism** including **town criers**, storytellers, poets, and ballad singers; use of writing and the circulation of manuscripts; early forms of **printing** believed to be developed in China, Korea, and Japan.

*c.*1450   Gutenberg develops a system of **printing** involving moveable type, paving the way (eventually) for **print journalism** and print **media**

1476   Caxton establishes a **printing** press at Westminster

17th century and beyond: Production and circulation of **chapbooks**, broadsides, corantos, newsletters, books, almanacs, **pamphlets**, **newsbooks**, and eventually **newspapers**.

1641   Perhaps the first **newsbook** appears during unrest in build-up to the English Civil War: *Heads of Severall Proceedings in this Present Parliament From the 22 of November to the 29, 1641*; many more newsbooks follow

1642   Outbreak of the civil war (or revolution) sees all sides using printed material to spread **information**, ideas, and **propaganda**

1644   John Milton's *Areopagitica*

1647   **Levellers** at the **Putney debates** call for a **free press**

Mid-17th century and beyond: The **Enlightenment**.

1662   **Licensing Act** passed

1690   Possible publication of a forerunner of *Berrow's Worcester Journal*

Late-17th and 18th centuries: Circulation of news and correspondence in **coffee houses**, helping to create a **public sphere**.

1693   *Ladies' Mercury* appears, possibly the first **women's magazine** in the world

1695   The lapsing of the **Licensing Act**

1695   Possible publication of a forerunner of *Stamford Mercury*

1701   *Norwich Post* first published, possibly the first provincial newspaper in England (**local journalism**, **regional media**)

1702   *Daily Courant* newspaper first published on **Fleet Street**

1709   *Worcester Post-Man* published (later *Berrow's Worcester Journal*)

1712   Imposition of **stamp duty** on newspapers (**taxes on knowledge**)

1713   *Stamford Mercury* published

1737   *Belfast Newsletter* first published

1754   *Leeds Intelligencer* first published (later the **Yorkshire Post**)

1762   **North Briton** first published (**radical press**)

1763   Outbreak of **Wilkes and liberty** protests

1785   **Daily Universal Register** first published

1788   **Daily Universal Register** becomes *The Times*

1791   **First Amendment** agreed by all states in USA

1791   **Observer** first published

Early to mid-19th century: Growth of the **radical press**, war of the unstamped newspapers (**alternative journalism**), development of commercial **mainstream journalism** (**penny press, pops**); some complain that the **golden age of journalism** has passed while others insist it is the most exciting time ever to be a **journalist**.

1802   **Cobbett's Political Register** first published (**radical journalism**)

1817   **Scotsman** first published

1817   **Black Dwarf** first published

1819   Peterloo Massacre prompts the **Six Acts**, including increased **stamp duty** on newspapers

1821   **Manchester Guardian** first published

1822   **Sunday Times** first published

1824   Duke of Wellington declares: **'Publish and be damned'**

1827   **Freedom's Journal** appears as first US Afro-Caribbean newspaper (**black media**)

1828   **Cherokee Phoenix** appears as first Native American newspaper (**indigenous media**)

1828   **Spectator** first published

1829   **Providence Journal-Bulletin** first published

1830   Major campaign launched against **stamp duty** (aka **taxes on knowledge**)

1831   **Poor Man's Guardian** appears as an unstamped radical newspaper

1831   *Sydney Herald* (later **Sydney Morning Herald**) is first published

1835   Havas news agency (later **Agence France-Press**) established

1836   **Newspaper Society** formed

1837   **Northern Star** launched in support of the Chartist movement (**radical press**)

1838   *Bombay Times and Journal of Commerce* (later the **Times of India**) first published

1841   **Jewish Chronicle** first published (**ethnic minority media**)

1843   The **Economist** first published

1843   **News of the World** first published

1844   *The Times* reports royal birth thanks to the **telegraph** (use of **new technology**)

1846   Launch of **Associated Press**

Mid-19th and beyond: Growth of black newspapers (**black media**) in the USA.

1850	First English translation of the *Communist Manifesto* (**Marxism**) published in the *Red Republican* (**radical press**)
1850	*Harper's* magazine first published
1851	*New York Times* first published
1851	**Reuters** established
1854	William Howard Russell sent to cover Crimean War (**war reporting**) for *The Times*
1855	*Daily Telegraph* first published
1861	**Taxes on knowledge** end
1868	**Press Association** established
1869	*Western Mail* first published
1870	*Women's Suffrage Journal* appears (first wave of **feminist media**)
1870	Education Act leads to increasing literacy in the UK and the growth of popular **mainstream journalism** (**pops**)
1877	*Washington Post* first published
1878	The *Hindu* first published
1879	*California Owl* (later *California Eagle*) first published
1880s	Newspapers slowly begin to use **photographs**; also emergence of **new journalism**
1882	Pioneering football special newspaper (*Green 'Un, Pink 'Un*) published in Birmingham (**sport reporting**)
1884	National Association of Journalists formed (later the **Institute of Journalists**)
1885	W. T. Stead's **investigative journalism** at the *Pall Mall Gazette*
1887	Nellie Bly's **undercover reporting** for the *New York World*
1888	*Financial Times* first published
1889	*Wall Street Journal* first published
1892	Beginning of **black media** in UK
1895	*Daily Record* first published
1895	**Circulation war** between Hearst and Pulitzer's New York newspapers marks beginning of **yellow journalism** (aka **yellow press**)
1896	*Daily Mail* first published
1896	**Pathé News** sees the emergence of **newsreels**

20th century: Women's suffrage, two world wars, radio **broadcasting**, and the birth of **television journalism**.

1900	*Daily Express* first published
1903	*Daily Mirror* first published
1907	*Votes for Women* launched as first wave of feminism builds (**feminist media**)
1907	**National Union of Journalists** formed
1907	Launch of **United Press International**

1910	Arrest of Dr Crippen thanks to the **telegraph**
1911	*Daily Herald* first published
1911	UK **Official Secrets Act**
1912	American Association of Teachers of Journalism formed (later the **Association for Education in Journalism and Mass Communication**)
1912	Creation of the **DA-Notice** system
1914	Launch of *Woman's Dreadnought*, later the *Workers' Dreadnought* (**oppositional reporting**)
1917	**Pulitzer Prize** established
1920s	Emergence of **radio journalism**
1921	C. P. Scott's *Comment is Free* article
1922	British Broadcasting Company (**BBC**) formed
1922–3	Founding of the **Frankfurt School** (**critical theory, media effects, Marxism, media studies**)
1923	*Time* magazine first published
1924	US *Daily Worker* first published (**Leninist theory of the press**)
1927	British Broadcasting Company becomes British Broadcasting Corporation (**BBC**)
1930	**BBC** radio **presenter** declares there to be 'no news' worth reporting on one day (18 April)
1930	*Daily Worker* (UK) first published
1932	Launch of the Empire Service (later **BBC World Service**)
1933	**Newspaper Guild formed**
1934	**Newspaper Guild** agrees its **code of conduct**
1936	**NUJ** agrees its **code of conduct**
1936	*Life* magazine first published (**photojournalism**)
1937	**National Federation of Press Women** is formed
1938	*Grazia* first published (**women's magazines**)
1939–45	**Underground press** appears in Nazi-occupied Europe
1940s	Emergence of **television journalism**
1940	*PM* launched as a highbrow **tabloid**
1941	*Daily Worker* and *The Week* both suppressed under UK wartime **censorship**
1942	**Voice of America** launched
1942	*Dainik Jagran* launched
1945	*Ebony* launched
1946	**Orwell's six rules of writing** appear
1946	*People's Daily* launched
1947–9	First **Royal Commission on the Press**
1948	**Universal Declaration of Human Rights**
1948	**BBC** begins to broadcast TV news

1949	*Daily Mirror* defends **sensationalism** and overtakes *Daily Express* as the UK's biggest-selling daily newspaper
1949	**Deutsche-Presse-Agentur**
1950	**European Convention on Human Rights**
1950s	**McCarthyism** and the 'great fear'
1950	Lock-out at the *Las Vegas Review Journal* leads to founding of rival *Las Vegas Sun*, which takes on **McCarthyism**
1951	**National Council for the Training of Journalists** established (**training, journalism education**)
1952	Rupert Murdoch inherits the Adelaide *News* and so begins the **Murdoch empire**
1953	*I. F. Stone's Weekly* appears
1953	**BBC** launches *Panorama*
1953	**General Council of the Press** established
1954	Ed Murrow exposes **McCarthyism** on **CBS**'s *See it Now*
1955	Launch of **ITN**
1955	*Village Voice* first published (**alternative press**)
1956	UK military action in Suez opposed by *Observer* and *News Chronicle*
1957	*Today* programme first appears on **BBC** radio
1959	*Manchester Guardian* changes name to *Guardian*
1960	*News Chronicle* closes
1961	*Private Eye* first appears
1961–2	Second **Royal Commission on the Press**
1963	**General Council of the Press** becomes the **Press Council**
1963	*World in Action* launched
1963	*Insight* team created at *Sunday Times*
1963	*Oz* first published in Australia (**underground press**)
1964	*Daily Herald* becomes the *Sun*
1964	*Guardian* moves its operation from Manchester to London
1965	Galtung and Ruge's paper on **news values** is first published
1966	*Daily Worker* becomes the *Morning Star*
1966	US **Freedom of Information Act**
1966	*The Times* prints **news** rather than **advertisements** on its front page
1967	**BBC** begins broadcasting local radio
1967	*Rolling Stone* first published (**interviews, gonzo journalism, immersion reporting**)
1968	Launch of *60 Minutes*
1969	**Murdoch empire** buys the *News of the World* and the *Sun*
1970	The *Sun* starts running *Page Three* pin-ups
1970	Women employees sue *Newsweek* for sex **discrimination**
1970	**Reporters Committee for Freedom of the Press** launched

1970	*Irish Post* first published (**ethnic minority media**)
1971	Formation of the **Asian Media Information and Communication Centre**
1971	Obscenity trial over the 'schoolkids' issue of *Oz*
1971	**Pentagon Papers**
1972	**Watergate**
1972	*West Highland Free Press* first published (**alternative media**)
1972	*Spare Rib* and *Ms.* both appear for the first time (second wave of **feminist media**), as does *Cosmopolitan* (**women's magazines, glossies, lifestyle journalism**)
1972	**Younger Committee** reports on **privacy**
1972	*Gay News* launched (**gay media**)
1972	**Investigative journalism** at the *Sunday Times* exposes **Thalidomide scandal**
1972	Gaye Tuchman publishes research on **objective journalism** as a **strategic ritual**
1973	Launch of **IRN**
1974–7	Third **Royal Commission on the Press**
1975	Journalists' strike over **ethics** at the *Australian*
1975	Formation of the Australian Association for Tertiary Education in Journalism (later the **Journalism Education Association of Australia**)
1975	**National Association of Black Journalists** formed
1976	Murdoch buys the *New York Post*
1976	**Project Censored** launched
1976	*Sniffin' Glue* heralds the emergence of do-it-yourself **fanzines**
1977	The *Sun* overtakes *Daily Mirror* as the UK's biggest-selling daily newspaper
1978	*Daily Star* launched
1980s	**Newsrooms** switch from typewriters to computers (**new technology**)
1980	The **Little Jimmy** scandal at the *Washington Post*
1980	*Columbus Dispatch* publishes prototype dial-up 'online' newspaper
1980	Launch of **CNN** marks beginning of **rolling news** followed by emergence of the **CNN effect**
1981	The **Murdoch empire** buys *The Times* and *Sunday Times*
1981	**Committee to Protect Journalists** launched
1981	*China Daily* first published
1982	*USA Today* first published
1982	Launch of the *Voice* newspaper (**black media**)
1982	Launch of *Channel 4 News*
1982	*Sun* headline *Gotcha* during Falklands **conflict**
1983	*Sunday Times* and *Stern* run the fake **Hitler diaries**
1983	*Warrington Messenger* dispute
1984	**Whistleblower** Sarah Tisdall is jailed for six months (**anonymous source**)

1984	**National Association of Hispanic Journalists** and the **Native American Journalists Association** both formed
1985	*Real Lives* strike at **BBC**
1985	**Reporters Without Borders** formed
1986	**Wapping dispute** begins (**new technology**)
1986	*Independent*, *Today*, and *Sunday Sport* all first published
1987	Rise and fall of *News on Sunday*
1988	*Death on the Rock*
1988	UK government imposes **broadcast ban** re: Northern Ireland 'troubles'
1988	Herman and Chomsky's *Manufacturing Consent* first published (**propaganda model**)

Late 20th century: **Glasnost** and perestroika in USSR. Emergence of the public **internet** and use of **email**, the world wide web (**websites**), **online journalism**, **computer-assisted reporting** (later **data journalism**); also **public journalism** and the **Asian values in journalism** movement. Third wave of **feminist media**; also the emergence of **lads'** mags.

1989	The *Sun* blames Liverpool supporters for the **Hillsborough disaster**
1989	Launch of the *Sunday Correspondent*
1989	Launch of *Sky News*
1989	UK newspaper **proprietors** are warned they are drinking in the **Last Chance Saloon**
1989	*Eastern Eye* first published (**ethnic minority media**)
1990	*Take a Break* launched
1990	**National Lesbian and Gay Journalists Association** formed
1990	First **Calcutt Report**
1991	**Press Complaints Commission** replaces **Press Council** and establishes **Editors' code**
1992	**Squidgygate** and **Camillagate**
1993	Second **Calcutt Report**
1994	*Daily Telegraph* launches the online *Electronic Telegraph*
1994	*Diva* first published
1994	**Women in Journalism** formed
1995	*Metro* free newspaper launched in Sweden
1996	**Al Jazeera** launched
1996	*Fox News* launched
1997	**Paparazzi** blamed following death of Diana, Princess of Wales
1997	**Association for Journalism Education** formed (**academization of journalism, hackademy, journalism education**)
1997	*Wall Street Journal* introduces **paywall** for online content
1998	*Hack Heaven* in *New Republic*
1998	Sales of the *Daily Mail* overtake those of the *Daily Mirror*

1998	***Drudge Report*** exposes the relationship between Bill Clinton and Monica Lewinsky
1998	UK **Human Rights Act**
1999	First appearance of ***Indymedia*** (**alternative media, open-source publishing**)
1999	Release of **Blogger** software (**blogging, citizen journalism**)

21st century: The first two decades are dominated by the growth of user-generated content and **social media** and their effect on all forms of journalism.

2000	UK **Freedom of Information Act**
2000	***City Slickers*** exposed at the ***Daily Mirror***
2000	**Journalism Education Association of New Zealand** formed
2000	A paediatrician is forced from her home during **name-and-shame** campaign by the ***News of the World*** against paedophiles
2000	***OhmyNews*** launched in South Korea (**citizen journalism**)
2000	Launch of the journals ***Journalism Studies*** and ***Journalism: Theory, Practice, and Criticism*** (**journalism studies**)
2001	**StumbleUpon** launched (**social bookmarking**)
2003	**International News Safety Institute** formed
2003	***Daily Mirror*** campaigns against Iraq War; death of **anonymous source** David Kelly; establishment of **Hutton Inquiry**
2003	***Independent*** pioneers the **compact** format in the **quality press** and for a while promotes itself as a **viewspaper**
2003	Jayson Blair **plagiarism** scandal at the *New York Times*
2003	**Ofcom** created
2003	**WordPress** launched (growth of **blogging**)
2004	**Hutton Report** published, followed by **Neil Report**
2004	**Facebook** launched (**social networking, social media**)
2004	*New York Times* apologizes for insufficient **scepticism** in the build-up to the US-led invasion of Iraq
2004	Indian Ocean tsunami marks emergence of **user-generated content**
2005	***YouTube*** launched
2005	***Huffington Post*** launched
2005	Mark Felt reveals himself to have been **Deep Throat** in the Watergate investigation
2005	National **Sunshine Week** launched in USA
2006	Anna Politkovskaya killed in Russia, focusing attention on continuing **deaths of journalists**
2006	Arrests mark the beginning of the **hackgate** scandal at the *News of the World*
2006	Launch of **Twitter**
2006	Launch of *BuzzFeed*
2007	***WikiLeaks*** first appears
2007	**BBC Trust** replaces **BBC governors**
2007	*Wall Street Journal* bought by **Murdoch empire**

2007	*Politico* founded (**digital media**)
2009	*Seattle Post-Intelligencer* becomes digital-only
2009	James Murdoch attacks the **BBC** in keynote address at Edinburgh TV Festival
2009	MPs' expenses scandal revealed by *Daily Telegraph*
2009	**Trafigura**
2010	*WikiLeaks* releases *Collateral Murder* video followed by **cablegate**
2010	*Independent* launches spin-off title, *i*
2010	*ProPublica* breaks ground for **online journalism** by winning a **Pulitzer Prize**
2011	**Hackgate** scandal erupts over Milly Dowler story; *News of the World* closed; **Leveson Inquiry** launched
2011	**AOL** buys *Huffington Post*
2012	BBC's Jimmy Savile crisis results in **Pollard Review**
2012	**Leveson Report** published
2012	**Finkelstein Report** in Australia
2012	*Mail Online* becomes the most visited English-language newspaper website in the world
2012	The daily *New Orleans Times-Picayune* switches to a three-day week
2012	Warren Buffett's **Berkshire Hathaway** starts buying US **newspapers**
2012	**Speak Justice** campaign launched
2013	Chinese journalists' strike over **censorship** at *Southern Weekly*
2013	PPA publishes first combined **circulation** chart for print and digital **magazines**
2013	UK **Defamation Act**
2013	**Independent Press Standards Organization** proposed in UK
2013	*Newsweek* switches to digital-only publication
2013	**News Corp** split in two; **News International** becomes **News UK**
2013	*Washington Post* bought by Jeff Bezos and *Boston Globe* bought by John Henry
2013	*Sun* becomes first UK **redtop** to introduce online **paywall**
2013	**Whistleblower** Bradley Manning is jailed for 35 years (*WikiLeaks*) and changes name to Chelsea Manning
2014	Government funding of the **BBC World Service** ends
2014	Some journalists are still moaning that the **golden age** has been and gone while others insist it is the most exciting time ever to be a **journalist**.

Selective index of people

Below is a list of some of the people featured in the dictionary and an indication of some of the entries in which they are mentioned; most entries will point in the direction of further relevant information. The people listed include journalists, proprietors, scholars, and others.

More History titles from OUP

The Oxford Companion to Black British History
David Dabydeen, John Gilmore, and Cecily Jones

The first reference book to explore the full history of black people in the British Isles from Roman times to the present day.

'From Haiti to Kingston, to Harlem, to Tottenham, the story of the African Diaspora is seldom told. This Companion will ensure that the history of Black Britain begins to take its rightful place in mainstream British consciousness.'

David Lammy, MP, former Minister for Culture

A Dictionary of Contemporary World History: From 1900 to the present day
Jan Palmowski

Discover the facts behind the headlines with this indispensable A-Z of world history during the last century.

'Concise, current information ... highly recommended'

Choice

The Concise Oxford Dictionary of Archaeology
Timothy Darvill

The most wide-ranging, up-to-date, and authoritative dictionary of its kind.

'Comprehensive, proportionate, and limpid'

Antiquity

More Literature titles from OUP

The Oxford Companion to Charles Dickens
edited by Paul Schlicke

Reissued to celebrate the bicentenary of Charles Dickens's birth, this companion draws together an unparalleled diversity of information on one of Britain's greatest writers; covering his life, his works, his reputation, and his cultural context.

Reviews from previous edition:
'comes about as close to perfection as humanly possible'

Dickens Quarterly

'will prove invaluable to scholars, readers and admirers of Dickens'

Peter Ackroyd, *The Times*

The Oxford Companion to the Brontës
Christine Alexander and Margaret Smith

This Companion brings together a wealth of information about the fascinating lives and writings of the Brontë sisters.

'This book is a must ... a treasure trove of a book'

Irish Times

The Oxford Companion to Classical Literature
edited by M. C. Howatson

A broad-ranging and authoritative guide to the classical world and its literary heritage.

Reviews from previous edition:
'a volume for all seasons ... indispensable'

Times Educational Supplement

'A necessity for any seriously literary household.'

History Today

More Art Reference from Oxford

The Grove Dictionary of Art

The 34 volumes of *The Grove Dictionary of Art* provide unrivalled coverage of the visual arts from Asia, Africa, the Americas, Europe, and the Pacific, from prehistory to the present day.

'succeeds in performing the most difficult of balancing acts, satisfying specialists while ... remaining accessible to the general reader'

The Times

The Grove Dictionary of Art — Online
www.groveart.com

This immense cultural resource is also available online. Updated regularly, it includes recent developments in the art world as well as the latest art scholarship.

'a mammoth one-stop site for art-related information'

Antiques Magazine

A Dictionary of Modern and Contemporary Art
Ian Chilvers and John Glaves-Smith

This major new edition boasts worldwide coverage of modern and contemporary art from 1900 to the present day.

The Oxford Dictionary of American Art and Artists
Ann Lee Morgan

The first single-volume dictionary of American art in thirty years.

'Concise, clear and very informative ... There is really nothing comparable'

Choice

OXFORD

Oxford Paperback Reference

The Concise Oxford Companion to English Literature
Dinah Birch and Katy Hooper

Based on the best-selling *Oxford Companion to English Literature*, this is an indispensable guide to all aspects of English literature.

Review of the parent volume
'the foremost work of reference in its field'

Literary Review

A Dictionary of Shakespeare
Stanley Wells

Compiled by one of the best-known international authorities on the playwright's works, this dictionary offers up-to-date information on all aspects of Shakespeare, both in his own time and in later ages.

The Oxford Dictionary of Literary Terms
Chris Baldick

A best-selling dictionary, covering all aspects of literature, this is an essential reference work for students of literature in any language.

A Dictionary of Critical Theory
Ian Buchanan

The invaluable multidisciplinary guide to theory, covering movements, theories, and events.

'an excellent gateway into critical theory'　　　*Literature and Theology*

Oxford Paperback Reference

A Dictionary of Marketing
Charles Doyle

Covers traditional marketing techniques and theories alongside the latest concepts in over 2,000 clear and authoritative entries.

'Flick to any page [for] a lecture's worth of well thought through information'

Dan Germain, Head of Creative, innocent ltd

A Dictionary of Media and Communication
Daniel Chandler and Rod Munday

This volume provides over 2,200 authoritative entries on terms used in media and communication, from concepts and theories to technical terms, across subject areas that include advertising, digital culture, journalism, new media, radio studies, and telecommunications.

'a wonderful volume that is much more than a simple dictionary'
Professor Joshua Meyrowitz, University of New Hampshire

A Dictionary of Film Studies
Annette Kuhn and Guy Westwell

Features terms covering all aspects of film studies in 500 detailed entries, from theory and history to technical terms and practices.

OXFORD